Free People, Free Markets

Also by New Academia Publishing

Free People, Free Markets

Their Evolutionary Origins

by Ralph L. Bayrer

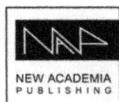

New Academia Publishing
Washington, DC

Library of Congress Control Number: 2009935178
ISBN 978-0-9823867-4-3 paperback (alk. paper)

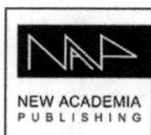

New Academia Publishing, LLC
P.O. Box 27420
Washington, DC 20038-7420
www.newacademia.com - info@newacademia.com

Contents

Praise for
Free People, Free Markets

Ralph Bayrer's new book, *Free People-Free Markets: Their Evolutionary Origins,* is a timely reaffirmation of freedom's central role in the creation of American prosperity and the most celebrated advances of western civilization. Relying on thorough scholarship and clarity of argument, Bayrer makes the compelling case that mankind's progress in the last millennium rests on a narrow foundation of freedom, a lesson people forget at their peril.

—John McCain

Acknowledgments

I am greatly indebted to a number of people whose input and support made this book possible. Foremost is Professor Phillip Scribner who provided an intellectual framework for understanding the unfolding of societal evolution and who was more than generous in his efforts reviewing formative drafts of this book. Equally generous was Douglas Seay, who brought his extensive understanding of history and political science to bear in critiquing multiple drafts of this work. Furthermore, Paula Jo Galbraith's communications skills were invaluable for improving its clarity, strength of argument, and flow. Also, I wish to acknowledge Carole Sargent's assistance in finding a publisher. And, of course, the patience and loving support of my life partner Ken George was essential for the completion of this long-term endeavor.

Introduction

> To understand our civilization, one must appreciate that the extended [economic] order resulted not from human design or intention but spontaneously: it arose from unintentionally conforming to certain ... practices, many of which men tended to dislike, whose significance they usually fail to understand, whose validity they cannot prove, and which have nonetheless fairly rapidly spread by means of an evolutionary selection – the comparative increase of population and wealth – of those groups that happened to follow them. ... This process is perhaps the least appreciated facet of human evolution.[1]

Adam Smith's question of two centuries ago—Why do some countries prosper and others do not?—remains unanswered in key respects and is even more pressing in today's world of growing disparities of wealth between developed and undeveloped countries. Indeed, given the money, the effort, and the intellectual capital invested in understanding and attacking the roots of poverty around the globe, the persistence of the question mystifies.

After all, any number of key studies, such as the *Index of Economic Freedom*, have clearly identified the essential predicates underlying the success of affluent countries in unambiguous terms. And all countries have access to science and to international capital markets. A number of countries, as we shall see, have fully drawn on such resources and have rapidly developed economically in the space of a generation to approach the first ranks of standard of living. Yet, by all measures, more countries than not continue to stagnate or even fall further behind.[2] How can this be explained?

The answer is not found in conventional economic theory, as noted by economist Elhanan Helpman, who stated that economists have been studying the wealth of nations without interruption since Adam Smith[3]. While the discipline of economics may have mastered many critical elements of modern economies, it has had difficulty formulating a complete model, akin to physics still lacking a unified field theory. That absence was pinpointed by Peruvian economist Hernando de Soto's comment, when he lamented that the West "never preserved a blueprint of its own evolution."[4] This acute observation suggests that while it is possible to identify key policies and institutions necessary for an affluent society, until one knows how these *evolved* originally, we may not be able to understand why each is essential and why they take hold in some countries and not others. That understanding is hindered because such measures were contentious as they emerged over centuries in the now affluent countries, and they continue to be resisted in less developed countries today.

It turns out that this puzzle was addressed, albeit in passing, by Nobel Prize-winning economist Friedrich von Hayek, as is evident in the opening quotation. Hayek's key insight was that the absence of a blueprint and an imperfect understanding stem from the fact that the elements comprising a new economic and social order were not consciously planned, but arose spontaneously and incrementally to meet needs of the day. New ways were innovated by participants in economic transactions because they met pragmatic needs and were adopted even when their underlying economic rationale was not fully understood and even if they were seemingly at odds with prevailing mores of society. Those outside the marketplace often looked down on such practices as being at odds with tradition. Thus, while practitioners increasingly adopted the new approaches and values, they were not codified, documented, or legitimatized in a manner that could be considered an unimpeachable "blueprint" and, as a practical matter, are continually subject to debate. And because new practices emerged in this manner, they tended to be veiled in the pages of history.

In addition, Hayek emphasized that to understand the nature of the modern economy it was essential to view it sociologically, in terms of the ability of members of society to cooperate productively.

He characterized the modern free market system as an *extended order of human cooperation*, having a number of key attributes. First, productive activity would be increasingly freed to be shaped by basic economic forces such as supply and demand, comparative advantage, and free market prices, rather than governmental fiat. Second, greater latitude would be accorded the inventor, the entrepreneur, and the individual himself. And thirdly, societal value systems would evolve beyond the instinctual and communal to systems that are more impersonal and contractual, which became possible only because societal norms increasingly emphasized mutual trust and expectations that others will live up to their commitments. As this book will show, the key features of the extended order are prominent in developed countries and stunted in undeveloped ones. This likelihood was anticipated by another early economist who said that Adam Smith saw "a Scotsman in every man," suggesting that he "formulate[d] laws of economic behavior that might be regarded as axiomatic only in fully developed societies."[5]

In such a light, one would expect to see significant societal differences regarding interpersonal cooperation and vis-à-vis the institutions underlying free markets in developed and underdeveloped countries, respectively. And, indeed, surveys of individual values taken around the globe demonstrate this clearly. For the case of underdeveloped countries, take Lawrence Harrison's characterization: "In the typical peasant society, an individual or a family can progress only at the expense of others. The typical peasant sees little or no relationship between work and technology on one hand, and the acquisition of wealth on the other: one works to eat but not to create wealth. The Anglo-Saxon virtues of hard work and thrift are meaningless in peasant society. ... Peasants are individualistic, and each social unit sees itself in continual struggle with its neighbors for its share of scarce wealth. An individual or family who advances is viewed as a threat to the stability of the community, which behaves like crabs in a barrel. Similarly, the peasant avoids leadership roles, fearing that his motives will be suspect."[6]

Then, contrast this view with conclusions regarding advanced societies derived from the *World Value Surveys*. The Survey results show that measurable cultural values markedly change as societies become more industrialized. As populations become more urban, move into new occupations, become more literate and educated, and reside in an altered political milieu, world views move along a trajectory characterized by "a shift from traditional values toward rational-bureaucratic norms; an increasing emphasis on economic achievement; rising levels of mass political participation and major changes in the types of issues that are most salient in the politics of the respective types of societies." More specifically, the surveys measured a decline in adherence to tradition and absolute religious norms as populations became more socially mobile, individualistic, economic oriented, and secular. Importantly, "social status became something that an individual could achieve, rather than something into which one was born."[7]

So, we see a congruence of views identifying a historical process of evolutionary change: von Hayek's paths of evolutionary change of practices, institutions, and interpersonal behavior, and the *Values Survey's* trajectories of value change—i.e., in terms of how individuals view themselves, their role in society, and the wider norms and institutions of society. But how is it that some countries followed that path and others did not, and in numerous cases rejected it?

To the extent that the world views and value systems of the undeveloped countries can be considered what was once the norm for the world's early cultures and civilizations, contrasting these with those of developed countries can provide markers of key paths evolution took to produce the extended order. And, with those markers in hand, we can re-examine the pages of history to uncover those evolutionary paths and even produce the outlines of the blueprint sought by de Soto.

To that end, this book describes how the extended order arose out of mankind's atavistic past to produce: free markets, institutions securing liberty, the possibility of more empowered individuals, and modern science. It examines in some detail all of the world's major cultural groupings to show how values, world views and institutions necessary to the workings of the modern world did or did not evolve, and why. That analysis helps one to gain insight into a host of related issues: why some poorer countries continue to languish, why attempts at nation building confound us, and why trillions of dollars of Western financial assistance to less developed countries have failed to assist. In other words, by examining the world views of different cultural groups, the specific hurdles they face in adopting the predicates of the extended order become much more evident. At the same time, we get to appreciate the virtues of our affluent societies so as to better protect and nurture them.

But to undertake this exploration something more is needed, namely a model of how societal evolution occurs, along with illustrations of how it unfolded historically. To understand the evolutionary process, the book turns first to the work of the philosopher Phillip Scribner,[8] who describes how societal evolution works within the context of broader evolutionary theory. He argues that the evolutionary rules evident in the concept of survival of the fittest apply at the human group level as well as at the species level. In effect, when humans evolved capacities for speech and reason a new entity—the societal animal—was created. Through their capacity for cooperation, groups can work to achieve goals just as purposefully as individuals. And because societal animals are in constant competition with one another for survival, an evolutionary dynamic occurs, with fitter groups surviving preferentially to others.

Scribner identifies cultural values and modes of argument as central to the social evolutionary process. He argues that groups most open to innovation and change will advance most rapidly through a natural selection of values and the arguments. He makes an analogy that arguments, institutions and values are part of the genome of the societal animal, comparable to DNA in living organisms. In that light, cultures that honor reason, value debate, and tolerate change are amenable to evolving rapidly. The test of evolutionary success—i.e., fitness, is the relative capability of the group to further its reproductive success, particularly by controlling sources of sustenance, such as food and energy, and to protect itself from aggression.

Second, with regard to societal evolution in practice, we are able to track group selection back to man's origins, even to his primate legacy. Studies show that man's earliest existence was highly precarious; indeed humans may have been close to extinction as recently as 50,000 years ago, in part because of incessant tribal warfare. Yet competitive warfare had the virtue (from a parochial modern human perspective) of driving the process of group selection. But natural selection remained a slow process until mankind learned the ways of settled agriculture around eight to ten thousand years ago. Once that happened, a multitude of new ways of organizing activities and forms of governance became possible – offering greater possibilities of protection against predatory groups and providing the basis for generating and accumulating wealth. These possibilities facilitated, in evolutionary terms, a radiation of societal creatures. The most rapidly evolving groups moved up the evolutionary scale from hunter-gatherers, to tribal units, to city-states, and eventually to empires.

Empires rose and fell over millennia. A number of these managed to establish widespread stability, which when accompanied by extensive trade, produced a modicum of affluence relative to mankind's early existence. Several enjoyed such affluence circa 1100 A.D: Europe, following the fall of the Roman Empire, was on the upswing with the "Renaissance of the Twelfth Century"; Islam achieved a peak of affluence during the Abbasid Empire after a consolidation of widespread victories; and China reached a high plateau of civilization in the Sung Dynasty, which also coincided with a "Golden Age" in Japan.

But they were seemingly caught in a *value trap*, which precluded significant societal advance. For example, the most advanced civilizations of the time—i.e., European, Islamic, Chinese, Japanese, and Indian—held very similar fixed traditions including autocratic governments, tightly regulated trade, and guild systems that rigidly organized crafts and manufacturing. Without a potential for science to unfold, commercial activity to be unleashed, and new compatible forms of governance to be found, no dramatic increase in affluence was possible.

The West, however, relatively suddenly broke out of this traditional value trap by evolving new institutions and worldviews that allowed its societies to grow more prosperous and strong. That process was largely unplanned, but not random—it had a direction and a coherence that is discernable in the context of evolutionary group selection. It transpired that the West possessed unique circumstances favorable to evolutionary advancement—a Greco-Roman-Christian cultural heritage situated among fragmented power centers, which were ineffective in stifling competitive change. The outcome was, in Hayek's formulation, the *extended order* of human cooperation characterized by free markets, representative governments with institutions securing liberty, and empowered individuals.

With this template, we are equipped to examine just how new values emerged in the West, primarily over the last millennium. Of four principal avenues of societal evolution—commerce, governance, science, and individual empowerment—commerce led the others, bringing them in its wake. Accordingly, the investigation begins by examining the flowering of commerce. Growing affluence and the new institutions for generating that affluence called forth other evolutionary advances in society. For example, the emerging commercial and industrial classes brought pressure for new forms of representative government to protect their wealth from arbitrary and predatory government. And with affluence, of course, came more opportunity for society to transcend a preoccupation with basic survival needs to produce more vibrant arts, philosophy, and eventually science. In the West, this led to Humanism, the Renaissance, and the Protestant Reformation, epochs during which individuals found greater scope for entrepreneurship and creativity of all kinds, while they demanded an increasingly greater say in governance. During the last few centuries a creative hothouse for social evolutionary change arose, creating expanded competition among ideas, practices, arguments, and worldviews.

Science is an especially important and illustrative microcosm of the evolutionary process, epitomizing an intellectual survival of the fittest. And modern affluence simply would not be possible, even with evolutionary advances in the other arenas, without the availability of science and its applications.

In short, the evolution of the extended free market system was an experiential process wherein innovations, when successful, gained adherents even when they ran counter to tradition, which they often did. Of central consequence was the cultural shift whereby values of ancient lineage—e.g., compassion and solidarity, were preserved in the extended family and local community, but gave way to contractual, impersonal ways in larger society.

The above analysis can also help us better understand the nature of the world's residual poverty. Specifically, contrasting the performance of economically successful and unsuccessful present-day cultures against this evolutionary framework reveals the role of cultural antecedents. For example, when societies outside the West possess a threshold of necessary values—essentially having a pragmatic similarity to the Protestant ethic, as do some Confucian traditions—it can be achieved in a generation. But without an evolved set of values and institutions, development is discouragingly difficult. And finally, to help understand the nature of that difficulty, the book examines the powerful undertow of atavistic worldviews retarding the adoption of evolved values.

This argument is presented in the space of eight chapters:

1. Wealth of Nations: The Cultural Nexus. Chapter I re-poses in modern terms Adam Smith's question of two centuries ago regarding the source of the wealth of nations: how is it that when all countries have access to science, to successful policy models, to global capital markets, and substantial financial aid, more countries than not fail to take advantage of these, and the economic development gap between developed and less developed countries continues to widen?

To frame the question, the chapter identifies indispensable elements of successful affluent countries and shows how developed and less developed countries fall into different cultural groupings regarding the extent to which they have adopted these elements. It goes on to identify key pragmatic differences in the cultural world views of the different groupings that could account for the varying performance. To provide greater specificity of value differentials, the chapter draws on recent cross-cultural data bases, notably the *World Values Surveys* analyzed by Ronald Inglehart. And implicitly, value differentials between advanced and undeveloped countries identify the key paths of evolutionary change taken by developed countries over the last millennium or so: first by the Protestant West, but quickly by some others, notably those with a Confucian heritage. The most telling avenues of cultural evolution that come to light are those associated with free markets, institutions securing liberty, the rise of science, and the empowerment of the individual. This framework guides the investigation of subsequent chapters, which show just how evolution unfolded along each of those avenues.

2. The Evolution of Societies. Chapter II presents the theory of societal evolution and shows how it unfolded from mankind's prehistory to the pre-modern era. Societal evolution is a process of Darwinian *group selection* in which groups that are more evolutionarily fit survive preferentially in competition with others. For the theory, the chapter draws on the work of philosopher Phillip Scribner, which describes how group selection works within the context of broader evolutionary theory and identifies the critical roles of cultural values and modes of argument in that process.

Viewed through that prism, groups can be seen to evolve through changes in practices and institutions that prove themselves to be more efficacious than those previously extant. This is an experiential process that often runs counter to tradition and evokes modified world views to accommodate new ways. Evolutionary leaps have occurred at key junctures of human existence—e.g., the movement from hunter-gatherer societies to fixed settlements and from settlements to city-states and then empires. A number of major civilizations—e.g., Roman, Persian, Islamic, Hindu, and Chinese, progressed through this evolutionary process, achieving rich cultures and modest levels of prosperity but eventually tended toward evolutionary stagnation. About one thousand years ago, however, a burst of evolutionary societal change began in the West, which is the subject of ensuing chapters.

3. Commerce: Driver of Change. A driver of societal evolution is man's propensity for enterprise and commerce, what the economist Ludwig von Mises termed *human action*. Evolutionary advance accelerated 1,000 years ago when Western Europe embarked on a mercantile revolution that produced greater wealth, power, and important new worldviews. In part, this evolution occurred in the West and not elsewhere because the fragmented and dispersed power centers of the West had less incentive and less capability to interfere with the natural instinct to create, build, invest, and innovate. Relatively free chartered cities and new towns arose in ways that promoted trade, protected wealth, and found more efficacious ways of deploying capital.

At the same time, the needs of expanding commerce led to the spontaneous rise of innovative instruments and institutions, such as money, banks, contracts, and courts to enforce contracts. In the West, in generally unseen ways, new worldviews corresponding to the utility of modern commerce and enterprise displaced value systems that had once been universal.

4. **Securing Ordered Liberty**. The growth of commerce and enterprise led to the evolution of political institutions as the mercantile classes sought ways of protecting their wealth from the predatory state. The new institutions built on traditions reaching back some two and a half millennia: principles of liberty and ordered government were identified in ancient Greece, were given early institutional form in the Roman Republic, and were preserved by tradition in the Dark Ages. But it was the British who evolved the most effective and enduring institutions for ordered liberty—a working system of constitutional law, representative government with checks on power, property rights, and the rights of the individual vis-à-vis the state. The United States built on this structure with a written constitution, a federal form of government, and more explicit checks on the exercise of power.

5. **The Emergence of Science**. Pure science, as opposed to technological creativity and efforts cataloguing the natural world, is the essential factor for making widespread affluence possible, and it arose uniquely in the West. Phillip Scribner argues that science could not have emerged without an enabling metaphysics, and that the metaphysics formulated in the West was primarily developed by Christian thinkers drawing on early Greek speculation. The new approach for gaining knowledge entailed a non-superstitious and non-mystical way of viewing the world, requiring a belief that the workings of nature, while not immediately visible to our senses, could be discerned through inductive reasoning, rigorous experiment, and applied mathematics. In addition, for science to emerge on a significant scale, society had to have a modicum of affluence and a culture that

tolerated debate. From the first intellectual grasp of the scientific method around the 12th century, several more centuries elapsed before Europe developed the tools—instrumentation and mathematics—essential for productive scientific enterprise. But once the institutional base was laid, scientific discovery exploded along evolutionary lines, powered by widening competition among ideas. Science, married to a free market system, liberated mankind from a heritage of poverty and precarious existence.

6. **The Empowerment of the Individual**. Via Greek philosophy, Roman republican principles, Judeo-Christian emphasis on a God-given conscience, Humanism, and the Protestant Reformation, the West evolved a culture in which the individual's ability to think and act for himself was freed from close control by his social group. In practical terms, this facilitated the decentralization of power associated with liberty, unleashed entrepreneurial forces, and accelerated man's creativity.

7. **Cross-Cultural Performance**. The world's other cultures have responded to the West's evolutionary advance in starkly different ways, depending on their cultural readiness for the extended order. Confucian cultures exhibited a particular readiness: Japan coolly determined what was required to catch up and launched the Meiji Restoration, and the Seven Tigers of Asia largely followed that model in more recent years. Latin America, however, with the exception of Chile, lags economically and haplessly resists many dictates of free markets. Islam, after confused efforts to catch up, appears in some quarters to wish to retreat to the primitive religiosity of 700 A.D., and Africa is mired in a post-colonial mindset marred by self-defeating victimology.

8. **Innate Resistance to Change**. The relative failure of some countries to advance, despite the general availability of science and clear prescriptions of sound macro-economic policies, can be traced to the contrary pull of atavistic traditions. Understandably, values crucial to past survival are not readily discarded, certainly not through abstract argumentation. To replace these familiar beliefs with new ones,

societies first require experiential demonstration of their validity. Yet, even where populations have been beneficiaries of efficacious new practices, retrograde forces persist. Examining some of the cultural battles underway in the United States provides a clearer understanding of why value change is so difficult, and why, ultimately, outcomes are determined pragmatically—i.e., when the Darwinian fitness of the institutions and policies in question has been demonstrated and accepted.

This book was written to cast new light on the evolutionary process that produced modern affluent societies in a way to inform policy makers regarding matters at home and abroad. But it serves another purpose as well, by highlighting the cultural and institutional roots of modern affluent society so as to better equip us to nurture and defend the values and the practices of our culture.

As the book is being written, the world is experiencing one of its recurrent economic downswings—after a prolonged period of unprecedented growth. Such recessions grow out of institutional mistakes and investor excesses, but are self-limiting (without further institutional mistakes). While they are dismaying and painful in consequences to many, the inevitable calls questioning the capitalist model demonstrate a bewildering ignorance of the free market track record. To paraphrase Churchill's famous aphorism, free markets are the worst kind of economic system except for any other.

Of perhaps greater concern are broader ideological attacks on the Western model, whether it be from groups generally hostile to 'globalization', fanatical Islam, or "Bolivarian socialism." All too often, key elements of Western society respond to such attacks more with fecklessness than resolution. They seem to be insufficiently cognizant of the dictates of the modern economy, as they are preoccupied with ill-founded moral relativism, myopically concerned with residual areas of social shortfall, past moral lapses, and ungrounded good intentions.

While robust debate is a healthy and essential feature of democratic societies, a pervasive lack of vision can ultimately be dangerous. To be sure, danger is not yet at our doorstep and Western societies are demonstrably in the vanguard of an evolutionary process in which societies tend to grow more 'fit'—i.e., wealthier, stronger, and more creative. One way or another, the evolutionary process will continue, but in any society there can be shocking setbacks. The book's concern is that, through a lack of confidence in their cultures, Western societies will derail the process, as they once almost did in the first half of the 20th century, by needlessly empowering destructive forces at substantial cost to themselves, and to the entire world. To counter that possibility, this book would rally support for the essential underpinnings of modern society: for free markets and free people. Consider the words of Jose Ortega y Gasset[9]:

> "If you want to make use of the advantages of civilization, but are not prepared to concern yourself with the upholding of civilization—you are done ... Just a slip, and when you look around, everything has vanished into air."

1
Wealth of Nations: the Cultural Nexus

The West "never preserved a blueprint of its own evolution."[10]
–Hernando de Soto

Adam Smith's question of two centuries ago—Why do some countries prosper and others do not?—remains unanswered in a key respect and accordingly needs a reformulation along the lines: Why do some countries become progressively more wealthy, creative, and free while many others, despite any number of attempts, remain static or even retrogress? For the fact is that despite all that has been learned regarding the successes and failures of economic development, more undeveloped countries than not fail to adopt 'best practices' of advanced countries. The economic gap between advanced and poor societies continues to widen, even though a trillion or more dollars of aid has been provided by the developed to the undeveloped countries. This phenomenon begs the question: if all countries have access to science, to successful policy models, to global capital markets, and substantial economic aid, how are we to understand why they fail to take advantage of them? More puzzling still is the fact that many of these less advanced societies actually repudiate successful economic models despite their undeniable success in vanquishing poverty, eradicating disease, and liberating entire populations from despotism. And they then blame their poverty and their own failure to act on the imagined greed and oppression of the wealthy countries.

These contradictions call out for a search for their 'root causes' of failure and dysfunctional behavior. While the intellectual capital invested in this exploration has been truly impressive, the central question still lacks a satisfying answer. There must be something deeper than conventional economics at work that holds poorer countries back, that undermines their ability to act. It turns out that the economist Friedrich von Hayek had perceived the answer, which this book will flesh out, that the missing piece of the puzzle lies in understanding the role culture plays in shaping a country's development path.

Von Hayek's insight is that a country's capacity for economic development has an essential sociological and cultural component that has generally eluded the mathematical approach of econometricians. As a practical matter, many countries lack the predicates assumed by the models, namely settings in which something approaching pure competition exists and in which individuals generally can be considered as utility maximizers. Indeed, just on common sense grounds, it is intuitively clear that when societies are generally suspicious of wealth, leery of outsiders beyond the family and clan, lack a tradition of rule of law, are not optimistic about the future, discourage individual initiative, and are prone to superstitious thinking, there will not be fertile ground for investment, either internally generated or from external sources. A society must first evolve a nurturing value system compatible with development before it can happen.

This chapter will lay out evidence that a country's culture plays an important role in determining whether it prospers economically or stagnates. First, it demonstrates how recent research has determined which policies and institutions are essential to a country becoming affluent and that developed and less developed countries fall into cultural groupings in terms of their success or failure, respectively, to adopt these. Next, it spells out the cultural differences—worldviews and value systems—relevant to economic development that exist between rich and poor countries. Finally, it indicates how a process of societal evolution can account for those differences.

PREDICATES FOR ECONOMIC DEVELOPMENT

The predicates for economic development turn out to be unexpectedly straight-forward as shown by several reports produced over recent years, notably: "The Index of Economic Freedom" (Index)[11], and "Economic Freedom of the World" (Report)[12], both published annually. Each surveys the countries of the world to rank them against objective criteria that focus on freedom of markets, rule of law, restrained central state, and sound macro-economic policies. Both reports characterize these attributes as elements of 'freedom', in practice meaning freedom from the predatory state, and freedom for personal initiative, for entrepreneurship, and for devolved decision-making.

What are these criteria and what are the underlying economic considerations (as presented in the 2006 Index)?

Judging Economic Freedom: The Underpinnings of an Advanced Economy

Let's take a closer look at to what factors the Index assesses to judge economic freedom:

(1) **Trade policy:** assesses average tariff rates, non-tariff barriers such as import quotas and licensing requirements, and corruption in the customs service.

(2) **Fiscal burden of government:** measures the top income tax rate, the tax that the average taxpayer faces, the top corporate tax rate, and government expenditures.

(3) **Government intervention in the productive economy:** measures government consumption as a percentage of the economy, government ownership of businesses and industries, share of government revenues from state-owned enterprises and government ownership of property, and economic output produced by the government.

(4) **Monetary policy:** considers the average inflation rate from 1995 to 2004.

(5) **Capital flows and foreign investment:** assesses foreign investment codes, restrictions on foreign ownership of business, restrictions on the industries and companies open to foreign investors; restrictions and performance requirements on foreign companies, foreign ownership of land; equal treatment under law for both foreign and domestic

companies, restrictions on the repatriation of earnings, and availability of local financing for foreign companies.

(6) **Banking and finance:** assesses government ownership of banks; restrictions on the ability of foreign banks to open branches and subsidiaries; government influence over the allocation of credit; government regulations; and freedom to offer all types of financial services, securities, and insurance policies.

(7) **Wages and prices:** assesses minimum wage laws; freedom to set prices privately without government influence; government price controls; the extent to which government price controls are used; and government subsidies to businesses that affect prices.

(8) **Property rights:** considers freedom from government influence over the judicial system, the adequacy of a commercial code defining contracts, sanctioning of foreign arbitration of contract disputes, government expropriation of property, corruption within the judiciary, delays in receiving judicial decisions, and legally granted and protected private property.

(9) **Regulation:** assesses licensing requirements to operate a business; ease of obtaining a business license; corruption within the bureaucracy; labor regulations such as established work weeks, paid vacations, and parental leave, as well as selected labor regulations; environmental, consumer safety, and work health regulations; and regulations that impose a burden on business.

(10) **Informal market:** considers smuggling; piracy of intellectual property, as well as agricultural production, manufacturing, services, transportation, and labor supplied on the black market.

The preface to the Index notes the strong interplay between the individual factors: "Any improvement in one area leads to improvements in another. Likewise, any decline of freedom in one area undermines economic freedom in another. The overall lesson is both simple and profound: To enjoy the benefits of economic freedom, a country must embrace a fundamental commitment to that aim.

A nation cannot undertake economic reform piecemeal and expect economic freedom to flourish."[13]

An Empirical Basis

These ten factors emerge less from a fully integrated theory of economics[14] than from centuries of economic experience. For the moment and in the absence of a grand set of economic laws, let's examine some narrower but experientially supportable aspects of economics to buttress the validity of the ten factors.

In the broadest sense, the chief test for an economy is its productivity as well as whether it produces goods that meet the needs and desires of its populace—i.e., the consumers. While some critics may deplore this view as too materialistic, as David Boaz noted, most individuals will prefer "life to death, health to sickness, nourishment to starvation, abundance to poverty."[15] One might add education to ignorance, and clean environments to polluted ones. The more productive an economy is, the more these preferences can be met.

Experience and logic dictate that the most productive economies are those in which physical and social resources flow to their optimum uses, many of which are found in capital investment to leverage man's individually limited capabilities to boost productivity. Accordingly, relevant tests of the optimum functioning of an economy look closely at the formation and the use of capital. And such an examination leads to the conclusion that optimum economic systems nurture freedom—freedom to act entrepreneurially, as well as freedom from predation, either from excessive taxation, expropriation, criminality, or from foreign threats and political insecurity. More specifically, such a system is based on the following considerations:

- A financial system should facilitate the accumulation of capital through savings and a free flow of that capital through investors and through intermediary institutions such as banks. Such a system needs to provide for return on capital commensurate with the risk taken, has to protect capital by rule of law, and permits the flow of capital to most productive uses without cumbersome regulation. (Index factors # 5 and 6)

• A free market should be unencumbered such that free play of the forces of supply and demand generates prices that provide clear signals to producers and consumers: rising prices encourage new production and discourage consumption; falling prices have the reverse effect. More abstractly, Hayek argued that the free market, through its price signals, effectively draws on the distributed intelligence and knowledge of all participants in the economic system. David Boaz elaborated: "Prices don't just tell us how much something costs at the store. The price system pulls together all the information available in the economy about what each person wants, how much he values it, and how it can be best produced. Prices make that information *useable* to both producer and consumer. Each price contains within it information about consumer demands and costs of production, ranging from the amount of labor needed to produce the item to the cost of labor to the bad weather on the other side of the world that is raising the price of the raw materials needed to produce the good. Instead of having to know all the details, one is presented with a simple number: the price."[16] This system is invariably superior to one of central planning because decision-makers, with the most at risk and closest to consumers and markets, will generally have the earliest and most detailed knowledge of relevant circumstances. (Index factor #7)

• Free trade with other countries should be unencumbered to maximize the productive effects of 'comparative advantage'. The economist David Ricardo described this economic principle as the law of association that demonstrates what the consequences of the division of labor are when an individual or a group, more efficient in every regard, cooperates with an individual or a group less efficient in every regard. Von Mises summarized it as follows: "The division of labor between two ... areas will ... increase the productivity of labor and is therefore advantageous to all concerned, even if the physical conditions of production for any commodity are more favorable in one of these two areas than in the other. It is advantageous for the better endowed area to concentrate its efforts upon the production of those commodities for which its superiority is greater, and to leave to the less well endowed area the production of other goods in which its superiority is less."[17] David Boaz's example is if Friday can catch twice as many fish as Crusoe but can find three times as many ripe fruits in a day, then both of them will be better off if Crusoe specializes in fishing (even though relatively less productive) and Friday specializes in foraging.[18] Under the same reasoning, societies should encourage individuals to focus on their greatest talents, trading the produce of these talents for the greatest benefit to themselves and to society overall. (Index factor #1)

• A free investment system should permit the flow of capital according to market signals. Neither inappropriate government regulation nor monopoly forces should be allowed to stifle the workings of comparative advantage or the innovative role of entrepreneurs. Competition should be unfettered to maximize innovation and to produce lowest costs to consumers. As a corollary, 'creative destruction'[19] must be tolerated, despite short-term pain. (Index factors #3, 9 and 5)

• Property rights must be protected by rule of law — a principal role of sound government. Tom Bethell in *The Noblest Triumph* lays out the role and central importance of property rights in the accumulation and deployment of capital. Simply put, if the fruits of one's labor and of one's savings are not protected, producing and saving are discouraged, thereby diminishing the production of wealth and the availability of capital. Equally importantly, investment will be discouraged and property will depreciate rapidly. As long ago as ancient Greece, Aristotle noted that what belongs to everyone belongs to no one and will be neglected. (Index factor # 8)

• The system should work to minimize externalities (costs) due to regulation and uncertainty. It is axiomatic that investment requires a rate of return commensurate with risk and uncertainty; the higher the risk, the higher the necessary return. For example, if the future value of a currency is uncertain due to inflationary forces, investors will require a higher rate of return to hedge against that uncertainty. Similarly, high rates of taxation effectively increase the cost of production so that net revenues have to be higher than otherwise to produce a desired rate of return. Corruption and wasteful regulation will drive up costs and reduce the productive value of a given investment. In short, the most productive economies will tend to be those where externalities—e.g., costs due to unsound currencies, wasteful regulation, political instability, and crime – are minimized, where contracts can be honestly enforced, and where profits are not unduly taxed. (Index factors # 2, 4, 9, and 10)

• Direct government intrusion in economic activity should be minimized. Lacking the constant pressure of competition and the penalty imposed by the market on mistakes and bad policy, government tends to employ resources less productively than the private sector. Moreover, protected bureaucracies breed timid operatives—civil servants more concerned about avoiding mistakes than with finding creative approaches that defy conventional wisdom. In addition, governments are invariably susceptible to political pressure—e.g., protecting a service to a favored group whether it makes economic sense or not. (Index factor #3)

• The tax burden should be minimized consistent with providing *essential* government services. Taxing an activity discourages it, and as pointed out above, taxation takes financial resources out of the hands of the more productive sectors and places them in the hands of a less productive government. Chapter VIII presents evidence that even among the most developed countries those with the highest levels of taxation have the slowest rates of economic growth, suggesting that optimally the rate of taxation by governments at all levels should not exceed twenty percent of the GDP. (Index factor #2)

The lesson here is that societies need to give wide opportunity to human productive impulses and to provide a supportive environment in which to act on them. When government places a heavy tax on productive behavior, distorts price signals, undermines economic rights, increases uncertainty, discourages movement of capital, discourages innovation, and places regulatory hurdles on new enterprises—all of which is dysfunctional behavior measured by the ten factors—economic growth languishes.

Having established the criteria, let's see how the world's countries align against them.

The Economically Advanced Countries are Those Who are 'Free'

The most economically developed countries are invariably those that are most 'free' in the sense postulated by "The Index of Economic Freedom." Figure I-1, taken from the Index (2008), summarizes the relative *freedom* of each of 157 countries in terms of freedom from government economic coercion and interference with the natural functioning of a free market. The countries with the darkest

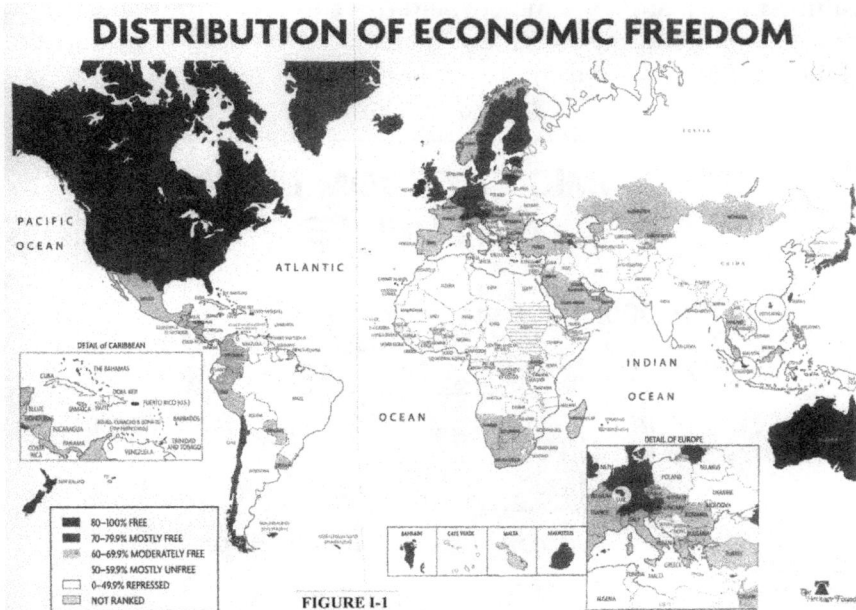

DISTRIBUTION OF ECONOMIC FREEDOM

80–100% FREE
70–79.9% MOSTLY FREE
60–69.9% MODERATELY FREE
50–59.9% MOSTLY UNFREE
0–49.9% REPRESSED
NOT RANKED

FIGURE I-1

Holmes, Kim R., Feulner, Edwin J., and O'Grady, Mary Anastasia. *2008 Index of Economic Freedom.* Washington, DC: The Heritage Foundation and New York: The Wall Street Journal, 2008.

coloring are considered free; those slightly lighter are mostly free; while those mostly unfree, unfree, or repressed are lightly shaded to white respectively.

The Index demonstrates a close correlation between high ranking on the freedom index and a high level of affluence, as seen in Figure I-2, which depicts each ranked group of nations against its per capita GDP (from the 2006 Report). A clear conclusion to be drawn is that the freer the nation, the wealthier the nation is likely to be, with the caveat that a country has to do most things right—i.e., countries in the mostly unfree category which follow only some correct policies fare as poorly as the repressed category of countries.

If one merely scans the shaded maps of the Index, one sees that the West as well as Japan and the 'seven tigers' of Asia are among the affluent. The least free and poorest countries tend to be those of the Arab world, of sub-Saharan Africa, and those still in thrall to Communist ideology such as North Korea, Viet Nam, and Cuba. Latin America shows a mixed pattern of free and unfree. Clearly, rich and poor countries are not distributed randomly around the globe but appear in culturally similar clusters.

ECONOMIC FREEDOM LEADS TO AFFLUENCE

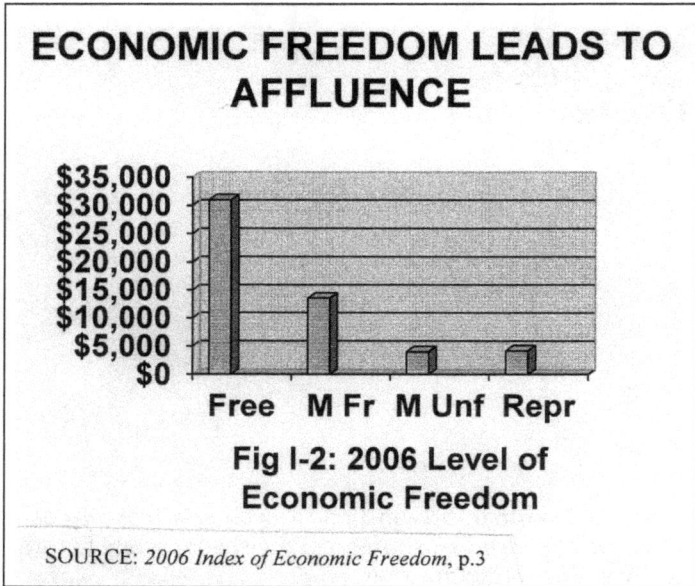

Fig I-2: 2006 Level of Economic Freedom

SOURCE: *2006 Index of Economic Freedom*, p.3

Unfortunately, more countries fail to adhere to these precepts of economic freedom than those that do. For example, using the ten identified factors as measurements of the degree of economic freedom, the Index (2006) concludes that of the 157 countries assessed, 72 are 'free' or 'mostly free' (largely adhering to most of the factors), while a larger number of 85 are 'mostly unfree' or 'repressed' (see Figure I-1).

Governments in the latter category routinely interfere with the market—creating coerced, or unfree, results—because of counter views: positions that challenge the efficacy of the market, claim the market ignores important human considerations, or argue there are 'market failures' that only governmental action can correct. Typical counter views are predicated on a belief that individuals are helpless vis-à-vis vested interests and that corporate entities will exploit the consumer and the worker without extensive government regulation. Perhaps even a more powerful counter-factor is the concept of 'fairness,' or social justice in response to poverty and disparity of wealth within a society. These latter views prompt government intervention to attempt to re-order natural outcomes through taxation, tariffs, and regulation to achieve outcomes that appear politically more desirable. Yet, however emotionally powerful these considerations might seem, they fail in achieving their goals because they are economically dysfunctional.

As economist Milton Friedman famously pointed out, "there are no free lunches." Given that most economic actors make decisions based on the best information available and do so in freely negotiated agreements, in most instances they will act for the best advantage of all parties in the transaction. Contrary action, coerced by the government, will introduce inefficiencies and other hidden costs. The political question arises as to whether government intervention is justified because it produces greater compensating social objectives. The short answer is that those compensating benefits are illusory. The most obvious evidence is that those countries that most pursue government distortions of the market are those that remain poor.

But that answer is somewhat unsatisfying in that it fails to illuminate fully why that should be. A deeper answer, which will take the length of this book to support, is that poor countries pursue self-defeating ends by placing undue priority on ancient human sentiment sympathizing with the poor and desiring fairness, without appreciating or understanding the role of the evolved values of free modern economies that would more effectively attain their objectives. To be sure, enduring human values—of mutual help and fairness—need to be preserved, but in their place: the extended family, in churches, in community organizations, and in philanthropies. That being said, a country's collective culture—worldviews and value systems—must move beyond a fixation on traditional values if they wish to become affluent. How a goodly number of countries moved beyond ancient sentiment in critical areas to achieve the benefits of modern society will be described in later chapters.

Another Dimension of Affluent Societies: Human and Social Capital

In terms of understanding the underpinnings of affluent societies and the failures of poorer ones, the institutional and policy factors discussed above represent necessary, but not sufficient, elements. An additional crucial dimension that distinguishes the two groups involves the role of culture in producing human and social capital, which determines the effectiveness of how members of society interact within a set of institutions and policies. The economic contribution of these forms of capital is captured by World Bank research summarized in its publication, *Where is the Wealth of Nations?*[20]

That report makes estimates of all the constituent parts of wealth in the world's countries, and concludes that the greatest piece of that wealth—intangible wealth—is produced by human and social capital. To arrive at a value of intangible wealth, the Bank first estimates a country's total wealth as that imputed by gross national income, then tallies up the components of tangible wealth, i.e., natural resources, capital investment, housing stock, infrastructure and so forth, and finally determines the difference, a residual of intangible wealth.

Table I-1, taken from the report, summarizes estimates of total world wealth by income-category of countries, showing the share of tangible capital vis-à-vis natural and produced capital.

TABLE I-1 Total Wealth, 2000
-- $ per capita and percentage shares --

Income Group	Natural Capital	Produced Capital	Intangible Capital	Total Wealth	Intangible Capital Share
Low-income countries	1,925	1,174	4,434	7,532	59%
Middle-income countries	3,496	5,347	18,773	27,616	68%
High-income OECD countries	9,531	76,193	353,339	439,063	80%
World	4,011	16,850	74,998	95,860	78%

SOURCE: The World Bank, *Where is the Wealth of Nations? – Measuring Capital for the 21st Century,* p.4

The Table shows that the greatest portion of wealth in all countries is intangible wealth, and that as countries grow more affluent, the basis for their wealth shifts increasingly from natural resources and invested capital to intangible capital.

One conclusion reached is that tangible wealth alone does not produce or necessarily correlate with the size of national income streams, but that other factors embodied in intangible wealth determine how productively tangible wealth is employed to produce a country's income. Specifically, the Report states:

> [Intangible capital] includes human capital, the skills and know-how embodies in the labor force. It encompasses social capital, that is, the degree of trust among people in a society and their ability to work together for common purposes. It includes those governance elements that boost the productivity of the economy. For example, if an economy has a very efficient judicial system, clear property rights, and an effective government, the result will be a higher total wealth and thus an increase in the intangible capital residual.[21]

The Report analyzes this concept further to pinpoint some sources of greater societal efficiency. Specifically, it traces efficiency to human capital and institutional quality, finding, for example, that the most influential contribution to such categories are years of schooling and rule of law, respectively.[22] Some of these findings coincide with the conclusions of *The Index of Economic Freedom* regarding the payoff in economic growth of sound policies and institutions. But an additional, but less measurable, piece of the picture is the strong suggestion that cultural factors play an important role as well—i.e., the degree of trust among people in a society and their ability to work together for common purposes. The following illustration[23] shows how such factors also can have substantial influence in determining economic outcomes.

While the World Bank Report has identified important factors contributing to a society's intangible capital, it leaves unaddressed implied questions of why many low-income countries continue to fail to adopt policies and institutions essential to building such capital as well as what the ultimate sources of societal capital such as mutual trust are. To pursue those questions requires a deeper investigation of the cultural underpinnings of society.

THE ROLE OF CULTURE

The prior examination of developed and undeveloped countries showed that they do not appear randomly about the globe, but rather in clusters having common cultural antecedents—culture being considered in the sense employed by some anthropologists referring to an "entire way of life of a society: its values, practices, symbols, institutions, and human relationships."[24] Some recent value surveys of countries around the globe allow us to examine in more detail the role of culture in determining economic outcomes.

Cultural Differences between Developed and Undeveloped Countries

Particular light was shed on the role of culture by a symposium of prominent scholars in the field of economic development in the summer of 1999 at the Harvard Academy for International and Area Studies. The symposium examined cultural factors that strongly correlate with the economic status of countries.[25]

One of the key papers related to that point was presented by Ronald Inglehart,[26] whose report[27] drew on the World Values Surveys. While these surveys collected data on a large number of variables, he found that that numerous variables could be aggregated, with a high degree of correlation, along just two 'dimensions'.

> **Culture's Role in Determining Relative Economic Performance – The Indian Textile Example**
>
> *A Farewell to Alms* examines the relative performance of the Indian textile industry vis-à-vis competitors world-wide during the first half of the twentieth century, and thereby highlights the role of cultural norms in determining an economy's productivity. It demonstrates that most factors of production were the same across the globe's highly competitive textile industry. For example, the same modern machinery, usually exported from Britain was used; often skilled managers from Britain accompanied the equipment; and costs of capital were comparable. Nonetheless, efficiency in Indian factories was only a fraction that of the United States, Britain, and Japan, with the consequence that although wage rates were only a small fraction of those in richer countries, the overall cost of labor was greater.
>
> Economic studies of the Bombay industry in the 1920s and 1930s showed that the differences in attitudes and behaviors between Indian workers and their counterparts in high-wage countries accounted for the differences in productivity. Gregory Clark summarized the conclusions of such studies: "The cotton mills in England were noted for the early introduction of strict systems of factory discipline. Workers, even those who were on piece rates, were expected to appear at opening time each morning, to work all the hours the mill was open, to stay at their own machines, and to refrain from socializing at work. Indian mills by comparison were undisciplined. This lack of discipline and high absenteeism continued at least into the 1960s.
>
> The Indian Factory Labour Commission report of 1909 is full of testimony by employers regarding conditions in the mills. A substantial fraction of workers were absent on any given day, and those at work were often able to come and go from the mill at their pleasure to eat or to smoke. … The mill yards would have eating places, barbers, drink shops, and other facilities to serve workers taking a break. Some others allegedly brought their children with them to the mills. Workers' relatives would bring food to them inside the mill during the day. … [While] there are few reliable estimates of the fraction of time workers were absent from their machines: the manufacturers put the figure at 10-30 percent of total work time."
>
> [Manufacturers, of course, experimented with various expedients to address the productivity shortfall, but none succeeded in reducing overall labor costs, still presumably influenced by cultural variables.]
>
> SOURCE: Gregory Clark, *A Farewell to Alms*, Chapter 17

- *The traditional vs. secular-rational dimension.* This dimension measures adherence to values associated with religion, family ties, deference to authority, political conflict, and consensus vs. confrontation in decision-making. Inglehart stated: "Societies at the traditional pole emphasize religion, absolute standards, and traditional family values; favor large families; reject divorce; and take a pro-life stance on abortion, euthanasia, and suicide. They emphasize social conformity rather than individualistic achievement, favor consensus rather than open political conflict, support deference to authority, and have high levels of national pride and a nationalistic outlook. Societies with secular-rational values have the opposite preferences on all these topics."

• *The survival vs. self-expression dimension.* Inglehart stated: "This dimension involves the themes that characterize post-industrial society. ... Societies that emphasize survival values show relatively low levels of subjective well-being, report relatively poor health, are low on interpersonal trust, are relatively intolerant toward outgroups, are low on support for gender equality, emphasize materialist values,... are relatively low on environmental activism, and are relatively favorable to authoritarian government. Societies that emphasize self-expression values tend to have the opposite preferences on all these topics. ... Societies that emphasize self-expression values are much more likely to be stable democracies than those that emphasize survival values."

By plotting the aggregate scores of 65 societies on a 'cultural map' drawn in these two dimensions (see Figure I-3), he found that

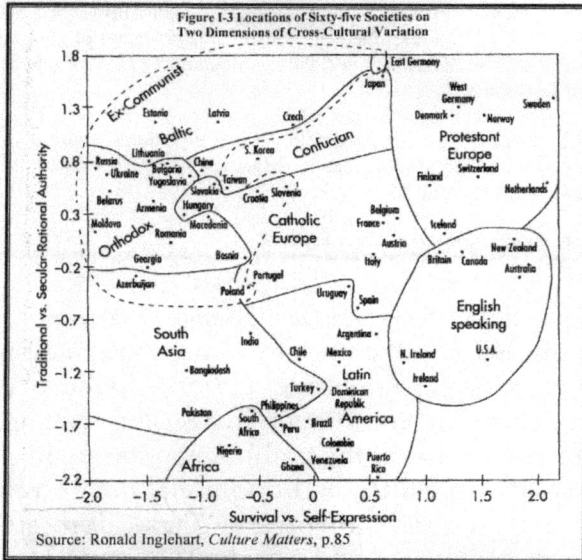

Figure I-3 Locations of Sixty-five Societies on Two Dimensions of Cross-Cultural Variation

Source: Ronald Inglehart, *Culture Matters*, p.85

societies cluster by culture, which reflect ethnic, religious and political heritages. On one hand, this merely validates our intuition that
one would expect countries with similar cultures to have populations with similar world-views. On the other hand, it confirms a
more potentially controversial view that rich countries differ from
poor by virtue of their cultural heritage.

To show this conclusion more explicitly, Inglehart has overlaid
the previous map with GNP per capita gradient lines—shown here
as Figure I-4. Affluent countries and cultures lie toward the upper
right while poorer countries are at the lower left of the chart. To be
sure, two clusters, Confucian and historically Catholic, extend over
a significant variation of income, because some countries in those
cultures have already succeeded in development while others lag.
Therefore, one can infer that while a country's culture may not initially have had values hospitable to economic growth, the exigencies of the process cause their people to absorb new world-views
over time.

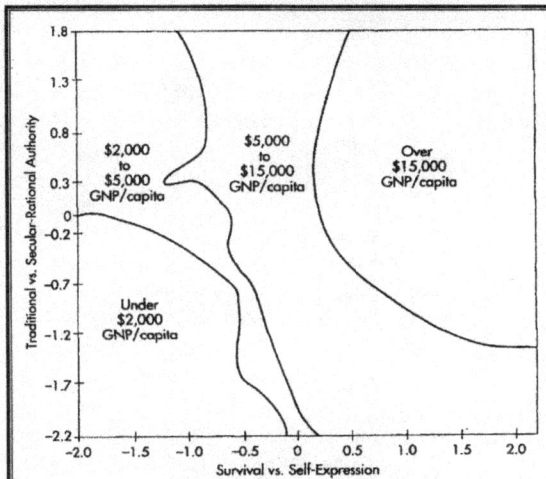

Figure I-4 Economic Level of Sixty-Five Societies
Superimposed on Two Dimensions of Cross-Cultural Variation

Source: Ronald Inglehart, *Culture Matters*, p.89

SOURCE: Economic levels are based on the World Bank's
purchasing power parity estimates as of 1995; see *World
Development Report, 1997*, pp. 214–215.

Inglehart singles out one value, interpersonal trust, to illustrate the underlying importance of values to economic growth. To do this, he portrays the percentage of a population that trusts people in general against the GNP per capita of a society, as shown in Figure I-5.

It is evident that the more economically advanced countries exhibit a greater degree of mutual trust among their inhabitants (as was the case in the World Bank Report cited earlier). In further support of this emphasis, he refers to several economists who show why interpersonal trust is essential for building the social structures on which democracy depends and the complex social organizations on which large-scale economic enterprises are based

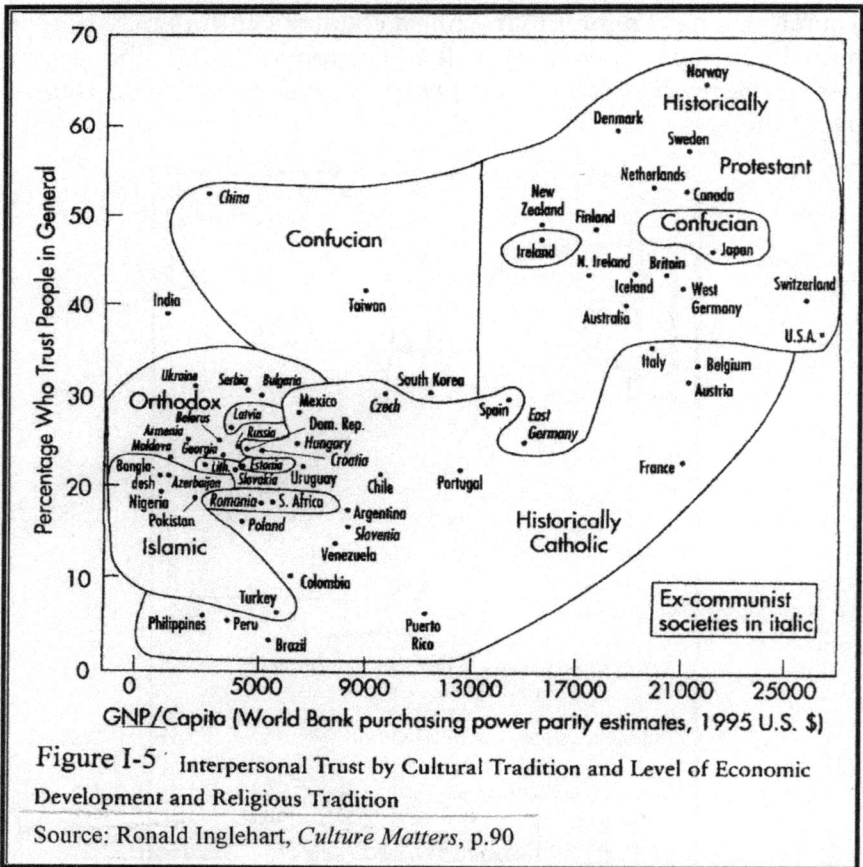

Figure I-5 Interpersonal Trust by Cultural Tradition and Level of Economic Development and Religious Tradition

Source: Ronald Inglehart, *Culture Matters*, p.90

– a theme that will be echoed in Chapters III and IV of this book. Essentially, trust is a surrogate for a number of subsidiary values critical to building and maintaining a modern economic order, as argued by Francis Fukuyama.[28]

"Social capital can be defined simply as an instantiated set of informal values or norms shared among members of a group that permits them to cooperate with one another. If members of the group come to expect that others will behave reliably and honestly, then they will come to trust one another. Trust acts like a lubricant that makes any group or organization run more efficiently.... The norms that produce social capital must substantively include virtues like truth telling, meeting obligations, and reciprocity." Fukuyama goes on to note that all viable social groups require elements of trust. What varies, however, is what Fukuyama characterizes as the "radius of trust", i.e. for practical purposes, do individuals trust others beyond the family; the clan; the village; the ethnic group; or indefinitely to others perceived as sharing the same cultural values? He notes that the greater the degree of trust within a societal entity, the lower the "transaction costs" (such as due to regulations, auditing, and legal actions) will be.[29]

The correlation between interpersonal trust and culture is as dramatic as is the correlation between it and affluence. For example, the figure demonstrates that virtually all historically Protestant and Confucian societies rank higher on interpersonal trust than virtually all historically Catholic societies. And ironically, despite the Communist rhetoric of creating a cooperative, socially-oriented populace—i.e., the new "Soviet Man," virtually all ex-communist societies rank relatively low on personal trust—lower than would be indicated by their ethnic and religious heritage.

But positively, Inglehart indicates how such a value conducive to economic development might grow in importance within a population as it experiences the benefits and demands of a growing economy. This can be seen in the survey's findings that Catholics rank as high as Protestants on interpersonal trust in mixed societies. That suggests that the utility of such trust is so high that the societies manage to inculcate these values in most of the adherent population—probably through example and experience.[30]

Paths of Cultural Change

Apparently then, for less-developed societies to evolve to modern economic states, they will have to move along a path of cultural change—from traditional social norms, toward increasingly rational, tolerant, trusting, post-modern values. The starting point is a world-view of traditional-survival societies, also described by anthropologists as a 'peasant society' mindset, which was described in the Introduction and common to most societies that have not yet developed. As described by anthropologist George Foster, "the typical peasant sees little or no relationship between work and technology on one hand, and the acquisition of wealth on the other: one works to eat but not to create wealth. The Anglo-Saxon virtues of hard work and thrift are meaningless in peasant society. ... Peasants are individualistic, and each social unit sees itself in continual struggle with its neighbors for its share of scarce wealth." [31]

Then, contrast this view with conclusions regarding advanced societies derived from the *World Value Surveys* that were described earlier in the Introduction – i.e., their economically advanced populations become more socially mobile, individualistic, economic oriented, and secular.[32]

Thus, in adapting to the demands of freer, more complex, and demanding economies, societies have learned experientially how to empower the individual, rely on more impersonal contractual ties, constrain authority, and learn to live with the uncertainties and the give-and-take of free societies. But because the new ways are in continuing tension with man's age-old value set, Hayek argued that despite their demonstrated efficacy, evolved values often do not sit easily with members of post-modern societies:

> The structures of the extended order are made up not only of individuals, but also of many, often overlapping, sub-orders within which old instinctual responses, such as solidarity and altruism, continue to retain some importance by assisting voluntary collaboration, even though they are incapable, by themselves, of creating a basis for the more extended order. Part of our present difficulty is that we must constantly adjust our lives, our thoughts and our emotions, in order to live simultaneously within different kinds

of orders according to different rules. If we were to apply the unmodified, uncurbed, rules of the micro-cosmos (i.e., of the small band or troop, or of, say, our families) to the macro-cosmos (our wider civilization), as our instincts and sentimental yearnings often make us wish to do, we would destroy it. Yet if we were always to apply the rules of the extended order to our more intimate groupings, we would crush them. So we must learn to live in two sorts of worlds at once.[33]

In effect, according to Hayek, mankind developed civilization by learning to follow rules that forbade one to do what instincts demanded, and freed him to a critical degree from needing to achieve a social consensus before acting.[34] Indeed, those living in the productive arena of the extended order gain from *not* treating one another as neighbors, rather adhering to rules of private property and contract instead of solidarity and altruism.[35] In effect, to the extent that entrepreneurs and visionaries gain freedom of action from the immediate social context of shared vision and goals, a more rapid response to changing circumstances in innovative ways becomes possible.[36] And as advanced societies progressed, their societies became increasingly more powerful, wealthier, and more liberated, as they relinquished old ways for new.

Readers may object that this beneficent view of modernization may ignore too much of what is important to being a human being. What about healthy extended families, and centuries if not millennia of artistic traditions and deep philosophic roots? These are indeed important to the human condition. But if one also desires a high standard of living, state of the art health care, leading academic institutions, creative arts, and so forth, an advanced economy is required as well. Some societies may opt for simpler, less affluent existences, which is their choice. But when countries make non-productive choices—i.e., ones rejecting the policy reforms essential for the functioning of free markets, they should not castigate others, usually the West, for resulting disparities in wealth among nations.

Moreover, to resist this argument on a belief in an essential equality among cultures is a disservice to poorer countries. This is not to argue that the current model of modernization is the end-all and be-all of possible societies. Other cultural models may well replicate necessary institutions of currently advanced societies to achieve comparable material progress, and then draw on other values unique to their cultures to pull ahead. The nature of evolution is that one cannot predict if and when newer values and capabilities might emerge, or if some existing values will take on increased utility under future unforeseen circumstances. But any path to stronger and more perfect societies will in all likelihood have to build on the achievements of currently advanced societies for some time to come.

In any event, it is clear that the value set or culture of a society plays a strong role in determining its ability to modernize. In addition, we have seen that countries move along a *path of value change* as they modernize and become affluent. The nature of that path becomes clearer when seen in evolutionary terms.

An Evolutionary View of Culture

Contrasting the historical record of developed and less developed countries led Hayek to conclude that the emergence of the modern free market system was the result of an *evolutionary* process of societies learning to organize their modes of innovation and cooperation more efficiently. He characterized the modern economic system as an *extended order* of human cooperation, which he considered to be an objective advance on humankind's atavistic ways of organizing society.[37] How did he see the extended order unfolding?

Von Hayek saw it unfolding through trial and error leading to superior new practices and institutions. Adam Smith, he said, identified the limitations on our capability of perceiving the details of the extended order in his references to the 'invisible hand', which alludes to the role of the pricing system in market exchange. Prices are shaped by circumstances of which we are only vaguely aware, and they lead us to satisfy the needs of others whom we do not know. In effect, according to von Hayek, "all this is possible because we stand in a great framework of institutions and traditions—economics, legal, and moral—into which we fit ourselves by obeying certain rules of conduct that we never made, and which we never understood in the sense in which we understand how the things that we manufacture function." [38]

The rationale for considering the process evolutionary was, of course, that it reflected the concept of survival of the fittest, i.e., it led to a comparative increase of population and wealth in those groups that followed certain innovative practices that often ran counter to established worldviews and value systems previously universal to civilized man. Moreover, Hayek intuited a process of unconscious self-organization in societies similar to biological phenomena.[39] Prime examples of such spontaneous unplanned creation are language, law, morality, and monetary institutions.[40] And in the *extended order*, as in biology, evolutionary change tends toward a maximum economy in the use of resources,[41] leading to effective new practices and institutions, producing in turn evolutionarily fitter societies. Taking the biological evolutionary insight further, Hayek concludes: "The extended order is probably the most complex structure in the universe—a structure in which biological organisms that are already highly complex have acquired the capacity to learn, to assimilate, parts of suprapersonal traditions enabling them to adapt themselves from moment to moment into an ever-changing structure possessing an order of a still higher level of complexity."[42]

Implicit in this view is that the very institutional framework and value system governing the ability of individuals to cooperate efficiently was unplanned, unscripted—hence, de Soto's lament that the West left no 'blueprint' of its evolution to guide developing countries.

So, if we wish to understand the origins of the extended order and why less developed countries remain unreceptive to its imperatives much may be learned by examining the evolutionary process as it unfolded with regard to societies. But how should that examination be undertaken? First of all, a methodology is required, for which this book draws on an approach formulated by Professor Phillip Scribner as is summarized in Chapter II. The particular utility of his approach is that it considers societal values as playing the role of the genome of the societal animal, and values are something that we can assess and track over time.

A second consideration is where the focus of our attention can profitably be directed given the vast universe of variables making up the human condition. Guidance to that end comes from the early part of this chapter. We saw from both *The Index of Economic*

Freedom and the *World Values Survey* how populations in developed and undeveloped countries differ with regard to views of free markets, of governmental authority, and of the freedom assigned to the individual. Accordingly, the book will explore how certain indispensable new worldviews, characteristic of developed countries, came about: (1) a respect for free play of market forces despite man's age-old distrust of the merchant and the trader, (2) institutions that secured individual liberty and restrained the predatory state in ways that overcame a heritage of despotism, and (3) the liberation of individual enterprise and artistic creativity from the confines of conformist tradition.

In addition, because the modern affluent world simply would not be possible absent the fruits of science, even if all the policies and institutions necessary to the extended order were in place, the book will show how science evolved in a world that had been mired in mysticism and superstition. As will be seen, the development of science represents the epitome of an evolutionary process that results in the survival of the fittest.

The next chapter begins the investigation by laying out a theory of societal evolution and portrays its unfolding during mankind's early existence.

2
The Evolution of Societies

The living world emerged when inorganic matter stumbled on a way of passing on intricate, unpredictable information, and found that it could achieve immortality for that information by its ceaseless repetition. … In the same spirit, our own nominally civilized, cultivated, intelligent, and reflective level of life emerged when organisms stumbled on a way of passing on intricate, unpredictable information to others around them and following them. It did so by inventing language and effectively binding together all human organisms, past, present, and future into a single mega-organism of potentially boundless achievement. – Peter Atkins[43]

As seen in Chapter I, Friedrich von Hayek concluded that modern economies arose during a prolonged evolutionary period via a process that intrinsically was unplanned and unscripted, thereby leaving the details veiled in the pages of history.[44] If we can lift that veil, we can gain a deeper understanding of just how the evolutionary process unfolded in the realms of new economic practices and new worldviews that produced the modern affluent world. And, thereby, we gain a better grasp of both the essential underpinnings of modern society and the hurdles confronting less developed countries.

To such an end, this chapter: (1) lays out a theory of societal evolution, and (2) employs it as a prism through which to examine human pre-history and early settled civilizations to see how societal evolution unfolded in practice. With that foundation, we will be positioned to explore the key avenues of evolutionary change identified in Chapter 1.

SOCIETAL EVOLUTION – THE CONCEPT

Societal evolution through the process of group selection is arguably subject to laws similar to those that govern the evolution of species, termed by Darwin "natural selection." Although the application of this paradigm to groups is relatively undeveloped and controversial, it can greatly enhance an understanding of the evolutionary expansion of the extended order. To that end, we will examine the evolutionary process as it is widely understood—i.e., as it applies to species—and then extend it to societies.

Evolution of Species

A standard portrayal of the workings of evolutionary forces is laid out by Phillip Scribner[45]: "Darwin (1809 – 1882) discovered a mechanism that can explain the evolution of species and their traits in an obviously naturalistic way. Darwin saw that if variations on traits occur randomly in members of a species, and if those traits are inherited by their offspring, evolutionary change could occur simply as a result of the greater reproductive success of those with traits that are useful. That is what he called "natural selection." Over time, the natural selection of random, heritable variations would give species traits that adapt them to their environments. … At first, there were only very modest organisms, but evolution has given rise over time to more and more impressive organisms, eventually including beings like us." Alexander Rosenberg's more rigorous definition of the evolutionary dynamic is seen below in the endnote.[46]

This view of evolution, although widely accepted, goes only as far as the evolution of species and not of groups or societies. Moreover, the standard view regards evolution as largely a random process, driven by mutations and changes in the environment. But new evidence and arguments, marshaled by Scribner, suggest that while mutations and environmental events are certainly random, their interplay is subject to discernable rules that provide a directional bent.

Evolutionary Stages—from Molecules to Societal Groups
A broad overview of the stages of evolution that culminated in advanced humans is depicted in a diagram developed by Scribner (seen in Figure II-1).

This portrayal highlights several key aspects of the evolutionary process, depicting *stages* of evolution in ascending order of complexity. Each succeeding stage represents a significantly higher order of complexity in terms of its structure[47] and capacity for an entity's interaction with its environment. As a stage initiates via crucial mutations, the first new organisms start out simple, uniform, and weak. But with evolutionary change, as new traits emerge, organisms become complex, diverse, and powerful. Moreover, Scribner notes that each stage can be objectively separated from the others, because, as shown by fossil records, each begins with a radiation of new species (during initial brief periods, many new species appear) to be followed by long periods of slow change (life forms might continue to emerge, but their number and complexity are constrained by the limited possibilities inherent at that stage). And

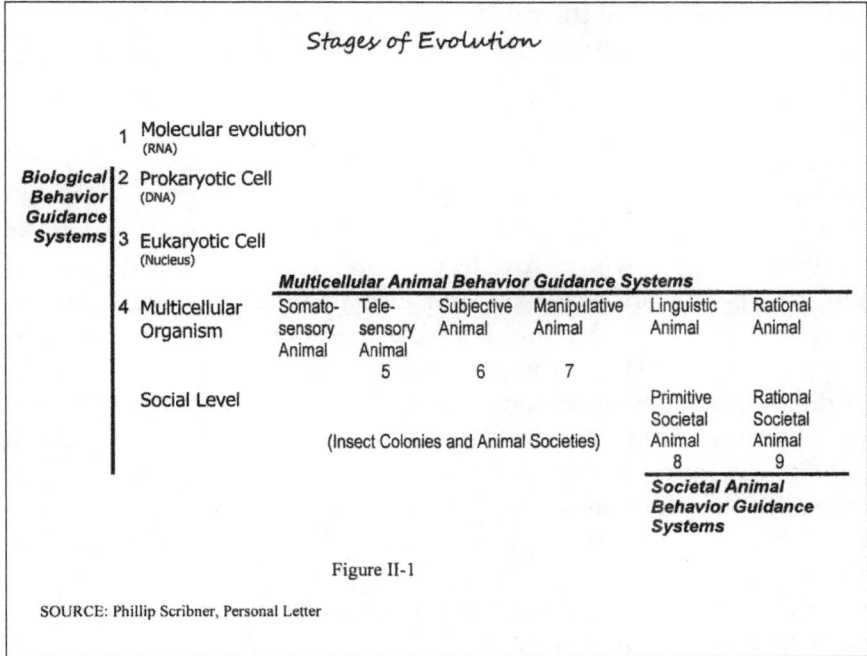

Stages of Evolution

Biological Behavior Guidance Systems	1	Molecular evolution (RNA)						
	2	Prokaryotic Cell (DNA)						
	3	Eukaryotic Cell (Nucleus)						
			Multicellular Animal Behavior Guidance Systems					
	4	Multicellular Organism	Somato-sensory Animal	Tele-sensory Animal	Subjective Animal	Manipulative Animal	Linguistic Animal	Rational Animal
				5	6	7		
		Social Level					Primitive Societal Animal	Rational Societal Animal
				(Insect Colonies and Animal Societies)			8	9
							Societal Animal Behavior Guidance Systems	

Figure II-1

SOURCE: Phillip Scribner, Personal Letter

significant further evolution is not possible until fundamentally new mutations emerge that lead to more complex life forms that are more powerful in exploiting environmental niches.

A key utility of this schema is that it provides a basis for understanding the origins and significance in evolutionary terms of the emergence of a new entity, the *societal animal* seen in Stages 8 and 9. As will be described below, when man evolved a higher level of neurological organization, offering the potential for language and reason, purposeful social effort became possible. Through culture and common values, the societal animal coordinates its members to achieve goals much like a brain coordinates the limbs of a body to serve the needs of the individual. And this new entity is just as subject to evolutionary forces as species are. The awesome implications of these evolutionary developments are implied in the Atkin's quote introducing this chapter: "[Evolution] did so by inventing language and effectively binding together all human organisms, past, present, and future into a single mega-organism of potentially boundless achievement."

Let's briefly examine the process of evolution at the early stages of life on this planet, and then consider how the forces at work apply to groups.

The First Replicators
Richard Dawkins provides a useful view of the beginnings of life and the inevitability of evolution.[48] Dawkins describes this process as having begun even before there were such things as genes and DNA. It began once certain replicator molecules emerged in the primordial soup of the simple stable molecules, which existed on earth in its earliest days in the form of air, water, carbon dioxide, and ammonia. Scientists have found that when energy in the form of ultraviolet light or electric spark is added to mixtures of these substances, more complex stable molecules are formed. Indeed, laboratory experiments have produced amino acids in the form of purines and pyrimidines, which are building blocks of the genetic molecule, DNA, itself.[49]

Eventually, perhaps over hundreds of million years, a special molecule was formed from such building blocks. Dawkins terms this molecule a replicator because it could replicate itself. All that was required was for the building block elements of the replicator to have an ongoing affinity for their own kind. Then, in the primordial soup, building blocks of similar molecules gravitated to the replicator and began to orient themselves in the same order as in the replicator, joining together in a form as stable as the replicator molecule and breaking away as a newly formed replicator molecule. Probably numerous such combinations were created, all contending for building block molecules in the soup. And the process worked as well if the building blocks had a special affinity for somewhat different building blocks, in which case a 'negative image' of the replicator molecule was formed. DNA molecules, it turns out, use positive-negative replication.[50]

But some replicators were more 'fit' for survival and propagation than others and grew in relative numbers, thus beginning the evolutionary process. In this early competition among replicator molecule types, mutations occurred that provided molecules with adaptive capabilities. Dawkins suggests these might involve chemical defenses and/or protein coats, and with such coats the molecules became 'survival machines'.[51] The most successful survival machines eventually were those that were constituted by large numbers of genes, which were sufficiently compatible with one another (despite ongoing intramural competition for survival) and which provided for greater evolutionary potential in terms of new powers. These processes are seen in Stages 1 through 3 of Figure II-1, depicting increasing levels of biological complexity from the first RNA molecular replicators to the Eukaryotic Cell (Nucleus).

Dawkins describes evolution as competition among replicators (usually genes) for "vehicles" (usually bodies). Good replicators had to have three properties: fidelity, fecundity, and longevity. If they did, then competition among them, differential survival, and, hence, natural selection for progressive improvement was not just likely but inevitable.[52]

Living Organisms
The next stages, 4 through 7, produced increasingly sophisticated creatures that more powerfully interacted with their environment to survive. For example, these creatures (animals) differ from life

forms that absorb energy at hand in that they acquire usable energy by seeking and ingesting energy-rich objects. These creatures had to have evolved a behavior guidance system—a nervous system—that allowed them to act on objects in space and to know which objects to ingest or otherwise act upon.

A key evolutionary advance prerequisite for thinking creatures occurred in Stage 6 when animals came into existence with a brain having a neocortex. Scribner suggests that a key aspect of this brain structure in evolutionary terms is the capacity for imagination. He states that a whole new range of relevant conditions would be brought under control if, instead of reacting instinctively to a situation, an animal could think about the effects of an action—e.g., of locomotion in various directions on the relation of its body to other objects in space. Moreover, the capacity to imagine different outcomes makes possible, he says, for animal behavior to be guided by desires, which motivate them to achieve one or another of those outcomes. To such ends, the animal guidance system can select behavior to control relevant conditions such as acquiring energy and avoiding predators.

Most notably, in Stage 7 of evolutionary development, mammals acquired 'manipulative imagination', which gave primates—and pre-humans—the capacity to consider the effects of handling objects, such as tools. This stage occurred about 40 million years ago, with a radiation of evolutionary more advanced creatures, the anthropoids, which displaced more primitive primates such as lemurs and tarsiers in most ecological niches.

Societal Animals

It was the last stages 8 and 9 (the linguistic and the rational) of this evolutionary sequence that produced evolved humans, an effectively new life form capable of rational, coordinated behavior. Scribner outlines how the increasing neurological development of the brain in the prefrontal neocortex (where behavioral schemata are stored for use by the behavior generator) allowed this development to occur.

The linguistic stage came about from the brain's capacity to use language as a system of representation, producing a dramatically more powerful capability for cooperation, and represents the beginnings of the societal animal. To be sure, initially this was a primitive capability inasmuch as it involved only simple sentences. But still it permitted individuals to coordinate their actions with others. Moreover, it motivated subjective animals to develop a sense for cause and effect, and eventually to understand efficient causation.

The rational stage became possible once the brain could provide individuals with a faculty of 'psychological imagination', or the ability to represent what is actual against a background of what is possible. A feature of the rational stage is the ability to use verbs of a propositional attitude such as 'believes' and 'desires'. Scribner calls this state the *reflective level of neurological organization* and asserts that it provided man with a rational imagination. Such imagination allowed individuals to consider causes for behavior—and causes led to reasons, which, in turn, enabled man to understand arguments. Consequently, *reason* was brought into human capability. Reason uses language in a very powerful animal behavior guidance system, which governs behavior at both the individual and social levels.

To be sure, a vast number of changes involving human evolution occurred over the eons, but Scribner's stages highlight the changes that totally altered the nature of man, resulting in the potential for reasoning, communicating, cooperating, and ultimately coordinating activities for mutual ends—and to make possible *societal* evolution. Scribner argues that via these new capabilities the *societal animal* emerged. Just as the primate brain coordinates muscles throughout its body so that the body as a whole can act on other objects in space, so the linguistic interaction among the members of a group coordinates the behavior of its members so that the group as a whole can act on other objects in space. Moreover, man's new capacity to rely on external aids such as writing (to store and pass on information and arguments to new generations) augmented and amplified the workings of the physical brain so that for all practical purposes it can be said to have evolved to a still more powerful level.

As a living, replicating entity, the societal animal is inevitably subject to the evolutionary forces driven by the survival of fittest—i.e., groups can evolve preferentially, based on having relatively fitter behavioral traits. To be clear, this concept of societal evolution is not to be linked to the concepts of social Darwinism current a century or more ago that led to discredited practices of eugenics. In societal evolution the group becomes evolutionarily more fit because of its values and practices not because of changes in genetic makeup.

Evolution: Inevitable and Progressive

Scribner elaborates on evolutionary theory to show how change has a directional bias. This bias is by no means teleological in nature; it is simply a process wherein a succession of mutations inevitably occurs, producing greater fitness incrementally. To be sure, not all mutations are beneficial and successful. But, in aggregate, fitter entities will develop along lines that enhance access to energy and as well as control of the conditions governing reproduction.

His thesis admittedly conflicts with current dominant views of evolution, which argue that there are no grounds for viewing evolution as progressive. Scribner defines essential aspects of the dominant view by noting that it rests on the concept of 'accidentalism', which recognizes two factors: First, environmental change is what is thought to cause natural selection. If selection pressures are imposed on species by changes in the environment whose causes are external to evolution itself, the course of evolution cannot be predicted by Darwin's mechanism alone. Instead, evolution is simply "tracking changes in the environment," in the words of contemporary Darwinists. Second, when a change in a species' environment occurs, there is no guarantee that the best adaptation will occur in response. Thus, natural selection operates on random variations, and only on those that happen to be available at the time. There may be other variations that would be better, but since they are not tried out (or tried only later, after another variation has already evolved), they cannot be selected. Thus, evolution cobbles together a makeshift "fix" for the immediate situation. It is basically random variations that happen to succeed in the face of external changes in the environment. Because species must make do with what is available at the time, biologists now see the traits and species found in nature more as effects of accidents and makeshift compromises than as something that shows they are an 'advance'.

Scribner proposes an alternative view, which he believes is not incompatible with the views originally held by Darwin: an idea of natural selection inspired by Malthusian theory which held that human populations grow geometrically while sources of food grow only arithmetically. In those circumstances, the natural selection that occurs is, in Darwin's words, via a "struggle for survival".

Since energy is always limited, and species are in ongoing competition for access to that energy, natural selection of relevant mutations should be a ubiquitous feature of the evolutionary process. In this light, evolutionary change occurs, not just in response to changes in the environment, but is ongoing, producing a gradual accumulation of traits that is progressive. Scribner argues: "[A]s long as there are new, heritable traits within the range of traits

---

An Illustration of Reproductive Causation

Scribner uses the example of fish evolving into amphibians. "Reproduction among fish of various kinds would eventually cause a scarcity in the usable energy and other resources available in the water. Those fishes in which random variations happened to try out traits that enabled them to move their bodies across land, would find plants that provided a new source of usable energy. Those fish would tend to succeed in reproducing, while otherwise they might have failed.

"Something like this apparently happened among lungfishes about 345 million years ago. These fresh water fish had already evolved lungs, perhaps to absorb oxygen from the air when the water was stagnant and deficient in oxygen, and they had "lobe fins," or large fleshy bases for their paired pectoral and pelvic fins, making it possible for them to move across land. At first, they were relatively uniform, simple and barely able to complete cycles of reproduction requiring locomotion across land, but reproductive causation would make them increasingly complex, diverse, and powerful. As random variations on their inherited multicellular structure tried out new traits, one new trait after another would be added. Each new trait would make them more powerful at controlling conditions that affected their reproduction, and as their complexity and power increased, new ways of controlling conditions could be tried out by random variations. Thus, fins would gradually evolve into legs, enabling them to crawl more efficiently across land, and since land plants provided many different sources of usable energy, the different ways of acquiring energy would lead to the evolution of different species of amphibians. ...

"Such a proliferation of species is called a "radiation," and it would occur again and again. When a more basic random variation on amphibians finally tried out internal fertilization (instead of fertilization in water) and made it possible for eggs that remained on land to house a form of embryological development that did not involve a larval stage, reptiles would be able to acquire usable energy from new sources on land. Two legged locomotion would be the start that gave dinosaurs their day in the sun. Those with wing-like limbs would begin the radiation of birds."

SOURCE: Phillip Scribner, *Western Philosophy and the Nature of Goodness*

being "tried out" by random variations that would make organisms better able to control the conditions that affect their reproduction,... evolutionary change of this sort could go on for a long time, adding one new trait after another, making them complex, diverse and powerful."[53] He terms this subset of natural selection 'reproductive causation'.

Thus, newly evolved creatures compete against earlier forms of that species—i.e., competition of the fittest occurs mainly within species and not between them. The chief competition within a species occurs where members fight others for reproductive opportunity and for access to food. Accordingly, fitness reflects explicit operational features—i.e., when a species evolves successfully it has gained a new capability of exploiting its energy environment in some determinate way that is superior to that of prior forms of the species.

Group Selection

The view that societal animals are subject to evolution through the process of group selection is just as controversial as the concept of progressivism. Yet the possibility of group selection is consonant with the Darwinian view that all life forms evolve by the differential survival of replicating entities. Darwin considered this possibility when he wrote: "There can be no doubt that a tribe including many members who, from possessing in a high degree the spirit of patriotism, fidelity, obedience, courage, and sympathy, were always ready to aid one another, and to sacrifice themselves; for the common good would be victorious over other tribes, and this would be natural selection."[54]

Such views failed to gain currency because of the difficulty in finding specific models in which group selection could have occurred. David Sloan Wilson[55] writes that that the concept remained in play, although by the 1960s a consensus had emerged that group selection was such a weak force that it could be ignored—that though it is theoretically possible for groups to evolve into adaptive units, it almost never happens in the real world.[56]

One central conceptual difficulty faced by group selection supporters had to do with possibilities of altruistic behavior (or lack thereof). The theoreticians believed that, for group selection to work, there would have to be individuals in the group who would favor the group's interests over their own—i.e., they would exhibit altruistic behavior. Such behavior, however, would seem to doom the survival of the genes that produced this kind of behavior because the associated individuals would be at a disadvantage for survival vis-à-vis other members of the group. Since natural selection clearly does operate at the level of individuals, the genes of truly altruistic individuals would be "unselected" with time. In this line of reasoning, if the interests of the group could not be favored over the interests of individuals, the group would never consist of anything but some amalgam of individual interests.

According to Wilson the theoretical pendulum has been swinging away from that position for the last several decades. More recent paradigms consider the possibilities of natural selection operating at the group level of the biological hierarchy. For example, if certain behaviors strengthen a group vis-à-vis other groups to the point that that group survives preferentially, then those behaviors will simultaneously favor the survival of the individuals practicing those behaviors vis-à-vis individuals in other groups that lack those behaviors. Therefore, while the struggle for survival of the species is inescapably tied to the fate of the individual, the competition is increasingly manifested by competition among groups—i.e., competition for survival has 'moved' up the biological hierarchy; from the individual to the societal group.

Culture: The Genome of the Societal Animal
A central hypothesis of the concept of societal evolution is that it operates via a society's 'culture'—i.e., its values, practices, and institutions, and accordingly that culture can be viewed as the genome of the societal animal. In this view, positive behaviors, which can be regarded as cultural mutations, arise in one group by chance or by rational deliberation, and quickly become the dominant behavior pattern of the group. As the efficacy of the behavior is widely appreciated, it is established as a new norm, and peer pressure reinforces it. Accordingly, such cultural evolution can proceed much more rapidly than species mutation, which requires generations to go by before a trait becomes predominant in a group.[57/58]

More specifically, Scribner argues that the rational stage of man's evolution provided the basis for societal evolution. In effect, man could perceive the relative efficacy of arguments and, thus, arguments packaged as 'culture' could evolve more powerfully by a process of rational selection. The competitive pressures driving natural selection within a culture would be produced by individual attempts at forming a coherent worldview of all of life's variables, in which they relinquish less useful or contradictory ideas in favor of more successful ones.[59]

This process begins as society acculturates the individual. Scribner writes: "the individual internalizes the culture of his spiritual animal as a normal part of his development after birth, including not only the language and the capacity to generate arguments..., but also the [content of] arguments and conclusions that have accumulated as the culture."[60] The core set of values in a societal animal is inherited as tradition—e.g., the language itself and the sets of beliefs and intentions that come to be shared by members of the group. The culture evolves as individuals present new insights—'random variations'—for others to consider. When these have obvious pragmatic value, or they appear to give a more coherent view of the world, they are adopted by others.

Hayek also subscribed to the idea of cultural or societal evolution: "cultural evolution is brought about through the transmission of habits and information not merely from the individual's physical parents, but from an indefinite number of 'ancestors'. The processes furthering the transmission and spreading of cultural properties by learning also ... make cultural evolution incomparably faster than biological evolution. Finally, cultural evolution operates largely through group selection."[61]

It follows that those cultures better equipped to appropriately deal with new ideas are likely to evolve more rapidly than others. In particular, Scribner argues that civilizations would not undergo much cultural evolution unless their culture happened to value argument and independent judgment. Such openness to ideas runs counter to the mindset that was required for early human survival, in which mutual agreement in being able to coordinate members was essential. In a survival mindset, disagreements tend to be repressed, unless they cannot be avoided for some reason, and such inhibitions may be so limiting that the process of rational selection has limited scope, with societal evolution being substantially slowed.[62]

Scribner also notes that, as a practical matter, cultural evolution is sustained in societies that not only foster the exchange of arguments but also provide enough members with the leisure to argue at length about matters far removed from immediate practical needs, and in which writing has evolved to the point that a record of the exchange of arguments can be passed from one generation to the next.

In this light, evolution occurs over a continuum of societal change rather than through the reproduction of successive generations, as is the case for living species. If culture is the genome of the societal animal, then its evolution takes place in the minds of the members of the societal animal—i.e., through changes in values, beliefs, and practices. As such, society next year can be marginally more evolved than society today and society a generation from now may well be virtually a different cultural entity.

Fitness of Societal Animals

Any argument in support of societal evolution through group selection must consider the attribute of fitness[63] in societal animals. Does it exist? Is it tangibly definable?

At a minimum, Scribner's concept of fitness for species—i.e., power to control conditions affecting reproduction—can be extended to societal animals as well. With regard to societal animals, fitness can be argued to be those attributes that allow humans to control the means of physical sustenance and the conditions that nurture the reproduction and survival of their societal animal. Equally important, the societal animal must be capable of protecting itself from predatory aggression by others, because survival of the fittest is demonstrated, ultimately, through biological competition among societal animals.

Thus viewed, the basis for recurrent philosophical debates becomes apparent. In one camp, are societies that prize innovation and creativity along with the traits, values, and practices that enhance the commercial productivity of society. This view implicitly recognizes these characteristics as ones that best make a society fit—i.e., affluence and innovation amply provide, when called upon, the means for repelling aggression and attaining security.

The opposing camp places much greater emphasis on the second half of the definition—i.e., on physical security and intellectual conformity, which considers, among other things, how fiercely cohesive society is and how willing members are to fight for their societal animal, even if little evolution occurs or if greater physical well-being languishes. In this case, fitness is more tightly tied to meeting certain psychological needs of society, such as immediate tangible security or greater certainty in a dangerous world, at the expense of creativity, individualism, or material wellbeing. Given that even until the present day, predation on others through war has been the lot of man, it is evident why this second part of the definition of fitness has held sway.

A few examples can highlight this ever-present tension. When previously superior Athens succumbed to Sparta during the Peloponnesian Wars, many concluded that Sparta's rigid ways were superior for the preservation of society to Athens' philosophically and socially more open ways. Even Plato's "Republic" outlined a 'virtuous' society as one modeled in many ways on Sparta. More recently, Hitler was convinced that unifying the German *Volk* under archaic value systems of racial purity and military might would overcome effete and decadent non-Aryans. Even more recently, many academics believed the focus and determination of the Communists would eventually overcome unplanned and 'feckless' democracies. Fundamentalist Islam today is raising a similar banner against a 'decadent' and 'materialistically shallow' West.

Even if one grants the likely superiority of the free society model, debates will continue on how societies within that mold should evolve further for greater fitness. For example, Prime Minister Lee of Singapore points to the West's high crime rates, the relative weakness of families in segments of its populations, its relatively unrestrained sexual activities, a vulgarism of the arts, and perhaps a general lack of discipline as serious debilitating weaknesses. In another case, Deepak Lal[64] respects the material achievements of the West, but he suspects that other nations such as India can emulate our market system and financial institutions, and then grow stronger because of more caring and effective extended families.

Coming from still another direction, many Western Europeans feel that the United States is too uncaring about the poorer members of society and has unleashed Schumpeter's 'creative destruction' in too unrestrained a fashion—i.e., without adequate social safety nets, thereby weakening the whole of society.

There are, of course, also some worldviews that might suggest that in many ways we do not need to progress at all. Some religious views, such as Buddhist or Taoist, argue that such material progress is irrelevant, that only the internal evolution of the individual is meaningful. Such views will likely always exist, perhaps benefiting the individual, but they do not incorporate the key attributes of fitness and thus remain marginal to the larger march of culture and civilization.

Which of the opposing conceptions of fitness will win out cannot be resolved by analysis alone. Yet, if one grants the existence of fitness for the societal animal, then intuiting its nature is of some consequence and is an objective of later chapters. In any event, fitness is an outcome determined by unceasing competition among societal animals.

Competition for Survival
The earlier discussion indicated that while genetic competition occurs between members of a species, once groups could compete, aggressive competition moved up the biological hierarchy, so that the fitness of one group became proven through contests with other groups.

In *Constant Battles*, Steven LeBlanc describes how "prehistoric warfare was common and deadly, and no time span or geographic region seems to have been immune." Moreover, such warfare was relatively more deadly than even the carnage of the twentieth century's world wars. He states that in primitive societies, war was a much stronger demographic reality, with about one-quarter of all men losing their lives in battle. The Rousseauian view of peaceable noble savages living in edenic harmony with the environment is totally fallacious.[65]

That an edenic view is unwarranted can be gleaned also from the behavior of our closest primate relatives, the chimpanzees who engage in warfare between bands apparently on behalf of the 'selfish gene'[66]. Matt Ridley in *The Red Queen* describes how many animals, primates and men included, strive to gain social power to increase mating possibilities.

He concludes that similar early warfare by humans was a consequence of attempts to attain women and reproductive opportunity rather than territory. (Think of Helen of Troy's role in the Trojan wars.) The anthropologist Napoleon Chagnon saw similar behavior in modern times among aboriginal tribes in Venezuela. He found that they were not fighting over scarce resources; they were fighting over women. Specifically, "among the Yanomamo, war and violence are both primarily about sex. War between two neighboring villages breaks out over the abduction of a woman or in retaliation for an attack that had such a motive, and it always results in women changing hands."[67]

How natural selection takes place as tribal societal animals compete can be seen elsewhere in contemporary times, e.g., in New Guinea. Ridley reports on work by the anthropologist Joseph Soltis, who analyzed the life of New Guinea tribes who had had little earlier Western contact. From their long history of violence, he was able to analyze hundreds of conflicts over a fifty-year period. From the pattern of victory of some tribes and the extinction of others one could observe the process of societal evolution. For example, Soltis noted that, "among the Mae-Enga people of the central Western Highlands, twenty-nine conflicts over fifty years among fourteen clans caused five of these clans to disappear. … In all, Soltis calculates that New Guinea clans died out at the rate of between two and thirty percent every twenty-five years." Of course, not all the vanquished perished; many were absorbed by the victorious tribes and so adopted their cultures. He estimated that this rate of extinction would be swift enough only to drive a mild form of cultural group selection.[68]

Jared Diamond described how these values played out: "For example, in New Guinea until recently, each tribe maintained a shifting pattern of warfare and alliance with each of its neighbors. A person might enter the next valley on a friendly visit (never quite without danger) or on a war raid, but the chances of being able to traverse a sequence of several valleys in friendship were negligible. The powerful rules about the treatment of one's fellow 'us' did not apply to 'them,' those dimly understood, neighboring enemies. As I walked between New Guinea valleys, people who themselves practiced cannibalism and were only a decade out of the Stone Age routinely warned me about the unspeakably primitive, vile, and cannibalistic habits of the people I would encounter in the next valley."[69]

Such tribal warfare remained endemic even with the rise of civilization, as seen, for example, in the incessant warfare of early Sumerian civilization and in the era preceding the first Chinese empires. The continuous warfare of feudal Europe and feudal Japan was little different.[70] In other forms, mindless, instinctual competition between societal animals continues to the present day. Indeed, Diamond lists 26 genocides in the last century—more than half involving no Western nations.[71]

Mankind eventually evolved ways to rein in such genetic impulses so that societal animals could flourish. In part, that is the subject of Chapter IV that describes the growth of principles of liberty and of the checks and balances of representative government. But genetic competition in the sense characterized by the selfish gene is inevitable. In developed countries, its manifestations effectively shifted to the economic arena, where capitalism and the extended order are often fiercely Darwinian.

Morioris vs. Maoris: A Zero-sum Game

The clash between more advanced and less advanced cultures is no more evident than that which occurred between the Moriori and the Maori tribes in the South Pacific. Diamond notes that these tribes were originally from the same cultural stock – i.e., Polynesians who were part of a farming, fishing, and seafaring people from the Bismarck Archipelago. The Maori settled in New Zealand and the Moriori, on the Chatham Islands hundreds of miles away.

During the ensuing several hundred years, the groups evolved in different directions. The Maori developed more complex technology and political organization. The Moriori, because of unfavorable climate and natural resources, reverted to being hunter-gatherers.

The Moriori remained a small population, which reduced potential conflict from overpopulation by castrating some male infants. They were a small, unwarlike population with simple technology and without strong leadership. In contrast, the Maori increased in numbers and were chronically in conflict with their neighbors.

When the Maori rediscovered the Moriori hundreds of years later, the result was horrific. As Diamond describes the encounter: "on November 19, 1835, a ship carrying 500 armed Maori arrived, followed by another shipload of 400 on December 5th. Groups of Maori began to walk through the Moriori settlements, announcing that the Moriori were now their slaves, and killing those who objected. An organized resistance by the Moriori could still then have defeated the Maori, who were outnumbered two to one. However, the Moriori had a tradition of resolving disputes peacefully. They decided in a council meeting not to fight back but to offer peace, friendship, and a division of resources.

"Before the Moriori could deliver that offer, the Maori attacked en masse. Over the next few days, they killed hundreds of Moriori, cooked and ate many of the bodies, and enslaved all the others, killing most of them too over the next few years as it suited their whim.

SOURCE: Jared Diamond, *Guns, Germs. and Steel*, p. 53

In summary, when humans developed powers of speech and reason, a new entity, a societal animal, with powers of purposeful cooperative action came into being. Multiple societal animals further evolved through aggressive competition, with successful survivors—the most fit—displacing the losers. The most fit invariably were those that were most skillful at generating wealth and/or that were most militarily successful. Either of these areas of skill was subject to innovation and creativity, usually realized through trial and error. As new practices were proven successful, societies developed corresponding new ways of looking at the world, and their traditions evolved to incorporate those relevant new values.

SOCIETAL EVOLUTION: AS IT UNFOLDED

Once gaining the power of reason, mankind was subject to societal evolution by virtue of his living in groups. Enough is known of humankind's primate ancestry and pre-history to enable us to trace the outlines of societal evolution from its early beginnings through the great acceleration that accompanied settled civilization.

At the Beginning

Anthropological studies provide an overview of both early human societal evolution and the key aspects of its cultural genome.

Early Societal Evolution
While societal evolution has been explosive in recent times, at first it lagged the pace of human physical evolution. For example, physiologically, the human animal's brain capacity is thought to have doubled over the span of the last million and a half years of evolution, yet evidence of more efficacious social entities did not appear until about 50,000 years ago. The reason for the lag: significant human societal evolution was not possible until the humans evolved the necessary linguistic and rational capabilities, which emerged relatively late in the species' physical evolution.

The extended period of physical evolution is seen in the several million years that were required from the first appearance of man's primate ancestor to the first appearance of modern man. Fossil remains and carbon dating indicate that human beings diverged from their closest primate relatives, the modern chimpanzee, about 7 million years ago (estimates range from 5 to 9 million years ago). They also indicate that our predecessors[72] had achieved a substantially upright posture about 4 million years ago, and began to increase in body size and brain size about 2.5 million years ago. The species closest to us had achieved roughly our size but only half of our brain capacity about 1.7 million years ago. Not until about half a million years ago did human fossils diverge from the older *Homo erectus* skeletons, having enlarged, rounder, and less angular skulls. These were sufficiently close to us that these fossils were reclassified as *Homo sapiens*. Their tools were crude, but they had discovered fire.

When *Homo sapiens* emerged from *Homo erectus*, few specific new social or behavioral capabilities were evident to mark this transition. The potential power of the larger brains took considerably more time and some additional mutation to manifest itself. Humans continued to use approximately the same crude stone tools that *Homo habilis* had used two million years prior; there is no evidence that they developed bone tools, ropes, or fishhooks in this long interval. Indeed, it suggests that as recently as 100,000 years ago, man was still an ineffective big game hunter because he had not yet developed the weapons and group coordination required for hunting larger animals.[73]

Lacking a capacity for efficacious cooperation, as well as more sophisticated tools and weapons, man led a precarious existence. Since the less evolved Neanderthals (who were nonetheless more muscular and equally nimble) were able to co-exist with humans until as recently as 50,000 years ago, one can surmise that the potential capabilities of more evolved humans had not yet come into play.

Forty thousand years ago may have been the tipping point between pre and modern humans, possibly as a result of some important mutations that improved man's speech and communication abilities.[74] During the Upper Paleolithic revolution, the evolutionary pace picked up: tools became varied and more complex and cave art appears for the first time. In addition, trading over long distances, artifacts of clay and bone, and elaborate new stone designs all seem to appear at once. Concomitant with the signs of new capabilities, man inhabited more and more environmental niches, likely forcing Neanderthals into extinction over the subsequent few millennia.

Recent genetic research reinforces the view that mutations played a key role in this evolutionary process. For example, evidence suggests that mutation in the FOXP2 gene on chromosome 7, which is necessary for the development of normal grammatical and speaking ability in human beings, occurred as recently as 200,000 years ago. This mutant form proved to be so successful in enhancing the reproduction of its possessors, likely in the form of greatly improved social interaction, that it now exists to the utter exclusion of all previous versions of the gene.[75]

But it is highly unlikely that this one gene accounted for the new capacity acquired by humans for symbolic and abstract thinking. There must have been changes in a number of other genes as well.[76] Scribner attributes these greater capabilities and the more rapid social evolution to a more evolved neocortex, which gave man the power of reason. This power was the foundation for culture and for social capabilities vastly exceeding anything seen before.

The Inherited Cultural Genome
Early human societies had value systems (the cultural genome), however primitive, that enabled them to function cohesively—i.e., as societal animals. That many of the values were likely inherited from primate ancestors can be seen in parallels of behavior between primate groups and humans. Matt Ridley provides examples of how chimpanzees and other primates relate to one another in undertaking purposeful activities, including actions based on mutual sharing and anticipated reciprocity. He emphasizes, however, that although we are primates and we learn about our roots by studying our relatives, we should not take comparisons too far as we are not the same in most ways.[77] Moreover, while the term inheritance is used, apes, monkeys and chimpanzees are not our ancestors; they are merely offshoots from the same ancient tree of primates.

One key comparison is with regard to social order. Ridley points out that all of our ancestors were social and that there was a hierarchy within each group, more marked among males than females.

Moreover, our ancestors' hierarchies were the relatively least rigid and most egalitarian of the primates—i.e., more like the chimpanzee and less like the monkey.

Ridley identifies aspects of chimp society that probably were common to early humans. Chimp society is more fluid than that of other primates, with coalitions forming and reforming to modify the social hierarchy. Ridley observes that relations within these coalitions seem to be based on reciprocal expectations—i.e., "If A intervenes on behalf of B, either to defend him when attacked or to support him when he starts a fight, B must later do so on behalf of A or the coalition will fall. The ... chimps clearly play tit-for-tat."[78]

Another feature of chimp behavior that humans can readily recognize in themselves regards fighting. Chimpanzees form macro-coalitions to defend their territory from other bands, and maintaining these coalitions requires leadership by the alpha males. Cohesiveness of the group is a high priority, demonstrated, for example, when the alpha male intervenes to prevent internal fights by playing a pacifying role. And when a group of males goes on a raid, he behaves as if he must get the backing of his coalition partners before launching an attack.[79] Moreover, chimpanzees and preliterate tribal humans were highly xenophobic—an *us versus them* mentality. Feuding and warfare were incessant.

Day-to-day life also provides interesting parallels. With regard to food, Ridley writes that "sharing is remarkably egalitarian. Dominant individuals are more likely to give than receive. Rank matters less than reciprocity. If A often gives foliage to B, then B will often give to A. There is a pattern of turn-taking: A is more likely to give food to B if B has groomed A recently, but not if A has done the grooming favour. A chimp will punish another that has been stingy by attacking it."[80]

Ridley also cites Frans de Waal who concluded that chimpanzees possess a concept of trade. They share in order to curry favor, receive reciprocal benefits in the future, and generally defend their reputations for virtue. Waal writes: "Sharing among chimpanzees is embedded in a multi-faceted matrix of relationships, social pressure, delayed rewards, and mutual obligations."[81]

The parallel with human behavior is quite clear. What was a pattern of mutual expectation among primates became 'values' when man developed the power of reason.

Tribal Life

While there is no direct evidence of the workings of early primitive human societies, there is informed speculation. Modern anthropologists' analyses of aboriginal tribes—e.g., in New Guinea and in Amazonia—have revealed shared patterns and practices that are characteristic of primate societies. New discoveries in genetic theory and insights from game theory provide complementary perspectives. Taken together, Ridley concluded that early human life had as strong a bias toward cooperative behavior within the group as it had a posture of competition and antagonism toward other groups.

In terms of our innate instinct for competition, he summarizes the thinking that underlies the idea of the selfish gene. In this theory, our ultimate purpose is to survive and to pass on our genes to our progeny. These drives shape our sexual appetites and the way we form family units, as well as our aggressive behavior toward others. This further explains our larger loyalties to our immediate and extended families. Recognition of this array of instincts has been reflected in philosophy and political theory, as for example, in Thomas Hobbes' conclusion that these innate drives were so pervasive that only a strong state can prevent life from being "nasty, brutish, and short".

Ridley, however, believes that life is not a Hobbesian zero-sum game because a strong genetic impulse exists for us to be virtuously cooperative in dealing with one another and that it predates civilization. He argues that even primitive society required trust and a sense of mutual obligation among individuals and that these are prerequisites for survival and for society to progress. These factors, among other things, made possible collective defense, the division of labor, and trade. Yet, why were they not overwhelmed by selfish propensities, by the inclination to get a 'ride free' on the coattails of the group? The answer is that they were all better off and had a greater chance of survival by cooperating.

Clues to how early human cooperation worked can be gleaned from anthropological and zoological studies regarding primate behavior in the wild and hunter-gatherer societies in New Guinea and the Amazon in the modern era. Anthropological work shows that hunters share large game freely, even with those who do not participate in the hunt. The motivation, however, may not be entirely altruistic; large amounts of meat exceeding the needs of the immediate families of the hunters would otherwise spoil. In sharing, the hunters gain in prestige, and this can be used to reap other benefits, often in the form of sexual favors.

Values for sharing, however, are not all encompassing. For example, it is evident that food that is gathered and even small game caught by the individual are largely reserved for the family group. Thus that which requires group cooperation is shared, and that which can be accomplished individually may not be. And when items are shared outside the family, there is a strong sense of reciprocity and expectation of future favors.

Such value systems have great utility for group survival. For example, this pattern of hunting and sharing maximizes the ability to catch large game and to ensure the highest calorie and nutritional input for the group as a whole. In recognition of this reality, groups internalize supportive values either in implicit expectations or in codified behavior.

These behavioral systems are based on expected reciprocity and work only when the participants expect to interact repeatedly. By and large, humans readily recognize about 150 fellow beings in terms of reciprocal behavior. This is the size, as Ridley puts it, of a typical hunter-gatherer band, of the average religious commune, and of the typical address book.

The accompanying cultural systems establish a 'moral' community wherein 'right' coincides with group welfare and 'wrong' with self-serving acts at the expense of other members of the group.[82] Wilson cites work from a number of researchers[83] who have attempted to show how such moral systems follow a specialized, genetically evolved cognitive architecture, including features of conformity. Wilson also cites work by Ellickson that demonstrated how people spontaneously establish, enforce, and largely abide by social norms in the absence of a formal legal system.[84]

With regard to group selection and cultural evolution, Wilson states: "In moral communities, social norms can create a degree of behavioral uniformity within groups and differences among groups that could never be predicted from their genetic structure and which is highly favorable for among-group selection."[85] Further, "if adaptations evolve by differential survival and reproduction, it makes sense that group-level adaptations evolve by the differential survival and reproduction of groups."[86]

Ridley turns to computer modeling and game theory to show how early human society might have evolved the appropriate values for tribal cooperation and subordination of short-term opportunism. These models draw upon "The Prisoners' Dilemma" that tests an individual's selfish interest vis-à-vis his obligation to others and thereby sheds light on social interactions. In the exercise, two prisoners are interrogated regarding a crime. If each fails to incriminate the other, both receive, at most, a light sentence for a lesser offense. If one, however, incriminates the other, the accuser gets a slap on the wrist, while the accused receives a heavy punishment. If each incriminates the other, both get a heavy, but not the heaviest, sentence.

To glean clues to the propensities for human behavior in such situations, analysts have developed a computer model. If both prisoners remain true to one another, they receive three points. If each accuses the other, each receives only one point. If one accuses and the other does not, the accuser receives five points, and the silent member of the pair receives zero points—"the sucker's payoff". Ridley notes that if two players are involved, there is a strong predisposition for one to accuse the other. In this case, the accuser gets the maximum possible score. But if both accuse, they both get something—not the maximum number of points, but something. If the game is modeled with a number of players, the outcome demonstrates that ruthless selfishness indeed pays. Yet the total number of points to be gained is highest if they both cooperate—i.e., six. So in terms of system-wide benefits, the group would be better off if individuals did not accede to common impulses of self-interest.

Insight into how society attains the greater benefits is gained if players get to play many times and if they get to observe the past behavior of other players. Often a different strategy proves to be the winning one: a slightly forgiving and beneficent "tit for tat" strategy, in which one tries to play with players who had previously demonstrated trustworthiness but would retaliate when encountering cheating.

The latter strategy seems to correspond to actual social interactions in our society. Those of us who cooperate well tend to achieve the most. And we have social sanctions to discourage the cheating behavior that undermines cooperation. It is easy to imagine how these social skills were learned in early cultures and passed on generation to generation.

Ridley cites extensive psychological testing that seems to reinforce the concept of understood reciprocity. In one set of tests, groups of individuals previously unknown to one another took part in prisoner dilemma types of exchanges after spending a half hour getting acquainted. The testers found that individuals who had relatively brief interactions quickly sized up which players were likely to cheat and thus were untrustworthy.

In summarizing these results, Ridley states, "The human animal does appear to have an exchange organ in the brain… [The brain] is equipped with special facilities to enable it to exploit reciprocity, to trade favors and to reap the benefits of social living."[87]

From Hunter-gatherer to Settled Farmer

A major evolution of the societal animal—a 'radiation', if you will—occurred as human beings made the transition from hunter-gatherer societies to settled agricultural civilizations. This evolution gave societies greater control over energy and food, thereby helping to ensure their survival and reproductive success. And in providing larger and more secure sources of food, settled agriculture established the basis for civilization itself. But given the radical changes involved, it is not surprising how difficult the overall transition was for the human species. Particular difficulties were the limited number of hospitable environments and the precariously long period of time required for humans to master the new ways that were clearly superior to previous forms of social organization.

Few Potential Locations
Jared Diamond[88] argues that there may have been only five locations on earth in which farming civilizations arose de novo: in Eurasia, the Fertile Crescent and China; in the Americas (thousands

of years later), Mesoamerica; the Andes; and the Eastern United States. But because farming methods spread among humans when their utility was recognized, it's not absolutely certain what was de novo and what was imitation. Hence, Diamond allows that such methods could have arisen independently in Africa's Sahel zone, Ethiopia, and New Guinea as well.

One chief obstacle to settled agriculture was the paucity of indigenous plants and livestock suitable for sustaining human life. Another was the lack of experience with raising crops in the face of disease, predators, and weather, as well as with taming and nurturing animals. Accordingly, those early humans who first attempted the transition were not always rewarded with higher calorie consumption. To gain an appreciation of the evolutionary leap, a few specifics are telling.

Although plants exist everywhere in the world except the Polar Regions, most indigenous vegetation is not suitable for sustaining human life, being either indigestible or too low in nutritional value. Diamond indicates that, on average, biomass suitable for human consumption constitutes only 0.1 percent of the biomass found on an acre of land. If human cultivation could increase the amount of suitable biomass to constitute more like 90 percent of the biomass per acre, however, one acre could typically sustain 10 to 100 times more herders and farmers than uncultivated land could support hunter-gatherers.[89]

Suitable plants—cereals and grains (grasses) and peas, lentils and beans (legumes)—that meet human needs[90] existed naturally in just a relatively few locations on the planet because only a few climates promoted such plants. Mark Blumler's work on world distribution of large-seeded grass species listed the 56 heaviest grass species and concludes that, of these, all but seven were originally found only in the five regions in which human cultivation of food originated.[91]

Not only was it important for these plants to be naturally available, but it was key that they be available with an ease and abundance that attracted human attention. Diamond notes: "A second advantage of the Fertile Crescent flora is that the wild ancestors of many Fertile Crescent crops were already abundant and highly productive, occurring in large stands whose value must have been

obvious to hunter-gatherers. Experimental studies in which bota-
nists have collected seeds from such natural stands of wild cereals,
much as hunter-gatherers must have been doing over 10,000 years
ago, show that annual harvests of up to nearly a ton of seeds per
hectare can be obtained, yielding 50 kilocalories of food energy for
only one kilocalorie of work expended. By collecting huge quantities of wild cereals in a short time when the seeds were ripe, and
storing them for use as food throughout the rest of the year, some
hunting-gathering peoples of the Fertile Crescent had already settled down in permanent villages even before they began to cultivate plants."[92]

But it was the domestication of cereals and pulses that launched
settled food production: wheat and barley with peas and lentils in
the Fertile Crescent; corn with several bean species in Mesoamerica;
and rice and millets with soybeans and other beans in China.[93]

Successful settled agriculture required livestock as well as
plants to meet human nutritional needs. Although man had successfully domesticated small mammals (e.g., dogs and cats) and
many birds, none were important sources of food and none could
provide transportation and work capabilities. Only large terrestrial
herbivores met this need.

Only 14 species of large animals—i.e., weighing over 100
pounds—were domesticated before the 20th Century, and only five
of these had become widespread and important—i.e., the cow,
sheep, goat, pig, and horse. The minor nine, as Diamond puts it,
were found only in limited areas of the globe: the Arabian camel,
Bactrian camel, llama, donkey, reindeer, water buffalo, yak, ban-
teng, and gaur. Of the wild ancestors of these 14 species, 13 were
confined to Eurasia (including North Africa), and only one, the lla-
ma/alpaca, was found in South America.

It was not that there weren't other candidates for domestication. Indeed, Diamond suggests that while 148 candidates could be
found around the world, only 14 were suitable for domestication.
Why? It was because of their diet, growth rate, breeding problems,
disposition to captivity, tendency to panic, and/or social structure.
Regarding diet, for example, for practical reasons, large animals
raised for food had to be herbivores rather than carnivores, since
while it takes around 10,000 pounds of corn to grow a 1,000-pound

cow, a 1,000-pound carnivore requires 10,000 pounds of herbivore raised on 100,000 pounds of corn.[94]

Slowness to Change

Although the advantages of a settled agricultural society are obvious to modern man, the transition from a society of hunter-gatherers to farmers took thousands of years. Recall the example of the evolution of the lungfish, which laboriously made its way on land for the first time. Without further evolution, it would have remained a clumsy affair. Similarly with humans, the first attempts at settled agriculture were awkward. It was with human learning and experience that it became a clearly superior form of life.

Indeed, initially most peasant farmers and herders were not necessarily better off than hunter-gatherers. Time-budget studies have shown that primitive farmers spent more rather than fewer hours per day at work than hunter-gatherers did. Moreover, archeologists have shown that the first farmers in many areas were smaller and less well nourished, suffered from more serious diseases, and died on the average at a younger age than the hunter-gatherers they displaced.

Viewed in that light, the decision to change doesn't make sense. The answer to the seeming paradox lies in man's manifold capabilities and the unique options facing individuals. At the beginning, it was not an either-or proposition. Rather, humans followed alternative strategies of mixing hunting-gathering with agriculture. Some hunter-gatherers, because of the ready availability of food, had become relatively non-nomadic in their lives. Moreover, their long experience of gathering made them well aware of the variety of potential foodstuffs in the plants. The question is: how did they come to spend time cultivating these plant species?

According to Diamond, the cultivation of additional foods took place sequentially, depending on availability and ease. Early on, people simultaneously gathered wild foods and cultivated others. Only when crops met nutritional needs did gathering become a sideline. This long process was driven by economics as much as by knowledge. Even primitive man could judge how his time should be allocated to produce the greatest payoff, e.g., when to hunt, to gather, to sow, to weed, and to harvest. He concentrated on those activities that had the biggest payoff in nutrition. When cultivating skills and horticultural knowledge increased sufficiently, crops provided the greatest payoff.[95]

Diamond notes that environmental opportunities shaped this process. In the Fertile Crescent region, where alternative hunting-gathering opportunities tended to be more meager than elsewhere, settled agriculture first emerged—around 8,500 B.C.

The passage of time and the gaining of experience facilitated the transition. For example, technology was developed for collecting, processing and storing wild foods: flint blades fixed into handles for harvesting; mortars and pestles for removing husks; techniques of roasting to prevent sprouting in storage; and underground pits, plastered for waterproofing, for storage. In addition, through trial and error, man learned how to genetically modify plants (by very crude means) to make them more useful. In addition, humans controlled the natural selection of their domesticated animals to make them more suitable for human needs—e.g., stronger, or capable of producing more milk or yielding more meat.

The shift to settled agriculture created the basis for denser populations and for civilization itself. As Diamond pointed out, one acre of land under cultivation can sustain, typically, 10 to 100 times more humans than one acre can sustain hunter-gatherers. He notes that livestock feeds more people in four distinct ways: by furnishing meat, milk, and fertilizer and by pulling plows. Through milk alone, mammals yield several times more calories over their lifetime for human nutrition than if they were slaughtered and consumed as meat.

Moreover, before animal domestication, the sole means of transporting goods and people by land was on the backs of humans. After domestication, animals were used to move heavy goods in large quantities, as well as people, over long distances.

These changes in turn had a direct impact on human social organization. Diamond notes that settled agricultural life shortened the birth interval. A nomadic mother could carry only one child along with a few possessions. She could not afford to bear her next child until the previous toddler could walk fast enough to keep up with the tribe. In practice, nomadic hunter-gatherers spaced their children about 4 years apart, while settled farmers tended to space children about 2 years apart.

Once settled agriculture demonstrated its feasibility, it was emulated more quickly by neighboring groups. Diamond notes that the hunter-gatherers in southeastern Europe had adopted the Southwest Asian cereal crops, pulse crops, and livestock as a complete package by around 6000 B.C., and all three spread rapidly through central Europe before 5000 B.C.[96]

Value Systems in Settled Communities
Once man moved to settled agriculture and livestock-tending settlements, new ways of relating were required. The values that had arisen worked well enough for man to survive in tribal settings, but how did such values work in more extended, settled-agricultural societies?

New circumstances and experiences drove change, and where change led, societal values followed. For example, farmers had to become planners: they had to learn how to anticipate and to husband resources—e.g., they had to preserve seed for next year's harvest and also part of the harvest as a cushion against drought and natural catastrophes. They looked at the world differently than hunter- gathers and required different behavior and values on the part of their families and their neighbors. Questions invariably arose regarding poaching and the use of the communal areas. Even more demanding were questions regarding the right to use land, or outright ownership. Moreover, while tribal culture tended to be relatively egalitarian, larger settled communities moved to more complex, socially-tiered, forms of organization.[97]

The entire movement to settled civilization can be seen in the context of group selection. Diamond states: "The fact is that, over entire continents and other large areas containing hundreds of competing societies, some societies will be more open to innovation, and some will be more resistant. The ones that do adopt new crops, livestock, or technology may thereby be enabled to nourish themselves better and to outbreed, displace, conquer, or kill off societies resisting innovation. That's an important phenomenon whose manifestations extend far beyond the adoption of new crops ..."[98]

Such was the state of mankind ten thousand or so years ago.

Civilization: City-States and Empires

Social evolution continued, but very slowly, in the direction of greater fitness as measured by relative wealth and strength. It led first to the development of city-states and then empires via evolutionary changes made possible by agricultural surpluses, trade, and innovations in governmental forms. The main impetus to evolutionary change was the agricultural surplus made possible by man's growing mastery of his environment, which, in turn, sustained other activities—i.e., administration, warfare, and religion, and making new forms of governance possible, notably city-states.

City-States

Beginning around five thousand years ago, city-states began to coalesce from single farming communities, first in Asia Minor, South Asia, and China. Professor Brian Fagan notes that these assumed many forms, generally with a fortified core population surrounded by a scattered rural population. In contrast to earlier agricultural communities, these had a higher level of organizational complexity, including public buildings, institutions governing law and order and the regulation of trade.[99] Economically, this allowed individuals to develop specialized crafts, which made possible an increasing array of innovations and increased the community's production and standard of living. In addition, the rise of city-states facilitated the growth of longer-range commerce, which was shaped by the forces of comparative advantage, and enhanced the productivity of all participating communities. In turn, agricultural surpluses and trade gave rise to the need for records, which slowly evolved into writing and numbers—with their explosive consequences for further societal evolution.

In more specific terms, Fagan describes the rise city-states in the Tigris-Euphrates estuary:

> - At first, the 'Ubaid people grew barley and dates, herded cattle, sheep, and goats, and depended on simple irrigation by means of canals built by communal labor. By 4,700 B.C. the town of Eridu sported a mud-brick temple and a larger population.

- As early as 3,500 B.C., another town, Uruk, which enjoyed far-flung trading connections with the Iranian highlands, grew rapidly, soon becoming a city with satellite villages extending out several miles. The remaining countryside became the hinterland of the city.
- By 3,400 B.C., the first signs of writing appeared, developed from a system of clay tokens used to regulate trade.
- During the fourth millennium B.C., a system of trade linked these Mesopotamian cities with eastern Iran, the Indus valley, Anatolia, and the Nile.[100]

Hayek took note of the evolutionary dynamic underlying the value changes accompanying the new order: "The various structures, traditions, institutions and other components of this order arose gradually as variations of habitual modes of conduct were selected. Such new rules would spread not because men understood that they were more effective, or could calculate that they would lead to expansion, but simply because they enabled those groups practicing them to procreate more successfully and to include outsiders."[101] The process required the gradual displacement of village/tribal tradition by learnt rules, embracing and enforcing beneficial innovations. Hayek stressed the importance of "the spontaneous evolution of rules of conduct that assist the formation of self-organizing structures," but he hastened to add that the process is often aided by follow-up deliberate organization.

Using commerce as an example, we can see how changes in worldviews and values came about: "Prospectors and miners, traders and middlemen, the organization of shipments and caravans, concessions and treaties, the concept of alien peoples and customs in distant lands—all these are involved in the enlargement of social comprehension demanded by the technological step of entering ... a bronze age."[102] These innovations particularly required that man's ever-present xenophobia be overcome, as it was by new values such as hospitality, protection, and safe passage. For example, Hayek refers to the early Greek custom of the *xenos*, the guest-friend, who was assured individual admission and protection within an alien territory. He believes that early trade was very much a matter of personal relations between individuals of different communities.

As a consequence, the increased opportunities to deal with members of other communities helped break the "solidarity, common aims and collectivism of the original small groups."

Empires
Despite growing prosperity and strength, the system of city-states was as war-ridden as the prior system of tribes. The next stage of societal evolution spanning further millennia came through warrior leaders who could meld the cities into empires. This allowed for the capture of the economic benefits resulting from curtailing incessant warfare, of larger and more secure territories, and wider-scale commerce. Fagan describes this process in China:

> - Urban clusters and states first developed in northern China during the time of the Xia and Shang dynasties (2,000 B.C. to 1,027 B.C.). There was no centralized state, merely a culturally similar collection of about 130 separate entities.
> - Regular periods of warfare between 770 and 458 B.C. gradually consolidated these states into fewer than 22. By this time armies numbered in the thousands, and chariots, cavalry, and iron weaponry had been developed.
> - The period from 458 to 221 B.C. was known as "Warring States," during which conflict was incessant. By 300 B.C., only four major states survived.
> - In 260 B.C., the ruler of Qin defeated his greatest rival. His successor finished off the rest and declared himself the first emperor of a united China in 221 B.C.[103]

Similar processes led to empires arising in Mesopotamia, Egypt, India, and Mesoamerica. Societal evolution was spurred by the need for new institutions of administration, new forms of religion, and new ways of relating to neighboring civilizations. Another and newer impetus for cultural evolution was the wealth and leisure among the elite that led to inquiry and reflection, and, in turn, early philosophic speculation, which aided in the development of man's powers of reason. Indeed, when the exchange of ideas and the use of contrary arguments reached an advanced level, a systematization of thinking, i.e., philosophy, emerged with revolutionary potential for societal animals. The full potential, of course, took millennia to emerge.

Enduring Genetic Influence

More negatively for the possibilities for further societal evolution, the forces of genetic selection expressed themselves differently in the new societal context. The varying reproductive opportunity between tribes and despotisms arose from a deep source. Mating behavior is determined not only by genetic makeup, but also by circumstances, notably the relationship of early humans to their sources of food and power arrangements within society. In primate and human societies, when a male controls a territorial source of food, society tends to be polygamous—i.e., women are willing to share a mate if that mate commands resources which will help ensure the survival of offspring. On the other hand, when food is widely distributed and no one male has a significant edge over another, women tend to select mates who are reliable helpmates in raising their young. In this latter situation, males have to resort to subterfuge and to raiding women from other tribes to increase the chances of passing on their genes.[104]

Humans' closest genetic cousins are the chimpanzees, and early man lived in similar circumstances. They inhabited grasslands and woodland savannas, existing through hunting and gathering, and evolved cooperative behaviors. Tribesmen to this day have maintained essentially single-pair bond systems. When the social/environmental context expanded to that of empires, where despots controlled the wealth—a situation similar to that of the apes—human social behavior shifted accordingly.

Anthropologist Mildred Dickemann found that in highly stratified Oriental despotisms, when they had the requisite power, men seemed to behave exactly as one would expect if the goal were to leave as many descendants as possible. They tended to seek polygamy, while women strove to marry men of high status. Laura Betzig's belief is that people are sexually adapted to exploit whatever situation they encounter. Her work has led her to postulate that man will tend to treat power not as an end in itself but as a means to achieve reproductive success. In examining 104 politically autonomous societies, she found that in almost every case, power predicts the size of a man's harem. Small kings had one hundred women in their harems; great kings, one thousand; and emperors, five thousand.[105] This pattern even appeared in the feudal West,[106] where monogamy was the traditional norm.

Thus, while the new empires were more powerful than their antecedents in evolutionary terms—as a consequence of growing commerce, interconnectedness of peoples, and the power of philosophy—other values involving governance and the individual assumed forms that tended to inhibit further societal evolution. For example, man's early egalitarianism was eroded and empires were invariably governed by despotisms, which were determined to protect their prerogatives and were unreceptive to change. The net result was that the great civilizations moved along a path to greater empowerment of the societal animal up to a point, and then tended randomly to rise and fall according to circumstances. In terms of cultural evolution, they stagnated in what could be termed a value-trap. It would be the West that would enjoy both the circumstances and the cultural heritage, allowing mankind to break free.

Mankind became a new form of living entity, the societal animal, when primate man developed powers of language and reason. The societal animal, as any organic replicator, evolved according to the same basic rules that govern the evolution of species, resulting in the survival of the fittest. The genome of the societal animal, however, did not consist of DNA; it was its culture, made up of the values, traditions, and institutions enabling it to work cohesively for common purposes. The successful societal animals that emerged through a process of group selection achieved greater fitness, seen in terms of ability to control life-sustaining resources and to counter threats from others.

Man's early cultural genome was likely inherited from his primate ancestry and then was rationally incorporated as part of tribal life. The crucial initial values were those that encouraged cooperation and solidarity. These then evolved when new practices and institutions arose through a process of trial and error, and produced in their wake new values. Major evolutionary leaps occurred at key junctures of human existence—e.g., the movement from hunter-gatherer society to fixed settlements, and from settlements to city-states and empires.[107]

A number of major civilizations, e.g., Roman, Persian, Islamic, Hindu, and Chinese progressed through this evolutionary process, achieving modest levels of prosperity, but exhibiting signs of evolutionary stagnation. About one thousand years ago, however, an explosion of evolutionary societal change began in the West, which is the subject of ensuing chapters.

3
Commerce: Driver of Change

Economics has ... been concerned with how an extended order of human interaction comes into existence through a process of variation, winnowing and sifting far surpassing our vision or our capacity to design. ...

Of the revival of European civilization during the later Middle Ages it could be said that the expansion of capitalism—and European civilization—owes its origins and *raison d'etre* to political anarchy. ... It was not under the more powerful governments, but in the towns of the Italian Renaissance, of South Germany, and of the Low Countries, and finally in lightly governed England, i.e., under the rule of the bourgeoisie rather than the warriors, that modern industrialization grew. – Friedrich von Hayek[108]

Understanding the evolution of the economic extended order in the West, how it came about, and why it is important involves examining four areas of critical change during the last millennium: the emergence of commerce and free markets, the securing of liberty, the rise of science, and the empowerment of the individual. While the changes in one were linked to changes in another, commerce was paramount. Trade together with a mercantile revolution led the way, making the other avenues of change, if not possible, more probable. For example, much of the impetus for rule of law and property rights was created by the rising mercantile class. The rise of science would need as a prerequisite the resources and leisure class associated with the growing wealth in the West. The empowerment of the individual required the security, the affluence, and a more educated populace associated with the other three.

Commerce, guided by the forces of comparative advantage, drove the process of economic transformation. It was not a matter of societies just doing more of what had always been done—i.e., working, saving and investing. A major transformation of societal structure, economic institutions, and worldviews—roughly corresponding to Hayek's extended order—had to come about, one that corresponds to the value differentials between poorer and more advanced countries (see Figure I-3). That shift was from social conformity to individual initiative; from a deep-seated respect for authority and tradition to openness to innovation; and from a close adherence to the extended family to a tolerance of outsiders and a greater degree of trust in other members of society. The shift was a product of centuries of experiential learning, not of academic and theological musings or logic employed in the abstract. So, to understand the transition, the experiences—i.e., the history—of those times, must be understood as well.

In the broadest sense, the process consisted of man's innate instinct for economic enterprise flourishing in an appropriate societal niche—i.e., one compatible with competitive innovation and the accumulation of deployable capital. Until 1,000 years ago, all civilizations had lacked the prerequisite conditions for an extended order to arise, being too wedded to fixed archaic values and too predatory. Fortunately at that time the West began an evolutionary proliferation in the commercial arena that allowed it to escape prior limitations. To see how this process unfolded, we will establish a baseline by identifying key aspects of man's innate commercial impulses, and showing how they had been systemically stymied in the major civilizations.

UNIVERSAL ECONOMIC IMPULSES AND UBIQUITOUS RESTRAINT

Mankind's striving for economic betterment is about as universal as are efforts of society to rein those impulses in.

The Innate Human Drive for Enterprise

If not squelched by government or peer pressure, commerce and enterprise are innate aspects of man's nature. Simply put, humans will work to improve their material well-being and security, thereby enhancing the likelihood of their own survival as well as the survival of their offspring.[109] Other than within various religious sects, the impulse was shown to be culturally universal by Max Weber's encyclopedic work *Economy and Society*. In contrasting other cultures with those thriving under the Protestant Ethic, he states: "to assume that the Hindu, Chinese, or Muslim merchant, trader, artisan, or coolie was animated by a weaker "acquisitive drive" than the ascetic Protestant is to fly into the face of facts. ... There is no proof whatever that a weaker natural "endowment" for technical economic rationalism was responsible for the actual difference in this respect."[110]

Not only did the larger civilizations cited by Weber experience extensive trade, but the impulse for trade was evident among the earliest human tribes as described by Jared Diamond. Evidence is clearer still about the pervasiveness of trade throughout the ancient world—from Mesopotamia to the early ancient Greek and Phoenician cities. In effect, simple calculation allows one to be guided by the law of comparative advantage in the furtherance of trade and commerce[111].

Just as remarkable is the ubiquity of relatively complex commercial networks in most societal settings. Friedrich von Hayek argued that naturally cooperative behavior and human creativity focused on situational needs, will produce a spontaneous order to facilitate and enhance human action. Such an order is by definition one that does not require government direction, or even participation. It has produced in the course of history trade, money, banking, commercial codes, and commercial courts. With this insight, he anticipated the evolutionary argument:

> Neither all ends pursued, nor all means used, are known or need to be known to anybody, in order for them to be taken account of within a spontaneous order. Such an order forms of itself. That rules become increasingly better adjusted to generate order happened not because men better understood their function, but because those groups prospered who happened to change them in a way that rendered them increasingly adaptive. This evolution was not linear, but

resulted from trial and error, constant 'experimentation' in arenas wherein different orders contended. Of course there was no intention to experiment—yet the changes in rules thrown forth by historical accident, analogous to genetic mutations, had something of the same effect.[112]

Adam Smith perceived the undirected spontaneity of the economic process as well, as, for example, where the market through the mechanism of prices signals where shortages exist and where a given amount of effort can be most fruitful. He also argued that as individuals endeavored to maximize their own income, they ineluctably increased the income of the nation as well, as though "led by an invisible hand to promote an end which was no part of his intention."[113]

Limitations Imposed by Value Systems and Predatory States

While all great civilizations attained a modicum of affluence, they all reached institutional limits caused by archaic value systems, hostile institutions, and predatory governments. Weber perceived this phenomenon in noting: "Whatever impediments exist result from rigid tradition, such as existed among us in the Middle Ages, not from any lack of ability or will. Such impediments to rational economic development must be sought primarily in the domain of religion, insofar as they must not be located in the purely political conditions..."[114]

Value Systems

At early stages of societal evolution, societies are invariably wedded to atavistic traditions with values and world views that served them well to survive in a hostile world but which make it difficult for vital features of the extended order – i.e., a far more efficient, decentralized, and responsive way to order economic affairs – to evolve. As seen in Chapter II, pre-modern societies, even in empires were supported by a village/ peasant class structure not far removed from earlier tribal life. As such, their egalitarian values distrusted individual ambition and particularly distrusted individual amassing of wealth. Accordingly, traders and moneymen were suspect and the institutions that finance trade, enable accumulation of productive capital, and protect property rights were not understood, even considered unjust. And their day-to-day lives were unlikely to change such world views; indeed, the typical peasant sees little or no relationship between work and technology on one hand, and the acquisition of wealth on the other: one works to eat but not to create wealth.

Then as societies emerged from their peasant origins, new economic ways demanded new roles for the individual that were unfamiliar and less congenial because they were less autonomous and more regimented. Working for others, especially performing, repetitive manufacturing functions could seem demeaning. While workers were compensated by increased material well-being even under the relatively harsh conditions of the early industrial revolution, individuals and communities were often slow to readjust their mindsets to recognize that everyone in the end benefited from such societal changes. Von Mises addresses this point:

> [i]f and as far as labor under the division of labor is more productive than isolated labor, and if and as far as man is able to realize this fact, human action itself tends toward cooperation and association; man becomes a social being not in sacrificing his own concerns for the sake of a mythical Moloch society, but in aiming at an improvement in his own welfare. Experience teaches that this condition – higher productivity achieved under the division of labor – is present because its cause, the inborn inequality of men and the inequality in the geographic distribution of the natural factors of production, is real. Thus we are in a position to comprehend the course of social evolution.[115]

Therefore, early manifestations of the extended order confronted philosophical and psychological barriers throughout society. Moreover, it had to overcome negative effects of the ubiquitous predatory state.

The Predatory State

When a state, out of imperial ambitions, a protection of vested interests, or merely because of the corruption of power, overtaxes and over-regulates natural human economic endeavors, wealth generation is discouraged and affluence drains away. The destruction of wealth is, of course, not an objective, merely an unintended consequence of the state acting from inappropriate values when addressing critical needs.

Deepak Lal states in *Unintended Consequences*: "A universal feature of polities is the ubiquitous predatoriness of the State. This merely reflects the necessary monopoly of coercive power and the inevitable maximization of net revenue that self-interested governors will then extract from their subjects."[116] [117] So, without appropriate restraints on political power, economic activity and the spontaneous order thereby engendered tends to be curtailed, if not throttled, by the state.

Brian Fagan's lectures[118] on 'human prehistory' show how universal this tendency has been, citing such geographically diverse examples as the ancient Egyptians, the Chinese, the Khmer, the Mayans, the Aztecs, and the Incas. In most instances, however, the causes of wealth extraction were twofold, i.e., aggressive tendencies by the ruler and the ruling class to expand personal power, as well as unending series of wars with all the expenses that wars entail.

In more modern democratic societies, deleterious forms of wealth extraction, viz. beyond the costs of providing vital governmental functions, is a form of rent-seeking whereby political factions attempt to retain or enhance power by catering to one group of people by extracting the wealth of others—usually the productive sectors. Some of that activity may be the necessary lubricant that keeps the political machine functioning and maintains social peace. Yet, as Lal showed abstractly, and as we shall see more concretely in Chapter VII, those actions, not sufficiently reined-in, can lead to economic stagnation and even ruin, even where many elements of the extended order have arisen.

The Roman Example

The Roman Empire can provide a salutary example of how government can gradually override the productive impulses of its people and eventually bring collapse, even to a great empire. The early Roman Republic was, for its times, a dynamic societal animal embodying disciplined, industrious values within a political structure providing an unusual degree of ordered liberty. But draining external wars, destructive civil war, and even military success—leading to a huge and ultimately undefendable empire—undermined the values of its inhabitants and destroyed its industriousness and prosperity. It is a story of how societal animals can decline.

During the Republic until the Punic Wars, Rome was a society of small agricultural proprietors, industrious and patriotic. Russell Kirk[119] describes them as follows: "they were earnest, tenacious, well-disciplined, frugal, often self-sacrificing when the state was in peril. A sense of duty and an attachment to honesty and honor worked upon their leading men. ... At the time when they defeated Carthage, the Romans were virtually incorruptible." Further, quoting Polybius: "If, among the Greeks for example, a single talent only be entrusted to those who have the management of any of the public money; though they give ten written sureties, with as many seals, and twice as many witnesses, they are unable to discharge the trust reposed in them with integrity. But the Romans, on the other hand, who in the course of their magistracies disburse the greatest sums, are prevailed on by the single obligation of an oath to perform their duty with inviolable honesty."[120]

These values of a naturally enterprising population, operating under *laissez-faire* policies, produced prosperity and the beginnings of an extended order. Herbert Muller[121] described the early economic promise of Rome: "Roman industry ... for a time gave signs of developing large-scale production. The ruins of Pompeii, for instance, reveal that among the many little shops of petty specialists were big bakeries that made over two thousand loaves a day, and a factory in which Pompeii's famous fish sauces were manufactured for export as well as the local market. Most household goods were apparently bought on the market, and some came from factories elsewhere. Moreover, Pompeii was frankly dedicated to the pursuit of wealth, with the blessing of the gods and the emperors. Its patron goddess, Venus Pompeiana devoted herself to protecting business, and she had no reason to complain of the emperors... Given this free enterprise, as well as the practical spirit of the Romans and the large amounts of capital available in the early empire, one might have expected industry to expand, spawning many Pompeiis. Yet it did not."[122]

Nonetheless, prosperity would outlast the decay of Roman virtue and the loss of republican liberty. During ensuing periods of stability, security, and expansion of trade, the Empire at its height experienced a high degree of affluence. Will Durant stated: "The improvement of government and transport expanded Mediterranean trade to an unprecedented amplitude.... It was the material zenith of the ancient world."[123] The lesson to be drawn from the continued prosperity, however, is not that liberty is dispensable in the interests of prosperity, but rather that stability and widespread trade can allow economic forces inherent in the division of labor and comparative advantage to function more effectively, bringing prosperity in their wake. Later sections of this chapter will identify comparable periods, of the order of centuries, during which the civilizations of all the major cultures enjoyed degrees of affluence while they maintained political stability and fostered extensive trade. But such affluence was inevitably fleeting as states became decadent and overly predatory.

In the case of republican Rome, Kirk believes that the chief cause of decay was the costs of the Punic Wars and, ironically, the successes Rome enjoyed in conquering Carthage, Macedonia, Greece, Asia Minor, and Gaul. The Punic Wars ruined the majority of Roman peasants; they died valiantly by the hundreds of thousands, and those who returned home found themselves hopelessly in debt, because of taxation and because of disadvantageous competition with the emerging slave-economy (growing out of the military successes). Innumerable slaves poured into Italy to man an increasingly impersonal plantation type of agriculture and to form an alien proletariat in the capital city itself. Estimates indicate that in 225 B.C. there were some 4.4 million free persons in Italy and 600,000 slaves. But by 43 B.C. there were perhaps 4.5 million free and 3 million slaves.[124] The slaves and the free proletariat no longer lived in the spirit of the value systems of republican Rome.

As Kirk put it: "Increasingly, the free Roman citizenry became little better than paupers, ready to follow some charismatic demagogue or ambitious military man; since the citizen-pauper had a vote, it became necessary increasingly to conciliate him by "bread and circuses" ..."[125] Accordingly, the changes that moving from Republic to Empire had wrought fatally undermined the old values, as well as positive world views.

Moreover, subsequent centuries of warfare, protecting the boundaries of an over-extended empire, entailed increasing levels of taxation and misguided regulation. The negative impact of taxation and regulation overcame the earlier economic benefits of stability. Simultaneously, the disappearance of a free agricultural population and the growth of the tremendous estates tilled by slaves or serfs resulted in a decline of productivity. The population, increasingly disempowered and poor, declined. Kirk stated: "Taxation, and the growing bureaucracy, devoured prosperity. Through lack of imagination and need for public revenues, during the third and fourth centuries, commerce and manufacturing were burdened and regulated insufferably. Attempts to replace private undertakings with state industry did not prosper."[126]

By the time of Diocletian, desperate measures were needed. Only by doubling the size of the army and concentrating power in himself and his colleagues could he hold back the barbarians on the frontiers and prevent the internal disintegration of the empire. These measures were accompanied by equally harsh control of the economy. According to Kirk: "City magistrates were made personally responsible for the collection of taxes, and fixed inescapably in their posts. ...Peasants were reduced permanently to serfdom. Wages and prices were fixed, and everything was regulated by central authority—so far as that power could be enforced. Grinding taxation impoverished every class."[127] In effect, the centralized, unchecked state succeeded in snuffing out innate human economic activity of working, saving, investing, and creating. Relatively few individuals remained who were sufficiently vested in Roman society that they could effectively counter and repulse the barbarian invasions.

COMMON ATTITUDES TOWARD COMMERCE ACROSS CULTURES

Around 500 AD, a remarkably similar set of value systems regarding human relationships in general and economic relationships in particular existed in widely different cultures. These grew out of the cooperative modes of behavior that enabled humans to survive in a hostile world as they emerged from their primate ancestry. Notably, cooperation was critical when food was scarce and cohesion was utterly essential in the face of wild animals and warring tribes. All cultures had internalized these values and they were reflected in the teachings of their great religious leaders—Confucius, Christ and Mohammed. These leaders and the institutions that grew from their teachings, while employing widely different philosophies, articulated values and views of appropriate human interaction that are, for the purposes of this narrative, similar. These religious leaders, each in their own way, may have been responsible for spiritual advances for man generally, but their teachings perpetuated ancient views that would hinder economic development, trade, and capital accumulation.

Exploring the validity of that position requires examining the attitudes toward commerce that held sway between 500 AD and 1000 AD, touching first on the value systems of Islam, China, and India, and concluding with those of Medieval Europe.

Islam

By the ninth century A.D., Islam, under the Abbasid Empire, had established one of the most prosperous civilizations on earth. "The Abbasidis succeeded ... [in] realizing their great scheme of knitting together the lands conquered by their predecessors into a uniform empire ... Islamization and Arabization made great progress, and at the same time the countries of the Near and Middle East became an economic unit, which distinguished itself by intense industrial and commercial activities. It is not an exaggeration to speak of a true economic miracle, performed under the guidance of the Abbasid government. ... The economic ascendancy of the Abbasid Empire over the other regions of Asia and Africa, and even more over Western Europe, was overwhelming, and it lasted a relatively long period—about two hundred years."[128]

The rise of Arabic as a common written language made it easier for merchants from distant parts of the empire to communicate. Plying their trade throughout the region, merchants were usually unencumbered by duties or the need for special travel documents. The rise of large cities increased the demand for a variety of products.[129] Iraq's prosperity in particular, with its rich tax base and thriving commerce, was an important element contributing to the political power and cultural brilliance of the high caliphate.[130] The late Umayyads and the Abbasids created a unified professional bureaucracy, including a treasury that balanced receipts and expenses, an accounting office, an intelligence service, and a chancery office to handle official correspondence.[131]

This prosperity did not grow out of any improvement in agricultural productivity or any growth in mechanical inventiveness but as a consequence of the establishment of peace, security, and economic integration, which permitted commerce to improve well-being and affluence, a process some have termed *Smithian* growth — i.e., growth fueled by slow growth of productivity benefiting from political stability, technological innovation, and economies of scale and comparative advantage made possible by large markets.

But subsequent centuries would see this prosperity decay as Islamic civilization fell victim to an inability to evolve its institutions and practices. Trade-based expansion did not outlast the Abbasids — i.e., after the 12th century — as social, political, and economic deterioration took place. While establishing a large market with economies of scale and relative physical security spurred initial economic growth, it was not enough to sustain it.

The reasons for the Islamic empire's decline were similar to those contributing to the decline of other civilizations. First, there was a sclerosis resulting from the efforts of vested interests' (government and commercial) struggle to protect those interests by stifling change, which slowly undermined the economic viability of the system. Moreover, under hereditary despotic governments, subsequent leaders rarely have the capabilities of the founder and are invariably more isolated from the people. Finally, increasingly less capable, these governments are inevitably subject to jockeying for power by regional, military, and administrative factions, producing instability.

According to *The Oxford History*, for example, when Iraq's agrarian prosperity began to wane in the tenth century because, among other factors, of a deterioration of vital irrigation works, increasing salinity of the soil, and sheer administrative mismanagement, the rulers found themselves unable to pay the bills of their extensive operations. This in turn sparked the infighting among military and administrative factions that characterized the decline of Abbasid power.[132]

This pattern of rise and fall would characterize most of the major civilizations in history from Egypt to China. But Islam never found the means of renewal after the fall of one or another of the caliphates. Why not? The answer would appear to reside in Islamic institutions as well as in archaic value systems inhospitable to the extended order and entrepreneurship.

Most profoundly, the system was relatively frozen because all the precepts of the Quran purportedly came directly from God through Mohammed. The precepts were so specific that they did not lend themselves to the type of argumentation and opposing thought—i.e., heresy—that so characterized Christianity from the first few centuries. Moreover, Islam ceded political power to the conquerors who were awarded jurisdiction of land not unlike the feudal barons in Europe, and possessed "other characteristics of a distinctly feudal spirit: the obviously unquestioned acceptance of slavery, serfdom, and polygamy; the disesteem for and subjection of women; the essentially ritualistic character of religious obligations; and, finally, the great simplicity of religious requirements and the even greater simplicity of the modest ethical requirements."[133]

And there was much in the Islamic value system that was hostile to trade and the creation of wealth. Islam was a culture trapped in the values of a tribal culture that may have been hospitable to preserving knowledge but not for extending learning and not for accommodating institutional evolution. Although Islam drew upon Judeo-Christian antecedents and preserved learning—philosophy and medicine from the Greeks in the West and mathematics and astronomy from the Indians in the East—it made *change* difficult.

Especially in the economic arena, its values effectively impeded the rise of entrepreneurial activity, the accumulation of capital, and the creation of financial institutions needed for the modern state. Negative values and institutions can be traced to the culture's predatory origins, namely the extensive conquering and plundering of neighboring lands. The Islamic state, as a conquest society, had a very simple constitutional justification: from its inception, all land was claimed to be the property of the sovereign by right of conquest. From the Ummayads and the Abbasids down to the

Ottomans in Turkey, state monopoly of land became a traditional legal canon of Islamic political systems. [134] As a result, private property was insecure, and arbitrary taxation and confiscation of private property became a feature of life in the Muslim world at a very early period.[135] And, without secure property rights, capital will not accumulate, nor will it be readily deployed.

The Quran's emphasis on the group vs. the individual also seriously restricted entrepreneurial activity in Islamic societies. Quranic values oppose the *ruiner*, i.e. the selfish individualist, who jeopardizes the moral integrity of the Muslim community. "In Islam this moral distinction between socially conscious virtue and asocial individualism replicates the dichotomy between faith and unbelief that separates the social environment of Islam from that of non-Muslims."[136] Indeed, across the board Islam promotes passivity and discourages individualist behavior. The very meaning of the word Islam is surrender and submission to the will of God.

Further teachings tie individual motivation to group consensus rather than to individual initiative. There is an emphasis on sharing with the family and the poor. Indeed, two concrete demands of the Quran that reinforce this mindset are the requirements for tithing and giving alms and the prohibition on usury, the latter of which acts as an insurmountable barrier to achieving a modern economic state._

All in all, Islam had much in common with other cultures of its time in its views of social cohesiveness and economic relationships among individuals. It distrusted personal initiative, it emphasized charitable values over the acquisitive instinct, and it disapproved of most instruments of impersonal financial transactions.

Asian Cultures

If one examines Chinese and Indian civilizations a thousand years ago, one can find similar value systems that posed major obstacles to economic growth.

Chinese Civilization

A visitor to earth a thousand years ago could have perceived China under the Sung dynasty as the most advanced civilization and could easily have assumed that it would continue its superiority. The period of the Sung Dynasty was a time of intensive growth of population and economy fueled largely by an agricultural revolution following an expansion into southern lands in the Yangtze River valley and the development of a new wet rice technology.[137] Other key sources of growth "were a revolution in water transport; increased monetization, including the introduction of paper money …; and based on local markets, the growth of "a national hierarchy of markets linking almost the entire Chinese economy." Linking the Chinese rural economy with the market converted the Chinese peasantry "into a class of adaptable, rational, profit-oriented petty entrepreneurs."[138]

This growth was accompanied by remarkable technological advances similar to those in the early western industrial revolution. In agriculture, examples include the dam, the sluice-gate, the noria, and the treadle water pump. In industry, they learned how to use coke instead of charcoal as fuel and developed a technique for making iron using coke. Indeed, China's level of iron output in 1078 was not matched by Europe until the beginning of the eighteenth century.[139] This period of relative affluence was Smithian in nature.

The commercial value systems and day-to-day life were not dissimilar to other large civilizations. Specifically, life on the farms and in the cities had numerous similarities with Europe, India and Islam. China in the Sung Dynasty (at the time of the late Middle Ages in Europe) also had a manorial system for its agriculture.[140] Chinese towns organized their economic activities into industrial guilds. "These guilds … limited competition, and regulated wages, prices and hours; many of them restricted output in order to maintain the prices of their products." The Chinese had similar attitudes to money and trade vis-à-vis Medieval Europeans, Moslems and the Hindus. To be sure, the Chinese were considered to be 'natural merchants', had established widespread trade, and were among the first to develop a supporting system of paper money and credit to support that trade. Nonetheless, according to Durant, Chinese philosophy and officialdom agreed in despising traders … It was the custom to rank scholars, teachers and officials as the highest class, farmers as the next, artisans as the third, merchants as the lowest; for, said China, these last merely made profits by exchanging the fruits of other men's toil.[141]

But China's growth and innovation flagged in a manner similar to the decay of other large civilizations. Stagnation of the Chinese economy and the loss of intellectual vigor, however, specifically have been viewed as one of the great historical puzzles. It is referred to as *The Needham Problem.* Yet, a number of likely answers are apparent—i.e., the pernicious effects of a too centralized state, an atavistic value system regarding commerce, and a resistance to change.

A Too Centralized State
For example, several scholars relate this stagnation to the creation of the Confucian mandarinate, which was charged with implementing the official doctrine that held that the emperor "should consider the Empire as if it formed a single household". ... "Systematic restraint upon industrial expansion, commercial expansion, and military expansion were built into the Chinese system of political administration."[142] The impact of this arrangement was that "as long as officials could bring overriding police power to bear whenever they were locally or privately defied, the command element ... remained securely dominant ... [I]n every encounter the private entrepreneur was at a disadvantage, while officials had the whip hand. This was so, fundamentally, because most Chinese felt that the unusual accumulation of private wealth from trade or manufactures was profoundly immoral ... official ideology and popular psychology thus coincided to reinforce the advantage officials had in any and every encounter with merely private men of wealth."[143] The implicit arrangement between business and the state bureaucracy was a *predatory partnership* akin to more modern "crony capitalism".

While this specific culture was unique to China, predatory aspects of an absolutist state were not. As elsewhere, the Imperial state restricted trade and expropriated the wealth of merchants. The cities and the feudal provinces never gained administrative quasi-independence, and thus there were no safe niches in which innovations could flourish. When faced by war—e.g., Mongol invasions—the wealth extraction by the state grew more intense.

Because it was an Imperial state with an extensive bureaucracy, China could take negative economic values and governmental schemes to extremes. Daniel Boorstin's telling example of policy in the Sung Dynasty illustrates the baneful effects that a misguided central government can have when no significant power centers exist to counter destructive ideas.

An Atavistic Value System Regarding Commerce

Importantly, there was no philosophic base to challenge the political-economic state of affairs. China was home to a number of humanistic or non-theological religions such as Confucianism, Taoism, and Buddhism, as well as ancestor worship and widespread superstitions. While diverse in nature, all the religions shared the same values, drawn instinctively from man's primitive origins. Basically, they taught that in matters economic, man should help man,

---

Boorstin's Example of Unrestrained Executive Power

For 500 years, the Chinese had traded as far a field as with the Islamic world. Their maps showed the Nile, the Sudan, and Zanzibar. In 1405 the emperor had a flotilla of as many as 317 ships built, and enlisted some 37,000 crewmen to man the flotilla. Over twenty-eight years, seven expeditions took place – from Sumatra in the east to Zanzibar in the west. But whatever localized successes this approach might have had, the net result was an economic drain on the Chinese treasury. Thus, while the flotillas exemplified the maritime prowess of the Chinese, they were essentially a whim of the state and not part of the society's organic growth of trade.

And whims can come and go. Under a new emperor, the Mandarins noted the net costs of these flotillas, and they were halted. Meanwhile, the thousand-mile long Grand Canal reaching from Tiensin in the north to Hangchow in the south had been perfected into a full-capacity, all-season seaway, diminishing the need for seagoing vessels. Moreover, the long standing conviction of the Chinese that they had no need for outsiders took greater hold. With acute suddenness, the central government implemented a policy of the 'Great Withdrawal', and upon the return of the last flotilla, an imperial edict imposed savage punishments on Chinese who ventured abroad.

"By 1474 the main fleet of 400 warships had declined to 140. Shipyards disintegrated, sailors deserted, and shipwrights, fearing to become accomplices in the crime of seafaring were hard to find. The ban on foreign maritime ventures was extended to include coastal shipping. ... By 1500 it had been made a capital offense even to build a seagoing junk with more than two masts. In 1525 coastal officials were ordered to destroy all such ships and to arrest mariners who continued to sail them." Ironically, this was precisely the Age of Henry the Navigator and European sea goers who were circumnavigating the globe.

SOURCE: Daniel Boorstin, *The Discoverers*, p. 200

and not profit from his need. So, whenever the government moved to exploit the commercial sphere, itself seen as exploitive, there was little basis for principled resistance.

Moreover, without an experiential wisdom of a commercial class, other dysfunctional views of economic affairs repeatedly raised their heads to the great cost of society. Hayek suggested that such sentiments, often corresponding to quasi-socialist principles, are derived from our atavistic past. For example, according to Durant the Legalists, a rival school of Confucius believed: "Even tradesmen are not too intelligent, but pursue their interests very often to the detriment of the state; perhaps, said one of the Legalists, it would be wiser for the state to socialize capital, monopolize trade, and prevent the manipulation of prices and the concentration of wealth.[144] While such actions were still in the arena of theory at this time, subsequent emperors attempted to implement such policies, usually with dire results.

For example, Wu Ti, the greatest of the Han emperors (140-87 B.C.), experimented with socialism by establishing state ownership of natural resources, and made the production of salt and iron and the manufacture and sale of fermented drinks state monopolies. Further, to break the power of middlemen and speculators, he established a national system of transport and exchange, and sought to control trade to prevent sudden price fluctuations. All incomes had to be registered with the government and merchants had to pay an annual tax of five percent. The explicit purpose of these measures said Ch'ien, a contemporary historian, was to prevent rich merchants and large shop-keepers from making big profits and to regulate prices for the benefit of the consumer.[145]

Another later example of government meddling in the economy for well intentioned, but misguided reasons occurred when Wang An-shih (1021-86) attempted anew to better the welfare of his people with socialistic policies. He held as a general principle that "the government must hold itself responsible for the welfare of all its citizens. He said The State should take the entire management of commerce, industry and agriculture into its own hands with a view to succoring the working classes and preventing them from being ground into the dust by the rich." He rescued the peasants from the money-lenders by providing low interest loans for the planting of crops; boards were established in every district to regulate the wages of labor and the prices of the necessities of life; and commerce was nationalized, with the produce of each locality bought by the government partly for local needs and otherwise sold in state depots throughout the realm.[146]

However well intentioned these ideas were, this system failed for much the same reasons socialist systems usually do. First of all, the system required high levels of revenue. Just taxing the rich was insufficient. The large bulk of the population, the poor, would have to contribute in kind as well. They had to provide a soldier in times of war, and had to place their livestock in the service of government in times of military need. Second, a vast bureaucracy was needed to administer the numerous regulations intended to achieve 'fairness'. Honest men could not be found to administer the system and corruption spread throughout China. Soon, Durant reports: "Conservatives ... denounced the experiment as inherently unsound; they argued that human corruptibility and incompetence made government control of industry impracticable, and that the best form of government was a *laissez-faire* which would rely on the natural impulses of men for the production of services and goods."[147]

Lack of Individualism and Imperviousness to Change
Compounding the effects of dysfunctional economic values imbedded in the culture was the lack of individualism. According to Durant "the concept of the individual was weak, and lost him in the groups to which he belonged. He was, first of all, a member of a family and a passing unit in the stream of life between his ancestors and his posterity; by law and custom he was responsible for the acts of the others of his household, and they responsible for his. ... A web of ancient custom bound him, and a powerful public opinion threatened him with ostracism if he seriously violated the morals or traditions of the group."[148]

China's imperviousness to change in values and institutions can be traced to the Confucian influence, which especially shaped the values of the ruling elite. Although it was only one of a number of strong religious influences in China, it provided the most profound ethic for the upper classes and for the values of government over the span of millennia. Confucius was a philosopher rather than a theologian. Like Socrates, he was concerned with an individual's character and with his ability to think clearly, but his philosophy was more family centered and ritualistic. Importantly, he believed that if individuals could lead exemplary lives within the family unit, eventually this behavior would lead to enlightened governance from above. He wrote: "A man's character is formed by the Odes, developed by the Rites [the rules of ceremony and courtesy], and perfected by music.

Confucius, however, did not develop a comprehensive theology. According to Durant, The only metaphysics that Confucius would recognize was [1] the search for unity in all phenomena, and [2] the effort to find some stabilizing harmony between the laws of right conduct and the regularities of nature. "… Clarity and honesty of thought and expression were the first lessons of the Master."[149]

With regard to commerce, Confucius' teachings did not incorporate the biases against trade and profit seen throughout Chinese culture. Indeed, some scholars maintain that Confucian values were not directly antimarket but were only against ill-gotten and excessive wealth.[150] In Durant's summaries of Confucius' teachings, the only reference to economic matters was that the state should seek a wide distribution of wealth.[151]

But in terms of the evolution of the societal animal, Confucianism had an important downside. While Confucianism provided tranquility after a time of troubles, it ultimately became a shackle on evolutionary forces. More specifically, "[t]he rules of propriety, destined to form character and social order, became a straight-jacket forcing almost every vital action into a prescribed and unaltered mold. There was something prim and Puritan about Confucianism, which checked too thoroughly the natural and vigorous impulses of mankind; its virtue was so complete as to bring sterility. No room was left in it for pleasure and adventure, and little for friendship and love."[152]

Indian Civilization
In contrast with Chinese civilization, India lends itself less to broad cross-cultural comparisons because of its greater diversity of ethnic stocks and its greater heterodoxy of religion. Moreover, India was more subject to foreign invasion and did not experience

an enduring culturally-unifying central state similar to Imperial China. Will Durant stated that India should not be conceived as a single nation such as Egypt or Babylonia, but rather as a continent as populous and polyglot as Europe.[153] Nevertheless, two important observations can be drawn pertinent to the theme of this chapter. First, its culture was highly resistant to forces of societal evolution, and second, its attitudes toward commerce in that fixed society were similar to other civilizations—i.e., still derived from the days of early man.

The Fixity of Culture

While India's governing structures underwent periodic change as a result of foreign invasions and internal upheavals, its social structure was remarkably enduring. Indeed, India's social order of a thousand years ago—the period of this chapter's cross-cultural comparisons—had essentially been long established as a result of the Aryan invasions from the north as far back as the Second Millennium B.C. The pattern was set when the armed invaders settled and their tribes evolved into petty states, because India's topography militated against strong central rule. It has been said that it was easier to conquer than to rule India.[154] This led a form of governance akin to feudal Europe, where the barons' control of the land stemmed from a set of military obligations, but also included considerable autonomy.

The fixity of Indian social structure and culture can be traced to the circumstances in the aftermath of the Aryan invasions which overwhelmed the native stock of Nagas and Dravidians, greater in number and of different ethnic and color origin. To avoid assimilation, the invaders forbade marriage outside their racial group; to maintain dominance they established a rigid caste system. The top caste consisted of the fighters; the next were the Brahmans who initially were priests. However, during extended periods of peace, Brahmans became the educators, and in that capacity eventually displaced the warriors as the top caste. The next levels of castes were constituted by merchants and freemen, followed by the peasants who comprised most of the native population. At the bottom were the outcastes—unconverted native tribes—who became the "Untouchables" of more modern times.[155]

This societal structure was as durable as it was rigid in preventing significant evolution. Durant concluded: "Nowhere else can we find this astonishing phenomenon—so typical of the slow rate of change in India—of an upper class maintaining its ascendancy and privileges through all conquests, dynasties and governments for 2,500 years ... it gave to a country shorn of political stability by a hundred invasions and revolutions a social, moral and cultural order and continuity rivaled only by the Chinese."[156]

Nor would forces for change emerge from the religious sphere. To be sure, there was considerable religious ferment, particularly when Buddhism competed with Brahmanism. Yet the pervasive outcome was, according to Durant, a 'Hinduism' that was not one religion, but a medley of faiths and ceremonies that recognized the caste system and the leadership of the Brahmans, revered the cow, accepted the law of *Karma* and the transmigration of souls.[157] All in all, the religious beliefs were inward-oriented, had few socio-ethical dimensions, and were profoundly pessimistic regarding possibilities for change.

As described by Durant, this was true of Buddhism as much as it was of Hinduism. Buddhism was a 'slave' philosophy arguing that all desire or struggle, even for personal or national freedom, should be abandoned, and that the ideal in life was a desireless passivity. Hinduism, he stated: "depicted life as inevitably evil, and broke the courage and darkened the spirit of its devotees; it turned all earthly phenomena into illusion, and thereby destroyed the distinction between freedom and slavery, good and evil, corruption and betterment."[158]

Part and parcel of these beliefs was a lack of individualism. This could be especially seen in the legal code, which "continued to be group-oriented and non-egalitarian or ascriptive instead of being individual-oriented and universalistic."[159] These views were incorporated into Hindu books of law, which promulgated an organic, traditionalistic ethic of vocation, similar in structure to Medieval Catholicism, only more consistent.[160]

The Economic Order
Despite such a stultifying philosophic picture, daily life went on: life had to be sustained, food had to be grown, and goods had to be

produced. Human instinct for survival makes most men pay more attention to economic-related activity than to religious. Thus, it is not surprising that, in terms of economic life, Max Weber's extensive cross-cultural, sociological studies indicated that the universal human drive for betterment and commerce was as evident in Indian civilization as any other. Indeed, while good data is not available, certain contemporary accounts suggest that India after about 300 B.C. achieved levels of prosperity comparable with other advanced civilizations. As in the Abbasid Middle East and Sung China much later, political and ideological unification [under the Mauryas] may have spurred a period of Smithian intensive growth.[161] Extensive foreign commerce was evident as far back as 3000 B.C. and trade with India in the late Middle Ages was a spur for Western exploration of the globe.

At a more micro-economic level, Will Durant believes that village life was not dissimilar to that of other civilizations with a rural routine of seeding, tillage and craft industry. The fields were divided among constituent families, and the land could not be sold but could only be bequeathed to family heirs.

Town life also was similar to other civilizations as seen in attempts to provide security, certainty, and fairness at the expense of innovation and anything resembling free markets. Artisans and apprentices organized into powerful guilds to stifle competition. Prices were fixed and not permitted to fluctuate according to the laws of supply and demand. For example, an official 'Valuer' tested goods to be bought and dictated terms to the makers.

So despite periods of commercial prosperity, it appeared that Indians were just as tied to ancient values that emphasized security and predictability over competition and change. In this regard, Weber noted similarities of values regarding the economy between Hindu India and medieval Europe. Just as in Europe, Indian warrior nobility tended to regard as parvenu any person who had risen up the social scale as a result of the acquisition of money. Tied to such views, speculative acquisition of consumer goods was viewed unfavorably in Hindu legal books. Similarly the Hindu books of canonical law prohibit the taking of usury, at least for the two highest castes.[162]

Such anti-commercial views were unlikely to change, at least not from internal pressures. According to Max Weber, the caste taboos of the Hindus restricted intercourse among people far more forcefully than the value systems of other cultures. In particular, economic rationalization could not evolve where taboos had achieved such massive power, and which were notably traditionalistic, rather than rational.

These taboos' power were derived from their connection with the belief in transmigration, and especially with the tenet that any possible improvement in one's chances in subsequent incarnations depended on the faithful execution in the present lifetime of the vocation assigned one by the virtue of his caste status. Effort to escape this assigned role, and especially to intrude into the sphere of activities of higher castes, entailed the likelihood of unfavorable incarnation hereafter. This explains why precisely the lower classes, which would naturally be most desirous of improving their status in subsequent incarnations, clung most steadfastly to their caste obligations.[163]

Medieval Europe

Medieval Europe was similar to these other civilizations when it came to values governing day-to-day agriculture, manufacturing and commerce. It too still incorporated values from man's distant origins, albeit in more sophisticated formulations. But at the same time, Europe had inherited from its Judeo-Christian-Greco-Roman cultural legacy a worldview that would offer greater opportunity for evolutionary change to unfold.

Day to Day Life

The economy of Medieval Europe was as overwhelmingly rural and agricultural as the economies of all contemporary civilizations. Inasmuch as between 80-90 percent of the population did agricultural work to survive, that society was preoccupied with providing food.[164] In Europe, agriculture took place in the Manorial System inherent in feudalism: nobles were given control of the land, which was worked by serfs. But feudalism was not despotism. While the serfs were tied to the land and were very much under the control of the lords, they were not without rights. For example, they could expect to have the right to work the land passed on to their children, their payments to the lords were fixed, and their other responsibilities were enumerated. Moreover, lords were constrained in their behavior: they could not sell their serfs except as part of the sale of the manor, and the amount of labor the serfs owed the lord was limited.

The manors were economically largely self sufficient with activity governed by custom. Serfs essentially traded their labor for the use of land and there was little participation in a money-economy. But while barter was the predominant form of exchange, money was still required. For example, fees might be charged for the milling of grain or for the baking of bread; for payment to the lord in lieu of required labor for the payment of fines; and for purchases in the occasional trade fair.

It is not surprising that in this closed world, values were similar to those of early human groups. According to Rosenberg and Birdzell, "The lord of the manor was a father figure, reminiscent ... of ... primitive forms of family, clan, and tribal leadership to which the priest-kings no doubt owed their origins. In weaving the political, economic, religious, and social threads of community life into the pattern of a single fabric, under the leadership of a father figure, the Middle Ages reiterated the most ancient forms of community organization."[165]

Medieval towns constituted a much smaller percentage of the population. The relatively small manufacture and trade that existed occurred there. Because they could not be self-sufficient in the same way of manors, they had to rely on an exchange economy to a greater extent.

Despite the different economic role, medieval towns shared the values of larger feudal society. The paternalistic, rule-bound organization of the manor carried over to the towns. Most production took place under the exclusive monopolies of the guilds. "The Church's notions of 'just price' and a 'just wage' gave moral sanction to guild regulations covering prices, wages of apprentices and journeymen, standards of product quality and workmanship, admission to the trade, and a duty to ply one's trade at the established prices and wages. ... The holding of markets and fairs was permissible only under license, and their conduct was as rigidly regulated as the trade of the guilds themselves."[166]

All in all, institutional arrangements and regulations for small manufacturing and crafts were conceptually not dissimilar to those found elsewhere, notably in Chinese and Hindu cultures, aiming at security, certainty, and fairness.

Prevailing Value Systems

Underlying this relatively primitive economy was a value system as old as man. Indeed, at its heart it was the same economic world-view—e.g., with regard to: individuals in fixed roles in society, attempts to achieve fairness, and certainty through rigid regulation of all aspects of production and exchange. But one important difference from other cultures was the attempt by the Church to understand this state of affairs and to provide an intellectual, albeit theological, underpinning to it. In this regard, the Church played a role quite different from institutionalized religions elsewhere that made little attempt at a comprehensive metaphysical view of the world.

The Church's role was determined by the state of affairs following the fall of the Roman Empire following incursions by the Germanic tribes. New societal animals came into being. The declining Roman culture, which saw slavery, poverty, and alienation, was incapable of absorbing and neutralizing the populous German tribes in, say, the same way that China assimilated periodic invaders. And because the tribes lacked the values and traditions to establish a new, flourishing empire on their own, the barbarian leaders pragmatically drew on traditions and institutions of an empire that no longer existed (in the West anyway). They did so via the intellectual and institutional resources of the Christian Church, which provided the invaders with prestige, a store of learning, and a way of gaining the support of the conquered territories.

In its catholic ambitions, the Church attempted to develop a comprehensive theology beyond mere tradition to govern man in his earthly existence, with a goal of saving men's souls. The Church was prescriptive on most aspects of behavior, vocational and social as well as moral and spiritual. These prescriptions included man's appropriate positions and roles in society. Indeed, "A hierarchical social order was established by a range of definitions which started with the standard of duties for Christians in general. The more specific tasks and duties imposed on the various classes, and the occupational and professional groups of the population, were defined in accordance with this standard." Individual behavior and its rightfulness provided the starting point for all considerations, since the life of every human being was primarily regarded as preparation for the salvation of his soul and practices regarded as sinful had to be controlled." The Church strove to weave these teachings into a rigorous metaphysics based on *universals* so as to provide a logical basis for ancient and still prevailing values: communal responsibility, sharing, and fairness in transactions. Logical theorizing was most important in several economic areas.[167]

Key watchwords in this theory, *just price* and *just wage*, represented concepts that grew out of a desire to ensure fairness in transactions. It transpired that these were complex, non-self-evident ideas, beyond the capacity of the times to understand. Nonetheless, the Church's best attempt at a definition was based on a belief that things had intrinsic values that endured over time. To be sure, some Scholastic thinkers asserted that value should be linked to the utility of objects, but most believed that utility was merely a gloss on inherent objective value.

Building on these concepts of value, the rules to be observed in performing monetary transactions were derived by the Church from the Aristotelian principle of *commutative justice*. As interpreted by the Scholastics, this principle implied that equivalence of intrinsic values should obtain in all cases in which goods were exchanged for each other, and that the intrinsic value of the goods should be reflected in their prices.[168] In attempting to determine the logical basis for intrinsic value, the Scholastics agreed that price should reflect the work done by artisans as well as the cost of materials and tools. Costs of labor were to be determined by graded remuneration according to the skill and social position of the worker and the nature of the work. According to this construct, the value of goods was held to be independent of the passage of time. The difficult-to-discern more valid economic laws of supply and demand were not identified for centuries to come.

Pursuant to this line of Scholastic logic, a number of trading practices were condemned and prosecuted, including forestalling (buying up of goods before they reached the market), regrating (buying of goods in the market with the intention to resell them at a higher price), and engrossing (the monopolistic manipulation of prices).

Aside from the issues of commutative justice, Christian theology condemned any pursuit of gain for its own sake. Strict limits were placed on the tendency to expand a gainful enterprise or to increase one's earnings. Three serious logical difficulties arose, however, when trying to apply such principles to the activities of traders and merchants. The first related to the Church's belief that the more a community was self-sufficient and the less its citizens depended on the activity of traders and merchants, the closer it was to perfection. This view ran counter to normal ambition, and to adhere to this view, the community would have to forgo the economic benefits from comparative advantage in trading, thereby condemning itself to relative poverty.

A second set of difficulties were associated with financial calculation, such as how one could determine the licit remuneration of intermediaries between producers and consumers who did not add to the *intrinsic* value of goods. The logical problems associated with the lending of money were greater still. Since money was regarded only as an instrument for measuring values, how was a just price for the use of money to be determined?

Thirdly, the profit-making impetus for such activity in itself was suspect in the Church's eyes. As trade and a money-economy grew, transactions became more impersonal, less sentimental, and increasingly indifferent to specific needs of the individual. Weber, emphasizing this issue, stated: "But it is above all the impersonal and economically rationalized ... character or purely commercial relationships that evokes the suspicion ... of ethical religions."[169]

The Church's metaphysics was not up to addressing the multiplying problems associated with that trade and the emerging extended order. According to Rosenberg and Birdzell, "The market's uncertainties involve responses of buyers and competitors, how much the peasant or artisan will be able to realize from the finished work, the prices the merchant can get in the future for stock bought today, and all the consequences of unanticipated changes in supply and demand. The merchant with funds to use in buying and selling faces choices: what to buy, when to buy, when to sell, whether instead to lend some money to others at interest or for a share in someone else's voyage or other enterprise. Which of such choices will result in the most gain or the least loss is, perhaps, the greatest uncertainty of all. In a medieval society where economic roles were inherited, regulated, and priced by custom and law, such choices were alien to the system. The calculation of the most favorable choice verged on the immoral."[170]

But in terms of future developments, it is important to note that the basis for many restrictions was considered to be logical inferences from universals and not necessarily from Holy Scripture. The treatment of *usury* is especially illustrative in that regard. According to Pribram, usury was a *logical* sin. Virtually all Scholastic authors agreed that usury was forbidden by natural law and by natural law alone. Hence, usury was condemned in order to protect the authority of the Church's logical—as opposed to faith-based—conclusions from being undermined by the effects of erroneous thoughts. Thus, in principle, the issue could be viewed differently under future conditions through the application of logic and not violate scripture.[171]

Max Weber illustrated this point: "The original basis for the thoroughgoing rejection of usury was generally the primitive custom of economic assistance to one's fellows, in accordance with which the taking of usury "among brothers" was undoubtedly regarded as a serious breach against the obligation to provide assistance."[172] He believed that the Christian injunction against usury came from a mistranslation of the language that God will not reward the lender in transactions which present no risk. More elementally, individuals emotionally are averse to paying someone who is seen as not having actually produced something and the Church was reflecting such reactions in its behavioral codes.

But as a practical matter, Weber believes usury was not much of an issue in early Christianity and that the Popes and the Church generally were not reluctant to charge interest on loans. In other words, an important gap existed between philosophy/theology and practice. At the heart of the disjuncture was the inevitable reality that loans would not be available without the charging of interest, and thus, church teachings at the time may not have been in accord with the reality of much of day-to-day life.

This framework for economic life was designed to maintain social cohesiveness in the face of life's uncertainties, to promote mutual support, and to preclude one person taking economic advantage of another in trading and, above all, in times of need. The theology of the medieval Church reflected an ancient value system that worked in the context of the economically primitive medieval setting but would prove unsuitable for the extended economic order of modern economies.

Despite the Church's medieval teachings being at variance with economic laws, their saving grace was in the attempt itself to deal with economic matters in a logical construct. So, when unsettling logical problems emerged with the quickening of trade and the beginnings of manufacturing, a framework existed from which to consider new theories and new views. Much like a scientific paradigm, the model could, in principle, be modified with the accumulation of experience.

For a modern economy to become possible, values and arguments would have to change. Acceptance of laws of supply and demand would have to displace the concepts of price and wage controls. The charging of interest would have to be seen as essential for the accumulation and sound deployment of capital. Envy of the rich, opprobrium of the trader, suspicion of individual initiative, and disapproval of wealth accumulation would have to be overcome—through the lessons of experience and the forces of self-interest at all levels of society.

Somehow, the whole medieval cultural mindset with regard to economics would have to be left behind. It is to this *great escape* by the West that we now turn.

THE WEST'S ESCAPE

Major economic evolutionary changes emerged in Western Europe that, together with the changes in value systems and institutions, allowed the European societal animal to evolve to greater potency and effectiveness—i.e., to become more evolutionarily adaptive. Small patterns of trade common to all humankind expanded greatly. Growing trade spurred the development of markets, of banking, of new financial instruments and institutions. The demand for

---

SUMMARY OF ECONOMIC VALUES – CIRCA 1000 A.D.

All the major civilizations on earth around 1000 A.D. had remarkably similar attitudes toward economic affairs. In the case of Christianity, Islam, and Hinduism, these attitudes were explicitly embodied in their theology. In the case of China, the values appeared to be more an instance of cultural tradition. But they all had their origins in man's early primitive life. They served early societal animals well, and tradition maintained them.

Islam had much in common with Medieval Europe in its views of social cohesiveness and economic relationships among individuals. It distrusted personal initiative, it emphasized charitable values over the acquisitive instinct, and it disapproved of most instruments of impersonal financial transactions.

Both Europe's and India's cultures had military antecedents, had rigid codes designed to maintain the status quo as well as to minimize the uncertainties of life and establish a system of fairness. And both achieved periods of stable and enduring economic life.

Despite these similarities, there was one glaring difference: Islam, the Asian cultures, and the Hindu Indian cultures were, in large measure, impervious to fundamental change. Only Medieval Europe escaped the fate of older as well as contemporary empires as a consequence, in part, of beneficial fragmented political power, power centers that resisted the predatory power of the king through institutional checks and balances, and new value systems that were to come under the rubric of "The Protestant Ethic."

---

goods by merchants created a parallel supply by new manufacturers. Because much of this activity was at odds with the prevailing value systems of Europe, particularly as codified by the Catholic Church, we shall see how experiential learning in the processes of economic development and newfound power by those leading these processes generated new world views and new values.

Although the medieval period is the point of departure for describing this evolution, history does not have sharp disjunctures in which everything is 'new' after a certain date. The evolution described had roots going back to antiquity—Judeo-Christian religions, Greek philosophy, Roman law, and certain values of the

Germanic tribes regarding rule of custom, if not of law. Taken together, such features made western civilization unique and made what followed possible. Still, as we have seen, the world had at least three other societal animals at this time that had comparable, if not superior, wealth and technological expertise. But they lacked the internal values compatible with comparable evolution.

The Darwinian model presupposes that inventive man in pursuing his interests will continuously attempt new, and hopefully superior, ways of achieving his ends. Inventive approaches can be viewed akin to mutations in the biological world. Some will work as desired; others will fail. Some won't work well immediately, but may as experience is gained and circumstances become more favorable. For evolution in the economic arena to proceed, two critical elements are required: new approaches that make more effective use of resources for meeting needs, and a favorable political niche that does not emasculate or destroy the innovation—i.e., a society with a restrained predatory state and an openness to innovation.

Politically fragmented Western Europe possessed those conditions. Its sustained growth began when the economic sphere managed to gain a sufficient degree of autonomy from political and religious control.[173] In effect, forces that suppressed change in other civilizations were either overcome or pushed aside in the West.

Growth of Commerce

As discussed earlier, the Roman Empire, with its stability, rule of law, and infrastructure enjoyed widespread trade and relative wealth before taxation and economic controls strangled the basis of wealth generation. Then, with the Empire's fall and the rise of Islam, with its almost total control of the Mediterranean Sea, most trade of any consequence vanished from Europe. While Venice continued to trade with Byzantium and some necessities such as salt were traded over longer distances, most areas of Europe slumbered in quasi-autarchy.

Without trade there was no capital accumulation and no basis for manufactures of any consequence. Any capital at the time was generally in the hands of the Church, much in the form of silverplate. There are many recorded instances of the nobility regularly borrowing from the Church when in need. This borrowing was generally for consumption beyond their means, for the needs of military campaigns, or for buying property, but not to invest in production or other economic activity.[174]

How, then, did trade burgeon and become the basis for breaking the feudal order? The transition in Europe was slow—over 500 years or so of evolution had to occur before one could say that the feudal order was dead and the foundation of modern Europe set.

Change was fitful and unplanned, with one innovation or political event marginally affecting another in a positive manner, and then being reinforced in turn. This mutually reinforcing evolution was characterized by a slowly growing population generating demands for goods and new lands to cultivate; the chartering of new towns that enjoyed considerable freedom; the quickening of interregional trade; the clearing of the Mediterranean of inhibiting Islamic control, which allowed the efficient use of water transport; and the first stirrings of manufactures outside the confines of the small towns that produced more than the localities needed.

The Seedbeds for a New Commercial Order
The towns of Europe became the seedbeds for a new commercial order, but they had unprepossessing origins. 'Cities' in early Medieval times were largely centers of ecclesiastical administration and manorial administration, with those living there dependent on rents from their estates and on religious dues. They also provided refuge for the surrounding population during times of insecurity. With the dissolution of the Carolingian Empire, protection was needed from the Saracen incursions in the south, from the Normans in the North and West, and the Hungarians in the East. This role of towns was an adjunct to what was, basically, an agricultural society.[175]

The towns that were eventually to drive commercial evolution were the independent city-states, the relatively autonomous chartered cities, and the leagues of cities that emerged in Medieval Europe, a uniquely Occidental phenomenon.[176] They found oddly favorable political circumstances in the aftermath of the collapse of the Roman Empire. The failure of any subsequent empire such as Charlemagne's to centralize power bestowed a dispersed political arrangement, a serendipitous benefit growing out of the Dark Ages.

A new beginning was generated by a growth of population made possible by somewhat more secure political circumstances. Although Europe's population had declined, probably reaching its nadir in the ninth century—the Dark Ages indeed—it rose from the eleventh century on. By the beginning of the fourteenth century it had risen to more than 70 million. Feeding the growing population led to an exploitation of new, unsettled regions, enlargement of the amount of arable land in older regions, and an increase in the intensity of agriculture generally.[177]

The growing population began to have effects beyond the settling of new lands. As there were more children than could be accommodated by the manors, many departed to settle new lands and to join the military, others moved into the towns and still others sought to make their own opportunities in trade. The first significant symptoms of the revival of commerce were evident in the second half of the tenth century. The risks encountered by the wandering merchants caused them to seek the protection of the walled towns, particularly those situated along rivers or natural routes by which they traveled. Soon, the space offered by these burgs became too constrained, and the merchants moved outside to create a new burg—i.e., a *faubourg*. According to Pirenne, the activities of these new denizens represented a totally different sort of existence from that of the original inhabitants. Indeed, the term *bourgeois* is derived from these burg roots.

Towns increasingly gained some freedom from baronial powers that ruled during this era through various routes. For example, The Spanish monarchs found it to their advantage to establish walled cities as outposts of the Christian conquerors in their centuries-long effort to drive the Moors out of Spain. They found it desirable to grant the inhabitants of these cities *fueros*, or charters, which endowed them with extensive privileges.[178] On their own initiative, medieval towns typically obtained a measure of political autonomy by the purchase of charters from their suzerains. The charters, occasionally negotiated with the threat of violence, conveyed varying degrees of self-government. In countries with stronger central monarchies such as France, England, and Spain, the towns tended to ally themselves with the monarch vis-à-vis the feudal nobles, resulting in the loosening of town obligations to the nobles,[179] because the king's legal advisors held that each city on becoming a commune came under the direct administration of the king, no matter what other feudal jurisdiction in which the town might lie.

Nature of the Revival of Trade

Although the manorial system was largely self-sufficient – and self-sufficiency was considered to be virtuous – trade was still necessary. And bartering, guided by the laws of comparative advantage, is always present, at however small a scale.

Pirenne believes that trading activities experienced a sea change in Europe a thousand years ago. Much trade until then was adventitious or intermittent occupations of manorial agents. But increasingly, merchants were no longer determined by relations with the land. He characterized them as being in every sense of the word, a class of incontestably *new men*.

Although the accounts are fragmentary, he cites the example of St. Godric of Finchale as an example of how the nouveaux riches of that time arose. St. Godric was born toward the end of the 11th century of poor peasant stock in Lincolnshire and probably forced to leave his parents holding. He became a beachcomber because shipwrecks were numerous, and one fine day a windfall enabled him to get together a *peddler's pack* of wares. He then built a little store of money when he joined a band of merchants. That business prospered and he soon made enough profit to enable him to form a partnership with others to load a ship and engage in coastal trade along the shores of England, Scotland, Flanders, and Denmark. Their operations, in common with most profitable trade, consisted in taking goods abroad to where they were scarce and bringing back a cargo of goods in great demand at home. Particularly in times of famine, which were frequent and ubiquitous, large profits could be realized from a relatively small amount of grain.[180]

Clearly, the nature and extent of trade were reviving as seen in a few examples. Edward Cheney in *The Dawn of a New Era* portrays the breadth of trade quickening through Europe. This trade, of course, was spurred by the forces of comparative advantage operating on the reality that certain items were required everywhere, but found only in a few locations. He traced the trade flows of prominent items:

- Salt was carried from the Adriatic by pack horses to Serbia, Croatia and Hungary; one of the biggest regular convoys of the North carried salt from France to the Baltic to salt fish.

- Wine was in demand everywhere but could only be produced under southern sun. Bordeaux thrived on the wine trade and import duties a large part of British royal revenue.

- Shipyards around the Mediterranean had to get lumber from far inland or from the areas around the Black Sea.

- Iron, lead, copper and tin, silver and gold were produced in a few localities but were in universal demand to cover roofs, to make pewter, and in later years to cast cannon.

- Wool played perhaps the largest part in trade of any of these material products. While Sheep were raised everywhere, quality differences resulted in hundreds of thousands of bales and sacks being transported yearly from favored wool growing areas to the centers of textile industry – e.g. from Eastern England and northern Spain to the manufacturing towns of Flanders and northern France.[181]

In effect, there was a huge potential to be exploited, and European geography was conducive to the trade that could exploit it. Europe's large coastline relative to its land area, with many inlets and rivers, made coastal and tributary transport attractive long before the overseas voyages of discovery occurred. These geographical features were unusual, sorely lacking in most other civilizations.

One result of the nature of European trade was the need for economical transport of bulk commodities that went way beyond the spices and luxury goods of long-distance trade in earlier times. As another example of how trends do not arise in isolation but often grow in tandem, one reinforcing another, the growth of commerce in Europe was the catalyst for opening the Western Mediterranean Sea to trade.

Opening of the Mediterranean
During the Dark Ages, the Tyrrhenian Sea had largely become a *Moslem Lake* stifling trade from Southern France and Northern Italy

northwards.[182] This was not true, however, of the Eastern Mediterranean. The Byzantine Empire had kept those waters under its control, and, Venice, nominally aligned with the empire, controlled the Adriatic. Venice prospered mightily from that trade and provided an example for others, enticing Italian cities on the west coast such as Pisa and Genoa to seek similar wealth from trade. These latter cities undertook campaigns against Moslem powers for an extended period of time beginning in the tenth century. At first, and for some 70 years, the advantage lay with the Moslems. But over the following century, Italian cities advanced to the coast of Africa; forced the entrance to the port of Palermo; and took Mehda. By the beginning of the First Crusade in 1097, the Mediterranean was effectively cleared for European commerce.

With the whole of Mediterranean open for commerce in the south, and increasing waterborne commerce in the north—along the English Channel, the North Sea, the Baltic, and rivers such as the Rhine—a wide spread, relatively low-cost transport network for trade arose. The revival of maritime commerce stimulated agriculture and industry inland as part of a widening exchange economy.[183]

With the ongoing growth of population and the recovery of trade in the tenth and the eleventh centuries, one could speak of the *Renaissance of the 12th Century*, with its concomitant revival of the classics, literature, jurisprudence, and the beginnings of universities.[184]

Early Manufactures

These early manifestations of trade consisted of raw materials found in limited locations but needed everywhere. The expansion of demand became the basis for the beginnings of manufacturing. The first significant example was cloth manufacturing in the Low Countries. Although some primitive manufacturing of cloth took place as early as the Roman occupation of Flanders, the 'industry' was destroyed during the Scandinavian invasions, not to be revived until the renewal of trade.

As renewed demand, especially from England, soon surpassed the amount of local wool production, the whole of Flanders became a country of weavers and fullers in the 12th century.[185] The towns of

Flanders, which were devoted to clothe manufacturing, led the way in organizing production and carrying out wholesale commerce. For the first time in the Middle Ages one had entrepreneurs who, together with wholesale merchants, carried on an international trade.

Furthermore, in the 13th century, the textile industry in Flanders assumed a large-scale, semi-capitalist structure, in which thousands of workers produced goods for the general market, and earned profits for investors whom they seldom saw. In effect, a new social class arose as workers became wage-earners.[186] Much the same industrial evolution occurred in Northern Italy, where, for example, Florence was noted for its textiles, metalwork, and trade in armor.[187]

New Financial Institutions

With greater political stability and the opening of trade routes in the Mediterranean, human action in commerce was again beginning to flourish. Despite symbolic central power of the Holy Roman Empire, political power remained highly fragmented. Rulers, vying with others to benefit from trade and enterprise, desisted from preying on the new sources of wealth to a debilitating degree. Further, spontaneous order could be seen in the collective actions of merchants and manufacturers to evolve much more effective financial instruments and institutions. Important illustrations can be found in (1) the role played by trade fairs leading to the creation of primitive bills of exchange, (2) economic freedom gained by the towns, and (3) the beginnings of banking.

Trade Fairs
Trade fairs were qualitatively different from and not linked to local agricultural markets, which simply supplied the provisions for everyday life. Rather, they had more of a wholesale and financial character. They grew organically to meet the practical needs of merchants at a time when they were a peripatetic lot. Already in existence in the 11th century, they were centers of exchange that set out to attract the greatest number of people and goods independent of local considerations. Because of their size, it was impractical to hold

them more than once or twice a year, but when they were held, they were enormous drawing cards. For example, the Champagne fairs in the 12th and 13th centuries attracted merchants from the whole of Europe.

Although the sites were naturally determined by the flow of commerce, only territorial princes had the right to found them. This sponsorship, in turn, provided the fairs with important advantages not found elsewhere: the ground on which they were held was protected by a special peace under the protection of the prince; letters of obligation sealed with their seal were recognized as especially binding; the "franchise" exempted merchants from reprisal or debts stemming from outside the fair as long as it lasted; and the suspension of the canonical prohibition of usury and of the fixing of a maximum rate of interest was suspended.

Drawing on innovations that grew up in the more advanced Italian city-states, these fairs became the money markets of Europe. At every fair, a period of sales was followed by one of payment. These payments not only involved the clearing of debts contracted at the fair itself, but also settled credits contracted at preceding fairs. This was an early form of bills of exchange. The bills were written promises to pay a sum of money in a place other than where the debt was contracted. The Champagne fairs were so widely attended that most debts were made payable at them, no matter where contracted. This became the case not only with commercial debt, but also with loans contracted by individuals, princes, or religious houses.[188]

A notable example of the early role of primitive bills of exchange was associated with the English wool trade. Most countries forbade the export of gold and silver, which created difficulties for the transmission of substantial papal dues. To deal with this situation, English clerics would deposit coined money with Italian bankers in England and receive from them a primitive form of bill of exchange which could be sent by messenger to Rome, where it was payable in cash or credit. In the meantime the agents of the bankers in England would invest the money in wool or other native produce and ship it to Flanders, France or Italy to be sold to produce revenues to make good on other bills of exchange.[189]

While the fairs served an important purpose in the acceleration of commerce, in the immediate centuries to come trade became more institutionalized and capital intensive so that the need for them waned.

The Expanding Role of Towns

Venice, of all medieval cities, led the way in embracing new values that enabled Europe to become wealthy. Versions of its mercantile culture spread to cities throughout Western Europe concomitant with the expansion of commerce. And it provides perhaps the clearest example of how a favorable social Darwinian innovation can emerge and thrive in a protected niche. Venice introduced and promoted any number of commercial and financial innovations along with new modes of supportive governmental structure.

The city enjoyed a number of political and geographic factors that supported this development. Importantly, they never were overrun by barbarians and never fell into the economic stagnation of the Dark Ages. They eluded the grasp of the Carolingians and remained only loosely tied to the Byzantine Empire. Sitting at the top of the Adriatic Sea, they were never seriously threatened by the Saracens. Situated on islands, they were protected from threats from the land.

In trade, they benefited from the ongoing needs of Constantinople. So they, in contrast with most Western Europe, preserved a merchant class along with skills and risk-taking attitudes. Having eluded the worst of the Dark Ages, they never subscribed as fully to the Church's metaphysics regarding commerce. Indeed, they institutionalized values greatly at odds with the Christian values that held sway elsewhere. For example, Medieval Europeans distrusted trade in general, viewed acquisitiveness with suspicion, and attempted to avoid financial risks with stultifying regulation of prices and commercial transactions. Venetians, on the other hand, recognized that their wealth and security depended on being a commercial state and embraced the values and policies attendant to that role. As Pirenne noted: "No more striking contrast could be imagined between Western Europe, where land was everything and commerce nothing, and Venice, a landless city, living only by trade."[190] In today's world, Hong Kong and Singapore are comparable examples.

Religious or moral scruples seldom held Venetian traders from following a path to potential profit. From the end of the ninth century, they traded increasingly with lands under Moslem control in North Africa and Syria. They exported slaves (young Slavs) to the harems of Egypt and Syria. They shipped timber and iron to the countries of Islam, knowing that they could be used to build vessels and to forge weapons with which to fight against Christians. In vain did the Pope threaten to excommunicate the sellers of Christian slaves, or the Emperor to prohibit the supply to infidels of articles capable of being employed in warfare.[191] These activities, while morally objectionable in the context of Christendom, illustrate that the Venetians were the Ur-traders of their day.

The entire population was involved in and depended on trade. The doges themselves set the example and the most important families were major participants.[192] Cheyney provides useful illustrations of these relationships: "The government was that of a joint-stock trading company, the Doge its president, the Senate its board of directors, the populace its shareholders. The policy of Venice was consistently that which would best subserve the demands of her commercial interests."[193] The aristocracy in Venice was not one that lived on wealth of inherited estates. When a fleet was organized, its captains were drawn from the 200 or so noble families; the archers were often young members of the aristocracy. Most Venetians, even the highest, were merchants and most saw sea-service at one time or another in their lives.[194] With its wealth and power, Venice, was becoming a stronger societal animal increasingly emulated by others.

In the course of a few centuries, many other cities in Western Europe followed this commercial example. But they, recovering from the Dark Ages in a feudal status, had in many ways to begin afresh. The swelling of trade and the desire for further affluence provided the impetus, causing cities to fight vigorously against the financial constraints of the feudal order. As the power in the towns moved to the economic interests of the *new men*, the towns gained economic freedoms by becoming charter cities, and as men's economic interests evolved, so did their values. They sought personal liberty because without the power to come and go, to do business, to sell goods—a power not enjoyed by serfdom—trade would be impossible.[195]

One can imagine the slow process whereby old worldviews and values were eroded. From early times towns had to rely on the surrounding countryside for their foodstuffs. The towns regulated the marketplace tightly to secure for the townsfolk abundant provisions as cheaply as possible. Middle-men were suppressed, and the minutest precautions were taken to control prices.

But as towns grew larger, they had to look farther a field for their foodstuffs. In addition, as they grew wealthier, they looked to import a wider range of goods, which was impossible without the middleman—i.e., merchants—who bought wholesale either at the fairs or at the point of production, and sold retail to urban consumers. According to Pirenne: "This import trade could not be subjected to the regulation just outlined ... [Regulation] was powerless before the wholesale merchant, who unloaded on the town quays the cargo of several ships laden with rye, cheese, or casks of wine. What influence could it exert in this case on prices and how set to work to subject wholesale sales to a system made for retail trade? Here it was obviously face to face with an economic phenomenon to which it was not adapted. As soon as capital came into action it foiled municipal regulation, because it was beyond its reach."[196]

Thus did the first cracks occur in the principle of 'fair price'. Other cracks developed regarding the loaning of money vis-à-vis the prohibition of usury. Any number of subterfuges arose. For example, while interest was supposedly prohibited, payment for damages to the lender was permissible. So if the debt were not discharged on the day specified, damages were due. It was understood that the debtor would not pay on the agreed date thus allowing usury under the guise of a penalty for delay.[197]

The societal pressures from the new commercial culture would lead to evolutionary change in the nature of towns, with regard to forms of political autonomy, modes of taxation, and forms of self-government.

Gaining political autonomy might be purchased in some form, or might be obtained through the threat of force, or even armed conflict. Depending on the jurisdiction, autonomy might have to be wrested from feudal overlords or from ecclesiastical authorities. For example, with regard to feudal overlords, in some instances the cities might try to refuse or resist baronial or Episcopal tolls or taxes or offer money for a charter, but it often came down to force. Tours, for example, fought twelve times before its liberty was won.[198] In France the enfranchisement of the cities involved a violent struggle lasting more than a century, with struggles beginning at Le Mans in 1069. The bishop of Tournai fought a civil war for six years in 1190-96 to overthrow the commune. In 1235 at Reims the stones brought to build the cathedral were seized by the populace for missiles in revolt against the highest ecclesiastic in Gaul. Similar events took place in England and in Germany.

With regard to ecclesiastical cities, the battle for autonomy had both financial and religious grounds. For example, as Pirenne noted: "The fact that the bishops were obliged to reside in their cities, the centres of diocesan administration, necessarily impelled them to preserve their authority and to oppose the ambitions of the bourgeoisie all the more resolutely because they were roused and directed by the merchants, ever suspect in the eyes of the Church."[199] The quarrel between the Holy Roman Empire and the Papacy in the second half of the eleventh century gave towns wider opportunity to rise against their ecclesiastical prelates. The uprisings began in Lombardy and soon spread to the Rhineland and the Low Countries.

This jurisdictional autonomy gained by the towns was accompanied by administrative and fiscal autonomy. This is not to say that they were not part of larger principalities and did not have wider responsibilities, especially regarding defense in an age of frequent warfare. But the power to dictate the form and amount of taxation had shifted as a consequence of the town's administrative autonomy. Princes would encounter some resistance and the mutual negotiations would lead, as will be seen in the next chapter, to early forms of Parliament.

Equally importantly, the towns had to establish internal forms of self-government and learn how to tax properly—i.e., equitably and without being ruinous. In the event, the money was raised predominantly from the burgesses. The quota payable by each was calculated on the basis of his fortune, a form of principled taxation. Collaterally, for the towns to collect taxes and to undertake the municipal functions, it became necessary to elect councils of magistrates. The first outlines of these municipal organizations appeared in the 11th century and their essential forms were complete in the

12th. Pirenne states: "The work thus accomplished is all the more admirable because it was an original creation. There was nothing in the existing order of things to serve it as a model, since the needs it was designed to meet were new."[200] Once again we see Hayek's spontaneous order at work.

According to Durant: "By the end of the twelfth century the communal revolution was won in Western Europe. The cities, though seldom completely free, had thrown off their feudal masters, ended or reduced feudal tolls, and severely limited ecclesiastic rights."[201] With this evolutionary transition, many dispersed financial centers, free of dogmatic Scholasticism, arose and offered greater scope for commercial innovation.

Amassing of Capital and the Beginning of Banking
These new free cities provided a protected niche for the new wealth. With relatively secure property rights, capital could be safely accumulated for investment. Over centuries, artisans became traders; traders became merchants; and merchants became bankers. Also, many of the first bankers were descended from money exchangers—essential because of the plethora of currencies—who grew rich in one of the few niches of the economy relatively free from control. But as a general rule, medieval bankers were both merchants and money-lenders, naturally finding a use for their surplus capital.

The growing mercantile wealth created new connections between merchants and their overlords. Kings always needed the wherewithal to fight wars and local aristocracies; when confronted with cash-flow problems, they preferred getting an advance of money from the merchants to pledging their lands to abbeys or sending their plate to the mint. So while the aristocracies often looked down on the merchants, their self-interest caused them to look away, reluctantly support, and occasionally invest with them.[202]

During the earlier Middle Ages, Jews often lent money, being exempt from the religious proscriptions against usury. But once they were expelled from France in 1252 and from England in 1290, Italian bankers such as the Lombards began to fill this role. In turn, they too were expelled from England and France. But the need for lending services, the ever present need of royal treasuries for funds, provided opportunities for new economic entities to enter the commercial arena. For example, Venetian merchants, among others, were subsequently induced to lend money to English kings.[203]

The role of money-lenders was clearly not free of considerable risk. For example, if the debt of a monarch or the nobility grew too burdensome, the lenders were expelled from the land or, worse, arrested on spurious charges. Yet, the fragmentation of political power and the competition for wealth among many political entities in Europe sustained a general openness to change and precluded its suppression very often or very extensively.

Cultural Value Shifts

With time, more and more elements of society experienced direct financial benefits from the expansion of trade and the development of new financial instruments and institutions, which encouraged governments to promote these changes. The Medieval Church, however, was not comfortable with such changes in society, which was increasingly focused on the here and now rather than on the afterlife. Important segments of society were striving for wealth, and concepts of fair price and commutative justice were being eroded. The logically structured metaphysics constructed by the Church was being undermined by experience and the new attitudes generated by that experience. This process was seen in some quarters as challenging the basic teachings of the Church.

Presumably, the Church could have led a reactionary rearguard action on economic matters as it did later in the scientific arena—e.g., with regard to Galileo and his views on astronomy. One can envision parallels with the closing of the theological mind in Islam under the Abbasids or the constriction of the Chinese economy by the Mandarins. In actuality, the Church's teachings became more ambiguous. Beginning with Thomas Aquinas, its teachings began to permit alternative views of social life, and some of these were supportive of economic change. Not surprisingly, new views were most prevalent in those parts of Europe where commercial change was most swift and compelling—i.e., England, Northern Italy, the Low Countries and northern France. But the Papacy itself did not renounce some medieval teachings for hundreds of years—e.g., usury remained officially sinful until the nineteenth century. Re-actionary teachings retained their hold in other areas of Christendom.

Here, as elsewhere in the examination of economic change in Europe, the question of cause and effect is fascinating. Were the new views in the Church simply a consequence of reacting to the new practices, or did they, in an intertwined fashion, help give them important legitimacy? In any event, the ensuing changes in logical reasoning proved invaluable in validating pragmatic economic changes and helped provide the logical base for formulating economic theory in the coming centuries.

Ironically, the very attempt of the Church to develop rules and theory governing all of civic life would help bring about the unraveling of such rules. What precisely were the philosophic structures formulated by the Church, and what were the logical considerations that caused them to evolve?

The Medieval Worldview
The Medieval worldview gradually edged aside was a religious metaphysics with a strong neo-platonic aspect—i.e., it postulated the real existence of a hierarchical array of universal archetypes that were part of divine creation. These archetypes were the ideal prototypes for perishable entities existing on earth and perceivable by the senses. Further, the human mind was capable of perceiving the essence of the ideal universals through the senses, reflecting the dichotomy between the immortal soul and the perishable body.

From the universals relating to human beings were derived normative attributes corresponding to duties for all Christians. Specifically, society was viewed as a hierarchical order with defined obligations and tasks imposed on the classes as well as on the occupational groups of the population.

The Church took this task seriously as they did challenges to the views formulated. Karl Pribram stated: "If absolute truth could be arrived at with the aid of abstract concepts, it was evident that only one valid definition corresponded to each of these concepts. The Church claimed the exclusive privilege of deciding with finality on these definitions, and of condemning as heretical, any deviation from the officially proclaimed tenets and judgments."[204]

Since all the educational facilities were dominated by the Church, this worldview made for a societal mental-straight-jacket, indeed.

Aristotle, Thomas Aquinas, and Nominalism

By the 12th century, however, the Church's intellectual bonds on society were being sorely strained. Old tenets were being ignored in the evolving market place; new mercantile classes were arising; autarchic society was increasingly a memory; and the new universities were open to different views—views that burst on the scene with the rediscovery of Aristotle and his teachings. His metaphysics had been much less well known than Plato's to medieval scholars until the time of Averroes.[205]

Catholic students and scholars were exhilarated at discovering new ways of thinking, and Aristotle became highly esteemed in philosophical matters. In many ways, his logic introduced a fresh approach for the formation of fundamental abstract concepts. The Church felt it essential to respond to the threatening new intellectual enthusiasms. Rather than banning the new philosophies, it had Thomas Aquinas, a great Dominican theologian, modify Scholastic reasoning to accommodate Aristotelian methods of cognition. To this end, Aquinas' *Summa Theolgica* supplied a comprehensive set of theological, moral, sociological, and economic principles. His philosophic accommodation would have wide ranging ramifications for economics as well as for science (see Chapter V). Moreover, it would stand in sharp contrast to the 'closing of the Islam mind', which occurred when Islam, similarly, had been forced to confront the implications of the Greek philosophers.

Aquinas' formulations allowed a more pragmatic approach to economic matters, which unintentionally opened the way to aligning intellectual thought with the lessons of the extended order. The unworkable teachings of the Medieval Church regarding wages, prices, interest, and wealth per se were displaced in the fullness of time.

In part, this new intellectual approach was derived from Aristotelian logic, which redefined the functions of reason. The Neo-Platonists had relied on *emanations* and *illuminations* to link the human mind to the absolute source of all general notions. However,

Aristotle believed that the mind was endowed with the faculty of using methods of abstraction to derive general notions from the *essential* features common to a group or class of comparable objects. This shift of logical perspective revolutionized the thinking of the day. Universals were now found to be directly accessible to the human mind through processes of analyzing individual things: observation combined with the application of deductive method.[206]

Aquinas' adjustment to Scholasticism led to a clear distinction between revelation and reason as two separate sources of knowledge—i.e., a distinction between supernatural theology and natural theology. The latter was held to be accessible to human understanding. Furthermore, the newly available Aristotelian writings showed that outside of strictly religious issues, there existed a large body of questions that could be treated independently of metaphysical considerations with a certain degree of flexibility. Accordingly, considerable latitude could be granted to the expression of divergent views, and due regard could be paid to the opinions of other officially recognized authorities. The bulk of social and economic problems was assigned to this group and was dealt with in accordance with the principles of Aristotelian epistemology.[207]

Still and all, Aquinas had no intent to be a revolutionary. He was attempting to provide an overall philosophic structure for Scholasticism and medieval society. In the process, he was merely taking into account the newly accessible views of Aristotelian thinking, attempting to provide a logical basis for the concepts of just price, just value, the prohibition of usury, and the hierarchical structure of society in general. But the way was cleared for profound change.

These views likewise encompassed potential change in social institutions and practices. One such area included the governance of communities. Aristotelian Scholastics found different sources of justice and law. Foremost among these, divine reason was held to be the source of justice, and revelation provided a safe knowledge of divine law. The rules of natural law taught by sound reasoning, however, were considered another source of equally binding precepts. Hence reason assisted by revelation could be relied upon to teach what had to be approved of as good; together, they provided the basis for human law.

Importantly, law could be designed to adjust to the changing conditions of social life. In Aquinas's view, political communities arose from a social instinct, and were an empirical fact—not a transcendental principle. Accordingly, the organization of political bodies was attributed to human convention and considerable latitude was found to exercise pragmatic judgments in these matters.[208] In this context, the codification of Roman law at the time of Justinian in the sixth century was revived in the 12th and 13th centuries by the jurists of the University of Bologna, who believed that progress in human legislation was considered possible and desirable.[209]

Given the new potential for intellectual flexibility, albeit still constrained, a number of great minds began exploring alternative views to the then prevailing Scholasticism. Pribram classifies them under the rubric of 'nominalism'—i.e., as opposed to the universalism inherent in Scholasticism. Some of the key emerging views included those of Peter Abelard, Roger Bacon, and William of Ockham.

Abelard had questioned the underpinnings of universalist principles as early as the 12th century. He had concluded that valid knowledge could be derived from the study of individual things and phenomena, and that analyzing religious doctrines was not beyond the power of human reason. While he was forced to renounce these heretical propositions, the cat was out of the bag.

In the 13th century, the Franciscan monk Roger Bacon expanded aspects of nominalist reasoning to justify new approaches for studying the physical world. He emphasized that observation and experience were reliable methods of scientific analysis, and regarded singular things and phenomena as logically prior to universal ideas. About the same time other, less radical, theologians emphasized the subjective element involved in deriving general notions from individual phenomena by methods of abstraction. They pointed to the fact that the name given to a general concept was simply a product of the human mind.[210]

These broad changes in philosophical thinking inevitably led to new views on practical matters in trade and mercantile endeavor. For example, Jean Buridan, a disciple of Ockham and rector of the University of Paris, regarded human wants as the natural measure of the goods of exchange (as opposed to some inherent value). He outlined the principles of a predominantly subjective value theory without violating the Aristotelian principle of equivalence. He realized quite early that each partner to an exchange expected to get an advantage from the transaction. Similarly, the very concept of a just price was abandoned by the last Ockhamite scholar, Gabriel Biel, in the 15th century. He argued that no sales or purchases could be concluded unless each party expected to have a greater advantage from performing than from not performing the transaction. Reliance on objective standards was thus superceded by recognition that subjective individual assessments determined prices.[211]

Such early analysis proved important in man's increasing understanding of economic principles, even though a deeper understanding required centuries. But here were the first logical underpinnings of free markets. Not only were concepts like just price found untenable, but so also was the belief that the pursuit of gain was sinful. When doubt was cast on the rigid Scholastic moral categories, the distinction between justified earnings and the pursuit of gain could no longer be maintained.

There was nothing inherently inevitable about any of the new ideas. Rather, each idea and argument was akin to an intellectual mutant. If it found favor and was useful to others, it propagated. Otherwise, it did not. Where new ideas persuaded and endured, it was because they were substantially congruent with the new experiences and ways of an evolving society—i.e., they made sense. In the broadest sense, Hayek argued that analytic reason based on first principles counts for relatively little; tradition and experience for a lot.

Intellectual positions were likely to mirror the underlying experience of society. In England, Paris, the Low Countries, and Northern Italy, all areas of economic growth, universities favored change congruent with the needs of trade and economic growth. In economically stagnant areas such as the Iberian Peninsula and the Hapsburg Empire, older values of Scholasticism were predominant in the universities.

ENSUING WEALTH CREATION

The Europe emerging from the medieval period "left behind a society that possessed many features deeply embedded in human history. It [had been] a society that lived, worked, and traded by custom and rule, not by strategy or calculation. Its political and economic order, whether in manor or guild, had its roots in the father figure, the family, the tribe, and the household. Political and economic leadership was one and the same. The authority and obligations of king and seigneur were those of the shepherd over his flock, the father over his household."[212]

The full benefits of that emergence were not immediately experienced, however. Europe suffered greatly during the 14th century. The Black Plague killed as much as a third of the population, and the Hundred Years War between England and France further undermined the economies. Still, the foundations in values and the new ways of trading, banking, and manufacturing were in place. Moreover, the calamities did not cause the Europeans to retreat into a medieval mode of life.

One of the most significant permanent changes was the passing of Feudalism from the scene. Then, less dramatic but equally important, a steady expansion of manufacturing, trade, and institutional development occurred over the next several hundred years, until the beginning of the Industrial Revolution in the 18th century.

The Passing of Feudalism

Feudalism had grown out of the need to provide security and stability to the lives of people in dangerous and turbulent times. At its heart it was a military compact between king and vassal. But it also embodied an implied broader economic contract between the nobles and their vassals. Feudalism lost its reason for being with the emergence of new military tactics and the growth of a money-economy.

Preponderant military strength shifted from feudal chivalry to professional armies that combined infantry (pike men, crossbowmen, and musketeers) with siege artillery and cavalry. The skill and power of this arrangement came to exceed that of the part-time feudal levies. Thus, much of the rationale for the feudal social arrangement evaporated. In addition, quasi-independent barons could no longer effectively hold out against monarchs with their siege cannon. This was the beginning of the centralized nation states.

These arrangements depended on the new forms of the economy because professional armies required pay and the new forms of armament required industries to produce them. Clearly, governments of states with relatively larger money-economies had an advantage over others.

The more important effect of the passing of feudalism was the end of serfdom and the institution of a more efficient agricultural system. Feudalism was rooted in the manor system, characterized by a barter economy. Peasants had an inheritable property interest of sorts in the form of an expectation that the tenure would be renewed from year to year and would pass to their heirs. Early on, peasants could not sell their interest, which held them to the land, because leaving the manor meant abandoning a small holding that might have been in the family for several generations. Over time, it became possible for peasants to buy themselves free of their feudal obligations, sometimes by lump-sum payments and sometimes by substituting a periodic money rent. This liquidation of feudal dues and duties, together with the acquisition by the peasants of a saleable interest in the land they cultivated was a long process, rather than an event. The process tended to occur first in those countries in which commerce was most robust—i.e., in Holland, England, and France.

With the transition of agriculture into the money-economy, there was an inevitable evolution in the economic organization of agriculture, including the adoption of improved agricultural methods leading to an increase in the food supply.[213] For example, land was used more efficiently, with the strip system being abandoned in laying out new farms. Agricultural techniques slowly improved as well. Peasants practiced a three-field rotation of crops, with the soil triennially replenished with fodder or leguminous plants. Powerful teams of oxen drew plows more deeply. The 13th century saw the first experiments in cross breeding and acclimatization of breeds. The increasing productivity, which occurred over hundreds of years to be sure, not only fed the growing urban populations, but also released surplus rural workers to man the new manufacturing facilities.

These changes, where they happened, did so because they proved also to be congruent with the interests of the nobility. While their military role had passed, they still enjoyed a political role, which often required them to relocate the main residences to capital cities.

This shift, often accompanied by the desire for a higher lifestyle, created pressures for a financial wherewithal that was incompatible with the previous barter economy. They found that by altering the economic arrangements with their peasants, they could liberate wealth to invest in growing enterprises and to finance a new way of life.

The Ongoing Expansion of Trade, Industry, and Institutions

With the passing of Feudalism, private actors increasingly were given—or seized—opportunities to seek wealth through manufacturing and trade. Governments remained predatory, given that wars were frequent and taxes were essential to their prosecution, but they limited their interference with new ways of organizing economic activity. Innovation was widespread. When new ways were successful—i.e., profitable, they were emulated and spread in a Darwinian sense. Northern Italy, England, and the Netherlands provided the most nurturing niches for change and led the way. In a famous example, when Tsar Peter the Great of Russia recognized the significance of the changes ongoing in Western Europe, he went to the Netherlands and England to learn how to modernize Russia.

Western Europe's new class structure, characterized by the entrepreneur and the constituent parts of the bourgeoisie, came into being and transformed the cultures. These entities had a freedom to accumulate and deploy capital, and the associated factors of production, as never before existed in human history. Inspired insights by individual entrepreneurs were essentially the 'random variations' that occur in the process of social reproductive causation. Rather than competing for limited sources of energy, as would organisms, economic actors competed for capital and revenue. As the new entrepreneurship took hold, the Western World experienced an explosion of innovation in the market. New economic entities arose to exploit opportunities, only to be pushed aside by superior entities.

The broad outlines of the process of economic expansion were recognized by Marx and Engels in their *Communist Manifesto* of 1848:

The discovery of America, the rounding of the Cape, opened up fresh ground for the rising bourgeoisie. The East-Indian and Chinese markets, the colonization of America, trade with the colonies, the increase in the means of exchange and in commodities generally, gave to commerce, to navigation, to industry, an impulse never before known, and thereby, to the revolutionary element in the tottering feudal society, a rapid development.

The feudal system of industry, under which industrial production was monopolized by closed guilds, now no longer sufficed for the growing wants of the new markets. The Manufacturing system took its place. The guild-masters were pushed on one side by the manufacturing middle class; division of labour between the different corporate guilds vanished in the face of division of labour in each single workshop.

Meanwhile the markets kept ever growing, the demand ever rising. Even manufacture no longer sufficed. Thereupon, steam and machinery revolutionized industrial production. The place of manufacture was taken by the giant, Modern Industry, the place of the industrial middle class, by industrial millionaires, the leaders of whole industrial armies, the modern bourgeoisie.

Modern industry has established the world-market, for which the discovery of America paved the way. This market has given an immense development to commerce, to navigation, to communication by land. This development has, in turn, reacted on the extension of industry; and in proportion the bourgeoisie developed, increased its capital, and pushed into the background every class handed down from the Middle Ages.[214]

Rosenberg and Birdzell believe that Marx and Engels gave too much emphasis to trade with the new world and colonies to the neglect of burgeoning economic development within the European nation states. In addition, it seems misleading to attribute these developments to an objectified class named abstractly, the bourgeoisie. Bourgeoisie is at best a loose abstraction covering entrepreneurs and investment classes generally, but hardly is congruent with a purposeful entity. Rather, the concept covers innumerable individuals seeking their own ends according to the "invisible hand," and often at cross purposes with one another. Nonetheless, Marx and Engels provided a vivid picture of the sweeping changes that had occurred in Europe.

Moreover, when they wrote their work, Europe was experiencing only the initial benefits of steam power in manufacturing and transportation, when man had grasped the power to augment his limited strength and endurance (and that of animals) with the vastly greater power of fossil fuels. But subsequent waves of innovation and rapid economic growth would follow scientific discoveries with regard to electricity, chemistry, and the internal combustion engine. Indeed, from the beginning of the 19th century, economic growth in the West would become Promethean—i.e., growth would move from a fraction of a percent a year to a rate of several percent a year.

Where Do We Stand?

Western Europe's unique evolutionary course led to societies that were capable of producing previously unimaginable wealth for all. We have seen how the foundations for economic growth had been laid through an emerging class of merchants and bankers; governments that actively supported trade; commerce mediated by money and market price signals; a broader mindset that accepted calculations of best rates of return on capital; and shifts in religious thinking that accommodated these developments. The most remarkable aspect of this evolutionary development was, as emphasized by von Hayek, how spontaneously the extended order came into being when natural human productive instincts were freed from the fetters of predatory states and inhibiting cultural mores.

As Adam Smith noted, writing several hundred years ago, wealth is derived not from gold and silver, but from the productive capacities of people and how these mesh with the broad values and practices of society. Productivity is a function not merely of access to science and of factors of production.[215] Its source lies deeper in the way it organizes and deploys both its labor and its capital, as seen in private property rights, the rule of law, a capability to raise and deploy capital efficiently, openness to innovation and competition, and entrepreneurial tradition.[216]

Those societies, which have not evolved from man's early worldviews regarding commerce, languish economically—despite hundreds of billions of dollars in aid. And it is not easy for them to make the leap to modern economies. (See Chapter VII.) Indeed, even wealthy countries, which have largely internalized the full experiential benefit of the evolutionary changes, still have significant segments of the population that are hostile to the values and the institutions that make affluence possible. (See Chapter VIII.)

The reluctance of the former and the hostility of the latter are related to once critical value systems, and as such are understandable. The desire for security and predictability in life as well as charitable sentiments can appear at odds with the impersonal extended order. Indeed, the ferocious Darwinism of the extended order can be unsettling to the staunchest of heart.

Schumpeter's gales of creative destruction blow unabatedly in free economies: most new small businesses in the United States go bankrupt in a few years; the major corporations of a century ago wither, no longer exist or play a diminished role; large industries at the peak of the industrial age such as steel, coal, and automobiles have shed a large fraction of their workforces (but, of course, producing more through higher productivity). The loss of jobs and the need to make career transitions is emotionally wrenching, leading to political pressures to resist change through protectionism and regulation, and to question the free economy itself. But at the end of the day, the freer and more Darwinian that societies are, the richer, more creative, and more fulfilled their members are. Even the 'poor' of the United States today enjoy the material wellbeing of the lower middle-class of a generation ago.

A central lesson from this experience is that the process is evolutionary, not planned, and that the enabling value systems are not gained ex cathedra but are learned experientially—where societies permit those experiences to unfold naturally.

We have seen how the evolution of trade, a mercantile revolution, growing industry, and finally a free capitalistic system caused the West to modify certain values of its atavistic past to mirror a vital, risk-taking, increasingly affluent and powerful present. In the process, the West developed a new world view that necessarily displaced the value systems that had existed in Europe and in virtually all the major civilizations one millennium ago.

The growing affluence also had wider ramifications, evoking or making possible other elements of societal evolution, notably new forms of governance to protect and enhance the extended order.

4
Securing Ordered Liberty

In the main, the theme [of "A History of the English Speaking Peoples"] is ... the growth of freedom of law, of the rights of the individual, of the subordination of the State to the fundamental and moral conceptions of an ever-comprehending community. Of these ideas the English-speaking peoples were the authors, then the trustees, and must now become the armed champions. – Winston Churchill[217]

A second major avenue of evolutionary change enabling the extended order was the institutionalization of liberty through a constitutional order that incorporated representative government along with checks and balances on the exercise of power. These features of the extended order bypassed the pitfalls of despotism, historically the most common form of human governance, which had hitherto produced an evolutionary dead-end for societies.

When humanity left the hunter-gatherer tribal stage its age-old societal mechanisms for controlling intra-community aggression and predatory behavior became relatively ineffective in the new eras of city-states and empires. As seen in Chapter II, while tribal life tends to be egalitarian, the growth of empires brought into being hierarchical societies in which despotism, predatory governmental practices, and corruption became the norm. To be sure, life was physically more secure and economically less precarious. But for more efficient means of arranging the accumulation and deployment of capital to arise and for the creativity and productivity of its populations to be unleashed, radically new forms of governance would be required. This chapter will show how evolutionary forces led to such new institutions: institutions protecting individual liberty, shielding productive elements of society from the predatory state, and curtailing corruption of power.

The evolution of new political institutions, which unfolded in the West over the last thousand years, built on a Greco-Roman cultural inheritance. That inheritance of values—particularly respect for the individual and a belief that the ruler derives power from the people—made Europe a fertile area for the emergence of *institutionalized* liberty. Britain led the way in creating the institutions and values necessary for securing liberty, including constitutionally protected rights—especially property rights, the rule of law, representative government, and a system of checks and balances in government. Since it was the British model that was passed on to the United States, other British colonies, and eventually other parts of the world, its evolutionary development will be our primary focus.[218]

To comprehend what was a multi-millennial process, we need to examine early man's collective behavior, the West's cultural inheritance regarding individual rights and rule of law, and institutional development in Britain and the United States.

Early Collective Behavior and Its Evolution

The *selfish gene*, as we have seen, programs all living entities to manifest actions and behaviors that enhance their prospects for the reproductive success of themselves and their offspring. These behaviors are inherited from our primate forebears and include interpersonal aggression, inter-societal warfare, even genocide.[219]

Specifics of this grim reality were laid out by Steven LeBlanc, who describes how "prehistoric warfare was common and deadly, and no time span or geographic region seems to have been immune." Moreover, such warfare was relatively more deadly than even the carnage of the Twentieth century's two World Wars. He states that in primitive societies, war was a much stronger demographic factor with on average about one-quarter of all men losing their lives in battle. He found the Rousseauian view of peaceable noble savages living in edenic harmony with the environment to be totally fallacious.[220]

Inter-tribal aggression is clearly part of the group selection process that continues into the modern age. As noted in Chapter II, the anthropologist Joseph Soltis analyzed hundreds of conflicts in New Guinea over a fifty-year period and identified an ongoing extinction of groups in favor of presumably fitter groups. With regard to larger societal groupings, Jared Diamond states: "Since 1950 there have been nearly twenty episodes of genocide, including two claiming over a million victims each (Bangladesh in 1971, Cambodia in the late 1970s) and four more with over a hundred thousand victims each (the Sudan and Indonesia in the 1960s, Burundi and Uganda in the 1970s).[221] This list did not include the massacres in Rwanda, which claimed one million souls in 1994.

Given this violent reality, it is clear why humans, especially in less developed societies, placed—and continue to place—personal security high in their value systems. For without security against external enemies and internal predators, as the philosopher Hobbes noted, life would be nasty, brutish and short.

In light of such innate propensity to violence, how did early man evolve an essential societal cohesiveness? Clearly, the most successful societies had to discern ways of controlling aggressive instincts and fostering cooperation in order to enhance the survival prospects of their societal animals. Some modes of cooperative behavior were undoubtedly inherited from our primate forebears. In that regard, Ridley describes behavioral patterns among chimpanzees, our nearest animal relatives, whose societies have a hierarchical structure of sorts, wherein coalitions are formed to constrain the power of the most dominant animal. Indeed, in dangerous situations requiring coordinated group action, behavior akin to consensus building to manage risk can be observed.[222]

Human societies evolved a range of mores and institutions to control violence, including shared values and peer pressure. Those pressures created groups that generally proved to be quite egalitarian. David Sloan Wilson observes that: "Hunter-gatherers are egalitarian, not because they lack selfish impulses but because selfish impulses are effectively controlled by other members of the group," sociologically a form of "reverse dominance". In human hunter-gatherer groups, an individual who attempts to dominate others is likely to encounter the combined resistance of the rest of

---

Wilson's Example of Social Control within the Mbuti Tribe

"Njobo was an undisputed great hunter, knew the territory as well as anyone and had killed four elephants single-handed. He was a good enough Mbuti not to attempt to dominate any hunting discussion in the forest, merely to take a normal part. If he ever appeared to be overly aggressive or insistent he was shouted down and ridiculed, although highly popular. ... [A discussion of three others followed.] ... But while these four can be singled out as exceptional, they could either separately or together be outvoted by the rest of the hunters. On such occasions they were compelled either to give their assent to the popular decision or to refrain from joining the hunt that day. None of them had the slightest authority over the others."

Source: David Sloan Wilson, *Darwin's Cathedral*, p. 42)

---

the group employing reverse domination, ranging in intensity from gossip, to ridicule, to ostracism, to assassination. Self-serving acts are thereby effectively curtailed.[223]

Not all tribes were alike, nor did they all develop the same methods to deal with social problems. Different approaches led to different capabilities of the entire societal animal and thus became a potent means of group selection over time. Other more peaceable but equally effective expressions of the selfish gene emerged — e.g., the best hunters with the most meat to share gained more reproductive opportunity. With the expansion of competitive free markets, wealth increasingly displaced raw physical prowess as a basis for attracting mates.

Despite the pressures of competition, on balance the successful groups incorporated powerful mores for cooperation. Wilson cites research indicating that small groups of humans are psychologically disposed to bind themselves into functional units. He particularly cites a work *Order without Law* (Ellickson, 1991) which shows how people "spontaneously establish, enforce and largely abide by social norms in the absence of a formal legal system."[224]

This phenomenon is manifested in the practices of African tribes (having ancient antecedents) described by George Ayittey. Having to confront issues of self-governance universal to mankind, African tribes developed approaches that were consistent with egalitarian spirit of tribal life and were functionally similar to those of some

Greek city states as we examine later. Many had a chief, an inner council, a council of elders, and a village assembly. The inner council would formulate legislation, which for significant issues would be taken to the council of elders, a more formal body comprising all the hereditary headmen of the wards or lineages. Ayittey reports that routine matters were resolved by acclamation, whereas complex matters would be debated until the council reached unanimity. If the council could not reach unanimity on a contested issue, the chief would call a village assembly, where the people served as the final authority.

Regarding checks on the execution of power, Ayittey identifies features we shall also encounter elsewhere: "chiefs and kings were not above the law and had to obey customary laws and taboos. ... [There] were [injunctions] clearly designed to check despotic tendencies and misuse of power. ... Any violations could result in immediate destoolment (removal from office). ... [He] could be removed at any time ... if he was corrupt or failed to govern according to the will of the people—and so he can be even in modern times."[225]

This structure, in some respects, echoes features of Greek city-states. Yet, it was a form uniquely suited for relatively small groups. The challenge for larger civilizations was to evolve mechanisms that preserved essential values in larger and more impersonal environs.

Moving Beyond Tribal Units

The first moves beyond tribal units were the city-states that established governance over larger populations centered in a core city. These city-states were no less warlike than their tribal predecessors—perhaps the most renowned conflicts are those of the Greek city-states. Such behavior was universal: incessant warfare also existed among city-states in Sumeria, China, and Mesoamerica.[226]

While such warfare went on for millennia, eventually powerful leaders emerged who were able to unify multiple city-states into primitive empires, for example, in Sumeria, in the Harappan Empire of South Asia, in the first Zhou Empire in China, and in the Mayan and Aztec empires of Mesoamerica. To govern multiple cities and extended areas, new institutions and techniques had to be invented. A major consequence, most likely unplanned, was that the new entities were able to capture the economic benefits of greater stability and larger markets. As a result, the empires were considerably more evolutionarily fit than the city-state and tribal forms of society because of their collective armed strength and greater wealth, leading to their eventual predominance.

As larger societies evolved to capture economic and security benefits, they inevitably evolved new forms of governance. As Wilson points out, thirty people can sit around a campfire and arrive at a consensual decision; 30 million people cannot.[227] Wilson sees a process of cultural evolution at work as humanity developed new forms of government suitable for larger populations – i.e., if many human groups are confronted with the same novel problem, they will come up with different solutions, some much better than others. The more adaptive and utilitarian will prevail and be emulated by others. [228]

Moreover, Wilson strongly echoes von Hayek's thinking: "[M]any of the mechanisms guiding cultural evolution take place beneath conscious awareness. … [t]hese conscious processes are important agents of cultural change (Boehm 1996), but they are the tip of an iceberg of automated cognitive processes that take place beneath our conscious awareness, some of which are very sophisticated. That means that cultures can evolve to be smart in ways that are invisible to their own members."[229]

The rise of consolidated states had profound consequences for humankind. They provided a security that nurtured commerce and much greater wealth. They also fostered the development of written language, the creation and preservation of learning, as well as a host of artistic innovations. Without these developments, the philosophic stage of human evolution, which unfolded millennia later, would not have been possible.

To administer these empires, entirely new institutions of governance later were required. These usually entailed a king, a ruling class, standing armies, and a religious mystique of some kind. The stability provided by these institutions created substantial benefits for the respective societies that grew over time.

The Downside of Empires

Yet, for all the initial security empires provided, they were inherently unstable and thus tended not to endure beyond a few generations. Rulers became despotic and, with time, the corruption of power corroded the systems. The growing ranks of the nobility placed predatory demands on the rural classes, thereby undermining economic benefits made possible by the enhanced stability of the political order. Often, subsequent generations of rulers became weaker, and were pampered, isolated from their people and increasingly out of touch with critical problems. Inflexibility stymied the introduction of 'new blood' into the elite. While uncommon events, a few empires in Mesoamerica simply collapsed, with society regressing to small rural communities. Most failing empires succumbed to external predators.

Yet, despotic empires remained a prevalent form of human governance, enduring serially. As such they represented an evolutionary dead end for societal animals. They were more evolutionarily fit than the tribal societies they replaced, but their inherent inflexibility and predatoriness stymied further evolution, especially in governing forms. Less tangibly, but equally importantly, they squelched the innate human instinct for egalitarianism and, thus, individual initiative as well.

Despite the inherent instabilities for any given despotism, as a rule, most of civilized life existed under a succession of such entities, because as a practical matter, viable alternatives that could successfully confront the might of standing armies under authoritarian control had not yet evolved.[230] The West, however, building on a Greco-Roman heritage, was to make a dramatic breakout of the evolutionary dead-end through innovations that accommodated ever-innovative, robust free markets, and advanced the freedom of individuals.

THE WEST'S CULTURAL INHERITANCE

The West had an advantage over other civilizations because of its cultural inheritance from ancient societies that honored each individual, notably the Greeks and the Israelites, whose values were embodied in increasingly sophisticated forms in religious and philosophic writings, such as the Old Testament and the works of Greek philosophers. Many of these values were later made explicit in Roman law, and passed on to the societies of Western Europe following the fall of Rome. Will Durant concluded: "As Greece stands in history for freedom, so Rome stands for order; and as Greece bequeathed democracy and philosophy as the foundation for individual liberty, so Rome left us its laws, and its traditions of administration, as bases of social order."[231]

Greece

The evolution underlying our structured liberties in the West begins, as in so many other things, with the Greeks. Illustrative are Solon's attempt to create an effective and stable society in Athens, as well as Aristotle's speculations on the most appropriate forms of human governance.

Solon

Solon's role in the development of a new governmental structure for Athens is one of history's earliest examples of a substantive attempt at achieving a principled form of government. This effort is particularly surprising in that it occurred in an environment of incessant, ruthless warfare among the Greek city-states.

Although the Greek cities were more advanced in their governance than most tribal societies that preceded them, their behavior was, nevertheless, tribal. To the Greeks, freedom meant primarily the independence of their own city-states, not personal liberty. Russell Kirk notes: "They stood ready for war against barbarians and against other Greek cities of similar origins and institutions, should advantage seem to lie in aggression. Within every city, class hostilities, political feuds, and private ambitions rent the fabric of civil order every few years."[232]

In the early years of the 6th century B.C., Solon was confronted by an Athens that had lost much of its strength, was threatened by nearby neighbors such as Sparta, Corinth, and Megara, and was roiled by civil feuds. The situation of the city was so desperate that virtually all classes agreed to give him unprecedented authority to reform the traditional political mechanisms, along with power to administer the city. Accordingly, in 594 B.C. Solon was elected *eponymous archon*, the chief civil magistrate of Athens. Most of his peers undoubtedly would have seized the opportunity to make themselves a tyrant—as often happened—but Solon did not, believing that a commonwealth could endure only through righteous order.

Solon instituted a number of practical measures to ameliorate social strains by reducing debts, including liberating individuals who had been sold into slavery for debt. But it is his constitutional reforms that most interest us here. The reformed order was neither an aristocracy nor a democracy, but a system of checks and balances designed to stabilize the government. He increased the powers of the Assembly—i.e., the popular congregation of all free citizens and, to make it more effective, he created a new Council of Four Hundred to prepare and guide its business. Executive authority was left in the hands of the old Council of the Areopagus, a kind of senate recruited from former religious, military, and civil magistrates. He wrote that this combination of the old and the new councils would save the Assembly from rash action: "The ship of state, riding upon two anchors, will pitch less in the surf and make the people less turbulent."

In large part due to Solon's reforms, Athens became the leading Greek city-state in wealth and commerce.[233] When Solon voluntarily resigned from office, Athens once again drifted under the sway of tyrants. But many of Solon's reforms endured until the city overreached itself during the Peloponnesian War and was defeated and humbled by Sparta. To our modern eye, the reforms were insufficient. They were instituted by one individual from the top and did not endure long enough for their innate wisdom to be absorbed by the value system of the larger society. Nevertheless, they were a creative attempt to establish a vibrant economy and to counter age-old problems of governmental instability.

Aristotle

Aristotle appeared on the scene about two and a half centuries after Solon's constitutional reforms. Having viewed the functioning and travails of many governments, and aware of the pitfalls that could befall society through the corruption of power, the greed of the rich, the envy of the poor, and the turmoil that factionalism could bring, he developed a systematic view, expressed in his unfinished work *Politics*, of how enlightened man might govern himself for the general welfare.

Aristotle believed that the Greek *polis* was superior to any other form of social organization, but did not conclude that any one particular form of government was necessarily best for all people. As a result, he devised not an absolute model for governing, but an early framework for analyzing governing constructs.

Russell Kirk summarized Aristotle's thinking as three forms of "right government" meant for the general welfare: monarchy, aristocracy, and the commonwealth. By monarchy, Aristotle meant the leadership of one man of excellent virtue, under a body of laws that limit his power. He defined aristocracy as the predominance of a class of men of high birth, dutiful and filled with the spirit, which later would be called noblesse oblige. And a commonwealth denotes the exercise of power by a majority—but a virtuous majority, respecting the lawful rights of all classes.

These ideal forms had perverse deviations: democracy as rule by the crowd, for the benefit of the dominant majority; oligarchy as rule by the few for the good of that few; tyranny as an unconstitutional assumption of power by one man for his own satisfaction. Aristotle advocated a mixed government—the ingredients of the mixture varying with particular circumstances—to incorporate the virtues of each form.[234]

Whatever the mixture, Aristotle believed government should be dominated by the middle classes—not aristocratic families, nor the *demos*—the more numerous artisans and sailors without property. It was the middle class of Athens and of many other states that supplied the infantry, bore the brunt of fighting, were the most productive class economically, and provided a model for stable family life. Aristotle's underlying view was that a polity is a community of friendship in which men have everything to gain by peaceful cooperation, as if they were so many parts of the human body—a societal animal.[235]

It is a testament to his insight that Aristotle could identify so many of the critical elements of good governance so long ago during times of turmoil and rapid change throughout Greece. He was, however, only too aware that good intentions and knowledge of optimal forms of governance would take man just so far. Indeed, he catalogued some forces that undermined his precepts. First, he noted that the middle classes in those days were relatively small in number. "In the second place, factitious disputes and struggles readily arise between the masses and the rich; and no matter which side may win the day, it refuses to establish a constitution based on the common interest and the principle of equality, but, preferring to exact as the prize of victory a greater share of constitutional rights, it institutes, according to its principles, a democracy or oligarchy ..."[236]

Like Solon, Aristotle had key insights on the issue of private property. In this he parted from the beliefs of his teacher Plato, who argued that in an ideal society members of the ruling or guardian class should not have any property of their own beyond personal essentials. They were to live in barracks, like soldiers. They would have no private homes and would receive a modest income from taxes levied on workers. Plato believed that greedy rulers had ruined Greek cities in the past, and by preventing them from owning property, they would be restored to the path of virtue and idealism.

Aristotle, speculating on the proper system of property for citizens living under an ideal constitution, asked: "Is it a system of communism, or one of private property?" He pointed out that communal arrangements tended to cause "a good deal of trouble". "If they do not share equally in work and recompense, those who work and get less recompense will be bound to raise complaints against those who get a larger recompense and do little work."

He noted that when a large number of people are in a position to say "mine" of the same object, the result cannot be harmonious. When people have their separate spheres of interest, on the other hand, there is less ground for quarrels, and the amount of effort will increase as each man applies himself to what is his own.[237]

Aristotle, like Solon before him, had hit upon key elements of sound governance, but his concepts were not institutionally tested and may well have been too advanced for the prevailing values of the Greek society. Yet, he had planted the seeds of thought regarding property rights and sound governance.

Rome

Greece's legacy was mostly philosophical and speculative. Rome added law and institutions, notably: a constitutional construct, concepts of individual worth, the idea that the power of the government is ultimately drawn from the consent of the people, a codified rule of law, and the protection of private property rights.

Constitutional Construct

Russell Kirk provided an overview of the Roman constitutional construct, as variously expressed by Polybius, Livy, Virgil, Cicero, and the Stoics. Three chief elements composed the polity of the Roman Republic: the consular authority; the Senate; and the comita, or formal assemblies of the people. To give the people a more immediate check upon the Senate, popular tribunes were chosen, with the power to veto senatorial actions. Two annually elected consuls were the chief magistrates, their power almost absolute in time of war, while the Senate controlled the public purse and determined general policies in ordinary circumstances. The people, usually voting in "tribes," elected magistrates, approved or rejected legislation, and determined peace or war, and alliances.

This system incorporated checks and balances on political power, and provided for separation of political functions. The Roman constitution, said Polybius, was not formed upon abstractions, but developed organically in response to the circumstances of times of trouble.

In many ways, it was the "mixed government" praised by Aristotle, but which Aristotle had thought almost impossible to maintain on a grand scale. In other words, the Roman constitution was not purely monarchical, aristocratic, or democratic, though it contained features of all three patterns of government. Kirk concludes: "At its height, this republican constitution had the high advantage of uniting all the citizens for strenuous public efforts. It was particularly suited for enabling men of strong practical talents to rise to authority."[238]

Individual Worth

Given the widespread existence of slavery in the Roman Empire, as well as the likelihood that slavery's prevalence may well have been a major contributing factor in the decline of Rome, it might appear ironic to attribute concepts of individual worth to Roman culture. But forms of slavery were nearly universal at that time and often incidental to the form of government. Moreover, in Rome slaves had rights, and broader philosophies were engendered regarding the value of every human being.

An examination of individuality, equality, and personal liberty in the Roman Empire begins with Aristotle's precepts, which may have underlain the views of much of the Mediterranean ancient world. He contended that: "slavery was a natural and reasonable institution, because there was a fundamental difference and in-equality among men. Some were capable of determining their lives to some rational end, while others were only possessed of reason enough to apprehend it in others. The first were by nature free men, the second were naturally slaves, for it was better to be under the control of reason, even if it were that of a master, than to be without the guidance of reason..."[239]

Cicero, living in the time of Julius Caesar, strongly took issue with Aristotle's view. In his treatise on "The Laws", he sets out the principle of equality: "There is no resemblance in nature so great, he says, no equality so complete, as that which exists among men, there is therefore only one possible definition of human nature; for that reason, by which men are superior to the mere animals, is common to all, men differ indeed in learning, but they are equal in the faculty of learning; there is no man or race of men who cannot attain to that virtue. Nature has given to all men reason, and therefore law which is right reason commanding and forbidding."[240]

In the following century, the Roman philosopher Seneca re-em-phasized the belief that master and slave are equally human, with equal possibilities of developing virtue of all kinds, with nobility being determined by one's character. He stated: "It is fortune that makes a man a slave, slavery is only external, it only affects the body of a man, the body may belong to a master, the mind is its own, it cannot be given into slavery."[241]

These were not mere musings of philosophers; they were concepts that entered Roman jurisprudence, where slavery was viewed as an incidence of war, rather than an essential inequality. Ulpian, a Roman jurist, said that despite their absence of freedom under civil law, under natural law all men are equal. Gaius, a jurist of the second century, stated more concretely that neither the Roman citizen nor any subject of the Roman Empire was permitted to treat his slaves with immoderate and groundless cruelty and that by a law of the Emperor Antoninus, "the man who kills his slave without cause is held accountable to the law."[242]

These concepts were developed in parallel by Roman era Christianity. St. Paul in the Acts of the Apostles represented that all men are alike, for they are all the children of the one divine nature, and they are all capable of the highest, and are all made for the same divine end, the communion of the soul with God.[243]

Power Derived from the People

We owe to Rome's philosophers, especially Cicero, and its jurists, most notably Ulpian, the clear articulation that the power of government is derived from the people. And, it is that articulation that endured through the Dark Ages to help form the values we hold important today.

As noted above, Cicero was brought up in the Aristotelian tradition of three possible forms of government, monarchy, aristocracy, and democracy (or some mixture thereof). He thought democracy was the least satisfactory of the three but was also dissatisfied with the other two, because "the multitude under such governments can scarcely be said to possess liberty." This criticism was based on the conclusion that a government that did not recognize man's equality in reason and in possibilities of virtue cannot be good, and that without a share in political authority men cannot be properly said to possess liberty. Further, the great jurists of Rome handed down to the Middle Ages and the modern world the essential concept that there is no other source of political authority except the community itself; neither the authority of God, not the intrinsic superiority of the ruler, but the will of the community."[244]

Later, as emperors gathered more power around them, the great jurist Ulpian stated in his *Digest* that the emperor indeed had an unlimited legislative authority, but only because the people— i.e., the whole community—conferred this upon him. This conclusion was shared by the emperors Theodosis II and Valentinian II themselves, who said that the ruler is bound by the laws, for his authority is drawn from the law. Later, Emperor Justinian in the 6th century noted that the Roman people were the original source of authority.[245]

Carlyle sums up the concept of government whose power comes from the consent of the governed with the observation: "Political freedom implies that all political authority is derived from the community, the community which is composed of men who are capable of directing and controlling their public as well as private lives to ends determined by themselves."[246]

Rule of Law

Rome's development and codification of law represents one of its greatest bequests to western civilization. While originally shaped to provide order for everyday life, the design produced by the growing Roman Empire aimed at meeting the needs of diverse cultures. Moreover, its jurists, conforming to Cicero's dictum that "True law is right reason in agreement with Nature," provided a philosophical umbrella of natural law that allowed secular law to evolve to meet new circumstances and to include concepts that would nurture political liberty in future times.

Until Rome mastered the rest of Italy, the Roman people were subject to only the *jus civile*, the civil law for native-born Roman citizens. According to Russell Kirk, "this was a complex body of customary laws, not ordinarily promulgated through formal enactment by Senate and People, but rather developing out of long usage among the Romans themselves—much as, many centuries later, the English common law would arise as a kind of organic growth, from the precedents set by decisions in particular cases at law."[247]

But once Rome extended its power, it had to recognize a second body of laws, applicable to the multitudes of people who were not full Roman citizens, and therefore neither entitled to the privileges of Romans nor accustomed to the *jus civile*. In this regard, Cicero observed that in every known community there were certain precepts that were honored—e.g., precepts regarding violent assault on an innocent; the violent appropriation of property recognized as belonging to another; and which kind of transactions remain valid even in the face of fraud and lies.

Moreover, Cicero shared Aristotle's belief that the "principles of equity are universal and are everywhere the same." Cicero believed that these universal precepts exist because they are expressions of human nature itself. They are reflections of what is essential to a rational being. This concept would be incorporated in the Roman *jus gentium* (the ancient Roman law for aliens; in effect international law). By the end of the first century A.D. these precepts would form the basis for what became known as natural law.[248]

Yet in many instances, it was difficult to reconcile the differing forms of law prevailing among various "foreign" peoples, or to make those forms compatible with the Roman civil law. Therefore the *praetors* had to search for principles of justice that would apply to cases of differing legal systems, principles   founded on ethical norms, the general opinion of mankind, and the nature of rational man, viz., on theories of universal justice. Thus there developed a third body of laws: the *jus naturale*, natural law, as distinguished both from customary law (whether the *jus civile* or the *jus gentium*) and from statutory law (or 'positive laws' formally enacted by the people and confirmed by the Senate). Natural law was a loosely knit body of rules of action presumed to be derived from divine commandment, from the nature of man, or from the long experience of mankind in community" and thus superior to the political state[249]

From this theoretical base, the Romans codified law, beginning with Hadrian in 117 and continuing through Justinian in the 6th century. This codification incorporated the working ways of society, reflected the wisdom of Greek philosophy, and allowed for change to reflect the needs of different cultures. Justinian's *Institutes*, part of that codification, stated that the law of nature is the law instilled by nature in all creatures. Implicit in that formulation is the Stoic view that nature does nothing without a purpose, that there is an order and reasonableness to it, and that human affairs should be governed by the same rationality, the same orderliness. Humans are fitted by nature with an instinctive understanding of what is necessary to flourish by making us aware, at the most intuitive level, of core precepts. In this view, wherever civilized beings exist, they will live according to these principles.

Property Rights

Because of implications for the growth of western culture and western prosperity, the concept of property rights deserves special scrutiny.

Prior to the Roman Empire, no legal system had recognized unqualified private property. Ownership in Greece, Persia or Egypt had always been conditional on superior or collateral rights of other authorities or parties. Tom Bethell concluded: "The idea that principles of law were superior to authority and force, that justice was "blindfolded" and (ideally) indifferent to persons, was something new to antiquity. Beyond the Roman perimeter, either a collectivist tyranny or a subsistence-level communalism generally prevailed." The economic benefits that flowed from the existence of protected property rights helped generate the wealth and leisure that enabled Greek and Roman citizens to pursue literature, philosophy, and the arts. Further, that wealth gave Rome a comparative military advantage over its neighbors.[250]

A tangible sense of Roman property rights can be gained from the *Twelve Tables*, written law promulgated around 450 B.C. Although fragmentary, what survives is worth noting, given that no surviving legal text contains a Roman definition of ownership. Bethell concludes from an array of examples that property was more respected than liberty and more secure than life: [251]

> • Most property was presumed to be private. The legal scholars of the *Digest* specifically note the things considered to be public—e.g., religious temples, flowing water, river banks and the seashore, stadiums and theaters, city walls and gates.

- One register of property in Northern Italy from the second century A.D. listed 47 estates, of which 46 were in private hands.
- Urban property was frequently rented. Leases began on July first, and rent was due at the end of the rental period. Bethell notes that this was a good indication of the owners' confidence that the tenants would pay up.
- Valuable property such as land, houses, slaves and farm animals were said to be *res mancipi*, meaning that their transfer to another owner required a ritual, or court procedure. "Proof of title was therefore reasonably simple in Roman law," according to the historian John Crook.
- Rural property distributed to citizens by the state was surveyed and boundary lines marked out.
- Easements were routine—e.g., the law of trespass was ameliorated to allow the gathering of fruit fallen onto a neighbor's ground; and a right of passage had to be given to someone who could not otherwise reach his property from the road.[252]

However, when the Roman state began to tax individual assets intolerably and to over regulate its populace, and when farms were increasingly tended by slaves, the economy and even the populace contracted. Rome lost much of its comparative advantage over neighboring states and barbarian tribes. Nevertheless, even though property rights were insufficient in themselves to maintain prosperity, they had been an essential factor in early Roman greatness, and were a critical contribution to the value system passed on to Western Europe.

PRESERVATION OF VALUES THROUGH THE DARK AGES

By the 5th century A.D., the western part of the Roman Empire had collapsed under the attack from the barbarian German tribes. In contrast to China, where periodic invaders were eventually absorbed by the vastly more numerous Chinese, in Europe invaders became numerically dominant in many areas, particularly those that had experienced depopulation. As a result, Roman institutions and culture were widely destroyed or displaced. Often only fragments were preserved, with the Church playing a major conservator role, though to be sure, the survival of the Greek and Roman view of law was aided by the continued existence of the eastern empire as well. Specifically, Durant noted how Roman law continued to be codified in the Eastern Empire in the form of the Code, Digest, and the Institutes of Justinian. Also important, however, were "the silent tenacity of useful ways, [through which] Roman law entered into the canon law of the medieval Church, inspired the thinkers of the Renaissance, and became the basic law of Italy, Spain, France, Germany, Hungary, Bohemia, Poland, even within the British Empire—of Scotland, Quebec, Ceylon, and South Africa."[253]

'The silent tenacity of useful ways' was a major factor in preserving key elements of the Roman rule of law. Regardless of their intrinsic merit, laws and practices do not take root unless they resonate with the cultural values of a society and are congruent with traditional ways of life. Enough of Roman society survived in the West to preserve what later were to become key contributions.

The Dark Ages

In 410 A.D., Rome fell to Alaric the Goth. For the first time in 800 years, the city was taken and sacked by an enemy.[254] Over the next several centuries, the order once guaranteed by the Roman Empire gave way to anarchy and conflict, to an era known as the Dark Ages. Europe, having lost the security and stability provided by the Roman Empire, was attacked by opportunistic barbarians on all sides. As described by Durant: "Scandinavia was a pirates' lair, Britain was overrun by Angles, Saxons, Jutes, and Danes; Gaul by Franks, Normans, Burgundians, and Goths; Spain was torn between Visigoths and Moors; Italy had been shattered by the long war between the Goths and Byzantium."[255] Security was increasingly provided by local feudal leaders, as serfdom grew and the economy shrank. Life for most of the population consisted of what the largely autarchic manor could provide.[256]

Preserves of Roman Traditions

These events, however, did not occur systematically or simultaneously. A few areas were left undisturbed; others were settled by foreign populations relatively peacefully. In many places, key institutions such as the Church endured.

Even with the first invasions, the barbarians' principal objective was largely plunder, not devastation. Indeed, some of the first incursions were hardly invasions at all. Tactically, the Romans had invited German tribes to settle in many border areas of the Empire. When Roman authority waned, a relatively peaceful marriage of barbarian and Latin culture emerged. Durant notes that by 430 A.D., northern Gaul had become half Frank. Maintaining their German language and pagan faith, as Rome's authority waned, they believed they had shaken off the Roman yoke, seeing themselves not as barbarians but as self-liberated freemen. By the 6th century, Roman law had been displaced by the Salic law, which emphasized trial by ordeal and contest.

A similar situation emerged in the Visigothic Kingdom of Southwestern Gaul. In 506 A.D. Alaric II issued a *Breviarium*, or summary, of laws for his realm. A comparatively enlightened code, it codified relations between the Romano-Gallic population and its conquerors to rule and reason. A similar code was enacted in 510 A.D. by the Burgundian kings, who had peaceably established their power.[257]

Not all the Dark Ages were without light. Areas of stability and relative security—indeed strong states—arose here and there and from time to time. In particular, the Merovingian, the Lombard, and the Carolingian kings created intervals of order in France, England, Germany and Italy. These rulers established security in their realms, which was reinforced by the intellectual and institutional strengths of the Church. This allowed features of Roman civilization in many forms to be preserved and passed on. In particular, we can see recurring elements of non-despotic, quasi-consultative government, even under strong leaders.

Merovingian Kings (511 - 614)
Clovis inherited the Merovingian throne in 481 and soon took over Northwest Gaul, eventually extending his conquests until

they touched Brittany and the Loire valley. Clovis later moved to establish control over Visigothic and Burgundian Gaul as well as the Ripuarian Franks on the Rhine. His descendents expanded the Kingdom to include Provence and much of Germany.

He won over the Gallic population by leaving them in possession of their lands, and the orthodox Christian clergy by respecting their creed and their wealth. Unfortunately, as happened time and again, the unifying work of a great leader was undone by his descendents. But the mode of governance, viz., the monarch being constrained by the power of jealous nobles, lived on. In addition, this arrangement proved to be the basis for a new political order because, in exchange for supporting the king, the nobles had been rewarded with estates upon which they were practically sovereign. On these began the feudalism that dominated Europe for centuries.

The Frank and Roman worlds continued to fuse as Frank chieftains intermarried with the remnant of the Gallo-Roman senatorial class and generated the new French aristocracy, albeit a crude one.[258]

The Lombards (568 - 774)

Byzantine rule in Northern Italy was brought to an end by the Lombard invasion. As the turmoil of conquest subsided into law, they instituted key elements of a balanced and consultative government—e.g., the king was elected and advised by a council of notables and usually submitted his legislation to a popular assembly of free males of military age. Gradually, the commerce natural to the Po valley was resumed and, by the end of the Lombard period, the cities of northern Italy were rich and strong. While this region would see political turmoil in the years thereafter, the economic revival described in the previous chapter had strong roots in this region.[259]

Venice (451 - 1095)

With the Lombard invasion, the populations of numerous towns fled for safety to the fishing villages on the islands at the head of the Adriatic Sea, the center of which was to become Venice, a unique political and commercial entity. Increasingly, the commerce of northern and central Europe began to flow through Venetian ports.

While they acknowledged the over lordship of the Byzantine Empire, the Venetians were for all practical purposes a sovereign entity, incorporating essential elements of representative government. At first, a collective body of twelve tribunes, one from each of the principal islands governed. Later, given the need for a more united authority, a new position of Doge (i.e. Duke) emerged. Finally in 1033, an aristocracy of commerce ended the hereditary transmission of ducal power, adopted the principle of election by an assembly of citizens, and had the Doge govern in collaboration with a senate.[260]

Charlemagne (768 - 814)

Charlemagne was the greatest of the medieval kings and the grandson of Charles Martel (the Hammer), who had repelled invasions on all sides and saved Europe for Christianity by repelling the Moors at Tours. A true warrior himself, Charlemagne personally led some 53 campaigns to expand his empire, bringing under his rule all the peoples between the Vistula and the Atlantic, and between the Baltic and the Pyrenees, along with almost all of Italy.

Despite this martial focus, Charlemagne fostered the rule of law and consultative government. Semiannually, he assembled groups of property owners at various points around his realm, having first consulted with smaller groups of nobles and bishops regarding proposed legislation. He then presented the legislation for approval by the entire gathering. This was largely a pro forma exercise, but it provided a precedent for basing the king's rule on agreement by the nobles and the populace. In addition, Charlemagne devised the *jurata*, a sworn group of inquirers who decided local issues of ownership or criminal guilt. He also divided the empire into counties, each with its local assembly of landholders that met periodically to consider governmental issues and to serve as a provincial court of appeals.

Durant notes that Charlemagne was generous to the Church, which he used as an instrument of education and government. His coronation by the Pope strengthened the Church by making civil authority seemingly derived from ecclesiastical conferment. The interaction of church and state was to have consequences for a thousand years in that two centers of power emerged in Europe providing an effective check on the centralization of power.

Charlemagne divided the empire among his three sons, but the results were hardly more lasting than those of the Merovingian kings. Durant's judgment was: "One man, one lifetime, had not availed to establish a new civilization. The short-lived revival was too narrowly clerical; the common citizen had no part in it; few of the nobles cared a fig for it, few of them even bothered to learn to read. ... Within a generation after his death the 'missi dominici', who had spread his authority through the counties, were disbanded or ignored, and the local lords slipped out of central control."[261]

In some respects, this short-lived attempt to revive civilization should be mourned. But the political fragmentation left behind resulted in beneficial unintended consequences—e.g., niches of opportunity for trade, industry, and different forms of governance. Centralized authority never arose, and rulers continued, in some form, the tradition of consultation with their nobles.

Transmission of Key Principles

A number of entities, including the Church, preserved or extended important Roman governing concepts in Europe during the early Middle Ages, among which were resistance to despotism, the community being the source of political authority, rule of law, and consent of the governed.

A key legacy to feudal Europe from the Roman Empire was disapproval of and resistance to despotism. Carlyle noted: "This principle, that all merely human authority is limited, was derived from the Roman law, and was of the greatest importance in medieval thought and sentiment, for it meant that there neither was nor could be any such thing as an absolute political authority. It was St. Thomas Aquinas himself who said that while sedition was a mortal sin, it was not sedition to resist an unjust authority."[262]

With regard to political authority, the Roman view "was that there could be only one immediate source of political authority, and that was the community itself, that there was no other source, neither the personal qualities of the prince, his greater wisdom and intelligence, nor force, nor, normally, the direct appointment of God, but only the community."[263] But it was not merely a contemporaneous expression of the community. The law in addition had to be grounded in principle and not just be a product of legislative action, which is termed 'positive law'. Such principles were thought to be discoverable in the Law of Nature, which in its proper character is divine and unchangeable, and cannot be abrogated by positive law.

As a practical matter, for the jurists of the Middle Ages, law was not a product of legislation, but the expression of the custom of the community—i.e., tradition. When new positive law was formulated, it had to be confirmed by those who lived under it. These principles were set out as early as the 9th century by Hincmar of Rheims, the most important ecclesiastical statesman of the time. He said that kings must govern their people by the laws of their ancestors, which were promulgated with the general consent of the community. This principle was articulated again in the middle of the 12th century by Gratian (the first great systematic canonist) in his *Decretum*. These principles were repeated in many countries in the 13th century. Bracton, an Englishman, held that England was governed by unwritten law and custom. Beaumanoir, a Frenchman, wrote "All pleas are determined by the Customs ... The king is bound to keep, and to cause to be kept, the Customs of his country."[264]

Another set of principles nurtured in the Middle Ages was that a king could not take action against the person or property of any of his subjects except by process of law. Carlyle states: "This is expressed not only in the famous clause of Magna Carta (39) but in the equally important ... statement of principles of law in Spain. At the Cortes of Leon in 1188 Alfonso IX swore that he would not take action against any man except by judgment of the court, and in the Cortes of Valladolid in 1299 it was decreed that no one was to be killed or deprived of his property till his case had been heard by *fuero* [custom] and Law. This was also the constitutional law of France as testified by Gerson in the fifteenth century, and by De-Seyssel and Machiavelli in the sixteenth; cases between the king of France and a private person were subject to the jurisdiction of the Parlemens."[265]

Since a just government depended on the consent of the governed, institutions to represent the authority and will of the community—i.e., a system of representation—were needed. That system had to be adaptable not only to small communities, but also to the national states, which were then slowly taking form. Such forms of representation were evident in the great cities of Italy, Germany, and the Low Countries as early as the 12th century. Representative assemblies emerged in a number of locations across Europe. In Hungary, King Andrew was forced to sign the Golden Bull in 1222, which required a Diet to be summoned each year, allowed no imprisonment of a noble without a trial, and permitted no levy of taxes on noble or ecclesiastical estates.[266] In Spain, the Cortes of 1188 placed restraints on Alfonso IX.[267] Carlyle states that in Spain the representatives of the towns were first summoned to the great council of the kingdom a good hundred years before the Parliament of 1295 in England. Similar bodies arose in most parts of Europe.

Kings were often reluctant to have to consult with such bodies, and not until compelled by financial exigencies. But the jurisdiction of the bodies extended beyond the merely financial. Carlyle says of the English Parliament of 1322: "all those matters which were to be established for the kingdom and the people were to be treated, agreed upon, and determined in Parliament by the king, with the assent of the Prelates, Counts, Barons and the whole Commonalty of the kingdom". Similar language could be found in the provisions of the Cortes of Bribiesca in 1387, which laid down that royal briefs contrary to custom or law were to be treated as null and void, and that laws and ordnances were not to be annulled except in Cortes.[268]

Given the expanse of Europe and the span of centuries, such institutions were more the exception than the rule. In most instances, effective institutions did not survive the ensuing centuries, or were greatly attenuated under absolutist kings, such as those of France. Still, they persisted in the value systems of the day, and were preserved by philosophic thought. What was lacking was a system of checks and balances to control corruption, tyranny and revolution, as well as the general will to fight for these principles. The latter calls to mind Benjamin Franklin's famous reply to the question of what had been produced at the Constitutional Convention: "A Republic—if you can keep it."[269]

In retrospect, with this foundation of Greek and especially Roman traditions, Western Europe was fertile ground for the rise of new institutions of government. Under the pressures of the Reformation and ensuing sectarian wars, key innovations in government arose, notably in Britain, the Netherlands, and Switzerland, but the flowering of institutions crucial to maintaining liberty and democracy occurred most fully realized in England and the United States.

INSTITUTIONS

The West's Greek and Roman heritage of political values regarding the worth of the individual, the concept that political power flowed from the people, and a ruler was subject to law, was well established. Yet, by the end of the Middle Ages, Western societies had not yet developed the political institutions that secured these values and permitted them to function with stability in a world where ubiquitous demagogues stand ready to play on fears and insecurities of the people.

To be sure, important institutions had been created, and even employed, in the Roman Empire. The Republic's system of checks and balances between the executive and the Senate had served Rome well for some centuries, until the emperors increasingly took power in their own hands in face of the exigencies created by wars and barbarian invasions. But western societies had had no direct experience of such institutions for centuries.

New institutions for governance were arising in the West, inspired in part by more widespread political stability and by increasing affluence. The growth of commerce in the West nurtured new towns that attained a substantial degree of independence from their feudal overlords and required new forms of self-government. These established representative bodies to make decisions regarding taxes and to provide governance compatible with emerging mercantile values.

These cities were far more evolved than the ancient city-states, playing an important role in the evolution of the new nation states of Western Europe. In the politics of the time, cities generally made common cause with the king at the expense of the nobility. When kings required revenues for their incessant wars, they would look to the wealthy merchants of the cities as well as that of the landed nobility. From early on, the emerging consultative bodies included representatives from the towns and the commercial classes. In this way the emerging 'extended order' protected its interests and helped shape new institutions. This process occurred most clearly and effectively in Britain.

BRITAIN

In furthering the development of liberty, Britain must be credited with playing the paramount role in establishing key institutions. Britain built on the medieval inheritance to construct a robust institutional system of common law, an unwritten constitution, a representative Parliament, and a Bill of Rights that would secure liberty for the British people.

Even in early Anglo-Saxon times there was a healthy sense of the value of the individual. According to Russell Kirk: "[T]he Anglo-Saxon realm was made up predominantly of small freeholders and their dependents, or of people relatively free: slavery was rare, and the hard serfdom of the nations of the Continent was not prevalent generally. The Norman Conquest did not substantially alter the social character, for the Normans neither butchered nor enslaved the Anglo-Saxons, who remained by far the larger part of the English population. ... [There was] widespread household and village liberties, under the king's laws for the most part, as contrasted with the rule of petty princes and barons in the Continent..."[270]

Yet, this is at best a relative distinction. The country was still feudal and essentially aristocratic. The power lay in the hands of feudal barons often at war with one another. "The enforcement of justice was rude, when justice could be enforced at all; the weak might go to the wall."[271] Nonetheless, there existed a deeply ingrained belief in individual rights. A complete set of institutions to secure those rights would be 600 years and more in the making after the Norman Conquest, but when completed included extraordinary accomplishments: the Magna Carta, representative government, the Bill of Rights, Common Law, an intellectual tradition of 'continuity', 'moderation', and a tradition of the peaceful transfer of political power.

The Magna Carta

The Magna Carta was an early milestone in securing these rights. It arose not out of thin air but from commonly followed and accepted practices and attitudes. Articulated in concrete form, it bound a King to follow the provisions of the charter and by so doing, became a touchstone for binding subsequent monarchs. And, while it was expressly intended for securing the rights of the baronage, with time, under political pressures, those rights were extended to other classes of society.

Knowing the political and social context in which the Magna Carta was promulgated helps us understand its significance. England generally shared the values of medieval Europe regarding power flowing from the community and the king's being subject to the law. These values existed in the context of feudalism, which entailed reciprocal obligations between monarch and nobles, an arrangement providing for the common defense while it resisted the centralization of power. As Kirk put it: "[t]he barons' jealousy of royal prerogatives, and the kings' perennial suspicion of unruly barons, generally maintained a tolerable balance of power."[272]

When John became king in 1199, probably because of John's ambitious history, Archbishop Walter made him sign a coronation oath that "his throne was held by the election of the nation (i.e., the nobles and prelates) and the grace of God."[273] This turned out to be not much of a leash. A dozen years of licentious living, misrule, bad political calculations, and conflicts with Philip Augustus of France as well as with Pope Innocent III ensued. Wishing to attack Philip once again, he demanded of a recalcitrant nobility scutage, a money payment in lieu of military service. Instead, the nobles sent a deputation demanding a return to the laws of Henry I, which had protected the rights of the nobles and limited the powers of the king. Receiving no satisfactory answer, their armed forces confronted the king at Runnymede on the Thames in 1215.

There John was compelled to sign the Magna Carta, which contained a roster of protections for the nobles. Durant summed up the significance of this document as follows: "The Great Charter deserves its fame as the foundation of liberties today enjoyed by the English-speaking world. ... [I]t defined and safeguarded basic rights; it established habeas corpus and trial by jury; it gave to an incipient Parliament a power of the purse that would later arm the nation against tyranny; it transformed absolute into limited and constitutional monarchy."[274]

Churchill's description of events provides a sense of how warring parties of great ambition could, but rarely did, resolve a major conflict of political interests on the basis of principle, rather than raw power. "It was [the archbishop] who persuaded the barons to base their demands upon respect for ancient custom and law, and who gave them some principle to fight for besides their own class interests." Rather than attempting just another feudal change of power, they sought a new system of governing that provided the monarchy its necessary strength, but subordinate to law. Churchill concluded that: "It was this idea, perhaps only half understood, that gave unity and force to the barons' opposition and made the Charter which they now demanded imperishable." While the king had not been defeated militarily and might yet have escaped these bonds, he soon died and the Charter survived.[275]

The example of the Magna Carta also illuminates the importance of the willingness to fight, perhaps sacrificing one's life and fortune, to preserve the efficacy of principle.

Representative Government

Montesquieu said that the only grand change in the art of government that has come about since Aristotle's day is representative government. Russell Kirk added the observation that were it not for representative government, the great modern states would be, at best, imperial structures like the Roman Empire, or else they would dissolve once again into city-states and cantons in which the typical citizen could make his voice heard directly. Kirk believes that nearly all the 'free world' owes modern representative institutions to the English example.[276]

Even with the Magna Carta the English were not significantly more advanced in *representative* government than their Continental counterparts. British kings, like monarchs in various medieval societies, conferred with assemblies of nobles. But England began to improve on this arrangement in a number of respects. It developed constitutional procedures for determining representation; it enhanced the range of issues on which Parliament had to be consulted; and Parliament began to meet on a regular basis.

In the struggle for power found in all societies, it is rare to non-existent that all ambitious parties abide by principle in their efforts. So the Magna Carta might have proven to be no more than one more well-meaning document. The power dynamics of England, however, dictated otherwise.

King John and his immediate successors were relatively weak monarchs, which led to recurring contests between the king and the barons in which both sides had to reach out for support beyond the barons who sat in the Great Council—indeed, beyond the baronial estate altogether. To obtain that support, especially money, they had to consult with representatives of the commons, who were not the mass of peasants, but men of property and some standing—i.e., burgesses of chartered towns, freeholders in the countryside not bound by feudal allegiances, the sons of barons, and knights.

The Model Parliament
But an orderly efficacious institution for consulting with these groups still had to gel. Prior to established parliaments, the king and the ruling barons had irregularly invited representatives of the commons to take part in the deliberations of the realm. These representatives sat in a Great Council, which over time yielded some of its powers to a more general parliament. Then, in 1295, a "Model Parliament," representing all estates—barons, commons, and clergy—was summoned by Edward I. In addition to the members of the original Great Council and the great ecclesiastics, two knights from each county, two burgesses from each burgh, and representatives from the lesser clergy were included.

Yet, as with any new institution, there were a myriad of unsettled issues on how this new parliament was to function vis-à-vis the monarch—issues that were previously settled largely through armed struggle. For example, when Edward attempted to levy fresh taxes unilaterally, the barons compelled him to grant a "Confirmation of Charters," in which the king affirmed that, conforming to old custom, he would levy no extraordinary tax, beyond feudal dues, without the consent of his realm's estates.[277] Churchill summed up the significance of these events:

> At first it [Parliament] lacked substance; only gradually did it take on flesh and blood. But between the beginning and end of Edward's reign the decisive impulse was given. At the beginning anything or nothing might have come out of the experiments of his father's troubled time. By the end it was fairly settled in the customs and traditions of England that "sovereignty," to use a term which Edward would hardly have understood, would henceforward reside not in the Crown only, nor in the Crown and Council of the Barons, but in the Crown in Parliament.

Dark constitutional problems loomed in the future. The boundary between the powers of Parliament and those of the Crown was as yet very vaguely drawn. A statute, it was quickly accepted, was a law enacted by the King in Parliament, and could only be repealed with the consent of Parliament itself. But Parliament was still in its infancy. The initiative in the work of government still rested with the King, and necessarily he retained many powers whose limits were undefined. Did royal ordinances, made in the Privy Council on the King's sole authority, have the validity of law? Could the King in particular cases override a statute on the plea of public or royal expediency? In a clash between the powers of the King and Parliament who was to say on which side right lay? Inevitably, as Parliament grew to fuller stature, these questions would be asked; but for a final answer they were to wait until Stuart kings sat on the English throne."[278]

But this was more than 300 years in the future. Meanwhile some kings attempted to shake free of all parliamentary controls and return to absolutism. When Richard II attempted to do so, he was overthrown by Henry of Bolingbroke, who was crowned Henry IV. Kirk states that in assenting to the coronation of Henry, Parliament in effect asserted its power to dethrone and to elevate another to kingship—even if, as with Henry, it required a successor who was not in the direct line of primogeniture.[279]

Securing the Power of Parliament

The Epic battles to secure the rights of Parliament and to resist tyrannical royal behavior occurred in the 17th century after the death of Queen Elizabeth I. James VI of Scotland became James I of England and began the reign of the Stuarts, who had a taste for absolutism — indeed, James declared he ruled by divine right.

The political turmoil of the 17th century involved far more complicated issues than the balance of power between Parliament and the king. The struggles also involved the interface of politics and religion. This era followed the beginning of the Reformation, when Henry VIII broke with Rome and formed the Anglican Church; at the same time, Scotland became fiercely Calvinistic. So the actors in these battles were Royalists and Parliament men, Anglicans, Presbyterians, independents, martyrs and fanatics.

Churchill describes the temper of the times as one in which the educated part of the English nation expressed a far-reaching interest in Europe. The public's interests went well beyond earlier centuries' concerns with dynastic contests on the continent. They were aware of the intense religious conflicts between Protestants and Catholics and wished to champion Protestantism so as to preserve their new Anglican faith. These interests were given strong voice in Parliament, whose debates far transcended parochial interests. [280]

Despite James I's temperament, his rule did not provoke Parliament. The reign of his son, Charles I, was another matter. Old tensions between king and Parliament surfaced. Requiring money to support England's position in the religious and dynastic wars on the Continent, Charles resorted to taxation without Parliament's assent, to forced loans, to martial law, to the billeting of troops in private homes, and to imprisonment without warrant. Parliament drew up a "Petition of Right" in protest, calling for the King's commitment not to resort again to such measures.

But it was the religious issues that brought Charles down, including convoluted struggles in which Charles and the Archbishop of Canterbury resolved to prevent the disintegration of the Church of England by bringing the Dissenters (Protestants who refused to except the doctrines of the Church of England) to heel. This led to several deadly exchanges. A hostile Parliament had Charles' ablest minister and the Archbishop beheaded, and the House of Commons moved to deprive the king of command over the militia and threatened to impeach the queen, who was a Catholic. Parliament based its defiance not on the desirability of parliamentary sovereignty, but on the imminence of a feared Catholic uprising in England, and warned the country that victory for the King would be followed by a general massacre of Protestants.[281]

During the years of turmoil and civil war that followed, including the beheading of Charles I in 1649, a non-representative Commonwealth and Free State was created under Cromwell, one of despotic powers. According to Churchill: "The Royalists were crushed; Parliament was a tool; the Constitution was a figment; the Scots were rebuffed, the Welsh back in their mountains; the fleet was reorganized, London overawed."[282] This was a critical juncture for the continuity of constitutional government.

Yet, Cromwell did not intend a tyranny. Churchill noted: "Although Cromwell easily convinced himself that he had been chosen the Supreme Ruler of the State, he was ever ready to share his power with others, provided of course that they agreed with him. He was willing, indeed anxious, to govern through a Parliament, if that Parliament would carry the laws and taxes he required. But neither his fondlings nor his purgings induced Parliament to do his will. Again and again he was forced to use or threaten the power of the sword, and the rule which he sought to make a constitutional alternative to absolutism or anarchy became in practice a military autocracy."[283]

This form of government grew unpopular with the people, but there was no obvious successor to Cromwell. With his death, a yearning for stability brought Charles II, the son of Charles I, to the throne and the Restoration—the re-establishment of the monarchy and the Anglican Church of England.

The Glorious Revolution and the Bill of Rights

Charles II reigned peaceably enough, but the reign of his successor, his brother James II, resulted in the "Glorious Revolution," with consequences for representative government far more enduring than the earlier struggles of the century.

The essential cause of a new era of dissension in England was that James II was a staunch Catholic, which reignited the fears of Protestants regarding the possibility of a bloody counter-reformation despite James' coronation oath to preserve and protect the Established Church.

Following a rebellion by one of the Protestant nobles, however, James, who did not conceal his belief that his power was absolute, unleashed a series of acts that suggested the re-establishment of Catholicism was possible. He asked Parliament to repeal the Test Act, which excluded Catholics from office and from Parliament. Moreover, as a sign of his absolutist views, he requested Parliament to modify the Habeas Corpus Act, and to establish a standing army under royal command. Parliament refused. Nonetheless, James proceeded to appoint Catholics to office.

Despite the Pope's counsel to go slow, James accelerated his efforts, feeling he had few years of life to effect the changes important to him. He appointed Catholics to military posts, and created an army under officers who would be subject only to his orders. He suspended laws governing Catholic worship. Then when a Catholic son was born to James, an alarmed Protestant England feared that the birth would prevent his daughter Mary, who was Protestant, from inheriting the throne.[284] Consequently, England's major landed nobility approached Mary and her husband William, who was then leader of the Netherlands, to come to England and assume the throne.

Although he had no rightful claim to the English throne, William accepted the offer and landed in England with an armed force. After maneuvering, some of James' high officers deserted him, as did his other daughter Anne, who was married to Prince George of Denmark. Losing heart after virtually no bloodshed, James left England for France.

A Convention of assembled lords, bishops, and former members of Parliament offered the crown jointly to William and Mary and drew up a Declaration of Right. The latter was enacted by Parliament as a Bill of Rights, a document that greatly influenced the founding fathers of the United States in their preparation of the Declaration of Independence. The Bill of Rights spelled out the grievances that justified James' ouster, made an explicit assertion of the legislative supremacy of Parliament, and articulated the rights of the citizen in the face of arbitrary governmental power.

So formulated, it laid out a principled basis whereby the over-turn of a government can be justified. The English philosopher John Locke expounded on the events and the document with a series of conclusions:[285] that political sovereignty belonged to the people and not to the king; the people delegated their power to a legislative body, Parliament, but might withdraw that power on occasion; and executive authority, derived from the legislative, is dependent on Parliament. Further, government is agreed upon by free contract: governors hold their authority only as a trust from the people, and when this trust is violated, a people may use its strength rightfully to undo tyranny—although only under heavy provocation.[286]

The Bill of Rights established the principle of representative government firmly in England, but the practical effect was circum-scribed since the great majority of the people were not enfranchised to vote[287]. In effect, this "Glorious Revolution" represented the con-solidation of power in the hands of the landowning aristocracy, co-operating with the leaders of industry, commerce, and finance, as opposed to the Monarchy, the 'squirearchy' of smaller landed pro-prietors, who, together with some of the noble families and com-mercial classes, considered themselves 'Tories'.

The king, however, retained considerable power of initiative and action. Through the Crown's patronage and other political pre-rogatives, a king could manage Parliament much of the time down to the beginning of the 19th century.[288]

Common Law

England has also bequeathed to itself, its colonies, and the United States traditions that, while less tangible than the institutions dis-cussed above, are important for the functioning of a free society, notably those associated with common law.

Russell Kirk contrasts common law with statutory law. The latter is a product of statutes enacted by a sovereign political authority, whereas common law is founded upon custom and precedent, i.e., it is an "organic" development arising out of centuries of judges' decisions that were based on what the people believed to be just. As such, it is "customary" or "traditional" law. It can be ascertained in a complex body of legal precedents upon which all judges are supposed to base their present and future decisions – i.e., to rule on a present case, they must consult the body of established precedents in earlier analogous cases. Its application rests on the rule of 'stare decisis', "to stand by decided cases". Thereby, all judges are supposed to be bound by previous decisions, so that they are not permitted to create laws or to decide cases arbitrarily, or to favor particular persons in particular circumstances. It is the fundamental body of law in England and in the countries that have received it from England. [289]

As conclusive as this may appear, real life execution was often another matter. In Elizabethan England, as described by Durant, the courts were by common consent corrupt through bribery or through pressures from the monarch, since judges were removed at the Queen's pleasure. And, while trial by jury was maintained except for treason, the juries were often intimidated by the judges or other officers of the Crown. Moreover, treason was loosely defined to include all actions endangering the life or majesty of the sovereign, and such cases could be summoned before the Star Chamber (the Privy Council in its judicial capacity). There the defendant was denied jury trial, counsel, and habeas corpus, he was subject to exhausting interrogation or torture, and he was usually condemned to imprisonment or death."[290]

Thus the common law in action was hardly perfection. But it was better than the alternatives and improved with time. Lord Acton's view that power corrupts bears on this issue. He believed that the more political power is constrained by checks and balances, the greater the likelihood the legal system will function as intended. In this case, while the common law may have been often flouted, the principle endured. In times of crisis and change, men could reach for that principle.

Traditions of Continuity, Moderation, and the Peaceful Transfer of Power

In addition to building on the tradition of common law, England increasingly respected continuity, moderation, and the peaceful transfer of political power. Richard Hooker (1554-1600), a philosopher influential during the formation of the Church of England, emphasized the importance of moderation and balance in the political and religious life of the nation, as well as the central role of law, continuity, constitutional liberty, and tolerance. Russell Kirk summarizes his views: "Over thousands of years, a people learn certain truths about personal and public order: mankind forms a consensus of opinion on certain vital matters. It is not simply the people living in any one year whose opinions we must consult, but more amply the conclusions of all generations that have preceded us in time—a kind of filtered wisdom of the human species. ... Our Religion, our culture, and our political rights are all maintained by continuity: by our respect for the accomplishments of our forefathers, and by our concern for posterity's wellbeing. ... [I]t is not in the power of anyone to create a new church or a new society out of whole cloth."[291]

Montesquieu (1689-1755) added to this traditionalist view. Even though he was a French nobleman at a time of the growth of absolutism, he resided in England for two years and developed a great admiration for the English 'constitution'. Underlying his philosophy were his beliefs that law arises from custom and habit rather than "social contract". Accordingly, one country's historic experience cannot be readily transported to lands of a different culture, and customs and habits cannot be altered by legislative action alone. His ideas on federalism versus centralized government, the separation of powers, and checks and balances, strongly influenced the design of the U.S. Constitution.[292]

Similarly, the Scottish philosopher David Hume (1711-1776) believed that: "What we learn in this world we learn through custom, repeated experiences, rather than through pure Reason. ... Education really is the accumulated custom of the race. The ways of society are not the ways of reason, but of the customary experience of the species, beginning with small family-groups and growing upward into the state. It is perilous to meddle, on principles of pure rationality, with valuable social institutions that thus are natural developments, not logical schemes."[293]

The diffusion of such views throughout the body politic 'inoculated' the English against false promises of radical revolution, such as that of the French later that century.

These concepts took form only over many centuries. Throughout this era, the monarchical system dominated, coupled with an
autonomous and powerful aristocracy of landed nobles. For example, even strong kings looked for support from coalitions among
the nobility, who continued to control large numbers of troops.
In unsettled times, as Churchill put it: "Parliament was little more
than a clearing-house for the rivalries of nobles."[294] Lesser shifts of
political power were signaled by changes in the king's ministers.
When policies were seen to fail and became deeply unpopular with
key political factions in the country, the monarch would be pres-
sured to replace ministers, usually leading nobles, who represented
different views and interests.

The relative stability of this system was punctuated by violent
upheavals, bloodshed, and even the occasional deposition of the
monarch. Henry of Bolingbroke in 1399 usurped power from Richard II after many nobles and the emerging merchant class had become alarmed at Richard's increasingly autocratic behavior. In the
most extreme example, Charles I was beheaded in 1649 after having been defeated by forces led by Oliver Cromwell and the royal
government was replaced by a radical "republic."

Although Parliaments had existed since the 13th century, Parliament became paramount only after the Glorious Revolution. Even
though the king continued to exercise great influence, including the
selection of Prime Minister and the use of patronage, power gravitated toward shifting coalitions within the Lords and Commons.
In this emerging system, losers in the political contest knew that
they had the opportunity to contend anew in the future and regain
power. Equally important, they knew that their lives would not be
forfeit if they lost. Thereby Britain produced an efficacious institutional alternative to revolutions, coups, and war for transferring
political power.

Moreover, there were important practical aspects of the new tradition beyond avoiding the costs of internal warfare and instability.
Among the most important is the natural dynamic of a two-party
system in which the 'out' party continuously seeks an advantage
by criticizing weak or failed policies of the party holding power.
Through such scrutiny, government becomes less susceptible to the
'corruption of power'.

Thus it was that representative government evolved in Great Britain in an enduring form. Associated institutions and their implicit values were conveyed to the British colonies as well, and America was no exception. Indeed, it proved to have the most fertile soil for nurturing the seeds of a democratic society.

THE UNITED STATES

The English colonies in America as a whole inherited the British political traditions, but those colonies making up the United States went on after the War of Independence to develop a modified form of constitutional government. The efforts of the American colonists were based on their unique experiences in the New World, their perceptions of weaknesses in the British model, and their readings of historical experience regarding political philosophy and institutions. The philosophic and institutional choices made by the colonies grew out of their political setting.

The Political Setting

The American colonies arose in unique circumstances, and consisted of a population which had absorbed values passed from Greece and Rome to medieval Europe to enlightened England. By the time of their emigration to the new world, they enjoyed the liberties of free Englishmen and were accustomed to the relatively free markets that had developed in England and a few other places. Yet they were so far removed from effective political control of England that they were as free from the baneful effects of a predatory state as any civilized peoples ever were. They benefited from, as Russell Kirk put it, from 'salutary neglect'.

For most of the colonial period, the British government showed little attention to its subjects in North America. For one thing, in terms of trade and wealth they were of lesser importance than the colonies located in the Caribbean. For another, the colonies were founded on charters granted to British trading companies and great proprietors—i.e., as potentially profitable enterprises. Accordingly, Parliament relied on those receiving the charters to manage the affairs of the colonies. To the extent that there was any systematic policy from London, it came from the Board of Trade and Plantations.

This neglect probably also stemmed from the lack of interest by members of the British establishment. There were no nobleman (not one peer settled permanently in the colonies), no bishops, no ancient families of rural magnates, no generals, and no admirals (except on temporary duty).[295]

As a result, in this isolated, yet protected setting, the population prospered uniquely free from the exactions of a predatory state. Individuals farmed, worked, and traded—von Mises' *Human Action* at work. The opportunity for self-betterment attracted large numbers of settlers, who, while poor, possessed enormous vigor. Even in the harsh environment, the indigenous health and longevity soon exceeded that of the English population, and they thrived such that their birth rate resulted in doubling their numbers every quarter century.[296]

In terms of shared values, the colonies were remarkably homogeneous. Having left the class tensions behind in Europe, society was egalitarian and non-hierarchical. Since individuals in the colonies could rarely claim status on the basis of genealogy, an individual's personal merit and behavior was the basis of esteem.

Left to their own devices, the colonists developed local governments in accord with their values as free Englishmen, naturally following the model of English representative government. In some of the colonies, provision was already made in their charters for a representative assembly; in others, such assemblies began to be held by colonists themselves, without express authorization. Although at first these assemblies were expected by the Crown or the proprietors to be mere ratifying and tax-granting bodies, they successfully asserted their own powers.

There also existed in every colony an executive agency, a governor, either appointed by the king or the proprietors, or elected by colonial freeholders, as in Connecticut and Rhode Island. In struggles between a governor and his council on the one side, and an assembly on the other, the odds ran against any arbitrary governor. Since they had to rely on funds from the assemblies and were distant from England, the governors had to establish cooperative relationships. Kirk noted that in every colony the habit of representative self-government was so firmly established that by the 1760s royal or parliamentary decisions contrary to an assembly's will could not be enforced without the dispatch of military or naval forces from England.[297]

But these colonial assemblies were anything but radical bodies. They were composed overwhelmingly of the colonial gentry. Given the ready availability of land in the colonies and the small amount required to be considered a freeholder, the franchise was far broader than in England. There was little class conflict because small freeholders usually found that the richer gentry represented their interests. Political conflict tended to be between governor and assembly or between more settled regions and the western frontier.

At the local level, the colonists were also in the habit of self-government—via counties in the south, and via townships in New England. The county justices in Virginia were appointed by the royal governor, but in practice candidates came from a list submitted by the county courts. The semi-independent status of the counties had long-run effects on American history: the Virginians who helped draft the Federal Constitution had lived under a quasi-federal system in colonial Virginia, and had seen the advantages of strong local positions during conflicts with the king's representatives.[298]

The New England towns were more democratically run with the entire adult male population involved in decision-making. They were influenced by the participatory government that had grown up in the Presbyterian and nonconformist churches in England, but Massachusetts' Declaration of "Laws and Liberties" (1648) opened town meetings even to persons who were not members of the Puritan churches to present petitions, even if they were not permitted to vote. In effect, the meetings helped to train the whole population in participatory self-government.[299]

The Constitution

Given this political setting, what in the world would cause a non-radical, tradition-loving, freedom-enjoying people to engage in a revolution?

The simple answer is that they, even the immigrants from other nations, had absorbed the values of England. Just as the English had revolted against Charles I and James II when they found their rights encroached upon, so would the colonists revolt against George III and Parliament. The revolution was a fight to preserve the rights they had enjoyed, not a fight over abstract principles.

The struggle began as a dispute over who had the power to tax, Parliament or the colonies' legislative assemblies. Until the 1760s England had not attempted to tax the colonists. During the wars against the French, Parliament had requested financial support from the colonial assemblies. However, as the costs of the various wars became burdensome, England, not unreasonably, believed that, having grown more prosperous, the colonies should bear a greater part of the financial burden of efforts to ensure their own security. England tried to impose taxes directly, bypassing the colonial assemblies via the Stamp Act and the Tea Act. But the colonists resisted, and, England increasingly turned to force to uphold what it saw as Parliamentary rights.

The fundamental question was whether the Parliament might levy taxes on the Americans without the consent of the colonial assemblies. If Parliament enforced its views, the colonists believed their liberties would be encroached upon, possibly endangered. This consideration—that true liberty resides in each individual's right to labor for his well-being without unjust coercion of the government—was made the centerpiece of the Declaration of Independence, which stated that all men have the unalienable rights of life, liberty, and the pursuit of happiness.

Upon the successful conclusion of the Revolutionary War, sovereignty remained with the individual states, and a loose confederacy was attempted under the Articles of Confederation. It soon became clear to many that an executive agency was needed, as were means for a common defense, for resolving financial issues, and for assuring the basis for trade among the states and internationally. To deal with these issues and to create a stronger government among the thirteen states, a Constitutional Convention was convened in Philadelphia in 1787.

Philosophic Underpinnings

As many commentators have noted, the men assembled there were remarkable in the talent and perspective they brought to their task. While thousands of miles away from the centers of culture in Europe, they were well educated in matters of history, government and law. They were well aware of Solon, the Athenian experience, the history of the Roman Republic, the Magna Carta, the Glorious Revolution, the English Bill of Rights, French philosophic thought, and, of course, their own experience in self-government, and the rights of free Englishmen. They were equally aware of practical problems growing out of the frailties of human nature—hunger for power, factionalism, rent-seeking, and opportunism. These, an unavoidable aspect of life, had destroyed governments throughout history. A central question was how to create a strong executive without a king and still secure the liberties they had enjoyed, while reining in human frailties.

In addition to their combined practical experience in government, as educated men, they had read the words of a number of practical philosophers. Prominent among these was Montesquieu, whose belief in the continuity of institutions and the importance of custom was enhanced by his practical views on the construct of government. His "Considerations on the Grandeur and Decadence of the Romans", published in 1734, and "The Spirit of Laws", published in 1748, were quickly translated into English and eagerly read by educated colonists, including those who later assembled in Philadelphia.

Montesquieu wrote: "the highest achievement of any country's law is the enlargement of personal freedom. Law and freedom are not opposed; for there cannot be freedom without law, only violent anarchy; and without freedom, law is despotic, obeyed only out of fear."[300] But he believed that individual liberty and the rule of law are threatened by centralized power, as in France, and supported arrangements akin to federalism.

Montesquieu believed that the countries that had done the best job in reconciling the claims of freedom and law were the Roman Republic and the constitutional monarchy of England. These political-social entities had evolved the constitutional features of the separation of powers and a system of checks and balances. Their underlying rationales were that power can be restrained only by counterbalancing power; and that no man, political body, or office should possess unchecked power. Personal liberty and free communities depended on power being divided and hedged.

Practically speaking, the separation of powers entails apportioning authority to different branches of government: the executive, the legislative, and the judicial. By each checking and balancing the exercise of power by others, centralized and arbitrary rule can be prevented and liberty preserved."[301]

The drafters of the Constitution were not without experience in drawing up constitutions embodying these principles. Indeed, Virginia (1776) and Massachusetts (1780) had already done so.

Features of the Constitution
Over a four-month period in 1787, the delegates to the Constitutional Convention distilled their experience and philosophy into one document, the U.S. Constitution, which was designed to achieve two opposing goals, namely the creation of a central government sufficiently powerful to exercise control over the sprawling new country while simultaneously constrained in employing that power by a system of checks and balances. Among its key features are:

A federal republic: One of the main conceptual problems facing the convention was how to preserve an essential degree of authority for the largely autonomous states while establishing a sufficiently efficacious central authority. To that end, the new central government was limited to ensuring a common defense, conducting diplomacy, preventing struggles among the states or insurrections within the states, maintaining a sound national currency and fiscal policy, and promoting the general welfare. The states were to retain all authority not explicitly given to the central government in the Constitution. To further protect state interests, a Senate including two representatives from each state, elected by state legislatures, comprised the upper house of the Congress.[302] Thus, all legislation would require the collective assent of the states.

Checks and balances: James Madison's "Federalist Paper Number Fifty-one," speaks to the elemental need for explicit checks and balances in the structure of government:

But the great security against a gradual concentration of the several powers in the same department [i.e. branch of government], consists in giving to those who administer each department the necessary constitutional means and personal motives to resist encroachments of the others. The provision for defense must in this, as in all other cases, be made commensurate to the danger of attack. Ambition must be made to counteract ambition. The interest of the man must be connected with the constitutional rights of the place. It may be a reflection on human nature, that such devices should be necessary to control the abuses of government. But what is government itself, but the greatest of all reflections on human nature? If men were angels, no government would be necessary. If angels were to govern men, neither external nor internal controls on government would be necessary. In framing a government which is to be administered by men over other men, the great difficulty lies in this: you must first enable the government to control the governed; and in the next place oblige it to control itself. A dependence on the people is, no doubt, the primary control on the government; but experience has taught mankind the necessity of auxiliary precautions.[303]

Accordingly, the framers of the Constitution incorporated several key such checks: the President's veto power checked the legislative branch while, conversely, the Congress had the power to override vetoes and the unique authority to declare war. In addition, the Senate was assigned the power to accept or reject treaties and approve or reject executive branch appointments.

The framers of the Constitution were also careful to preserve the balance of power between the states and the new federal government. Accordingly, they established in the Constitution the principle of enumerated powers of the federal government. To underscore the importance of this provision, the Tenth Amendment to the U.S. Constitution states: "The powers not delegated to the United States by the Constitution, nor prohibited by it to the States, are reserved to the States respectively, or to the people."

Separation of powers between the executive and legislative branches: The presidency was designed to support a vigorous executive, who was both head of state and head of the government. His power was checked by an independent Congress, which the President could not dissolve and which met regularly, whether the President wished it or not.

The Congress of the United States, the legislative branch, took Parliament for its model in many respects. Like Parliament, it consisted of two houses. The House of Representatives was designed to represent popular opinion inasmuch as its representatives are directly elected by the populace. Like the House of Commons, it has initiating authority over taxation. As noted above, the Senate is constituted by members elected by the states who serve longer terms allowing them to be more independent of passing political passions and, thus, more deliberative. It was assigned primacy in treaty-making and in confirming the president's major appointees to office. The two houses checked each other since they both needed to pass a piece of legislation for it to be enacted.

Bill of Rights: An essential bulwark against the possibility of despotism requires a means of protecting an individual's rights as citizen. Such rights were implicit in the hard-won British tradition based on the Magna Carta and the Bill of Rights that formed part of the "Glorious Revolution", and they were explicitly included in some of the state constitutions. Yet the Constitution, as framed by the Convention, did not include a Bill of Rights. In large measure this was because most delegates believed that those rights were self-evident and were sufficiently embodied in American culture. Nonetheless, the debate during the ratification of the Constitution by the states highlighted concerns about their absence, and this led to an understanding that such rights would be incorporated in amendments to the Constitution soon after establishment of the new government. Notably, the first of these amendments states: "Congress shall make no law respecting an establishment of religion, or prohibiting the free exercise thereof; or abridging the freedom of speech, or of the press; or the right of the people peaceably to assemble, and to petition the Government for a redress of grievances." This was an intellectual cornerstone of the checks against arbitrary government, but left a question of how Congress could in practice be restrained from inappropriate action. The check on Congress was to be the judiciary, in particular the Supreme Court.

A Supreme Court: Unlike the executive and the legislative branches, the eventual role of the Supreme Court was unprecedented. The Constitution created its potential, but its efficacy was only realized by subsequent developments. In Article III, Section 1, the Constitution states: "The judicial Power of the United States shall be vested in one supreme Court and in such inferior Courts as the Congress may from time to time ordain and establish." This language is silent regarding a specific role of the court and left it to the Congress to give it form.

The framers of the Constitution and many members of the new Congress had been influenced, as noted earlier, by the writings of Montesquieu. He feared that even separation of powers and effective checks and balances might not suffice to ensure continuity of law and evenhanded justice. He believed that some "guardian of laws" protecting the constitution of a country was necessary.[304] In "The Federalist Papers," Alexander Hamilton echoed Montesquieu, writing that certain provisions of the Constitution "can be preserved in practice no other way than through the medium of the courts of justice, whose duty it must be to declare all acts contrary to the manifest tenor of the Constitution void. Without this, all the reservations of particular rights or privileges would amount to nothing."[305] In this view, the Constitution removed constitutional interpretation from the national and state legislatures.

But the realization of this potential would be realized only through actions of the Supreme Court itself, which was set up by The Judiciary Act of 1789.[306] The latent power of judicial review was first asserted by Chief Justice John Marshall in the case of Marbury vs. Madison, decided in 1803. His opinion stated: "The particular phraseology of the Constitution of the United States confirms and strengthens the principle, supposed to be essential to all written constitutions, that a law repugnant to the Constitution is void; and that *courts*, as well as other departments, are bound by that instrument."[307] Through this process a key check on the abuse of power in the American system came into being.

The history of the next two centuries demonstrated the extent to which the aspirations of the founding fathers were realized—i.e., a constitutional means to balance the need for order with the requirements of liberty. They had indeed crafted a form of government that reined in the potential of a predatory state while allowing generous space for industrious and creative human action to prosper. The Constitution had the robustness to accommodate a Civil War, participation in two World Wars, as well as a number of other contentious conflicts, allowing the United States to become wealthy, powerful, and free.

So it was that the creation of the United States and the enactment of its Constitution capped an evolutionary process of securing liberty that spanned two millennia, embracing efforts by the Greeks, the Romans, and feudal Europe, with Britain towering over them all. Each of these contributed philosophic insights and institutional innovations that permitted man to control the worst of his aggressive instincts and to regain the egalitarian spirit inherent in tribal life in a way compatible with extensive nation-states.

The new modes of governance married to free markets produced the richest, most powerful, and most innovative of modern societies. While no other civilization developed institutions compatible with liberty, a number of nations did emulate many of these features, thus benefiting from an evolutionary process begun in the West.

5

The Emergence of Science

The progress of science is marked not only by an accumulation of facts but by the emergence of the scientific method and of the scientific attitude. – *The Columbia Encyclopedia*

A third avenue of cultural change in the West was the emergence of science—science that allowed man to master the material environment and that transformed worldviews to produce stronger societal animals.

While every educated person has at least an intuitive appreciation for the nature and power of science, its origins and the basis for its power are much less well understood. Scientific knowledge—as opposed to technological prowess—is extraordinarily difficult to glean from nature. Thomas Kuhn observes that the teaching of science lends itself to a view that knowledge is gained in a linearly cumulative fashion by man's increasingly detailed examination of nature[308]. It would appear a self-evident process. It is not.

To be sure, man is naturally curious about the world about him. Most civilizations during periods of stability and affluence have undertaken detailed examinations of nature and the heavens—i.e., systematized and accumulated learning regarding natural phenomena. This activity, however, was mostly that of the 'encyclopedist.' There is a deeper view of science that will help us see why science as we know it arose in the West and not elsewhere.

Indeed, science is the ability to 'see' beneath and beyond what is observable to the eye and the senses. To begin, let's look at a working definition of "science" from *The Columbia Encyclopedia*:

> The progress of science is marked not only by an accumulation of facts but by the emergence of the scientific method and of the scientific attitude. The first step of the scientific method is the gathering of data by the observation of phenomena. By inductive reasoning a hypothesis or preliminary generalization is drawn from the data. The validity of deductions that follow logically from a generalization is tested by further observations and experiments. A verified generalization is considered a scientific theory or law; if contradictory facts arise, the theory may be modified to include the new facts or it may be replaced by a new concept. The scientific method is an expression of the scientific attitude which rests on rational impartiality and on a strict regard for accuracy, and controlled experiment.[309]

This approach and methodology may now seem obvious; nevertheless, it is a worldview and set of values that were hard won through centuries of experiential learning, often at odds with religion and conventional wisdom. Indeed, many worldviews militated against even the possibility of such knowledge, and most cultures were awash in the belief of supernatural forces at work on earth. For example, Islam believes that Allah orders all events, and Christianity believes in an all-knowing, all-powerful God that offers the possibility of miracles. Historically, most religions, relying on revelation, distrusted knowledge gained through the senses.

Indeed, our senses can mislead, and they are incapable of measuring temperature, pressure, acidity, speed, or time with any accuracy. Most phenomena swamp unmediated attempts at precise observation with myriad potential variables. Who would make the effort? Where would instruments for measurement come from? Were knowledge and understanding really attainable?

These were moot points until civilization achieved the affluence and leisure to consider such matters. With time, several civilizations did attain a stage of evolution—i.e., material wealth as well as philosophic ferment and creativity—prerequisite to true science.

Yet science emerged in the West and failed to do so in other civilizations because only there did key philosophic forms, largely metaphysical, emerge from the ongoing process of debate. The West's cultural inheritance from ancient Greece and medieval Christian theology provided the unique philosophic foundation from which science could emerge.

Moreover, because of fragmented political power and tension between religious and secular authorities, the West contained societies that were sufficiently—hardly entirely, but sufficiently—open to political and philosophic debate essential to the scientific enterprise. Western Europe increasingly provided a milieu in which arguments and a productive framework for arguments were regularly tested, with the fittest surviving—an intensely Darwinian process.

Just how this evolutionary process played out can be seen by contrasting how receptive leading civilizations were to scientific thinking, outlining the emergence of a favorable philosophic basis for science in the West and illustrating how that philosophic approach led to productive scientific discovery. The pervasive influence of those discoveries changed how people viewed the universe and their place in it.

PRE-SCIENCE: ONE MILLENIUM AGO

If Phillip Scribner is correct about the inevitability of certain forms of evolution, one can expect appropriate random variations of thought and prerequisite conditions for philosophy, the underpinnings of scientific inquiry, to have appeared more than once—and even simultaneously—among evolved societies. In that light, it is intriguing that Socrates in Greece, Confucius in China, Buddha in India, and the prophets in Israel, each representing a flowering of philosophic thought, appeared on the scene somewhat contemporaneously around 500 B.C. It appears that totally separate streams of societal evolution attained the affluence and other prerequisites for deeper philosophical speculation at about the same time. But only the Greeks provided the necessary metaphysical speculation that would, two thousand years later, lead to *science*.

How essential metaphysical speculation was—and is—to the unfolding of science becomes readily apparent in reviewing the scientific views and capabilities of China, Islam, and medieval Europe a thousand years ago. In that era, these three civilizations of all those on earth were the most affluent, valued knowledge the most, and were the most ingenious in the use of technology in meeting man's needs. In terms of material conditions, an impartial observer of a millennium ago would likely have assessed the prospects for science best in China, next best in Islam, and poorest in Europe. But this proved not to be the case.

China

By all accounts, China had achieved extraordinary accomplishments in many fields by the time of the Sung Dynasties (960-1279 A.D.):

> [China] produced excellent textbooks of agriculture and sericulture two centuries before Christ, and excelled in treatises on geography. ... Chang Ts'ang (d. 152 B.C.) left behind him a work on algebra and geometry, containing the first known mention of a negative quantity. Tsu Ch'ung-chih calculated the value of [pi] to six decimal places, improved the magnet or "south-pointing vehicle,"... Chinese mathematicians apparently derived algebra from India, but developed geometry for themselves out of their need for measuring land. The astronomers of Confucius' time correctly calculated eclipses, and laid the bases of the Chinese calendar... Medicine in China ... produced great physicians long before Hippocrates. ... Chang Chung-ning, in the second century, wrote treatises on dietetics and fevers, which remained standard texts for a thousand years. ... Ch'ao Yuan-fang wrote a classic on the diseases of women and children. Medical encyclopedias were frequent under the T'angs ... A medical college was established in the Sung Dynasty...[310]

Similarly, during this period China was the most technologically advanced civilization in the world.[311] They were ingenious in the use of technology in agriculture and industry: they invented the dam, the sluice-gate, the noria (peripheral pot-wheel) and the treadle water-pump to improve agricultural productivity. They had learned to use coke instead of charcoal as fuel and had a sizeable production of iron before the 11th century. They also made technological advances in shipbuilding, navigation, and gunpowder.[312] All in all, "between the first century B.C. and the fifteenth century A.D., Chinese civilization was much more efficient than [the] occidental in applying human natural knowledge to practical human needs."[313]

China's failure to move beyond this relatively advanced state of development gives rise to what a number of writers call the 'Needham Problem'. Joseph Needham's analysis of the development of science identified an historical puzzle that bears his name. Inasmuch as China a millennium or so ago was technologically further advanced than other cultures and was governed according to more rational principles than medieval Europe, how is it that science emerged in Europe and not in China? In this regard, Needham particularly noted China's rule of mandarins who were selected by an imperial examination designed to draw the best brains of each generation into the civil service. Despite this apparent advantage, "Needham's conclusion is that the social and cultural values of Asian 'bureaucratic feudalism' were simply incompatible with capitalism and, for that matter, with modern science."[314]

Thus, Needham seems to have concluded that traditional values combined with bureaucratic ambition can trump potentially productive change in decision-making at all levels. China's misguided bureaucratic bent coincided roughly with the neo-Confucian reorientation of philosophic outlook in the 14th century. At this time, the government was seeking to counter the inroads that had been made by imported Buddhism. Against the Buddhist assertion of the meaninglessness of life, the neo-Confucians sought to reorient social order and morality on a more positive philosophic basis. Unfortunately, the reorientation went from a view that accepted mercantile activity and pragmatic technical change to one that emphasized introspection, intuition, and subjectivity. (The West saw a weaker but analogous reaction with the Romantic Era following the Age of Enlightenment.)

The consequence of this philosophy for Chinese science was disastrous. As the result of a highly sophisticated metaphysics there was always an explanation—which of course was no explanation at all—for anything puzzling that turned up ... Given this attitude, it was unlikely that any anomaly would irritate enough for a framework of reference to be discarded in favor of a better one.[315]

At the end of the day, the Chinese culture valued consensus too much and distrusted argument and dissent too much to make philosophic progress in the scientific arena. Moreover, Chinese centralized power had the capability of suppressing unwelcome change.

Islam

Islam at its zenith during the Abbasid Empire (750-1058 A.D.) approached the Chinese in the extent of their achievements, if not in their creativity. Islam's initial openness to scientific enterprise was captured by the Arab historian Ibn Khalun (1332-1406), who stated:

> The intellectual sciences are natural to man, inasmuch as he is a thinking being. They are not restricted to any particular religious group. They are studied by the people of all religious groups who are equally qualified to learn them and to do research in them. They have existed (and been known) to the human species since civilization had its beginnings in the world.[316]

In reaching these conclusions, he drew on an Islamic heritage that had prodigiously preserved ancient knowledge, collected new knowledge about natural life on earth and about the heavens, but had already in his time begun to stagnate and drift away from the promise of science.

Preservation of Knowledge

In a number of fields—notably astronomy, mathematics and medicine—the Islamic world was instrumental in collecting the achievements of other civilizations and, in instances, extending them. For example, considerable effort was devoted to translating into Arabic scientific works from the Persian, Indian, and Greek.

The most important of these in terms of a philosophic base for science were those from the Greek. Because the caliphs realized the backwardness of the Arabs in science and philosophy and the importance of preserving the wealth of Greek culture that survived in Syria, many classics of Greek science and philosophy were preserved, often in Syriac translations and mostly produced by Nestorian Christians and Jews.[317]

The Abbasid princes institutionalized much of this effort. For example, al-Mamun established in 830 A.D. at Baghdad a "House of Wisdom" which included a scientific academy, an observatory, and a public library. It included a corps of translators. Just one of these serves as a dramatic example of this effort. The Nestorian physician, Hunain ibn Ishaq (809-73), translated a hundred treatises of Galen and the Galenic school into Syriac, and thirty-nine into Arabic. He translated Aristotle's *Categories*, *Physics*, and *Magna Moralia*; Plato's *Republic*, *Timaeus*, and *Laws*; Hippocrates' *Aphorisms*, Dioscorides' *Materia Medica*, Ptolemy's *Quadripartitum*, and the Old Testament from the Septuagint Greek.[318]

These efforts eventually were to flow to the West in the late Middle Ages.

Accomplishments

Durant provides an overview of the accomplishments of Islam in many academic fields, recognizing that much has been lost to history: "We shall probably rank the tenth century in Eastern Islam as one of the golden ages in the history of the mind."[319] ... "Avicenna was the greatest writer on medicine, al-Razi the greatest physician, al-Biruni the greatest geographer, al-Haitham the greatest optician, Jabir probably the greatest chemist, of the Middle Ages."[320] Let's look at some examples of these accomplishments.

• Muhammad ibn Musa wrote on the Hindu numerals; compiled astronomical tables that were standards for centuries; formulated the oldest known trigonometrical tables; drew up with sixty-nine other scholars, a geographical encyclopedia; and in his *Calculation of Integration and Equation* gave analytical and geometrical solutions of quadratic equations. In translation, this work was a principal text in European universities until the 16th century.[321]

• The Caliph al-Mamun engaged a staff of astronomers to make observations, to test the findings of Ptolemy and others. They took the sphericity of the earth for granted and calculated the circumference as well as the width of a terrestrial degree. Their latter measurement was 56 $^2/_3$ miles, just half a mile more than modern measurements.[322]

• Abu al-Rayhan Muhammad ibn Ahmad al-Biruni (973-1048) shows the Moslem scholar at his best. He was a philosopher, historian, traveler, geographer, linguist, mathematician, astronomer, poet, and physicist—doing major and original work in all these fields. He gave the best medieval account of Hindu numerals; formulated astronomical tables; noted the attraction of all things to the center of the earth; and remarked that astronomic data can be explained as well by supposing that the earth turns daily on its axis and annually around the sun as by the reverse hypothesis. He laid down the principles of specific gravity of objects, and he explained the workings of natural springs and artesian wells by hydrostatic principle of communicating vessels. And he laid out key aspects of the scientific method.[323]

• Moslems produced important precursors to chemistry, viz., precise observation, controlled experiment, and careful records. They analyzed innumerable substances, composed lapidaries, distinguished alkalis and acids, investigated their affinities, and studied and manufactured hundreds of drugs. Much of the work was done under the paradigm of alchemy, which while an incorrect model, contributed to myriad discoveries. Yet, perhaps because of the failure of the paradigm, the science of chemistry in Islamic nations succumbed to occultism. [324]

• Islam accomplished much in medicine—in observation, therapy, and drugs. Institutionally, they made great strides. They established the first apothecary shops and dispensaries and founded the first medieval school of pharmacology. Early on, 34 hospitals were established. Medical instruction was given at the hospitals, and no man could legally practice without passing an examination and receiving a diploma. Abu Bekr Muhammad al-Razi was a leading figure, writing some 131 books, half of them on medicine. His *Kitah al-Hawi* (Comprehensive Book) covered all branches of medicine in 20 volumes, a copy of which composed the whole library of the medical faculty at the University of Paris in 1395. His work was dethroned by later writings of Avicenna, who produced a *Canon of Medicine,* which was a gigantic survey of physiology, hygiene, therapy, and pharmacology. After being translated into Latin in the 12th century, it became the chief text in European medical schools, being required reading in some places until the 17th century. But, as in chemistry, theoretical understanding lagged. For example, being forbidden by religion to dissect human cadavers, anatomy had to rely on older works by the Greek physician Galen.[325]

This picture is one of extensive productivity and desire for physical knowledge. The Islamic world teetered on the brink of the scientific attitude. Durant describes al-Biruni as follows: "[h]is attitude was that of the objective scholar, assiduous in research, critical in the scrutiny of traditions and texts (including the Gospels), precise and conscientious in statement, frequently admitting his ignorance, and promising to pursue his inquiries till the truth should emerge. In the preface to the 'vestiges' he wrote like Francis Bacon: 'We must clear our minds ... from all causes that blind people to the truth—old custom, party spirit, personal rivalry or passion, the desire for influence.'"[326]

Nonetheless, as Deepak Lal summarizes Islamic achievements: "[t]here is not much evidence, however, of any new specifically Muslim technological breakthroughs. Both in science and technology, Islam brokered the transfer of ideas and techniques from the earlier ancient civilizations of Greece, India, and China. The efflorescence of Islamic science in the Abbasid period was largely derivative but notable nevertheless."[327]

Stagnation

Given these accomplishments, why did Islam not develop science, and why did even its investigations into the natural world retrogress? Did societal values turn hostile? Or did they never evolve far enough for science to take the necessary next steps?

The questions seem particularly intriguing because of initial similarities between Islam and Christian Europe. Both purportedly drew on a tradition that included the Jewish prophets, and both had access to the Greek heritage (one that first passed through Muslim hands to reach the post-medieval Europe). But scientific advancement in the Islamic world stagnated while it surged forward in Christian Europe. Why did these cultures take such divergent paths?

Simply put, Islam was less receptive to change and philosophic debate than Christendom. For example, man's speculations about his origins, purposes, ways of knowing, and ways of reason, at some point, have to be dealt with by established religions in terms of their teachings and traditions. Islam and Christian Europe confronted these questions in diametrically different ways. Islam, despite some Judeo-Christian antecedents, was a fundamentalist sect centered on the Koran, seen as the immutable word of God. As such, Deepak Lal believes that Islam was encumbered by cosmological beliefs—i.e., in worldviews embracing belief in the power of revelation and disbelief in free will, which hindered speculation and alternative views of the world. Christian Europe, on the other hand, developed a richer, more metaphorical theology that proved to be as fertile for speculation as it was for heresy.

Yet, Islamic civilization initially showed great promise for science. At first, when Islam settled down after its great conquests, the philosophically inclined inherited a myriad of influences. "Hindu speculations came in through Ghazni and Persia; Zoroastrian and Jewish eschatology played some minor role; and Christian heretics had stirred the air of the Near East with debate on the attributes of God, the nature of Christ and the Logos, predestination and free will, revelation and reason."[328] (Given the later atrophying of philosophic speculation, one has to consider that much of what is remembered as Islam's golden age was more the continuing spirit of Persian, Syrian, Nestorian, and Jewish cultures, before they were fully subjugated by Islam.)

Islamic societies eventually had to come to reconcile their still tribal values with these influences by grappling with universal philosophic issues, e.g., how we know things. Given the fallibility of our senses, do we adopt an epistemological approach based on reason and empirical inquiry or a mystical approach based on revelation?

Durant attributes the first broadly based attempts of Islam to reconcile the teachings of the Koran with broader philosophic questions to the school of "Mutazilites." He states: "[t]hey protested their respect for Islam's holy book, but they argued that where it or the Hadith contradicted reason, the Koran or the traditions must be interpreted allegorically; and they gave the name *kalam* or logic to this effort to reconcile reason and faith. It seemed to them absurd to take literally those Koranic passages, ... however adapted to the moral and political ends of Mohammed at the time, [that] could hardly be accepted by the educated intellect. The human mind could never know what was the real nature or attributes of God; it could only agree with faith in affirming a spiritual power as the foundation of all reality. Furthermore, to the Mutazilites, it seemed fatal to human morality and enterprise to believe, as orthodoxy did, in the complete predestination of all events by God, and the arbitrary election, from all eternity, of the saved and the damned."[329]

In any event, such learned men recognized the severe intellectual limitations inherent in religious doctrines formulated for small tribal societies. Durant cites writings of a group of philosophers formed in Basra about 983 A.D. called the "Brethren of Sincerity." They stated that: "[w]hen the mind has been emancipated by knowledge it should feel free to reinterpret through allegory, and thereby reconcile with philosophy, 'the crude expressions of the Koran, which were adapted to the understanding of an uncivilized desert people.'"[330]

For a time, Islamic civilization attempted to incorporate new knowledge and philosophic speculation. At a practical level, where philosophy and theology found their ways into practice through tradition, law, and institutions, attempts were made to broaden the understanding and application of dogma through legal reasoning. There was unanimity that the Koran and the Hadiths are divinely inspired and binding. However, since not all cases are covered by these sources, Islamic scholars early on found it necessary to find a broader application of doctrine via *fiqh* (the understanding or application of method), one form of which included analogical reasoning. Such theoretical attempts taken together produced a process of interpretation and exercise of independent judgment known as *itjihad*. The resulting intellectual conflict—partisans of literal scriptural reasoning on one hand, and those that support the extension of the Koran and Sunna into new domains on the other—produced various competing schools of Islamic legal thinking.[331]

There was an extended period of philosophic contention between the traditionalists and the rationalists. But before the end of the Abbasids, 'the closing of the Islamic mind'[332] was complete, with all of the fateful consequences. The decisive swing toward the Traditionalists came with the work of Abu Hamid al-Ghazali (1058-1111), whom Durant refers to as the greatest theologian of Islam—"its Augustine and Kant." He was widely educated and at an early age was given a chair at the Nizamiya College in Baghdad. He, according to his autobiography, experienced a crisis in faith and went into seclusion. Because he had lost the belief in the capacity of reason to sanction the Muslim faith, he turned from the outer world to an inner world of mysticism:

> In this mood al-Ghazali wrote his most influential book ...
> (*The Destruction of Philosophy*). All the arts of reason were
> turned against reason. By a 'transcendental dialectic' as
> subtle as Kant's, the Moslem mystic argued that reason
> leads to universal doubt, intellectual bankruptcy, moral de-
> terioration, and social collapse. ... In the end al Ghazali re-
> turned through mysticism to all orthodox views. ... [N]ever
> in Islam had the skeptics and philosophers encountered so
> vigorous a foe. When he died (1111), the tide of unbelief had
> been effectively turned. All orthodoxy took comfort from
> him ... After him ... philosophy hid itself in remote corners
> of the Moslem world; the pursuit of science waned; and the
> mind of Islam more and more buried itself in the Hadith
> and the Koran.[333]

To be sure, so momentous a change in a society and a culture cannot be attributed to a single individual. For him to have such an apparent impact suggests that he connected in a critical way with the *Zeitgeist;* with an Islamic *societal animal* in crisis.

Islam, drawing on huge military successes, viewed itself as doing the work of God and being sanctioned by God. Indeed, Islam taught that God determined all things. But eventually its further attempts at conquest were stymied by the French in the West and by Byzantium in the north. And internally, Islamic government became increasingly corrupt and distant from its people. Moreover, dogma was hard-pressed to come to terms with the newly translated Greek thought. As Durant notes, in a society where government, law, and morality are bound up with a religious creed, any attack upon that creed is viewed as menacing the foundations of social order itself.[334]

So, Islamic societies confronted a value conflict that other troubled civilizations had faced before and others would face later—i.e., they could continue to evolve through debate and change or they could return to older fundamentalist values, which seemed to be the source of past glory, or at least peaceful security.

In the event, Islam turned back. As it turned its eyes to the past, philosophy atrophied, books were burned, and "heretics" killed. True science never had a chance. In effect, the Islamic societal animal was not able to transcend the limitations of its essentially tribal culture to move into a philosophic stage of cultural evolution. Moreover, after the work of Averroes and others in Spain led to the transmission of ancient works to Medieval Europe, the learned traditions of civilizations conquered by Islam were extinguished. Virtually none of the traditions, or even works, of Islam's Golden Age has survived to modern times.

Medieval Europe

Christian Europe encountered a similar challenge but responded differently. Its challenge came later than Islam's, because, among other things, 1,000 years ago Europe had neither the wealth, nor the universities, nor the political security enjoyed by Islam. Indeed, during the Dark Ages, Europe had, in the absence of trade and a modicum of affluence, declined to a primitive state in scientific and philosophic thinking. It had lost contact with much of the fertile thinking of Greek philosophy and no longer enjoyed the day-to-day benefits of Roman institutions of law and learning.

Nonetheless, through the Catholic Church, it had preserved and extended the essence of a philosophic metaphysics, which proved to be essential for the development of science. But for this philosophic inheritance to bear fruit, for the practical development of science, sufficient stability and affluence in society were required. That prerequisite was attained with the 'Renaissance of the 12th century,' when new generations of philosophers found a supportive niche in society.

Europe's intellectual inheritance, a marriage of Judeo-Christian teachings and Greek philosophy, proved exceptionally fertile. Its uniqueness began with Judaism's departure from other religions of the ancient world. Other religions were forms of polytheism in which gods were parts of nature. The Jews, however, believed in a single God who created the natural world as an act of will, which implied that God transcends the natural world. Moreover, they believed that God established a covenant with the people of Israel: if they adhered to his laws, he would enable them to prosper. A consequence of these religious views was a belief that one could learn more about the transcendent God by learning more about His creation.

Contemporaneous with the Jews but taking a different tack, Greek speculation attempted to employ reason to perceive the basis of the world, notably through Plato's hypotheses about 'forms.' In his view, natural objects were somehow derived from abstract universal forms that account for the qualities that all like-things have in common. Scribner uses the example that 'equality' is what all equal things have in common and 'beauty' is what all beautiful things have in common. Plato called the realm of intelligible forms "Being" and the realm of visible objects "Becoming." Thereby was planted the concept that a reality existed, which was not immediately apparent to the senses. This approach led to logical difficulties, not the least of which was that the realm of 'Being' transcended earth and was essentially supernatural. Aristotle subsequently found such an approach unworkable, and shifted to a concept of 'universals.'

Nonetheless, Plato's attempts to work within this metaphysics and to extend the work of Greek philosophers guided some basic logical approaches to gaining a naturalistic understanding. "Within the realm of Being, [Plato] distinguishes mathematics from dialectic, the former proceeding deductively from hypotheses to conclusions and the latter proceeding upward from hypotheses to non-hypothetical first principle. ... Dialectic, the ascending kind of reasoning portrayed in the Socratic dialogues, provides a deeper understanding, for once it has reached its goal and grasped the first principle, all the rest can be seen to follow deductively without images."[335]

Plato's thinking entered Christian metaphysics through Saint Augustine, who acquired it from the works of the pagan philosopher Plotinus (204-270 A.D.). Augustine found Plato's dualistic construct useful to explain the relationship between God and nature. Here Plato's resort to a supernatural explanation suited Augustine (as it did not Aristotle), for he was able to equate the First Form in Being with God. God was the ultimate source of everything. He created the natural world by first creating formless matter and then imposing form on it. The Forms were ideas in God's mind. Out of his work emerged a metaphysics that encouraged man to think abstractly about the nature of the world. The world was God's creation, and one could 'know' God more deeply by understanding the nature of the world more fully.

This approach opened Christianity to Greek philosophy and reason. Christian Scholasticism in the medieval period was accordingly described as neo-Platonic. Indeed, Scribner believes that Augustine gave Western civilization a uniquely philosophical religion through his formulations. Still Augustine did not believe that all knowledge about the nature of the world stemmed from reason. He insisted that it also depended on revelation and faith in God. All in all, such a construct was a long way from science, but it opened the door to serious metaphysical speculation.

EMERGENCE OF A NEW PHILOSOPHIC OUTLOOK IN THE WEST

After the 12th century, Medieval Europe began tracing a path remarkably similar to the one followed by Islam in the conflict between religion and philosophy. But at a critical juncture, Europe took a different turn by following the path to the Age of Reason. The new path was made possible institutionally by the establishment of new universities and by joining an inherited philosophic outlook with newly discovered Greek thinking to create a new *scientific* way of viewing the world. Let's follow along that path, for it is a remarkable story.

Establishment of Universities and Communities of Scholars

Communities of scholars, whether in formal universities or more informal networks such as the Royal Society in 18th century England, are essential to the growth of science because they can invest concentrated energy into the pursuit of abstract questions; because they can efficiently share knowledge of new discoveries and new approaches to subject areas; and because, through mutual critique, they can test and refine conclusions.

In Europe, antecedents of universities were first encouraged by Charlemagne when cathedrals, monasteries, parish churches, and convents opened schools for the general education of boys and girls. Although many of these declined after the Carolingians, important cathedral schools flourished at Paris, Chartres, Orleans, Tours, Laon, Reims, Liege, and Cologne. In England, the University of Oxford was founded somewhat spontaneously, independent of any cathedral. There were also important schools in the south, notably the University of Bologna.

These universities were at first unlike our modern ones inasmuch as governance and institutional structure were at a minimum. Teachers and students were a peripatetic lot: in 1100, the school followed the teacher, by 1200, the teacher followed the school. At the close of the 11th century, learning was still centered on the seven liberal arts of the traditional curriculum: grammar, rhetoric, logic, arithmetic, geometry, music, and astronomy. In the 12th century, however, fields of learning expanded and the pursuit of knowledge became more structured: the new logic, the new mathematics, and the new astronomy were added, and the professional faculties of law, medicine, and theology were created.[336] What had been essentially a guild of teachers became a union of faculties. By the middle of the thirteenth century, in Paris, for example, the university was restructured so that the masters were divided into four faculties — i.e. theology, canon law, medicine, and the "arts."

Evolutionary Shift to a Scientific Outlook

New universities, with religious foundations, increasingly drew on Greek philosophy to augment a neo-Platonic worldview. As was the case for Islam a few hundred years earlier, the re-acquaintance with the works of the ancient world came from newly available translations. The reactions by the most influential scholars of the day produced Scholasticism, most fully articulated by Saint Thomas Aquinas. That process shaped the West's acceptance of a scientific outlook that had been foreclosed to Islam by its response to a similar set of circumstances.

Translations
The relatively closed intellectual world of medieval Christendom was illuminated by a wider exposure to the philosophy of ancient Greece by means of new translations of early works into Latin via the Arabic. But why hadn't Europe inherited the fruit of Greek thought directly via the Roman Empire? Durant noted that "Medieval Europe was divided into Latin and Greek halves, mutually hostile and ignorant. The Latin heritage, except of law, was forgotten in the Greek East; the Greek heritage, except in the Sicilies, was forgotten in the West." [337]

The result was that Western Europe had to rediscover Greek philosophy through translations. Having long been under the yoke of a religious orthodoxy, Europe, at least in the universities, reacted as though it had found a rich new world in these.

One important stream of translations came through the Jews migrating from Moslem realms into Christendom. As they lost knowledge of Arabic, they translated many works into Hebrew, the only language known by the entire 'scattered race.' For example, Moses ibn Tibbon translated from the Arabic Euclid's *Elements,* Avicenna's smaller *Canon*, al-Razi's *Antidotary*, and Averroes' shorter commentaries on Aristotle. In turn, these were translated into Latin.

The main stream of translations, however, was directly from Arabic into Latin. About 1060, Constantine the African translated al-Razi's *Liber Experimentorum*, Hunain's version of Hippocrates' *Aphorisms* and Galen's *Commentary*. In Toledo, shortly after the conquest of the Moors, Archbishop Raymond commissioned a translation of Arabic works of science and philosophy. Durant notes that most of the translators were Jews who knew Arabic, Hebrew, Spanish, and sometimes Latin. The busiest member of the group was a converted Jew, John of Spain. He translated a veritable library of works by Avicenna, al-Ghazali, al-Farabi, and al-Khwarizmi. Through this last work, Hindu-Arabic numerals were introduced to the West.

Durant considered that the greatest of the translators was Gerard of Cremona, also working in Toledo. He undertook 71 translations. These included Greek works of Aristotle, Euclid, Archimedes, and Galen, as well as several works of Greek astronomy, four volumes of Greco-Arabic physics, eleven books of Arabic medicine (including the largest works of al-Razi and Avicenna), fourteen works of Arabic mathematics and astronomy, and seven Arabic works on geomancy and astrology. Durant declares: "No other man in history has ever done so much to enrich one culture with another. We can only compare Gerard's industry with that of Hunain ibn Ishaq and al-Mamun's *House of Wisdom*, which in the ninth century had poured Greek science and philosophy into an Arabic mold."[338]

Later on, William of Moerbeke did a series of translations directly from the Greek into Latin that almost rivals the work of Gerard of Cremona. Partly at the request of St. Thomas Aquinas, he translated works of Aristotle, Plato, Hippocrates, and Galen.[339]

The Response of Western Scholars

Western European culture reached a situation similar to that in Islam: scholars in a society ruled by religious orthodoxy found access to the brilliance of Greek thinking and were increasingly intoxicated by the possibilities of new worldviews.

At first, this resurgence of intellectual speculation was restricted to theologians in universities governed by the Church. Speculation was kept within the confines of the faith—i.e., Greek philosophy had to be shown to be compatible with Christian dogma. Yet to do so logically necessitates that one partly relinquish an essentially faith-driven—or mystical—view of human knowledge for a more fact-based and empirical view. The Church and its theologians were not unaware of potentially fateful consequences of such a shift but felt that the popularity of Aristotle in all the Christian universities needed to be addressed and possibly countered. Indeed, Durant argues that Thomas Aquinas was led to write his *Summas* to halt the threatened liquidation of Christian theology by Arabic interpretations of Aristotle.

Christendom's confrontation of the implications of Greek thought can be glimpsed in the works of three men of the time: Peter Abelard, Albertus Magnus, and St. Thomas Aquinas. That process inevitably entailed freeing man's mind from all-embracing dictates of faith; it necessitated securing latitude for the exercise of reason. Thus the process had to confront the Church's long-term suspicion of the dangers of heresy, for in prior centuries, the Church had often squelched ideas that might threaten its claims to guide men's lives.

Peter Abelard, one of the eminent thinkers in the early 12th century, advocated the use of reason in pursuing truth. Around 1120 A.D. he wrote the *Dialectica*, a treatise on logic in the Aristotelian sense. He argued that truth cannot be contrary to truth; the truths of the scriptures must agree with the findings of reason, else the God who gave us both would be deluding us with one or the other.[340] His *Sic et Non* is, according to Durant, almost a declaration of independence for philosophy. Abelard wrote in *On the Divine Unity and Trinity:*

> For my students, because they were always seeking for rational and philosophic explanations, asking rather for reasons they could understand than for mere words, saying it would be futile to utter words which the intellect could not possibly follow, that nothing could be believed unless it could first be understood, and that it was absurd for anyone to preach to others a thing which neither he himself, nor those whom he sought to teach, could comprehend.[341]

In this view, the facts of science could not be in conflict with theological doctrine because they are truths about the same thing. Doctrine assumes that there is one Creator and one plan that can be perceived through different channels—i.e. of the theologian and the natural scientist. Much of this doctrine could be traced to St. Augustine, who argued that we have an obligation to know God and to understand the sense in which we have been created in his image and likeness. He believed you know the maker by His works. This formulation was accepting of what evolved into scientific inquiry, becoming one of the modes by which one knows God.

Nonetheless, St. Bernard and William of St. Thierry called attention to the dangers in Abelard's works. As a result a church council condemned a number of his propositions. Pope Innocent II issued a decree confirming the sentence of the council, imposing perpetual silence upon Abelard and ordering his confinement in a monastery.[342]

Such reasoning, however, was not easily suppressed. Other writers, excited by Greek philosophy, especially Averroes' presentation of it, continued to 'push the envelope.' Durant states that around 1240, Averrroism became almost a fashion among the educated Italian laity. Thousands accepted Averroistic doctrines that natural law rules the world without any interference by God.[343]

Under increasing intellectual pressure, the Church was defended by two different camps: the mystic-Platonic, mostly Franciscans; and the intellectual-Aristotelian, mostly Dominicans. The former argued, like most mystics, that the best defense of religion lay in man's direct consciousness of a spiritual reality deeper than all intellectual fathoming. They aimed at the good rather than the true.

Albertus Magnus undertook an Aristotelian defense. As Durant puts it, he loved knowledge and admired Aristotle this side of heresy. He surveyed all of his major works and undertook to interpret them in Christian terms. He employed Averroes' commentaries, cited Avicenna extensively, and drew on Maimonides' *Guide to the Perplexed*. In effect, he "gave Aristotle to the Latins." Furthermore he accumulated a storehouse of Arabic, Jewish, and Christian thought and argument, to be drawn upon by his pupil Thomas Aquinas.[344] More concretely, he was also deeply interested in the scientific spirit. He rejected the explanation of natural phenomena as the will of

God. He believed that "God acts through natural causes, and man must seek him there."[345]

St. Thomas Aquinas, who studied under Albertus Magnus in both Paris and Cologne, made a definitive attempt to reconcile much of Aristotelian philosophy with church teachings—i.e., to preserve all the possibilities of reason within the umbrella of faith. Importantly, in so doing, he defined a metaphysics that proved fruitful for the beginnings of scientific thinking.

In attempting to follow in his master's footsteps, Aquinas wrote extensively, publishing writings that would fill 10,000 double-column folio pages. His most extensive work was the *Summa Theologica*, an attempt to expound and defend Catholic doctrine using scripture *and* reason. At the very beginning of this work, Aquinas addresses the issue of what we know through reason and what we "know" through faith:

> Knowledge is a natural product, derived from the external corporeal senses and the internal sense called consciousness of the self. It is an extremely limited knowledge ... but within its limits, knowledge is trustworthy, and we need not fret over the possibility that the external world is a delusion. ... Since the intellect draws all its natural knowledge from the senses, its direct knowledge of things outside itself is limited to bodies—to the 'sensible' or sensory world. It cannot directly know the super-sensible, meta-physical world—the minds within bodies, or God in his creation; but it may by analogy derive from sense experience an indirect knowledge of other minds, and likewise of God. ... Nevertheless it is desirable to distinguish what we understand through reason and what we believe by faith.[346]

Karl Pribram, the economic historian, emphasizes the significance of this philosophical approach, which in some ways opened the door more fully to the practical power of reason. In accord with the Aristotelian principles of reasoning, the mind was seen as capable of using abstraction to derive general notions from the "essential" (the neo-Platonic) features common to a group or class of comparable objects. Accordingly, the universals which, according to neo-Platonic philosophy, were believed to exist independently of observable objects were now found to be directly accessible to the human mind through processes of analyzing the individual things. Thereby, a methodology arose that combined direct observation with deductions from abstract concepts.[347]

By melding Aristotelian methods with medieval theology, Aquinas made a clear distinction between revelation and reason as separate sources of knowledge and illuminated a metaphysical view of the world conducive to further investigation. Accordingly, he created a basis for believing that, outside strictly religious issues, a large sphere of questions could be treated independently of metaphysical considerations and with a certain degree of flexibility.[348]

Many orthodox Catholic theologians reacted much as orthodox Islam had a century earlier. According to Durant, the Franciscans were shocked by Aquinas' *intellectualism*, "his exaltation of intellect above will, of understanding above love." They believed that accepting this philosophy represented the triumph of Aristotle over Augustine and the victory of paganism over Christianity. Accordingly, their counterattack followed speedily. The Bishop of Paris issued a decree branding certain propositions as heresy, including three expressly directed against 'Brother Thomas.' A few days later, Robert Kilwardby, a leading Dominican, persuaded the masters of the University of Oxford to denounce various Thomistic doctrines. John Peckham, Archbishop of Canterbury, officially condemned Thomism, and urged a return to Bonaventure and St. Francis.

Aquinas, now three years dead, could not defend himself. But in what must be one of history's more dramatic turns, Albertus Magnus, although elderly, rushed from Cologne to Paris to defend the works of his student. He persuaded the Dominicans of France to stand by their fellow friar. After subsequent decades of intellectual conflict, the Dominicans convinced Pope John XXII that Aquinas had been a saint. His canonization in 1323 gave victory to Thomism. In 1879 Pope Leo XIII, and in 1921 Pope Benedict XV, while not pronouncing the works of St. Thomas free from all error, made them the official philosophy of the Catholic Church.

With Aquinas' broad metaphysics, medieval Scholasticism reached its apogee in its attempt to rationalize Christian doctrinal understanding of the universe, its purpose, and its end. As such, it could not leave out the scientific dimension of understanding the world.

Durant concludes that intellectually, Aquinas not only succeeded in reconciling Aristotle with Christianity but also won "an epochal victory for reason." As a practical matter, his triumph brought the Age of Faith to an end and opened the door to the Age of Reason. These momentous events occurred about a century and a half after 'the closing of the Islamic mind.'[349]

While the above portrayal is undoubtedly too deterministic, it can be regarded as a defining event of the age. The growing affluence of Europe, the large numbers of students at universities, the disputatious style of learning, and the growing exposure to Greek philosophy made these new modes of thinking inevitable. Once the foundations of epistemological philosophy had been laid and society had grown sufficiently affluent for individuals to pursue the necessary speculations, deeper application of reason and the evolution of science likewise become inevitable. In evolutionary terms, when efficacious random intellectual mutations occur in an opportunity niche, they proliferate.

Equally importantly, the political division in Europe between church and state made the squelching of unwelcome thoughts by the Church much more difficult than in Islam. Indeed, at some level, the Church may have recognized this reality and found Aquinas' work a tolerable, if imperfect, compromise.

THE BEGINNINGS OF SCIENCE

So the door was open to speculative and scientific reasoning in a way found in no other culture. While significant scientific discovery did not pick up steam until the 16th century, critical philosophic groundwork had been laid. But such matters are not all or nothing; once and for all. The Church would still force Galileo to recant his views and other scientific investigators would end up at the stake when their works seemed to threaten the faith.

Moreover, society at large still presented an inhospitable environment. Durant describes that milieu well in *The Age of Reason Begins*: "Thought has to live in a jungle of superstitions: astrology, numerology, palmistry, portents, the evil eye, witches, goblins, ghosts, demons, incantations, exorcisms, dream interpretations, oracles, miracles, quackery, and occult qualities, curative or injurious... To the poor in body and mind, superstition is a treasured element in the poetry of life, gilding dull days with exciting marvels, and redeeming misery with magic powers and mystic hopes."[350]

As late as the 17th century, Sir Thomas Browne, in 1646, required 652 pages to list the superstitions current in that day. In 1597 King James VI of Scotland (to become King James I of England) published a *Demonologie*, ascribing to witches the power to haunt houses, to make men and women love or hate, to transfer disease from one person to another, to kill by roasting an effigy, and to raise devastating storms. He advocated the death penalty for all witches and magicians. Between 1560 and 1600 some 8,000 women were burned as witches in a Scotland numbering a mere million souls, averaging about one every other day.[351] Only with increasing education and a growing awareness of the insights of science did such gross superstition begin to give way.

Laying the Groundwork for Progress

Reaching a threshold for substantial scientific endeavors, however, entailed changes and developments that were conceptual, practical, and institutional—and it required almost 300 years.

Conceptual Hurdles

At the risk of oversimplification, the conceptual hurdle involved establishing a broadly accepted methodology of problem definition, fact gathering, and verification. With the door ajar to natural reason, academics moved more surely on a pragmatic path of scientific method. Roger Bacon (1214 - 1292) was instrumental in illuminating that path even though he did not achieve major breakthroughs of his own. His work took place in the 13th century when scholars had rediscovered Aristotle and perceived the prospects for progress. Such a group of scholars, including Alexander Neckham, Robert Grosseteste, and Adam Marsh, formed at Oxford and began a 'scientific' tradition. Roger Bacon studied under them and was to inherit their tradition. He also studied in Italy learning Greek and

becoming acquainted with Moslem medicine. He fully acknowledged his intellectual debt to the work of his predecessors as well
as to Islamic science and philosophy generally, and, through these,
to the Greeks.

Durant highlights the importance of Bacon's contributions to
shaping scientific development. While science in Bacon's view employed experiment as its method, its aim was to present its conclusions in mathematical form. For example, he taught that "all
nonspiritual phenomena are the product of matter and force; all
forces act uniformly and regularly, and may consequently be expressed by lines and figures; 'it is necessary to verify the matter by
demonstrations set forth in geometrical lines;' ultimately all science
is mathematics. But though mathematics is the result... [t]he most
rigorous conclusions of logic leave us uncertain until they are confirmed by experience...." [352]

Centuries passed before this approach came into its own, but
it influenced a growing tradition. In that tradition, Francis Bacon
noted much later that it is easier to learn from error than from con-
fusion: If your data does not verify the mental construct, then perhaps the construct must be changed. But without a hypothesis to
be tested, one is bound to be bewildered by a vast array of possible
observables.

Kuhn terms these mental constructs that hypothesize how
a phenomenon works 'paradigms.' His work is replete with examples showing how early scientists formulated relatively crude
models to account for phenomena and, how, over time, data were
collected to try to verify the models. Sometimes the data led to a refinement of the model, but more often the model was relinquished
entirely in favor of a paradigm that had greater explanatory and
predictive power.

Practical Hurdles
In addition to conceptual methodology to pursue the validity of a
paradigm, one inevitably needs the practical means of obtaining
data *beneath the senses*, viz., by means of instrumentation. In addition, advances were required in mathematics if deeper physical
laws were to be formulated.

Instrumentation

For hundreds of years, most instrumentation was invented or just discovered by scattered efforts unrelated to scientific inquiry. But in most instances, scientists realized how such discoveries—lenses, clocks, and the utility of mathematics, for example—related to and served their needs.

Lenses

Daniel Boorstin notes that there is no record of when eyeglasses were invented. He surmised that the discovery was by chance by some glassmaker, perhaps when making disks for leaded windows. Perhaps he was testing a disk and found to his surprise that he could see better. But the utility of this discovery was overlooked for ages. From the first recorded use of eyeglasses before 1300 until the invention of the telescope 300 years later, there was no mention of their utility for scientific purposes.

It was probably not mere incuriosity. For one thing, there was no paradigm dealing with light refraction. Predisposed to 'perfect forms' such as the sphere, scientists encountered complex physical aberrations that led them nowhere in terms of theory. Further they had no useful theory about the physical nature of light. Their thinking was dominated by how people see rather than the phenomenon of light. For example, Plato and the Pythagoreans described seeing as a process whereby the eye's emanations somehow encompassed the object seen.

Moreover—and we will touch upon this later—Boorstin indicates that one of the deepest prejudices of the time was that truth and reliable knowledge could come only from the unaided and, particularly the *unmediated*, human senses.

So, further development of instruments was still to be the fruit of accidents. Galileo wrote in 1623: "We are certain the first inventor of the telescope was a simple spectacle-maker who, handling by chance different forms of glasses, looked also by chance, through two of them, one convex and the other concave, held at different distances from the eye; saw and noted the unexpected result; and thus found the instrument." Boorstin believes that this happening must have occurred more than once and history discloses one specific instance—in the shop of an obscure Dutch spectacle-maker named

Hans Lippershey in Middleburg about 1600. Two children were playing with his lenses. When they looked through two of them at the same time and gazed at a distant weathervane, they found it wonderfully magnified. Lippershey began making telescopes, and applied for what we termed a patent from the States General of the Netherlands. (Partly because of false claims by imitators, the States General turned him down.)[353]

Finally lenses were applied to scientific efforts—not yet to the theory of light, but to astronomy. In 1609, Galileo, then a professor and an accomplished instrument-maker in Venice, became aware of the offer of a telescope to the Senate and promptly made one for himself, improving on the design in the process.

He began to test the telescope in various applications, turning it to the heavens with revolutionary effect. He saw a myriad of stars and questioned whether the universe was infinite. He discovered four moons of Jupiter. He speculated that if Jupiter had satellites and the earth had a moon, perhaps the earth orbited the sun. He was aware of Copernicus' 'hypothesis' and had read Kepler's first book, but had not been ready to accept a heliocentric view of the solar system. The new explosion of data—thanks to the telescope—fully persuaded him otherwise.

The use of lenses soon led to the development of the microscope. At first Galileo tried using the telescope for this purpose but could not achieve the magnification he had when looking at the heavens. Moreover, the prejudice against mediating the senses persisted: while the magnified view of the heavens generally corresponded with what one could see with the naked eye, the sights from a microscope were counterintuitive. But others persevered: Robert Hooke published *Micrographia* in 1665, and by 1678 Leeuwenhoek was corresponding with the Royal Society on his findings.

Clocks
Man, early on in civilization, was conscious of the utility of measuring the passage of time. Various crude methods were employed: the passing of sand in an hour glass, the flowing of water from a bowl with a hole near the bottom, and the burning of candles. Boorstin cites an example from Roman courts where attorneys from

opposing sides were given equal amounts of time to make their arguments. They followed the Athenian practice of using a water bowl that emptied in about 20 minutes, a period termed *clepsydrae*. If the attorney needed extra time, he might ask for several.[354]

These methods were, however, unwieldy to break day and night into discrete segments for man's activities. The first practical mechanical means for measuring time were developed at monasteries to designate seven canonical hours of prayer during the course of the day. The first devices were weight-driven machines designed to strike a bell at measured intervals. Indeed, the word "clock" is derived from the Middle Dutch word for bell. But it was not until around 1330 A.D. that clocks registered the modern hour. By 1500, the Wells Cathedral in England was striking the quarter hour. And by the introduction of the pendulum, clocks could "read" minutes and then seconds of time.[355]

Once clocks were developed, they spread rapidly around Europe. Every town required a clock tower; every royal court demanded an elaborate device, showing planetary movements as well as time. The number of clock-makers grew apace, and the first pioneer-instrument makers consciously employed theories of clock-making to their needs. In ongoing attempts to improve the precision of clocks, inventers developed new devices such as the gear, the screw, the metal lathe, and gear-cutting machines. These devices made it possible in turn to develop other new scientific instruments—sextants, theodolites, micrometers, balances, barometers, microscopes, and telescopes.[356]

Such instruments made it possible for scientists to make the kinds of measurements that vastly expanded the scope of their inquiries. Once scientists could measure time with precision, all sorts of new observational capabilities were possible. Precise regularities could be observed, and proving hypotheses (predictions) became more feasible. And these hypotheses, particularly in the area of dynamics, increasingly lent themselves to the use of mathematics.

Clocks also captured scientists' imaginations in other, unexpected, ways. Kepler, for example, in describing the mathematics of planetary motion stated: "My aim is to show that the celestial machine is to be likened not to a divine organism but rather to a clockwork."

Example of Clocks in China

For a contrast in cultural outlook, it is illuminating to compare how clocks fared in the
West to how clocks fared in China. In 1090, Su Sung, a high Chinese civil servant
constructed a 30 foot high astronomical clock in the imperial gardens. A magnificent
achievement for the time, it embodied a huge clockwork driven by flowing water.

But when a new emperor came to the throne, the previous emperor's calendar, as
reflected in the workings of the clock, was declared faulty. Such declarations were
customary to establish the legitimacy of the new emperor; this particular declaration led
to the dismantling of the clock, so that it soon became the making of nothing more than a
legend.

Moreover, given the connection between the calendar and the legitimacy of dynasties,
astronomical observation was kept a prerogative of the imperial bureaucracy. Private
calendar-making and astronomical observation became acts of lese majeste'. Centuries
later, when Jesuit-missionary-astronomers from the West brought clocks to the Chinese
court, the Chinese found them fascinating, but regarded them as toys.

The cultural comparison makes two points: First, the practical impact of fragmented
political power in Europe was that no institutions existed that could readily squelch
innovations throughout society in the same way that innovation could be halted in China.
Second, within China's philosophic community, there was no empirical outlook that saw
the potential utility of a new device like a clock for measuring time more precisely.

SOURCE: Daniel Boorstin, *The Discoverers*, pp. 60, 62, and 76

Mathematics

The field of mathematics has many ancient antecedents: the Greeks,
the ancient Egyptians, the Hindus, and Islamic scholars. Especially in the Greek heritage there lingered a view that mathematical
principles helped explain the functioning of nature. Ancient Greeks
particularly intuited a relationship between mathematics and aspects of creation. One example was Pythagoras' philosophy of the
'divinity of numbers,'[357] which taught that reality of the world is
created not from something material, but from a deeper abstract
plan. That abstract plan, or template, is the realm of numbers, and
numbers somehow created the material world from the cosmos.
For example, the Pythagoreans placed particular meaning on the
first four integers—i.e., the basis for the point, the line, the plane,
and the solid. The cosmic *soul*, they believed, uses numbers to create material reality.

This concept was not considered a mere abstraction, however. For example, Professor Robinson refers to the utility of the Pythagorean Theorem in practical geometry and to Pythagoras' discovery of the relationship between musical harmony and mathematical principles. With regard to music, the Greeks realized that the human mind's perception of harmony and discord is not a coincidence. Chords are perceived as harmonious because the human mind is constituted to resonate with certain combinations of frequencies—i.e. combinations of numbers on a harmonic scale. In an analogy, creation itself could be seen as an essential harmonic undertaking—i.e. it is a formal relationship among abstract entities producing the lawfulness of the cosmos itself.

A wonderful correspondence thus exists between the abstract world and the world of reality, even if the material world is imperfect. This idea has excited scientists through the ages, and it is remarkable how many mathematical relationships were formulated long before science developed the technical means of identifying a corresponding reality—e.g., the mathematics that describe the shape of the conch shell or the crystalline formation of a snowflake.

Or consider abstractions such as Pi and the square root of minus one, an 'imaginary' number. While such entities have no physical manifestation, they are essential for understanding nature. Pi is required to calculate the circumference of a circle, or its area, and imaginary numbers have powerful application in modern physics. Taking the analogy further, the cosmos almost seems to be dictated by differential equations.

Pythagoras, drawing on the implications of the correspondence between mathematics and material things, held a transcendental view of all there is: numbers were a sign of the divinity of creation, there had to be an abstract plan, and that plan must be one of mathematical relationships. This was the debt Platonism owed to Pythagoras. And, as discussed, Plato's view of ideal forms underlying reality was to powerfully influence Medieval Scholasticism. Such values, in turn, influenced scientific investigators in their endeavors early in the Age of Reason.

More specifically, "epistemological philosophy fostered the evolution of mathematical arguments, because mathematics was the prime example of its deeper understanding. Without mathematics, physics would not have been able to discover the quantitatively precise laws by which it sees beneath the surface of perceptual appearances to the nature of matter. And without physics, the rest of modern science would not be possible."[358]

Similar views were evident in much early scientific work. Galileo said that mathematics was the language of nature and thus it was plausible to assume that the use of mathematics would enable rational subjects to see into the mind of God. Further, it seems fully appropriate that Leibnitz, Descartes, and Newton (see below) were great mathematicians as well as great scientists and philosophers.

Institutional Practices Promoting Continuity and Extended Collaboration

Scientific breakthroughs that occurred throughout the West could not and did not occur in isolation, but required continuity with past efforts and discoveries as well as a broad collaboration across a continent.

Continuity in Scientific Endeavor

Inescapably, scientific effort relies on sustained data gathering, the sharing of results, and access to speculations of the past. Scientific breakthroughs are almost always controversial because initially the insight is speculative and counter to previous beliefs, and it usually lacks extensive supporting data. The supporting evidence needed to prove, verify, or disprove a conclusion is usually created over extended periods of time by many practitioners. It is almost always the work of a generation; indeed, generations of scientists. Europe's universities, the depositories of knowledge and the seat of academic enterprise, with the establishment of academic disciplines, especially in natural philosophy, lent structure, purpose, and continuity to scientific efforts.

This was not the case in other civilizations. To see how the absence of essential purpose compounded by the lack of continuity hindered scientific endeavor, let's contrast the beginnings of science in the West with how China reacted to precursors to scientific

210   *Free People, Free Markets*

knowledge. We have discussed the advanced state of China's *technological* prowess 800 to 1,000 years ago, when the Sung civilization was probably the most advanced on earth, and cited 'the Needham question' as related to possible reasons for China's subsequent stagnation. Some of the specifics bear directly on the issue of the continuity of scientific endeavors.

According to David Landes, China had neither institutions nor an extended intellectual community to discover, preserve and transmit findings of a scientific nature. Indeed, lacking a scientific approach and framework, without hypotheses and a tradition of testing hypotheses, possibilities of 'progress' were slight. Speculation, even significant insights, would slip away. Landes concluded: "[t]his want of exchange and challenge, this subjectivity, explains the uncertainty of gains and the easy loss of impetus. *Chinese savants had no way of knowing when they were right.*"[359]

An Extended Community of Scholars
Continuity was also achieved in the West through a 'community of scholars' that provided the necessary shared values and the ongoing capacity for collaboration. In the physical sciences, seminal efforts usually exceed the capabilities of any one individual, no matter how brilliant. Significant amounts of data are usually required to 'prove' the validity of a paradigm. Moreover, some initially confirmatory data might be collected, but subsequent inquiry might disclose problems, requiring in turn modified or wholly new conceptions.

How did that community of minds come about in the West? As mentioned previously, universities arose around cathedral schools in the West, which had been promoted by Charlemagne, and these new universities, notably at Oxford and Paris, provided a protected 'environmental niche' for the fragile beginnings of those interested in 'natural philosophy.' With Latin the common language of scholarship, learned men of all Western Europe were able to communicate with one another, thus amplifying what would otherwise have been fragmented efforts. Moreover, this collaboration was enhanced by the practice of professors and students traveling from one country and one institution to another, bringing ideas and experience with them in an arena disposed to inquiry and debate, and the introduction of the printing press was, of course, invaluable in the dissemination of new knowledge.

But even though results accumulated, something more was needed. What von Hayek referred to as 'spontaneous order' in other fields came about here as well. Boorstin describes this order as a 'Parliament of Scientists.' One beginning was in Paris through the efforts of Marin Mersenne (1588-1648), who helped create what Boorstin refers to as an 'invisible college.' Such entities were invisible—no physical walls existed—much as Scribner's societal animal is. Yet there exists a manifest collectivity from the group's capability to interact.

Mersenne lived in the Minims Franciscan monastery near Paris. Boorstin reports that his personal charm and industry made the monastery a center of scientific life for Paris, and Paris an intellectual center of Europe. He gathered some of the most inquisitive minds of the day from Western Europe, and, indeed, it was there Pascal first met Descartes. His correspondence reached from London to Constantinople, bringing together the latest discoveries of Huygens, van Helmont, Hobbes, and Torricelli. An English friend might request any new observations—magnetical, optical, mechanical, musical, or mathematical—that had come his way, or Mersenne might send out word of Parisian experiments with telescopes, report on the chemistry of tin, and spread news on a sensitive plant from the West Indies. When foreign intellectuals visited Paris, they joined one of his conferences of interest and then returned to Italy, England, the Netherlands, or wherever, where they not only spread the scientific news but also remained members of his information network.[360]

Other informal networks arose in France, but it was in England that a more formal institution emerged to serve the growing need for communication among the swelling ranks of scientists. This institution was the work of Henry Oldenburg. While not possessing a great scientific mind, he was well educated, well traveled—he was very taken with Mersenne's salon—and well connected. Early on, he was acquainted with the scientists gathered at Oxford, who were to become the nucleus of the Royal Society.

In England after the Restoration, under Charles the Second's patronage, a group of English men of science met in 1660 to found a new academy, the Royal Society, for the advancement of the sciences. In 1662 Oldenburg was made Secretary. He filled this role until his death. Under his leadership, the Society reached out for new discoveries, solicited input from correspondents who did not attend the meetings, printed and distributed copies of important work, carried out translations, and supported the use of 'letters' as a means of reporting new work. Letters proved to be the most practical way of presenting incremental work speedily, while books were less timely, more expensive, and, in that day, often subject to censorship. In 1665, he published the first scientific periodical, *Philosophic Transactions*, which became a model for modern scientific publications.

The English clergyman Joseph Glanvill boasted that this "great ferment of useful and generous knowledge, makes a bank of all useful knowledge, and makes possible the mutual assistance that the practical and theoretical parts of physics affords each other. ... The Royal Society ... has done more than philosophy of a notional way since Aristotle opened shop."[361]

From the time applied reason was freed from dogma to the time science as we know it took off in earnest, several hundred years elapsed. Two to three centuries passed before the telescope, the microscope, and accurate clocks were available, before common standards of measurement evolved, and before different institutions and nations were able to compare results. But when these prerequisites came together, a favorable philosophical and material environment arose in the West, and institutions and shared values produced an increasingly productive scientific tradition.

Early Scientific Developments

In the 16th century, science stood on the brink of a radiation of ideas comparable to the radiation of species that followed when the first air-breathing fish struggled out of the ocean on ungainly flippers. According to Phillip Scribner the Darwinian model is especially apt to describe the evolution of science: one can "liken alternative theories to species of organisms which reproduce from one mind to another and compete with one another to occupy certain niches (that is, to explain certain aspects of the world). ... They are naturally selected when they convince other members of the scholarly community to believe them (that is, rationally selected). ... It is rational selection because of what those other members are looking for, not just any 'values', but certain values such as preferring a more coherent explanation, something that fits in better with other theories they accept, something based on mathematics or experiment, ..."[362]

Out of a vast array of activity, several developments contributed significantly to early progress in scientific discovery and are especially illuminating of the process: (1) advances in astronomy and mechanics; (2) advances in medical understanding; and (3) the beginnings of chemistry and electricity.

Each of these achievements is intellectually prodigious in its own right, and collectively can illuminate key concepts of scientific development. First, progress in each of these areas required an empirical worldview that held that a reality existed beyond what was immediately accessible to our senses. Second, the extant models of explanation, which had been inherited from antiquity, increasingly were seen to lack explanatory power. Third, whatever new model came into being would have to be consistent with the scientific process of data collection and hypothesis confirmation. Fourth, hypotheses would have to be formulated that could be checked by data that was observable through a process of inference. Fifth, new models are almost invariably disputed at first because they go against inherited 'wisdom' and because, initially, insufficient evidence is at hand to be absolutely dispositive. Overall, the *social system* would have to be open to new ideas and would have to tolerate debate about them—perhaps over the course of decades.

Astronomy
The history of man's growing understanding of astronomy provides a prime example of the scientific tradition in the West because much of the knowledge is counter-intuitive and can be gleaned only through the scientific method. The average individual asks, how do I *know* that the earth spins on its axis and rotates around the sun annually? What evidence is there for this in the senses? For centuries, men countered this view with the observation that if it were so and one threw a stone in the air it would come down at a different spot. Moreover, if one relied on perception alone, it seemed unlikely that the earth could be moving and yet feel so stable and secure. Indeed, the senses led many to believe that the earth was flat.

It required two millennia from the first speculations of the Greeks to the time of Galileo for the truth to emerge indisputably.

Early attempts at understanding began with myths. The ancient Egyptians observed how every day the sun-god Ra rode his boat through the sky. Every night, riding another boat through the waters under the earth, he arrived back to begin his daily journey again.[363] The ancient Greeks took this further and speculated that the earth was a sphere over which a rotating dome holding the stars rotated. Aristotle believed that precisely 55 concentric, nesting spheres constituted the heavens and accounted for all the planets and stars.

Interestingly, Aristarchus hypothesized the correct view—a heliocentric view—as early as the third century B.C. And as mentioned earlier, al-Biruni in the Islamic world also concluded that the available data could be explained by a heliocentric view. The views of both men, however, remained in the arena of speculation. Without further hard data, eventually to be gleaned with the availability of telescopes for example, geocentric and heliocentric models were equally arguable. Moreover, because the geocentric model was so much more established through Ptolemy's work and the systematic accumulation of data, it had immediate practical value that was initially lacking in a heliocentric view.

Ptolemy had taken the extensive astronomical readings of the Egyptians and others to produce a model of the heavens that had considerable utility, permitting the development of a calendar, a means for navigation, and a means for predicting the movement of heavenly bodies. Indeed, even today, it provides a reasonable approximation for predicting the movement of the observable planets in the sky.

However, with more accurate observations and the accumulation of evidence, the model became increasingly convoluted. Particularly, the system did not explain the irregularities in the observed motion of the planets and, in time, acquired a variety of complicated epicycles, deferents, equants, and eccentrics, which still could not explain anomalies. By the 16th century A.D., apparent problems caused the most inquiring minds to consider alternative models. That inquiry and its resulting developments are seen clearly through the works of Copernicus, Tycho Brahe, Kepler, Galileo, and Isaac Newton.

Copernicus
While Copernicus (1473-1543) was wonderfully versatile in his interests—his education included mathematics, physics, and astronomy—he was only an amateur astronomer and thus not an immediate prospect for advancing the heliocentric view.

Nonetheless, he was aware of speculation by Leonardo da Vinci, who had written: "The sun does not move .... The earth is not in the center of the circle of the sun, not in the center of the universe."[364] More importantly, he was uneasy with the cumbersome nature of the Ptolemaic model. Since the time of the ancient Greeks, there had been a sense that *simple* explanations were most in accord with the 'mathematical' underpinnings of life. Ptolemy himself argued that in seeking to explain phenomena, science should adopt the simplest possible hypothesis consistent with accepted observations. Copernicus' co-worker, Domenico da Novara, held that no system as cumbersome and inaccurate as the Ptolemaic had become could possibly be true of nature.[365]

It was an attempt to find a simpler explanation for astronomical data that led Copernicus to broach an alternative hypothesis to that of Ptolemy. He claimed that it was only a hypothesis and did not claim to have proof. Moreover, he recognized the religious implications and, accordingly, had his first summary work published as a "trial balloon;" his full work was not published in his lifetime. Among his conclusions were:

- There is no one center of all the celestial circles or spheres.
- The center of the earth is not the center of the universe, but only of gravity and of the lunar sphere.
- All the spheres [planets] revolve about the sun as their midpoint, and therefore the sun is the center of the universe.
- What appears to us as motions of the sun arise not from its motion but from the motion of the earth and our sphere, with which [motion] we revolve around the sun like any other planet.
- The apparent retrograde and direct motion of the planets arises not from their motion but from the earth's.[366]

As potentially revolutionary as these conclusions were, they were incomplete. Copernicus still subscribed to celestial spheres, and in his belief in simplicity, assumed that the orbits of the earth and the planets were that of circles (the elliptical orbits would be discovered later). Moreover, these conclusions did not add to the day-to-day utility of the Ptolemaic system. And because he produced little data of his own—confirming data was to come from others in the future—astronomers largely ignored this work.

Tycho Brahe
Tycho Brahe, a Danish astronomer born in 1546, three years after Copernicus died, provided extensive new astronomical data, which serendipitously would be of use to other scientists—notably Kepler—who would begin to discern 'proof' of Copernicus' hypotheses.

According to Boorstin, Brahe was a phenomenon in his own right. He was a precocious astronomer as a teenager. He studied at the Universities of Copenhagen, Leipzig, and Rostock. He inherited a large fortune from his uncle, which financially sustained his investigations. In addition, his reputation led King Frederick II to endow him with the Island of Hveen, along with an income, for the purposes of astronomical observation. These sources provided him with workshops, laboratories, and assistants. With time, he catalogued the positions of one thousand stars. (Mind you, this was before the invention of the telescope, and astronomical readings were still laboriously made by sighting of relatively crude instruments.) This work displaced Ptolemy's classic catalogue, but the data did not cause him to embrace the Copernican view.

When Frederick II died, financial support dried up, and Brahe moved to Prague. One happy outcome of the move was that one of his assistants there would be Johannes Kepler.[367]

Kepler
Kepler (1571-1630), a South German, attended the University of Tuebingen, where he studied astronomy and became an early enthusiast of Copernicus. He joined Brahe in Prague, and when the latter died, Kepler inherited all of his records but not his instruments. As a consequence, Kepler perforce had to employ the results

of Brahe's observations in his attempts to develop astronomical theories. According to Durant, Kepler's skill lay in testing hypotheses, and his wisdom lay in casting them aside when they proved incompatible with observed data. For example, in seeking to plot the orbit of Mars he tried 70 hypotheses through the course of four years before he discovered that the orbit of Mars around the sun formed an ellipse and not a circle. [368] He then quickly ascertained the same conclusion for the other planets for which he had data. From this work came his first two laws. First, each planet moves in an elliptical orbit, in which one focus is the sun; second, each planet moves more rapidly when near the sun than when farther from it, and a radius drawn from the sun to the planet covers, in its motion, equal areas in equal times. He ascribed the differences in planetary speed to the greater emanation of solar energy felt by the planet as it neared the sun. (This 'energy' would be recognized as gravity by Newton.)

After puzzling another 10 years, he arrived at his third law — i.e., the square of the time of revolution of a planet around the sun is proportional to the cube root of its mean distance from the sun. Kepler was so enthusiastic about the elegance of this result that he referred to the planetary motions as a "harmony of the spheres."

Durant states that Kepler transformed a brilliant guess by Copernicus into a hypothesis worked out in impressive mathematical detail, and bequeathed to Newton the laws that would lead to the theory of gravitation. He revealed the universe as a structure of law, as a cosmos of order in which the same laws ruled the earth and the stars. [369]

Galileo

Galileo (1564-1642) was born in Pisa and studied there at the university. His early work was in physics. He determined that the swings of a pendulum, regardless of their width, took equal times, but by lengthening or shortening the arm, the frequency of oscillation changed. Also, he showed that two bodies regardless of weight fall at the same speed and that that speed increases at a uniform rate. Further, he formulated the principles of the lever and the pulley and gathered data regarding dynamics and statics.

But it was in astronomy that he made his reputation. Kepler had written him with regard to his findings on the Copernican view.

Galileo found that that view was consistent with some of his own speculations, such as the cause of the tides, but he did not speak publicly in favor of the Copernican view, undoubtedly aware of the attacks that Copernicus had suffered.

Using the telescope on which he had made a number of improvements, Galileo began to make his own astronomical observations. The concrete results regarding the huge multitude of stars, the moons of Jupiter, and the phases that Venus exhibited fully convinced him of the validity of Copernicus' work. He then spoke out that he felt that Copernicus' findings were 'proven.' But the professors at Padua refused to credit these discoveries, and indeed, as Galileo wrote to Kepler, refused even to look through the telescope.

As these views moved from hypothesis to claims of reality, the Church began to feel threatened. Many theologians felt that the Copernican astronomy was so clearly incompatible with the Bible, that if it prevailed, the Bible would lose authority and Christianity itself would suffer. Because these findings struck at the Church's geocentric views of the heavens, a fateful collision between Galileo and the Church unfolded. Galileo suffered an inquisition and was forced to renounce his conclusions. While the Church, with its considerable authority, enjoyed a temporary victory in suppressing these views, it ultimately proved ineffectual. [370]

The cat was out of the bag, the network of scientists in Western Europe was too large, and the scientific method was too well established. Intellectuals had adopted the separation of faith from reason, and, of course, the Church held little sway in Protestant lands.

Newton

Sir Isaac Newton (1642-1727) attended Cambridge University, where he studied mathematics, optics, and astronomy. As he grew in experience, Newton rejected Descartes' belief that major truths could be elicited from *a priori* principles, developing his own 'rules of philosophizing' that drew on observation, scientific method, and research.

The first of his major achievements was in mathematics where he invented calculus,[371] followed by the development of the binomial theorem. The foundation of mathematics was to help him considerably in his more renowned work in physics.

Some of his early astronomical calculations suggested to him that Kepler's elliptical orbits could result if the gravitational force between two bodies varied inversely as the square of the distance between them. He did not at first publish this conclusion because it did not seem to be fully in accord with existing estimates of the earth's diameter and the distance of the earth from the moon. Moreover, he was not sure that approximating the masses of bodies as point sources for the purpose of calculations was appropriate.

When Picard in 1671 made new measurements of the earth's diameter and a new estimate of the distance between the earth and the sun, Newton realized that his methodology was correct and agreed with actual observation. He published these results as well as subsequent conclusions in his *Principia Mathematica*, which Durant cites as being one of the key events of modern Europe.[372]

Newton viewed his work as the mathematical principles of philosophy, i.e., endeavoring "to subject the phenomena of nature to the laws of mathematics." He formulated three laws of motion:

1. Every body continues in its state of rest, or of uniform motion in a straight line, unless it is compelled to change that state by forces impressed upon it.

2. The change of motion is proportional to the motive force impressed, and is made in the direction of the straight line in which that force is impressed.

3. To every action there is always opposed an equal reaction.

Armed with these laws, and the rule of inverse squares, Newton formulated the principle of gravitation. Using these laws, he explained the attraction of Jupiter upon its satellites; and of the earth on the moon, he calculated the mass of each planet; he worked out the mathematics of ocean tides; and he reduced the trajectories of comets to regular orbits (confirming Halley's prediction). In effect, the most distant star was subject to the same mechanics and mathematics as the smallest particles on earth.

His work encountered objections and doubts. Some of these were religious in nature. Others were concerned with his failure to determine what gravity 'was' and how it transmitted its force. Nonetheless, with the continued examination and application of his laws, the effects were revolutionary. Scientists gained increasing confidence about the possibilities of unlocking nature. Ernst Mach said, "All that has been accomplished in mechanics since his day has been a deductive, formal, and mathematical development ... on the basis of Newton's laws."[373]

Of course, Newton's theories were subsequently overtaken by Einstein's theory of relativity and the associated new paradigms. Relativity provided more accurate results when bodies were traveling at high speeds and was essential for sub-atomic and astrophysical research. But, undoubtedly, there had to be a Newton before there could be an Einstein.

Medical Understanding

The beginning of modern medicine is another example of how the use of the scientific method advanced knowledge and understanding of the natural world. A key development occurred when the widely accepted work of Galen was intellectually redirected by Paracelsus, and then more concretely established by the works of the new anatomists and by investigators of the circulation of blood such as William Harvey.

Galen

Galen (c. 130-200 A.D.) was a physician born of Greek parents in Pergamum and later a resident of Rome, where he became court physician to the Emperor Marcus Aurelius. He was a prolific writer; more than 100 of his works have survived, enough to fill 20 thick volumes. He was said to be a brilliant diagnostician.

For his time, his thinking was advanced in a scientific sense. He did a special study of the pulse, showing that the arteries carried blood and not air, as others believed. He believed that knowledge was cumulative and tried to learn from great men such as Hippocrates who had preceded him. He believed that conclusions should be based on direct observation whenever possible and that learning from books had severe limitations. He was an experimental physician; yet, as we shall see, he speculated about theories to aid in diagnosis even when hard data was not in hand, an approach that created problems for subsequent generations of physicians.

Two such problem areas confounding subsequent generations involved anatomy and the overall basis for health. With regard to anatomy, Galen was severely limited by the Roman proscription against the dissection of cadavers. Although he did much surgery on gladiators, on only two occasions did he have an opportunity to view the entire skeletal remains of a human. Otherwise, his anatomies were performed on monkeys for external anatomy and on pigs for internal anatomy, projecting these results on what would be found in man. Given that both Islam and Christianity also forbade dissections, the resulting errors were not disclosed for a millennium or more.

With regard to physiology, he passed on classical speculations, which were crude and inaccurate attempts at creating a model from which a physician could work. Disease according to these views was caused by an upset of the balance of the four cardinal "humors" — i.e. blood, phlegm, choler, and melancholy — in the body. Disease came from an excess or deficiency in one or another of them. It followed that there were as many different diseases as there were individuals because disease was a disorder of a person's unique humoral relations.

It is easy in retrospect to see that this model could lead nowhere useful. In one of history's ironies, generations of physicians who believed in Galen's pronouncements disregarded his caution about pedantic medicine and his urging to experiment. His works were practically canonized and declared authoritative both in Islam and in late Medieval Europe.[374]

Paracelsus

Paracelsus (1493-1541) was one of life's great rebels and discontents, a man of "mystic recklessness" according to Boorstin. Given the breadth of his interests, it is not surprising that he was often wrong, yet he helped find the path to modern medicine.

He took on the medical establishment of Western Europe for being pedantic, secretive, non-experimental, and often not helpful. He threw a copy of Galen's works on a student bonfire. He disparaged the *humoral* view of disease and instead championed a radically different theory that disease had some specific cause outside the body. "[W]hen he pointed outside the body, when he insisted on the uniformity of causes and the specificity of diseases, he was pointing the way to modern medicine. If his arguments were not correct, his insights and hunches were."[375]

His attacks had a practical as well as polemic side. Doctors at the time considered only herbal remedies. He urged that remedies from all of God's sources, the inorganic as well as the organic be considered. He did much work in mines and with metal workers, observing their special ailments and experimenting with remedies. "Miners' sickness, he explained, was a disease of the lungs and produced stomach ulcers. These came from the air that the miner breathed and from the minerals taken in through the lungs or the skin. He distinguished between acute and chronic poisoning, and noted the differences between the disorders caused by arsenic, by antimony, or by the alkalis. In a special section on mercury poisoning he accurately noted its symptoms...."[376]

A threatened medical establishment made him move on. The opposition of doctors prevented his writings from being published during his lifetime and his health was broken by poverty. But within decades, his views were to be diffused beyond the control of that medical establishment.

Vesalius

In the 14th and 15th centuries, barriers against dissection had eroded somewhat, at least to the extent cadavers of executed criminals were often available for that purpose. Nonetheless, given the lack of refrigeration, the process was unpleasant and hurried. Often the professor sat at a discrete distance as the surgeon-barber operated.

Although observation through dissection was increasingly possible, Galen was still held to be authoritative. Moreover, the acceptance of pragmatic new evidence was impeded by false models linking astrology to the human body. For example, popular diagrams of the *zodiac man* showed a connection between body parts and signs of the zodiac and indicated the best seasons for treatment.

Enter Andreas Vesalius (1514-1564). Vesalius was born in the Spanish Netherlands and studied at the University of Paris, developing a deep interest in surgery and anatomy. His diligence went far to change the understanding of the human body. He did hands-on dissections and prepared charts of what he learned. With the advent of publishing, his *Anatomical Tables* became widely known and a valuable teaching aid. Even so, past errors persisted because detailed examinations of the body did not extend to all parts of the body. With time, Vesalius realized that Galen had often described anatomy as found in apes rather than man. His charts made the necessary corrections and he then published *Structure of the Human Body*, a celebrated work. Ironically, but not surprisingly, his views were strongly attacked by his own teacher, Jabobus Sylvius, for irreverence toward the 'infallible' Galen. But the new chairs of anatomy at his university were disciples of Vesalius rather than Galen. And so knowledge progresses, at least as long as scientific values shape the academic culture.[377]

The Circulation of Blood
Galen also contributed to the medieval world an inaccurate model regarding the production and movement of body fluids. His views were somewhat derived from Plato, who said that three *pneuma* governed the body. Boorstin describes Galen's views as follows:

> After being inhaled, air was transformed into pneuma by the lungs, and the life process transformed one kind of pneuma into another. The liver elaborated 'chyle' from the alimentary tract into venous blood carrying the 'natural spirit,' which ebbed and flowed in the veins with a kind of tidal motion. Some of this natural spirit entered the left ventricle of the heart where it became a higher form of pneuma, the 'vital spirit.' This highest form of pneuma was diffused through the body by nerves, which Galen supposed to be hollow.[378]

Boorstin notes that Galen freely admitted the limitations of his model and that the elements of his system were elusive. Nonetheless, progress and understanding would have to await a sounder hypothesis. Ironically, such a hypothesis had already been made (likely more than once). The Arab physician Ibn al-Nafis had the idea of circulation as early as the 13th century. Later, Michael Servetus, whom Calvin had burned at the stake for heresy, described the pulmonary circulation of blood. But without the scientific method and follow-through, the truth could not be confirmed against competing models.

What was needed went beyond mere speculation. One required a systematic gathering of data in light of appropriate hypotheses. The scientific advance came when William Harvey gathered the necessary facts from his own original work and key work done by others. In his early studies, he described how arteries expanded when the heart contracted and he traced the blood carried from the left ventricle of the heart through the lungs. He then discovered other essential facts from the work of Realdo Colombo and Fabricius. Colombo showed that blood passed from the right ventricle into the left via the lungs, and defined the proper meaning of systole and diastole. Fabricius described the valves in the veins which permitted blood to flow in only one direction.

It became clear to Harvey, then, that the heart was a pump that made blood flow to nourish the organs. He was convinced that blood 'circulated' through the body, returning to the heart via the veins. But he was not able to demonstrate how the flood of blood from the arteries was returned to the veins. He simply lacked the instrumentation. He would be vindicated when the advent of the microscope permitted the discovery of the capillary system.[379]

Beginnings of Chemistry and Electricity

The fields of chemistry and electricity abound with examples of the successful application of the scientific method and the establishment of beneficial new fields of knowledge, and examination of early endeavors in these fields especially highlight the conceptual difficulties of finding useable models for directing research—but the immense payoff when the models are productive.

Chemistry

Chemistry involves the body of knowledge associated with the constituents of matter—atoms, molecules, elements, compounds, and the ways they interact. Chemistry grew out of investigative ways (but not theories) developed in alchemy.

True chemistry emerged only when earlier models were disproved by observation and analysis. For example, the theory of phlogiston was postulated in the 18th century by Georg Stahl, a professor at Halle. He interpreted combustion as the liberation of *phlogiston* from the burning material into the air. According to Durant, by 1750 most chemists in Western Europe accepted this theory of fire, but no one could explain why metals then weighed more rather than less after combustion.[380] Clearly the theory was incorrect, but much useful data were collected in trying to verify it.

New instrumentation helped. Stephen Hales devised the "pneumatic trough" in which gases could be collected in a closed vessel over water. Shortly thereafter, Joseph Black determined that one constituent of the atmosphere was *fixed air* (our carbon dioxide) and that this was a component of human exhalations. A prolific Swede experimentalist, Torbern Bergman performed over 30,000 experiments, identifying the chemical affinities of 59 substances. His student, Karl Wilhelm Scheele, is now acknowledged as the discoverer of oxygen, although his published work did not emerge until after that of Joseph Priestley.

Scheele succinctly stated the purpose of the new field of science—viz.: "The object and chief business of chemistry is skillfully to separate substances into their constituents, to discover their properties, and to compound them in different ways."[381] Scheele sent to publication in 1775 a manuscript entitled "Chemical Treatise on Air and Fire." He determined that the unpolluted atmosphere is composed of two gases: "fire-air" (our oxygen) and "vitiated air" (our nitrogen)—i.e., air that has lost "fire-air." Nonetheless, he still believed in Stahl's phlogiston theory.

Nevertheless, Joseph Priestley is usually credited with the discovery of oxygen. He had been experimenting with the gas released from the heated red oxide of mercury and concluded that it was air with less than its normal proportion of phlogiston. Ironically, he died believing in the phlogiston theory.

It was Lavoisier who made the critical connections. He determined that Priestley's gas was a distinct element and was a main constituent of the atmosphere. In an experiment involving the heating of tin with air in a sealed container, he determined that a vacuum was formed and air rushed in after the container was unsealed. He determined that in combustion, burning material took something from the air rather than released something. He named this something *oxygene*. He had in effect destroyed the phlogiston theory.[382]

Like Priestley (with whom he communicated), he determined that this gas was the kind that best supports animal life. He took these investigations further:

> Five sixths of the air we breathe is incapable of supporting the respiration of animals, or ignition and combustion: ... one fifth only of the volume of atmospheric air is respirable. Lavoisier thereupon founded organic analysis by describing respiration as the combination of oxygen with organic matter. In this process he noted a liberation of heat, as in combustion; and he further confirmed the analogy of respiration and combustion by showing that carbon dioxide and water are given off (as in respiration) by the burning of such organic substances as sugar, oil, and wax. The science of physiology was now revolutionized...[383]

Thomas Kuhn provides another example of a new paradigm through which chemistry was materially advanced. At the end of the eighteenth century scientists roughly adhered to an 'affinity' theory of chemical combinations, and were attempting to differentiate between what was a physical mixture and what was a compound. They had determined that some compounds ordinarily contained fixed proportions, by weight, of their constituents. But no chemist made use of these regularities.

It took John Dalton, who was a meteorologist and not a chemist, to provide the necessary insight. He was investigating the absorption of gas in water as a physical process in which affinity played no part. He thought he would be able to resolve his problems if he could determine the relative size and weights of the various atomic particles in his homogeneous chemical solutions. He found that in a 'chemical' reaction, atoms could combine only in one-to-one or in some other simple whole-number ratio. That assumption allowed him to determine the size and weights of elementary particles. As in other scientific advances, his conclusions were at first severely attacked, but eventually accepted. Kuhn noted that as a result of this work, "chemists came to live in a world where reactions behaved quite differently from the way they had before."[384]

Electricity

Before the 18th century, man had observed isolated phenomena related to electricity and magnetism. Ancient civilizations had noted the development of static electricity. Thales of Miletus (600 B.C.) was familiar with amber, jet, and a few other substances that when rubbed, attracted light objects such as feathers or straw. One also had the example of the magnetic needle used in navigation.

It was not until the eighteenth century, however, that growing scientific curiosity turned to electrical phenomena. Much of the initial effort went into amplifying and examining more closely the little natural phenomena available. Stephen Gray generated static charges by rubbing a glass rod. Further, he found he could transfer the charge to an ivory ball. With more experimentation he found he could transfer charges with some conducting materials and not others. Eventually he was able to conduct electricity, using strong twine over a distance of 765 feet.

Professors at Leiden discovered that an electrical charge could be stored in an empty bottle if its lower and exterior surfaces had been coated with tin foil. When several bottles were lined up a considerable charge could result. Du Fay in France found that two bodies, electrified by contact with the same body, repelled each other.[385]

Kuhn notes that in the first half of the eighteenth century there were almost as many views of the nature of electricity as there were practitioners—men like Hauksbee, Gray, Desaguliers, Du Fay, Nollett, Watson, and Franklin. Most of these views were guided by some version of the 'mechanico-corpuscular' philosophy that guided scientific research of the day, but had few specifics in common. Benjamin Franklin's model, which considered positive and negative entities inducing a fluid-like flow, became one of the first productive models.[386]In this context, Kuhn concluded that the significance of his famous work with lightening is obvious because it suggested which experiments would be worth performing and which, because directed to overly complex manifestations of electricity, would not. Kuhn states: "[f]reed from the concern with any and all electrical phenomena, the united group of electricians could pursue selected phenomena in far more detail, designing much special equipment for the task and employing it more stubbornly and systematically than electricians had ever done before. Both fact collection and theory articulation became highly directed activities."[387]

Durant notes that after these events, all Europe was alive with electrical theories and experiments. Any numbers of useful insights were gleaned. Priestley's brilliant contribution to theory was an analogy to gravitation. He suggested that the force experienced by two separate charges would vary inversely as the square of the distance between them. Volta came up with the Voltaic Pile, which was the first electrical-current battery.[388]

Yet, a deep scientific understanding was relatively slow in coming. It was not until the latter half of the nineteenth century that James Clerk Maxwell formulated the equations bearing his name. These were for electricity as revolutionary as Newton's Laws were for gravitation and dynamics. Once again, mathematics was married to physics to great effect.

Thus we see that scientific advancement, whether in astronomy, medicine, electricity, or chemistry requires far more than great minds having brilliant insights into nature. Beyond that, what is required is supporting values within society, communications allowing an ad hoc broad network of likeminded people to collaborate, and the apposite methodological approach. To exist, these elements must be congruent with the essential attributes of a societal animal. One cannot establish de novo a university or fund a great scientist in isolation and expect science to flourish. Many disparate elements must exist and must pull together. In this, government plays only an incidental role; von Hayek's spontaneous order is evident in a summation by Rosenberg and Birdzell. They perceive how the scientific method of posing and testing hypotheses and sharing results allows large numbers of practitioners to cooperate and participate in the advance of knowledge without an explicit organizational hierarchy. Individual inspiration determines where effort might be expended most productively and rewards come from the recognition of one's peers as to the value of discoveries. Rosenberg and Birdzell conclude: "[t]he resolution of conflicts on points of professional controversy was also a process of achieving professional consensus; no scientist would willingly have delegated the settlement of scientific disputes to a hierarchy. On the whole, it is apparent that the Western Scientific community was more, rather than less, efficiently organized by reason of its lack of a hierarchy."The general acceptance of the experimental method made it possible for hundreds and even thousands of specialists to build the results of their individual research into a single store of information, usable across all sciences. The introduction of the printing press greatly speeded the cumulation of this body of knowledge – as it had earlier speeded the ideas of Galileo and Bacon. Thus the West, alone among the societies of which we have knowledge, succeeded in getting a large number of scientists, specialized by different disciplines, to cooperate in creating an immense body of tested and organized knowledge whose reliability could be accepted by all scientists.[389]

The importance of science was not just a matter of enhancing man's abstract understanding. It also, of course, utterly transformed his ability to master his material environment and enhance his physiological and psychological well being. Chapter III described the expansion of commerce under the free market system. It was a marginal advance before science existed in a manner that could be practically applied.

The historian Angus Maddison estimates that there was no growth at all in per capita income in the first millennium and growth of some 0.17 percent per annum in the developed countries in the period 1500-1820 (far less in the non-Western world). But, with science, from 1820 to 1900 gross domestic product per capita almost tripled in Western Europe and more than tripled in the United States. Life expectancy had hardly increased until 1800, and then increased apace in line with economic growth.[390]

The benefits of the expanding scientific endeavor were in principle available to all countries. But it was those most open to the scientific method, those whose societies allowed for the most advantageous deployment of capital, and those who rewarded commercial innovation that benefited the most. We see here an underlying basis for the correlation shown in Chapter I between cultural values and a country's affluence, viz., the countries, which have moved the farthest along the tradition vs. rational-secular gradient, are the most affluent.

So while all advanced civilizations exhibited a deep interest in nature and a propensity for technological innovation, science only arose in Christian Europe. It arose there because only that culture had reached a necessary *philosophic stage* of evolution, wherein it incorporated a metaphysical view of reality that encouraged a systemic deeper investigation of reality beyond what was immediately available to the senses. In addition, the political systems of that culture proved to be advantageous to the emergence of science because they were too fragmented to effectively squelch potentially threatening speculation. Combined with the growth of universities in an increasingly prosperous society, the scientific method was established and fruitful scientific endeavors began on a number of fronts. The process unfolded over several centuries, eventually accompanied by a deep cultural value change—from the mystical to the secular, and from an adherence to authority and revelation to independence of individual thought and endeavor. This growing independence of thought extended far beyond the field of science to all spheres of life. Its role in the growing empowerment of the individual is treated in the next chapter.

6

The Empowerment of the Individual

By the morality of individuality I mean, in the first place, the disposition to make choices for oneself to the maximum possible extent, choices concerning activities, occupations, beliefs, opinions, duties and responsibilities. And, further, to approve of this sort of conduct—self-determined conduct—as conduct proper to a human being, and to seek the conditions in which it may be enjoyed most fully. It is in this approval—not merely on one's own account but in respect of others also—that the impulse towards individuality becomes a moral disposition. This is how human beings ought to live, and to be deprived of this exercise of individuality is recognized not only as the greatest unhappiness but as a diminution of moral stature. – Michael Oakeshott[391]

Individualism, as seen in an empowerment of the individual, is the fourth main characteristic that distinguishes the affluent West from poorer countries and one that sheds particular light on societal evolution. As we have seen, the populations of wealthier societies have high levels of subjective well-being, evidence high levels of interpersonal trust, are relatively tolerant toward outgroups, and are relatively distrusting of authoritarian government—values characteristic of a population that places high priority on self-expression and participation in decision-making.

Why these values have prevailed is not self-evident, given the enormous pressures in tribal life and larger civilizations to cohere and conform. Undoubtedly such values and associated behaviors,

232   *Free People, Free Markets*

which ran counter to tradition, were initially resisted, but when the benefits became evident over time, the new values were tolerated and even became celebrated. In light of the group selection model, these new modes of behavior and mores could have emerged only if their evolution made their societal animals more fit.

A greater role for the individual was certainly bound up with the evolutionary changes associated with free markets and free societies. For example, initiative emblematic of entrepreneurial-based markets demands autonomy and decision-making confidence in its leading participants. Similarly, the give and take of representative democracies must be tolerant of argumentation and individual judgment. If one had greater latitude to innovate in commercial matters, and one had greater political voice in protecting private interests, then it was only a matter of time before the individual gained greater autonomy in behavior—as long as deviations from the norm did not seriously undermine the security of society as a whole.

Even though it was the evolution of the extended order that was largely responsible for the growing empowerment of the individual, the process developed a momentum of its own. Accordingly, the specific avenue of evolutionary change resulting in the greater empowerment of the individual is worthy of examination in its own right.

To undertake that examination, we (1) provide a perspective for the evolution of individualism, (2) identify the beginnings in ancient civilizations, (3) examine the expansion of that heritage in late medieval times and during the Renaissance, (4) summarize the role of the Protestant Reformation, which *authorized* the individual to judge the meaning of scripture, thereby greatly freeing the individual from the tethers of 'group think,' (5) examine the role of western philosophy in crystallizing the new values, and (6) show how in recent centuries the power of new values led to the abolition of slavery, equal rights for women, and tolerance of gays.

THE EVOLUTION OF INDIVIDUALISM: A PERSPECTIVE

Michael Oakeshott's quotation introducing this chapter provides a pragmatic definition of individualism, which embraces a societal tolerance for individual creativity and initiative beyond the norm and beyond conventional wisdom. Much of it is at odds with man's early value systems, which required a predominant focus on an individual's responsibilities to the group. Even today in advanced countries, there is an inescapable tension between one's responsibilities to oneself and one's responsibilities to society as a whole. In less developed societies there may be less tension to the extent that individualism is often viewed as indulgent selfishness and is simply not tolerated.

To view the evolutionary avenue of change, we will examine the innate forces for conformity that were universal in early human existence and then identify cultural preconditions conducive to greater individual autonomy.

Conformity and Security

We saw the necessity for social cohesion by groups of early man living in a precarious physical environment and faced by constant warfare with other groups. Yet that cohesion was not achieved through autocratic authority; rather, decision-making was by consensus enabled by social conformity and social responsibility. Wilson's example of behavior in the Mbuti tribe describes how the will of the group prevails over the will of the strongest individuals.[392] In terms of adaptive behavior, this made perfect sense. Many modern sociological studies have demonstrated how the collective wisdom of a large number can be remarkably accurate—even surpassing the acumen of a given expert. So in a tribal context of hunting large game, necessarily a collective enterprise, the collective judgment regarding quarry and most promising locale had the highest probability of success.

Egalitarianism was a natural collateral value, which incorporated an instinctual aversion to hoarding and to private property and forms of status. In this context, egalitarianism is antithetical to individualism. Priorities required the individual to subject himself to the greater needs of the group and not think too highly of himself. In turn, he could count on the protection of the group and equal treatment with others. Elizabeth Cashdan notes of the Kung people: "If an individual does not minimize or speak lightly of his own accomplishments, his friends and relatives will not hesitate to do it for him ... and if a person is not generous, the norms of sharing are 'reinforced' by continued badgering and dunning for gifts."[393]

The Hutterites in Western culture provide another example of the sociological forces of conformity. The Hutterites, who originated in Europe in the 16th century and migrated en masse to America, have preserved a rigorous collectivism that has proven highly successful even on marginal farming lands. Matt Ridley states: "Their principle virtue is *Gelassenheit*, which means, roughly, 'grateful acceptance of whatever God gives, even suffering and death, the forsaking of all self-will, all selfishness, all concern for private property.' 'True love,' said their leader, Ehrenpreis, in 1650, 'means growth for the whole organism, whose members are all interdependent and serve each other.'" Ridley notes further that Hutterites mete out harsh discipline to those who exhibit egotism, implying that subversive selfishness remains a persistent danger.[394]

Modern day Islam also continues to emphasize hostility to individualism—e.g., the Quran stands in opposition to the 'ruiner,' i.e., the selfish individualist, who jeopardizes the moral integrity of the Moslem community. Indeed, the major thrust of Islam is to discourage individualist behavior. The very meaning of the word Islam is surrender and submission to the will of God.

The values exhibited here were once utterly essential for the security of the group in a hostile world and were strongly imbedded in societal psyches and mores. It is not much of a stretch to believe that similar world views were common to virtually all antecedent human societies. Thus, the transition to modern forms of individualism is all the more remarkable.

Preconditions for Change

Evolution in the West was to demonstrate how greater autonomy for the individual and devolution of decision-making in the interests of the extended order were compatible with societal security—indeed, made for a more flexible and responsive system that was ultimately more secure. What allowed these factors to evolve so efficaciously? Certain preconditions were required: society had to respect individual rights and had to become open to change and debate.

In contrast to other civilizations, the West's Greco-Judeo-Christian heritage provided a fertile beginning, having approached what Scribner termed the Philosophic Stage of human evolution, wherein arguments can become a powerful agent of change. He contrasted stagnant civilizations with those poised for evolutionary advance. He contrasted stagnant civilizations with those poised for evolutionary advance by distinguishing between societies that were or were not open to argument about essential features of their cultures. Average members of society throughout human existence tended to believe what everyone else takes for granted and to pursue the goals that are generally valued. But when societies sufficiently evolve – i.e., "the right conditions did hold, and regular and sustained argument about the whole range of situations did take place – there would be an inevitable tendency of culture to evolve in the direction of natural perfection for arguments of their kind."[395]

Accordingly, tolerance for debate is important in establishing an environment in which arguments can contend for survival. In this view, arguments are analogous to organisms, and fitness is demonstrated when an argument matches up with the world or with previous experience, or leads to behavior with favorable results. Akin to a new radiation of species, arguments start off simple, uniform, and weak and become increasingly complex, diverse, and powerful.

This is a natural selection process, amplified when a society is literate and can pass on the cumulative results of arguments, eventually producing principles. Scribner states: "discovering the true and the good is not, therefore, just a matter of accumulating beliefs about particular facts and making choices about how to behave in particular situations. It also includes the discovery of principles covering entire ranges of situations, uniting the arguments for them. Principles tend to become more general as rational level culture evolves."[396]

Concomitantly, reason, a powerful behavior guidance system, moves into a more central role in human affairs. While it makes the group more powerful, it also grants the individual a kind of autonomy. He now can act with initiative in the broad context of a situation, following only general guidance. Moreover, individual judgments can be made regarding what is "true."

This evolution began when mankind entered the Rational Stage of evolution where he could distinguish between his own needs and desires vis-à-vis those of others, and make independent judgments. The individual's need to realize his innate capabilities can, in principle, be fully rationalized with his meeting legitimate obligations to the larger society. To be sure, there will always be a larger need for social cooperation and cohesion—e.g., the individual's security ultimately depends on the continuing functionality of the larger group. But traditional group values may run counter to the needs of the individual in ways that are not, or are no longer, essential to the group's ability to function effectively. In such cases, change can be beneficial to both the individual and the community.

The ultimate test, however, is not so much philosophic as it is pragmatic. Does greater autonomy for the individual produce a fitter societal animal? It will where it enhances the *social capital* of society, producing individuals who in the aggregate are more creative, risk-taking, and entrepreneurial, without undermining society's essential cohesiveness. Debate regarding what is essential is ongoing and unavoidable.

To get us from the philosophic to the pragmatic, let's track the trajectory of growing individualism from early civilization through medieval Europe, the Renaissance, and the Protestant Reformation, to modern times.

Early Civilization

The starting point of our trajectory is about two and a half millennia ago. We saw earlier the intriguing coincidence of great philosophy emerging in different cultures at roughly the same time—i.e., the Jewish prophets, Socrates, Buddha, and Confucius all lived in the fifth and sixth centuries B.C. Each of earth's settled civilizations apparently had had a sufficiently long period of affluence and evolution to allow man's rational nature to move beyond survival issues to the beginnings of philosophy. Each of the civilizations—Israelite, Greek, Chinese, and Indian—found a unique path of philosophic investigation having dramatically different potential for the development of their societies.

Ancient Israel

Relying on the early (and significantly older) portions of the Old Testament, Herbert Muller concludes that the philosophic underpinnings of Judaism were primitive, and not that different from most early human cultures struggling for survival. Muller describes the God of the early Old Testament as a God of war and as an Oriental despot, fiercely jealous of his prerogatives. This God at first had little interest in the moral principles of his subjects, but made righteousness purely a matter of ritual (Exodus 34). Muller quotes Santayana, "it is pathetic to observe how lowly are the motives that religion ... attributes to the deity ...To be given the best morsel, to be remembered, to be praised, to be obeyed blindly and punctiliously – these have been thought points of honor with the gods, for which they would dispense favors and punishments on the most exorbitant scale."[397]

Thus, Israel in its early incarnation was as primitive and 'aphilosophical' as any of earth's struggling tribes. But a remarkable sea change occurred with the rise of the Old Testament prophets. Muller believes that at this juncture, the Israelites found Yahweh committed more to principles and less to war. By the time of the writing of the book of Amos, the essence of God was seen as requiring justice and righteousness. Muller believes that the prophet Micah represents this view with a sublime simplicity: 'He hath showed thee, O man, what is good; and what doth the Lord require of thee, but to do justly, and to love mercy, and to walk humbly with thy God?' Moreover, Isaiah made Yahweh the One God of all mankind. Muller states: "[a]lthough Yahweh was still an anthropomorphic God, the prophets remade him in an ideal image of man—of man as he aspires to be in his loftiest moments."[398]

This transition required individual man to gain greater introspection as to his role in life and the universe. Muller believes that the prophets allowed Judaism to rise "from the idol to the ideal, transforming an ordinary tribal religion into a unique ethical monotheism."[399] Moreover, he believes that the "moral value of this conception of history is plain. It puts the issue squarely up to man—i.e. for him to declare his responsibility for good and evil. Further, it demands that the rulers of this earth serve a higher law than the state."[400]

Nonetheless, in philosophic terms, it was a bare bones beginning. Muller states that the Jews "had a simple, absolute faith that the Lord *was*, that the whole universe testified to him, and that this was self-evident. They did not have to find him by introspection or mystical experience; they did not have to formulate a creed or rationalize their faith."[401]

Yet it seems that while the prophets launched no metaphysics, the new command to achieve personal righteousness helped engender Jewish Talmudic studies, requiring an intense application of logic to religious commandments and the needs of daily life. The rigor of this educational tradition helped give their societal animal a 'mindset' generating seminal works of philosophy and science over the centuries.

Ancient Greece

The Greeks, while they had their pantheon of gods, were more centered in man himself than in the supernatural. Their national motto at Delphi was not "Fear God" but "Know Thyself." In the 5th century B.C., approximately contemporaneous with many of the Jewish prophets, Socrates launched the rationalist mode of thinking central to Western philosophy for millennia. Socrates believed in an absolute "good" but allowed as how he could not yet define it, and laid out principles to guide such a journey of discovery.[402]

Muller finds the essence of Socrates' philosophic contributions as disclaiming any knowledge of the divine mind, and assuming that the proper 'service of God' was a constant search for wisdom, not an iteration of faith or simple submission. He believed that man should seek wisdom and virtue as something "not supernatural or transcendent—it was a positive human good, good for something in this life, good enough for this life alone. It was a good that all men could achieve by their own efforts, through reason, without the benefit of special grace." [403]

However admirable this may seem to us in retrospect, his skepticism was threatening to the traditions and established order of Athens. Independent thinking did not coexist well with still primitive social orders that perceived solidarity as essential to their continued existence. The Athenian Establishment ordered him to take hemlock. His friends urged him to flee Athens, which he could have done, but he chose to stay because of principle. As Muller states, he was the "first great apostle of intellectual and moral freedom, he remains a supreme example of intellectual and moral integrity."[404]

China

The emergence of Tao and Confucius philosophy in China was also approximately contemporaneous with the Jewish prophets and Socrates. Both of these philosophies identified ways in which the individual needed to think independently, but approached universal philosophical questions from a different perspective.

Lao-tze, Confucius' intellectual predecessor, formulated the Taoist way of life, in which he exhibited a strong distrust of government and intellectuals, anticipating liberal arguments of two millennia later. For example, Durant cites Taoists as believing:

> Knowledge is not wisdom, for nothing is so far from a sage as an 'intellectual.' ... The intellectual man is a danger to the state because he thinks in terms of regulations and laws; he wishes to construct a society like geometry. ... a ruler [who recognizes these pitfalls] regulates men as little as possible...[405]

While Taoism implicitly valued the role of the individual, it did not lead to the epistemological avenues of thought that Greek philosophy did—indeed, it tended to foreclose such speculation. Taoism ultimately believed that "Quiescence, a kind of philosophical inaction, a refusal to interfere with the natural courses of things, is the mark of a wise man in every field."[406] Moreover, Taoism is anti-intellectual, for it says that "silence is the beginning of wisdom ... the wise man does not speak, for wisdom can be transmitted never by words, only by example and experience."[407]

With regard to Confucius, Durant states: "The only broad philosophy that Confucius would recognize was (1) the search for unity in all phenomena, and (2) the effort to find some stabilizing harmony between the laws of right conduct and the regularities of nature." Despite his restrained philosophic ambition, these aims embodied crucial insights. While they may not have provided a basis for metaphysics, they were compatible with a search for understanding phenomena in the real world. Confucius emphasized that "clarity and honesty of thought and expression were the first lessons of the Master" and "obscurity of thought and insincere inaccuracy of speech seemed to him national calamities." Confucius argued the importance of defining one's terms, of not allowing wishes to discolor the facts and determine conclusions, and of impartially investigating the nature of things.[408]

As with Taoism, these teachings failed to set the Chinese on the epistemological track. But one can see clearly an evolution toward the individual's responsibility for seeking truth for himself.

India

A growing philosophic sophistication arose in ancient India that was also roughly contemporaneous with that which occurred in Israel, Greece, and China. The starting point was similar to that of most early human cultures. According to Durant, the oldest known religion of India was apparently an animistic and totemic worship of the spirits dwelling in stones and animals, in trees and streams, in mountains and stars. The earliest gods of the *Vedas* were the forces and elements of nature herself—sky, sun, earth, fire, light, wind, water, and sex. Conceptually, this was not that different from the gods of ancient Greece.[409]

With the composition of the *Upanishads,* however, which are as old as Homer, Indian civilization entered a more philosophic stage. These discourses were the product of various sages between the years 800 B.C. and 500 B.C. Although they represented no attempt at a coherent philosophy, they did represent, according to Durant, profound philosophic thinking. Their theme was all the mystery of this unintelligible world: "Whence are we born, where do we live, and whither do we go?" They told of a king who abandoned his kingdom and went into a forest to clear his mind for understanding and solve the riddle of the universe.[410] What could be more intensely introspective and individualistic; less concerned with the needs of the community? While introspective, it got Indian philosophy on a non-rational track. Brahmans were to "renounce learning and become as a child."

The Indian movement to introspection deepened with Buddha, who is believed to have been born circa 563 B.C. He taught that happiness is not possible here on earth or in the hereafter; that only peace can be attained; and that ambition and the search for pleasure can lead only to pain. Further, to achieve *Nirvana* one had to achieve the complete elimination of selfish desires and the annihilation of individual consciousness.

Buddha said that in the end we perceive the absurdity of moral and psychological individualism. While these strains of Indian philosophic thought led to a greater emphasis on the individual's spiritual needs vis-à-vis the needs of the community, they did not arrive at the in-worldly individualism that fuels societal evolution. Nonetheless, the impulse for greater understanding of life and the search for a code of moral behavior came from an awakening of man's reflective capabilities.[411]

The significance of such an awakening was not just that brilliant individuals engaged in the endeavor, but that the larger society was increasingly aware of the possibility of philosophic understanding. The Rational Stage of evolution was flowering. Durant states that when Buddha grew to manhood he found the halls, the streets, the very woods of northern India ringing with philosophic disputation. A large class of traveling Sophists "spent the better part of every year passing from locality to locality, seeking pupils, or antagonists, in philosophy. ... Large audiences gathered to hear such lectures and debates; great halls were built to accommodate them; and sometimes princes offered rewards for those who should emerge victorious from these intellectual jousts. It was an age of amazingly free thought and of a thousand experiments in philosophy."[412]

But these philosophic debates did not produce a coherent metaphysics; they generally led to a retreat from the world. The individualism of the Hindu and the Buddhist renouncer of the world embraced an "other-worldly" individualism. The rise of the "in-worldly" individualism had to await the arrival of Christianity in the West.[413] So, while the quest for wisdom went in many directions, the West proved to be unique in following the path of reason.

CATHOLIC EUROPE

While early Catholic Europe had many elements of a theocratic state stultifying to intellectual freedom, it also contained values that accommodated cultural evolution via intellectual inquiry. But for these values to flower, Europe had first to emerge from the primitive conditions following the fall of the Roman Empire, it had to rediscover Greek philosophy, and it had to turn away from a focus on the hereafter to values that honored man in the here and now.

The Inheritance

During the Dark Ages, Western Europe fell into a withdrawn feudal state. Life was reduced from relatively cosmopolitan circumstances under the Roman Empire to rural farming communities linked to small towns of artisans and clergy. The extended family and solidarity of the community established the value system. The Church's teachings, while based on a richer philosophic heritage, matched the circumstances of the times. Bertrand Russell, perhaps crediting the Church with a bit too much influence, described these times: "The outlook of most men, including the majority of philosophers, was dominated by a firm synthesis of dogma, law, and custom, which caused men's theoretical beliefs and practical morality to be controlled by a social institution, namely the Catholic Church: what was true and what was good was to be ascertained, not by solitary thought, but by the collective wisdom of Councils."[414]

These religious views permeated economic life as well as the mores governing individual behavior. According to Karl Pribram every community was endowed with defined classes according to functions, rights, and duties. While the artisans and traders were freemen, "their economic and social behavior was regulated by the officers of the guilds in which they were incorporated, and these officers were in turn supervised by the municipal magistrates." [415]

As we saw, economic activity was constrained by the Church's dogma regarding "just price" and "just wage." Such rigidity was feasible because of the autarchic and stagnant rural society of those days. The Church's alertness to dangers of heresy seemed to preclude an emergence from this theocratic environment.

Yet Europe was not a theocratic *state*. Practical power was retained by the descendants of the barbarian chiefs and the various kings who consolidated power in their wake. While Charlemagne was crowned by the Pope, the Emperors conceded little temporal power to the Church. Moreover, religious theology had for centuries accepted the division between religious and temporal claims on man, e.g., render unto Caesar things that are Caesar's and to God what was God's. In practice, the Church was focused on the hereafter, leaving mundane life to the jurisdiction of secular authority. According to Pribram, the Church connected the origin of political communities with a social instinct which was an empirical fact and not a transcendental principle. Accordingly, the exercise of governmental power by secular rulers was needed to control the behavior of sinful human beings, which could be accomplished more immediately and effectively by secular authority than by the church. [416]

A dual structure was proclaimed as early as the 5th century, when Pope Gelasius I (reigning from 492 to 496) declared: "Two there are by whom this world is ruled" — by Church, by State, the doctrine of the "two swords." [417] Accordingly, moral authority was not relinquished to the secular state; despotism was to be challenged when it encroached upon man's moral structure. Further in that light, Augustine advised one not to put one's spiritual well being in the hands of princes, kingdoms, or commonwealths. Taken together, these precepts opened the possibility of claims to a "higher authority" when confronting the power of the state.

Beyond the Church's separation from the institutions of government, its theology contained the promise of intellectual liberty by requiring an active understanding of religious teachings and a personal responsibility for behavior in accordance with those teachings. The theology of the day embraced a neo-platonic Christianity formulated by Saint Augustine in which God's injunctions were drawn from the teachings of Jesus. Importantly, while Jesus spoke in the traditions of the Major Prophets, he required more than merely observing the letter of the law. Notably, Jesus preached, "Thou shalt love the Lord with thy whole heart, with thy whole soul, and with thy whole strength, with thy whole mind, and thy neighbor as thyself." This injunction entailed greater introspection and higher sacrifice than did traditional Jewish teachings.

Moreover, as Scribner writes: "the belief that social roles had to be justified by basic principles about the nature of morality and justice that could be known by reason, and the belief that each rational subject has a free will which makes him ultimately responsible for his behavior (and the eternal fate of their souls) led to institutions that recognized the autonomy of individuals ..."[418]

Kirk argues that from this framework flowed the important values of the worth of the person, the equality of all men before the judgment-seat of God, and the limitations upon all earthly authority.[419] The need to determine one's obligations to God and the state challenged man's exercise of judgment, the hallmark of individualism. And to this moral autonomy was married a growing respect for reason.

There was another inheritance, more sociological than philosophic in impact, from a Pope in the 6th century, whose pronouncements had unintended consequences as they took the West further away from roots shared with other major cultures. Until then, the traditional Mediterranean and Middle Eastern practices governing domestic affairs "permitted, indeed encouraged, the practices of firstly, marriage to close kin; secondly, marriage to close affines or the widows of close kin (possibly by inheritance, of which the levirate was the extreme form); thirdly, the transfer of children by adoption; and, finally, concubinage, a form of secondary union." But in 597, Pope Gregory forbade all these practices. According to Deepak Lal, all the rejected practices concerned inheritance such that the ability of the extended family to retain its property was undermined, and individuals were increasingly able to escape the pressures of the extended family.[420]

Jack Goody also notes, "The Church's insistence on consent and affection, as well as on the freedom of testament, meant taking 'a stand against the power of the heads of households in matters of marriage, against the lay conception of misalliance, and, indeed, against male supremacy, for it asserted the equality of the sexes in concluding the marriage pact and in the accomplishments of the duties thereby implied.'"

Taken together, the 'extended family' was substantially altered. The result was late marriages, the fission of households on marriage, and employment of the unmarried outside rather than within households. Furthermore, Lal argues that these changes promoted greater individualism by allowing the young to choose their marriage partners, set up their own households, and enter into contractual rather than affective relationships of care for the old.[421]

The Renaissance and Humanism

As we saw, when economic life and prosperity began to return during the 12th century, Europe experienced a growth of universities, and these, in turn, led to the beginnings of science and associated changes of values. In effect, greater wealth permitted greater attention to the arts, to reason, and to intellectual discovery, building on the rediscovery of the philosophy of ancient Greece. With growing affluence, day-to-day life was less insecure and poverty-stricken, and the preoccupation with the afterlife held less sway. By the 14th century a major shift of worldview had occurred in a number of western societies; it came to be known as Humanism and was central to the Renaissance.

While such changes in cultures cannot be attributed only to single individuals, Will Durant describes Petrach (1304-1374 A.D.) as the "Father of the Renaissance."[422] He studied at the University of Bologna and had intended to practice law. But after some immersion in Virgil, Cicero, and Seneca, he abandoned law, steeped himself in classic poetry and romantic love. Durant states that his extensive poetry "caught the fancy of Italian youth, of Italian manhood, of the Italian clergy. ... His poems, his gay wit, his sensitivity to beauty in woman, nature, conduct, literature, and art, made a place for Petrach in cultured society ... his revival of interest in antiquity fostered the Renaissance emphasis on man and the earth, on the legitimacy of sensory pleasure, and on mortal glory as a substitute for personal immortality. ... By common consent he was the first humanist, the first writer to express with clarity and force the right of man to concern himself with this life, to enjoy and augment its beauties, and to labor to deserve well of posterity."[423]

Humanism flourished most in the 15th century, in which works concerning ancient Greece made their way, along with scholars, from the increasingly imperiled Byzantine Empire, which was to fall to the Turks in 1453. As Durant puts it: "It was under the Medici, or in their day, that the humanists captivated the mind of Italy, turned it from religion to philosophy, from heaven to earth, and revealed to an astonished generation the riches of pagan thought and art. ... The proper study of mankind was now to be man, in all the potential strength and beauty of his body, in all the joy and pain of his senses and feelings, in all the frail majesty of his reason; and in these as most abundantly and perfectly revealed in the literature and art of ancient Greece and Rome."[424]

As humanism permeated the educated classes, cultural values evolved as well. Durant says that the humanists, by and large, acted as if Christianity were a myth conformable to the needs of popular imagination and morality, but not to be taken seriously by emancipated minds.[425] Furthermore, "[t]he form, machinery, and the substance of modern erudition were established; ... the ideal of a gentleman [became] ... that of the fully developed individual attaining to wisdom and worth by absorbing the cultural heritage of the race. ... It was the humanists, not the navigators, who liberated man from dogma, taught him to love life rather than brood about death, and made the European mind free."[426]

"The Renaissance, by recalling classic culture, ended the thousand-year rule of the Oriental mind in Europe. From Italy by a hundred routes the good news of the great liberation passed over the mountains and seas to France, Germany, Flanders, Holland, and England."[427] Such philosophy, in spreading beyond Italy, culminated in works by Erasmus in the Netherlands and Thomas More in England.

Humanism was a process the Church did not strongly oppose, given its own recognition of the rational powers of man. The Humanists enhanced the belief in man's rationality, in his being made in the image of God. The Popes embraced the aesthetic impulses of the Renaissance and became patrons of painting, sculpture and architecture. Pope Leo X's architectural and artistic endeavors required enormous sums of money. To obtain those funds, the papacy sold indulgences—"papal tickets," written pardons for sins. It was this demand for money, the way it was demanded, and a religious reaction to humanism itself that brought on the Protestant Reformation and a dramatic advance in the scope for individual autonomy.

THE PROTESTANT REFORMATION

One can argue that the proximate cause of the Protestant reformation had more to do with money than it did with theology. Rome made repeated demands for funds—for the crusades, to fight the Turks, to rebuild Saint Peter's Basilica, and so forth. The rulers of England, France, Germany, and Spain protested that their countries were being drained of wealth; their national economies were being disturbed by repeated campaigns for luring money to Rome. Moreover, vast holdings of land by the Church diminished potential sources of revenue to these rulers. In addition, albeit on a more petty level, these countries resented plum positions in their lands going to Italian appointees rather than their fellow nationals.[428]

The effects of humanism, which had a dual impact, aggravated the resentment generated by financial matters: it weakened the piety of many members of Christendom and it seemed to account for the widespread corruption in Rome and throughout the Church. Just as the institutional Church appeared to drift from its early teachings, the incumbents of the papacy appeared increasingly corrupt. Kirk's description of Pope Alexander VI is a painful case in point:

> Pope Alexander was a monster of avarice, lust, and cruelty. With him, the papacy had sunk to its nadir. He gathered riches by selling church offices—and then, slowly poisoned the dignitaries he had appointed, that he might sell the posts again. 'Every night they find in Rome four or five murdered men, bishops and prelates and so forth,' the Venetian ambassador to the Holy See wrote home in the year 1500. ...This merciless pope was the product of the darkest corner of the Renaissance.[429]

Many felt that humanism needed to be fought rather than embraced by the Church and that the Church needed to return to its theological roots. The potential for reform was clearly 'in the air.'

Whatever the catalyst, the Protestant Reformation began almost inadvertently. Certainly its leaders at the outset did not intend to supplant the Catholic Church. Indeed, Martin Luther's initial actions attempted to address obvious abuses, particularly the selling of indulgences.

But it speedily drew on existing circumstances as well as on the growing intellectual discomfort with Catholic theology. For example, some believed it crucial to regain the core of Christianity in terms of the essential paths to faith in God and salvation. The reformers believed that the spirit of humanism brought about by the Renaissance, Rome's apparent acquiescence with that spirit, an over-reliance on ritual vis-à-vis religious truth, and widespread abuses by the Catholic hierarchy required a return to Christianity's roots—an emphasis on the essential sinfulness of man and on man's salvation by the arbitrary grace of God.

These kinds of concerns had already led to local religious rebellions to Catholic teachings in the prior century. In Britain, the Lollards, followers of John Wycliffe, had been suppressed only with much difficulty. In central Europe, the followers of John Huss, who was burnt at the stake in 1415 as a heretic, maintained their faith successfully against both royal and papal forces.[430]

It was also no coincidence that the full-blown Reformation followed on the heels of the beginnings of scientific inquiry, the Renaissance, and the discovery of the printing press. Understanding the evolutionary impact of the Reformation on the European societal animal requires (1) a review of the precipitating causes of the Reformation, (2) the main response of the Catholic Church, and (3) the key changes that occurred in the values and way of life of Protestant Europe.

Precipitating Events

On March 15, 1517, Pope Leo X promulgated an indulgence with fateful consequences. Although he had inherited full coffers from Julius II, he had just about emptied them. The new Saint Peter's Basilica had been started and required immense sums to complete.

Johann Tetzel, a Dominican friar, was charged with raising funds for the Church in Germany. He had considerable skill as a money-raiser, generally, and as a dispenser of indulgences, particularly. He offered an impressive formula: a plenary indulgence to those who confessed their sins and contributed according to their means to the building of St. Peter's. Several purchasers from Wittenberg showed purchased "papal letters" to Luther, a professor of theology at the university, and asked him to attest to their efficacy. He refused. Tetzel denounced him. The debate was launched.

Luther composed his arguments in the form of ninety-five theses. He tacked these on the church door, a common bulletin board, to announce public debates against all challengers. At this point, the debate centered on narrow theological points. According to Durant, Luther believed that the selling of indulgences trivialized the individual's reaction to sinful acts by lessening contrition. While he did not dispute the Pope's power to absolve the penitent from terrestrial penalties, he believed that the intercessory influence of papal prayers might, or might not be heard. Moreover, he believed that all Christians shared in beneficences associated with Christ and the saints without a papal letter of indulgence. [431]

There was nothing momentous or revolutionary here—a narrow theological point at best. The underlying culture had to have already been sufficiently unsettled to produce the explosionary transformation of the culture that it did. It was like a mixture near saturation, requiring only a foreign element to have the crystals precipitate out.

Indeed, at first there was little action. Complaints were made to Rome, and the Pope was, at first, indulgent toward Luther. Three years, with an increase in rhetoric, were to pass before Rome reacted strongly. Luther began to touch on widespread German grievances in the escalating rhetoric, and as unrevolutionary as his theses may have been, they became the talk of literate Germany. Thousands had waited for such a protest, and the pent-up anticlericalism of generations thrilled at having found a voice. Luther himself was dismayed at the unexpected and outsized reception.

Sides in the debate were drawn up. Tetzel replied with 106 anti-theses. Jakob van Hoogstraeten of Cologne suggested burning Luther at the stake. Johann Eck, Vice-Chancellor of the University of Ingolstadt charged him with heresy and undermining ecclesiastical order. On the other side, various ardent professors rallied to Luther's side. When the Pope's representative, Karl von Miltitz, reached Germany in late 1518, he was astonished to find half the country openly hostile to the Roman See. Yet as late as 1519 Luther wrote the Pope a letter of complete submission — and Leo replied in a friendly spirit.

Among Luther's supporters was Ulrich von Hutten. Drawing on German nationalism and the old tensions between the Pope and the Holy Roman Emperor, in one highly influential work, he voiced the national desire for independence from Rome. He described Rome as a "gigantic blood-sucking worm," and declared that "the Pope is a bandit chief, and his gang bears the name of the Church ... Rome is a sea of impurity, a mire of filth, a bottomless sink of iniquity." Subsequently, Luther drew on similar arguments of German nationalism.

The situation had grown increasingly threatening to the Church. On June 15, 1520, Leo X issued a bull, which condemned forty-one statements by Luther, ordered the public burning of his works in which they had appeared, and exhorted Luther to abjure his errors and return to the fold. Luther's pugnacity and tenacity were, however, now fully engaged, and he fought all the harder. In September he was excommunicated. There was no going back.

As a sign of the heated debate and widespread public involvement, the number of books published in Germany rose from 150 in the year 1518 to 990 in the year 1524. Four fifths of these favored the Reformation, while books favoring orthodoxy were hard to sell. Luther translated the Bible into German, making it more accessible.

While there were conferences and Diets, negotiations of all sorts, by 1522 events had led to fighting, such as the Peasants' War, fought between 1524 and 1526. Armed conflict did end for a period with the Treaty of Augsburg, which had been intended as a settlement of the religious question in Germany. Unfortunately, Catholics and Lutherans disagreed on the interpretation of the treaty and continued to organize into opposing groups: the Evangelical Union and the Holy League. Finally, a spark caused by the Archbishop of Prague's ordering a Protestant church to be destroyed in 1618 launched the Thirty Years War, one of Germany's bloodiest epochs. With time, the impetus for fighting changed from religion to power politics when the French, the Swedes, and Habsburgs joined in. By the time of the Peace of Westphalia (1648), half the population of Germany had died.[432]

Response of the Catholic Church

At first, the Catholic Church responded with the Counter Reformation—a pragmatic reform of abuses. But then the Church turned to denial, much as had Islam five centuries earlier. It began to view Protestants not as dissenters but as enemies of the faith, much like Jews and Moslems. And, as described by David Landes, the Inquisition was launched. Church and civil authorities took a number of actions to shore up belief and shield the faithful from Protestant heresy. Dangerous books were placed on an Index Librorum Prohibitorum (1557 in Rome, 1559 in Spain), and approved books required an official imprimatur ('let it be printed'). So serious did the authorities view the threat posed by books that the death penalty was introduced for importing books without permission and for unlicensed printing. Among the prohibited books were scientific works authored by Protestants – prohibitions that stifled intellectual inquiry for years to come. In collateral actions, Spaniards were not allowed to study abroad except at safe universities such as Rome, Bologna, and Naples. Moreover, scientists deemed subversive were silenced and made to denounce themselves.[433]

Changes in Values and Ways of Life

Luther's initial debate with the Church was centered on procedural abuses. But in the ensuing decades, the debate led by Luther, Calvin, and others turned to doctrinal disagreements.

Doctrinal Changes

Both Luther and Calvin argued that the Church's moral decay was the result of theological errors that had crept into the Church's teachings. What might these errors have been? Durant locates Luther's theology in the mainstream of religious evolution. His concerns went more to the Church's organization and the use of ritual rather to Catholic doctrine. In this he followed previous dissenters like Wyclif and Huss in rejecting the papacy, the councils, and any

guide to faith other than the Bible. Durant states: "[t]heologically
... [his beliefs were] ... anchored on Augustine's notions of predestination and grace, which in turn were rooted in the Epistles of
Paul, who had never known Christ. Nearly all the pagan elements
in Christianity fell away as Protestantism took form; the Judaic contribution triumphed over the Greek; the Prophets won against the
Aristotle of the Scholastics and the Plato of the humanists..."[434]

Two particularly important divergences from the then Catholic
orthodoxy had to do with concepts of free will and the sources of
true belief.

Free Will

Both Luther and Calvin said that the most profound difference between Papists and Protestants was the question of freedom of will.
The early Church, in the doctrine formulated by Saint Augustine,
had taught that man is wholly corrupt—that so far as man has free
will, this is only an opportunity to choose among evil acts. But the
Church had come to teach that in the depths of man's soul there
existed an essence of divine substance, potentially enabling man, if
given grace, to exercise his will for good.

The Protestants believed, like the earlier Church, that because
man is utterly corrupted by self-love, man enjoys no freedom to
act for the good. He can be saved from his total depravity only by
the arbitrary grace of God. While true faith in God should result
in good works, these are merely by-products. Thus, the reformers
concluded that the elaborate structure of penances, good works,
and the absolving of sins should be abandoned.

This shift in perspective might seem like a step backward regarding the growth of individualism. And so it might have been
had it not been for the corresponding shift in the view of authority
and sources of true belief. Moreover, this view of free will did, in
the hands of the Calvinists and the Reformist groups, lead to the
Protestant Ethic in spurring economic development as described
by Max Weber.

Source of True Belief

An equally important point of doctrinal controversy concerned the
source of true Christian belief. The Catholics turned to authority;

the Protestants turned to private judgment. According to Kirk, "[b]y Authority, the Catholics meant the teaching authority of the whole Church, over the centuries, as expressed in Scripture, in tradition, in the works of the Fathers and Doctors of the Church, in the consensus of church councils, in the sayings and acts of saints, in papal decretals." In contrast, the Protestants found authority in the individual Christian's interpretation of the Bible, in light of conscience. These interpretations had disparate and divergent sociological impacts – i.e., the Catholic maintaining an authoritative Church and a close-knit society; the Protestant leading to religious and social individualism.[435]

The Protestant perspective represented a revolutionary advance in the empowerment of the individual. While religion here provided leadership in this breakthrough, the underlying values and disposition must have already existed in society. The growing belief in the power of reason and the effects of Humanism, which placed man more in the center of the universe, played their roles. Ironically, the Protestants rebelled against Humanism, but inadvertently worked to further some of its central tenets.

Initially, however, one might have wondered whether the result would be otherwise. The impetus for the Reformation was to return to the roots of the religion—i.e., it was a powerful fundamentalist impulse such as occurred in the closing of the Islamic mind as it turned from reason to mysticism. Further, the Protestant stance on free will could have worked against a belief in reason. Moreover, the intense focus on faith and salvation seemed to pervade all aspects of life. One could almost expect the rise of theocracies. Indeed, in Calvin's Geneva this possibility reared its head, as it did among English Presbyterians, and, for a time, among the Puritans of Massachusetts Bay.

Kirk describes these views as follows: "they would have set up … the law of the Scriptures, through local courts composed of the devout—enforcing, incidentally, the Mosaic penalty of death for blasphemy, adultery, murder, and heresy. The Bible was the sole source of truth, the Geneva men proclaimed: all life, private and public, must be regulated by the Bible's ordinances. Whatever was prescribed in Scripture must be observed to the letter, and whatever was not mentioned in Holy Writ must be cast aside."[436] Does this not sound familiar? Even in this day, some Islamic countries turn to the law of Sharia, attempting to order life according to literal readings of the Quran.

However, in Europe, theocracies did not take hold. Such a concept proved to be totally incompatible with the growing empowerment of the individual. Once the individual became the sole judge of religious truths, the tendency was toward pluralism and self-reliance. This is another example of unintended consequences. In terms of our evolutionary theory, the Protestant mutation found an accommodating niche in the values of society and thrived, not on religious grounds, but because of pragmatic benefits.

Pragmatic Effects

Among the many changes accompanying the Reformation was the desire of individuals to exercise greater judgment in the conduct of their lives and to have greater say in the ways in which they were to be governed. It is telling that the Reformation took quickest and deepest root in those areas that had gone furthest down the path of expanding trade and freer markets. Three areas—notably England, the Spanish Netherlands, and certain German principalities—had especially experienced the growing wealth produced by the new ways, had greatest confidence in exercising entrepreneurial initiative, and were most willing to fight to preserve the benefits and the institutions—notably religious—that accommodated the evolving changes.

Kirk states that, out of the new convictions a "Protestant character" developed. Primary among the new values was self-reliance. "Self-reliance was encouraged, for in a sense every believer was compelled to judge of the Scriptures' meanings for himself, rather than looking to Authority. Self-examination and introspection developed because every man should be perpetually searching his own conscience, for his soul's salvation. ... Among Calvinists especially, indications that God had chosen a man to be saved were eagerly sought after; it was popularly supposed that one such indication might be a man's success in his worldly vocation, made possible providentially—so hard work and material accomplishment tended to be approved. [This was Weber's view in The Protestant Ethic.] ... Politically, the tendency of Protestantism was toward democracy. Luther preached obedience to legitimate princes; ... yet the idea of priesthood of all believers gradually would be transferred from the realm of religion to the realm of politics."[437]

Accordingly, a growing sense of self-reliance had important pragmatic effects regarding both greater individual participation in governance and widespread literacy. With regard to the former, experience in church governance enhanced self confidence and generated a desire to participate in the broader political arena. The tendency toward democracy was perhaps most pronounced among the Presbyterians of Scotland. Presbyterianism means government of churches by presbyters, or ministers and elders meeting in session in contrast to the authority of bishops common to the Catholic and Anglican churches. The adherents of this religion had to develop new forms of decentralized governance, itself an important evolutionary advance.

Specifically, there emerged the General Assembly of the Kirk, presided over by an elected "moderator" to supplant the old Episcopal establishment. According to J.M. Reid: "The Scots Kirk was unbelievably democratic. It did not aim at political democracy, although there was a radical strain among the first Reformers. The object of the men who made it was to reproduce as far as possible the sort of Church they found in the Bible. But in doing this through ministers and elders elected (or at least approved) by each congregation, men who again appeared in the courts of the Kirk or sent their chosen representatives there, they produced General Assemblies which could speak for the whole nation with far more backing than any parliament of those days."

The effects of this evolutionary advance were felt far beyond Scotland, since Presbyterians settled in large numbers in the American colonies, and their awareness of their rights and their independence of judgment prepared them for dispersed self-governance appropriate for sparsely settled regions far from the seat of power.[438]

Another far-reaching consequence of Protestant theology was the way it enhanced the literacy of the adherent populations through an emphasis on independent judgment and the encouragement of Bible reading. Significantly, this held for girls as well as boys. David Landes concludes that an important consequence beyond mere literacy was that there was a larger pool of candidates for advanced schooling and a greater assurance of literacy from generation to generation. As he puts it, "literate mothers matter."[439]

The Scottish example is again useful to highlight changes in education. John Knox's goal was popular education from elementary school through the four Scottish universities, with the consequence that literacy was higher in Scotland during the 17th and 18th centuries than in any other country. Moreover, the educational advances far exceeded the accomplishment of widespread literacy. As we have already seen, a "Scottish enlightenment" emerged in Edinburgh in the 18th century, producing luminaries such as the philosopher David Hume and the economist Adam Smith.

While Scotland had a relatively small population, Scots prospered throughout the British Empire in the 18th and 19th centuries disproportionately as administrators, soldiers, and merchants. In America as elsewhere, Scottish settlers had the advantage of sound schooling, with only the Puritans exceeding them in this regard.[440]

Catholic populations did not, for some generations anyway, follow this path. Catholics were catechized but did not have to read, and they were explicitly discouraged from reading the Bible. Max Weber identified this divergence existing as late as the end of the nineteenth century when he wrote *The Protestant Ethic*.

Beyond the religious values regarding the individual ushered in by the Reformation, other pragmatic changes influenced values as well. Because the Protestant lands led the way in a mercantile revolution, they led the way in developing more powerful roles for the individual in the economic arena. Rosenberg and Birdzell[441] theorize how value changes associated with trade and industry must have come about. They note that the most ancient of social institutions involved the extended family. In the Middle Ages, the business enterprise tended to be a family affair, built on a family fortune, with key managerial and technical skills provided by family and kin. Then as noted in Chapter III, economic transactions became increasingly impersonal, and at contractual "arms-length." As enterprises grew beyond the capacity of individual families, how did society make the value shifts required?

The economic entities of the Middle Ages provided little in the way of models for mercantile enterprises. Both the feudal order and the Church were hierarchies dependent on ritual and oath. They did not produce the practical relationships of trust and confidence needed for long-term economic association. Moreover, an atavistic and pervasive distrust of economic activity first had to attenuate.

Rosenberg and Birdzell focus on the new need for loyalty to an "outside" economic organism—an abstract enterprise. Group loyalty, mutual trust, and mutual reliance had to be developed. They speculate that such loyalties were common in military life on land and especially at sea. It was probably no coincidence that many English and Dutch merchants of the 16th and 17th centuries had been warriors or mariners, occupations where personal status among peers depended largely on fulfilling commitments and standing behind representations. Further, a large number of investors had to rely on the integrity and skill of the directors and managers of these new enterprises. Such trust presupposes a widely shared sense of business morality, and that sense of morality could hardly have been borrowed from the Catholic Church or from the older aristocracy. Indeed, the scorn of these older institutions with regard to trade only "encouraged the merchants to develop a code of honor pivoting on scrupulous care in timely payment of debts and on the loyalty to superiors—both points of striking weakness in the aristocratic code."[442]

In these ways, the Reformation was accompanied not just by greater literacy and a modified theology but by widespread skepticism, dissent, refusal of authority, and a multitude of viewpoints— the essence of individualism. The evolving worldviews would be reinforced by everyday experience and be reflected by new generations of philosophers.

THE EMERGENCE OF LIBERALISM AND "THE PURSUIT OF HAPPINESS"

We have now seen that a communal view of life, reflecting "survival" values, which existed throughout much of the Middle Ages, was eroding during the Renaissance and the Reformation. Oakeshott argues that historically the process in which the "morality of communal ties" was modified and finally superceded was a long one. He states that the new moral disposition, which he calls the "morality of individuality," did not unmistakably appear until the

16th century, and then only in Protestant Europe.[443] But by the end of the 18th century, the world saw in writing, if you will, in the American Declaration of Independence that men have unalienable rights, among which are life, liberty, and the pursuit of happiness.

During these two centuries or so, the effects of the Reformation, the experiential impact of new economic relationships, and greater autonomy for the individual challenged philosophers to make sense of the world in new non-scriptural ways. And, as we saw, the trenchant arguments of certain philosophers, notably John Locke, helped shape both the thinking of key statesmen in England and the English colonies and how larger society came to view the rights of the individual.

This was the era in which "modern philosophy" arose. Prior to the Reformation, the principal philosophic thinking and writings in the West were in the context of the Church's teachings. They were predicated on the existence of God and attempting to discern his desires for human behavior. The essence of "goodness" was attributed to God, without succeeding, as Phillip Scribner would argue, in rigorously determining what that goodness consisted of. Scholasticism, as articulated by Thomas Aquinas (and others) represented the epitome of Christian attempts to develop metaphysics for mankind.

Humanism, the Renaissance, the rise of science, and the Reformation shattered the utility of that metaphysics for many thinking people. The religious wars between Protestants and Catholics, the proliferation of Protestant sects, continuing struggles between Conformists and non-Conformists produced a deep desire for peace and tolerance—especially in England and the Netherlands. New ways were sought to explain man and to define the most appropriate behavior of individual to individual and of individual to society as a whole.

A number of great philosophic minds throughout Western Europe undertook divergent approaches to gaining a deeper understanding of man. These approaches shared an ambition of discovering first principles from which a foundation for truth could be erected. While these efforts looked to reason and empiricism, they were not anti-religious. Indeed, after the religious wars of the Reformation, societies tended to be intensely religious and philosophers had to be wary of the state, which invariably was linked to various established religions. Even though these philosophers failed to find the absolute truths they sought, they expanded upon man's understanding of the sources of knowledge and they helped crystallize societal values regarding the role and the rights of the individual.

These men had a tradition of philosophic thought extending back to the ancient Greeks to draw on. As we saw, Aquinas' metaphysics left the door open to empirical, non-revelatory sources of knowledge, notably "natural law," the fundamental questions of which had already been examined by Greek philosophy and refined during the codification of Roman law. Durant cites Epicurus' teachings as "[w]e can know nothing of the suprasensual world; reason must confine itself to the experiences of the senses, and must accept these as the final test of truth" and "if the senses are not the ultimate arbiter of fact, how can we find such a criterion in reason, whose data must be taken from the senses."[444]

The Stoics, however, highlighted a compounding difficulty. "Experience, however, need not lead to knowledge; for between sensation and reason lies emotion or passion, which may distort experience into error even as it distorts desire into vice."[445] Despite these problems, the Stoics believed in an underlying reality such that goodness is cooperation with God, or nature, or the "Law of the World."[446] In Roman times, Cicero wrote, "True law is right reason in agreement with Nature"[447] and Rome developed a body of laws, the *jus naturale*, which was distinguished from customary and statutory law.

Many centuries later, the English philosopher Richard Hooker (1553-1600) invigorated this line of inquiry by appealing to empirical facts about human nature to identify elements of the Law Rational. His analysis examined the origins of government and the bases for its legitimacy. He concluded that submission to government is voluntary, but individuals would obey the law if they saw that their individual good was at one with the good of the whole.[448] Such thinking tended to focus on the individual—one having free will and having the autonomy making him responsible for the life he led. Other proponents of natural law such as the Dutch philosopher Hugo Grotius (1583-1645) argued that individual rational beings have natural rights that are more basic than the authority of the body politic to impose sanctions and that government is, therefore, constrained to respect them.

Other non-religious attempts to find a theoretical foundation for human morality variously focused on the inevitable tension between reason and passion to discern principles for individual responsibility and for meeting societal responsibilities, and showed ways in which self-interest could be compatible with social responsibility.

In these developments, the Frenchman Rene Descartes (1596-1650) is usually considered the founder of modern philosophy. He took the tradition of rationalism and brought it into the modern era. He attempted to develop a metaphysics using rational intuition as the foundation of "clear and distinct ideas" about reality. Scribner says that Descartes' philosophy was a form of realism because it took as its foundation the ideas immediately present in the mind and tried to prove the existence and nature of a world beyond them.

Other great philosophers were more empirical and utilitarian in their formulations, with greater relevance for ethics and government. For example, the Englishman Thomas Hobbes (1588-1679) viewed human relations as a "social contract" in which individuals attempt to maximize satisfying their desires, not just in the moment, but over a lifetime. In this context, practical reason is the ability to see the consequences of one's behavior and to deliberate about the alternative means of attaining goals. In a world of scarce resources, for example, without foresight, individuals inevitably come into conflict with one another and aggression appears to be the best strategy. With foresight, however, one gains more from the enormous benefits of social cooperation than one loses from giving up the possibilities of violent unilateral action. Hobbes believed, however, that most men would not keep a social contract unless there was a sovereign with the power to enforce the contract.

Another English philosopher Joseph Butler (1692-1752) was more optimistic concerning the interplay of ambition and self-interest. He noted that individuals have benevolent as well as selfish desires, and our faculty of reason, which he calls "reflection or conscience," provides us with the means of determining which are to be satisfied. In so doing, reason is a "principle" with an "authority" to rule over desire, and it usually leads one to do what is morally right.

The German philosopher Immanuel Kant (1724-1804) also emphasized the role of reason employing the concept of *Categorical Imperative*, by which reason binds the will independently of other inclinations or interests. He believed that reason guides the will by establishing a sense of duty, and a guiding principle is to act only on those maxims (intentions, including goals) that could be applied as universal laws. Apropos to the concept of individualism, Kant said: "No man has the right to compel me to be happy in the peculiar way in which he may think of the well-being of other men; but every man is entitled to seek his happiness in the way that seems best to him, if he does not infringe the liberty of others striving for a similar end for themselves when their liberty is capable of consisting with justice"[449] — a central tenet of classical liberalism.

The English philosophers Jeremy Bentham (1748-1832) and John Stuart Mill (1806-1873) attempted to define morality on a less cerebral and more empirical, "utilitarian," approach, combining reason and desire. Thus, instead of being egoistic, reason might be universalistic and determine the morally good as what maximizes the satisfaction of everyone's desires. In the utilitarian calculus, the overall goal is to maximize pleasure and minimize pain for the greatest number in society.

The enhanced role seen for the individual can be especially seen in the works of John Locke (1632-1704), who captured the evolutionary changes sooner than most and was unusually in tune with the English political temper. Bertrand Russell concluded that "Locke is the most fortunate of all philosophers. He completed his work in theoretical philosophy just at the moment when the government of the country fell into the hands of men who shared his political opinions. Both in practice and in theory, the views which he advocated were held, for many years to come, by the most vigorous and influential politicians and philosophers."[450] Indeed, as we saw earlier, he had provided the theoretical foundation for the actions that led to the Glorious Revolution and the English Bill of Rights in two of his works, "Civil Government," and two "Treatises on Government."

Yet another work, the "Essay Concerning Human Understanding," explored the essential individualism of the mind. Locke believed that our ideas are derived from two sources: sensation, and perception of how the mind works. Because we can think only through ideas, and because all ideas come from experience, it is evident that none of our knowledge can antedate experience. Russell stated that this view represented a new doctrine because in that day the mind was supposed to know all sorts of things *a priori*.[451] And as Kirk noted, the Essay helped open the way to the rationalism of the 18th century.

Further, in "Civil Government" he argued that the desire for life, liberty, and property were innate qualities of man. Locke believed that private and public interests are identical in the long run, though not necessarily over short periods, and that a community of citizens will act, given liberty, in a manner to promote the general good.[452] In this, he was among the group of philosophers who viewed government as being one part of a "social contract," in which individuals are willing to give up certain rights for the common good in order to obtain greater security for the larger rights they possess as individuals. From this follows the conclusion that the power of the government can never exceed that which is required for the common good.

More specifically, he held: "The great and chief end of men uniting into commonwealths, and putting themselves under government, is the preservation of their property. ... the supreme power cannot take from any man any part of his property without his own consent."[453] At that time, *property* entailed much more than physical assets; it encompassed one's right to use and enjoy the benefits of one's thought, and efforts. And one's consent was, as a practical matter, given via one's representative in a legislative assembly. Locke took this logic one step further in the Second Treatise to argue that when a government violates such principles and becomes a despotism through arbitrary use of power, one has the right to overthrow that government.

Locke's influence was great with Whig thinkers for the next century. An evolved expression of his values was made by Edmund Burke around the time of the drafting of the U.S. Constitution:

If civil society be made for the advantage of man, all the advantages for which it is made become his right. It is an institution of beneficence; and law itself is only beneficence acting by rule. Men have a right to live by that rule; they have a right to do justice, as between their fellows, whether their fellows are in public function or in ordinary occupation. They have a right to the fruits of their industry, and to the means of making their industry fruitful. They have the right to the acquisitions of their parents; to the nourishment and improvement of their offspring; to instruction in life, and to consolation in death. Whatever each man can separately do, without trespassing upon others, he has a right to do for himself; he has a right to all which society, with all its combinations of skill and force, can do in his favor. In this partnership all men have equal rights; but not to equal things.[454]

Even though expressed by an Englishman, this was the philosophy underlying the establishment of the United States—its Declaration of Independence and its Constitution. It is a statement in accord with classical liberalism and modern libertarianism. It focuses on the rights of the individual to liberty in his thoughts, actions, and property.

Bertrand Russell described the resulting liberalism in broad brush:

Early liberalism was a product of England and Holland ... It stood for religious toleration; it was Protestant, but of a latitudinarian rather than a fanatical kind; ... It valued commerce and industry, and it favoured the rising middle class rather than the monarchy and the aristocracy; it had immense respect for the rights of property, especially when accumulated by the labours of the individual possessor. ... every community had a right ...to choose its own form of government.[455]

Thus, by the 18th century a philosophic basis for liberty and the empowerment of the individual had been laid out. While everyday life, for the most part, did not comport with the views of philosophers, those views were increasingly absorbed by societies and created forces driving cultural evolution in the West.

WIDER EMPOWERMENT IN THE MODERN ERA

The emergence of classical liberalism and the concept of individual rights to pursue happiness were all well and good, but the U.S. Constitution provided for slavery, the voting franchise did not include women, and only male property owners could vote. The founding fathers were well aware of the logical dissonance, but they believed that such compromises were required if there was to be a Union, including the Southern states, at all. So how did further empowerment proceed? Its unfolding involved the abolition of slavery, the coming of feminist rights, and acceptance of gay liberation.

The Abolition of Slavery

Slavery has existed in most human cultures; it was so ubiquitous that the Bible contains references apparently condoning the practice. Slavery occurred, however, usually as a result of the fortunes of war rather than from one group of people viewing another as inferior. Accordingly, as noted in Chapter IV, the Romans viewed slaves as having legal rights and as being the equals of free men in front of God, whereas in later times, the enslavement of black Africans was based on a racist view of the inferiority of those peoples.

As slavery had died out in the West soon after the fall of the Roman Empire, or at least had morphed into serfdom, which expired by the Renaissance, why did it reemerge with the discovery of the New World? The answer lies in its continuance elsewhere as well as in factors of climate and economics.

For example, when Europeans explored the Americas, it was clear white men could not toil and survive in the disease-ridden tropics. Thus, if the colonial powers were to make use of the agricultural potential of the New World in the tropics, it appeared that the use of slaves would be required. The economic stakes were not trivial. The sugar islands in the Caribbean were economically important to the British, the French, and the Dutch. As late as the French and Indian Wars, islands in the Caribbean were considered relatively more economically important than some of the British Colonies on the continent of North America.

The economic potential for slavery was far less at the time in the North American states. The dictates of climate were significant only in the southern states of South Carolina and Georgia, even though Virginia had significant numbers of slaves on the tobacco plantations. (But this constrained use of slaves was to change as Alabama, Mississippi, and Louisiana joined the union, and the profitability of cotton exploded with the invention of the cotton gin.)

Strong opposition to slavery arose first in England — very likely growing out of the philosophic views described earlier in this chapter. These views came to be held by many in the northern American states as well. Yet while England acted to outlaw the slave trade, the colonists, in forming their new union, temporized by outlawing the slave trade by a date certain, 1808, 20 years after the ratification of the U.S. Constitution.

The Founding Fathers rationalized the preservation of slavery by believing it would disappear on its own with time. This view, while opportunistic, was not without realistic expectation. Slavery had been waning. The price of slaves had declined, indicating a decline in demand. In the quarter century 1775-1800, the price dropped by 50 percent. All the states had ended the legal importation of slaves by 1803, and Congress was able to ban the trade from 1808 as envisioned in the U.S. Constitution.

But just short of the new century, Eli Whitney and the invention of the cotton gin changed the entire economic environment. The cotton gin provided an efficient, non-labor-intensive way of separating the cotton seeds from the cotton. With the cotton gin, a slave could produce fifty pounds of cotton a day instead of one. And with the introduction of the cotton gin and mechanical spinning machines, the price of cotton cloth in constant value of gold bullion was reduced by 99 percent. Demand soared. Cotton went from a relatively expensive product enjoyed by few, to an inexpensive, highly comfortable product desired by many.

Growing demand for cotton led to widespread growth of the plantation system in the South, and the demand for slaves increased commensurately. The price of slaves turned around and, in the next half century, shot up by a factor of almost twenty.[456]

When it became apparent that slavery was no longer waning, abolitionist sentiment began to organize in the North, with leadership from the religious community. William Lloyd Garrison

launched the publication of *The Liberator*. He wrote in a piece entitled "Declaration of Sentiments of the American Anti-Slavery Convention" (1833):

> Hence we maintain—that in view of the civil and religious
> privileges of this nation, the guilt of its oppression is un-
> equalled by any other on the face of the earth: and, there-
> fore, that it is bound to repent instantly, to undo the heavy
> burdens, and to let the oppressed go free.
>
> We further maintain—that no man has a right to enslave
> or imbrute his brother—to hold or acknowledge him, for
> one moment, as a piece of merchandize—to keep back his
> hire by fraud—or to brutalize his mind, by denying him the
> means of intellectual, social and moral improvement.
>
> The right to enjoy liberty is inalienable. To invade it is
> to usurp the prerogative of Jehovah. Every man has a right
> to his own body—to the products of his own labor—to the
> protection of law—and to the common advantages of soci-
> ety. It is piracy to buy or steal a native African, and subject
> him to servitude. Surely, the sin is as great to enslave an
> American as an African.
>
> Therefore, we believe and affirm—that there is no dif-
> ference, in principle, between the African slave trade and
> American slavery:
>
> That every American citizen, who detains a human
> beng in involuntary bondage as his property, is, according
> to Scripture (Ex. Xxi.16), a man-stealer:
>
> That the slaves ought instantly to be set free, and brought
> under the protection of law.[457]

Slavery became the central and defining political issue in the
United States for 50 years. With growing hostility in the north, the
southern strategy was to maintain control of the U.S. Senate, by
having as many Slave states in the Union as Free states. This allowed, among other things, a control over appointees to the U.S.
Supreme Court. Electoral strategy was centered on controlling the
Democratic Party.

The political issue came to an early head in the 1820s, when
the southern states, fearing the political dominance of the more

populous and growing north, talked of States Rights and possible secession. To counter this threat, Calhoun and Clay, prominently among other leaders, searched for expedients to preserve the Union. These expedients led first to the Missouri Compromise (1820), and later to the Kansas-Nebraska Act (1854).

By the mid-1850s, the southern strategy was increasingly unworkable. In 1856, the Republican Party was formed, drawing in Free Soil Democrats, former Whigs, and anti-slavery radicals, having an abolitionist core to its philosophy. Abraham Lincoln sharpened that policy and gained prominence for it in the famed Lincoln-Douglas debates of 1858. Lincoln gained the Republican nomination for the Presidency in 1860.

The South panicked. Their old strategy of controlling events through the Democratic Party might have continued to work, in that they could count on all the slave states plus a few northern states to form a majority. But the tide of public opinion was moving against them. The southern Democrats demanded a strong plank favoring the protection of slavery at the Democratic convention of 1860, but the northern Democrats would not go that far. The South fractured the Democratic Party by running a separate candidate, splitting the Democratic popular vote, and ensuring Lincoln's election.

The South panicked further as Slave states began to secede from the Union even before Lincoln took office. They compounded their errors by attacking federal positions at Fort Sumter—and the Civil War was on.

After years of bitter battle and horrific loss of life, the Southern cause was defeated. In 1863, Lincoln issued the Emancipation Proclamation freeing the slaves, and in the post-war years, the Thirteenth Amendment to the U.S.Constitution banned slavery.

Nonetheless, African-Americans were not brought into American society as free equals. The pernicious effects of slavery had prevented the slaves from developing the traditions of self-reliance, of education, and of democratic traditions common to the rest of American society. The two traditions were almost totally dichotomous. Even in the northern states, African-Americans tended to be devalued, and this gulf could not be breached simply by force of law. Time—generations of time—and evolution of all segments of society were required before the ideals of the abolition of slavery were realized.

Nonetheless, during the Reconstruction Period, the laws of "human action" continued working. The freed African-Americans built schools—even colleges—producing men and women of achievement. They went to work, and a small business class arose. With the passing of three generations, with the greater education of African-Americans, and with their wider participation in American life, the sensibilities of most Americans found civil restrictions on African-Americans increasingly anachronistic and intolerable. Accordingly, in the 1960s, a sweeping set of civil rights laws and initiatives were enacted to make minorities more fully equal participants in society. As a nation, we still have to deal with the negative aftermath of that era, but we are certainly in a far better place today. In practical terms, we have empowered an entire segment of the population to become more creative, productive, and entrepreneurial—creating a more powerful societal animal.

Women's Rights

Women did not enjoy the growing empowerment that men did from the Renaissance of the 12th century onwards. During those centuries, growing affluence of at least the upper classes, expansion of universities, growing literacy in general, the rise of science, and increasing entrepreneurship had become multiple strands of a new culture and a new world, largely in the hands of men.

In earlier times, women played a crucial, an honorable, and a fully productive, if not quite equal, role in society. When 90 percent of the population lived on the land in near serfdom and most of the others were artisans operating out of their homes, it was a moot point if women were somewhat less empowered. They played a crucial role in bearing and raising children, and were life-partners in running the farm and workshop. Many of us today can recall parents' and grandparents' lives where women may not have been "liberated" but were respected and equal mates.

Yet these circumstances were almost entirely in the confines of marriage and depended on the decency of the husband and pressures of an extended family. Women had little standing outside of marriage and virtually no legal protections. For example, as late as the 18ᵗʰ century in England, the most advanced state of the West, women were a legal nonentity. They had no claim on their own earnings; they could not enter a legal complaint; they could not re-tain council; they could not appear in court; and they could not vote. Children were presumed to belong to the father. Middle and upper class women were not expected to have an independent fi-nancial role. Jane Austen's name never appeared on her books; the Bronte sisters wrote under pseudonyms.

But women were not isolated from the empowerment trends of Western culture. Importantly, the Protestant Reformation pressed all adherents to be literate, to read the Bible, and to be judges of what faith required. Literate woman were able to follow the events of the Glorious Revolution and hear the arguments about the rights of man. They could read the works of Locke and other philoso-phers. Addressing the question of why such values did not apply to women was just a matter of time—an example of philosophy leading social change rather than the reverse.

What was perhaps unexpected was that the issue was addressed so clearly, articulately, and completely by one person, Mary Woll-stonecraft (1759-97), who wrote *Vindication of the Rights of Women*. She recognized the psychological importance of a woman achiev-ing some degree of self-actualization, and that she had to be a per-son in her own right, regardless of her position as wife or mother. Some degree of independence was necessary, requiring, in turn, the ability to earn her way. She wrote:

> How many women thus waste life away the prey of discon-tent, who might have practiced as physicians, regulated a farm, managed a shop, and stood erect, supported by their own industry ... Would men but generously snap our chains, and be content with rational fellowship instead of slavish obedience, they would find us more observant daughters, more affectionate sisters, more faithful wives, more reason-able mothers—in a word, better citizens.[458]

Others took up the theme. Angelina Grimke', an American Quaker, wrote in the mid-19ᵗʰ century: "My doctrine then is, whatever it is morally right for man to do, it is morally right for woman to do. Our duties originate, not from differences of sex, but from the diversity of our relations in life, the various gifts and talents committed to our care, and the different eras in which we live ... I recognize no rights but human rights—I know nothing of men's rights and women's rights; for in Christ Jesus, there is neither male nor female."[459]

But for the survival and growth of the societal animal, traditional ways cannot be discarded merely on the basis of argument. Leadership, experimentation, and proven benefits shape changing values. The new ways have to be seen to work.

How such change came about can be seen by examining the issue of women's suffrage. In both England and the United States the suffrage movement gained strength in the latter half of the 19th century. The first convention to discuss votes for women met in 1848 in Seneca Falls, N.Y. A resolution was adopted that women be given equal rights as citizens. Afterwards the National Woman Suffrage Association was founded by Elizabeth Stanton and Susan B. Anthony. Later that year (1869) the American Woman Suffrage Association was formed, headed by Henry Ward Beecher. The two associations later merged, and after more than 70 years, the Nineteenth Amendment to the U.S. Constitution granting suffrage was adopted in August 1920. Great Britain granted complete suffrage to women in 1928.

Other political battles were to follow. If women were to gain practical equality, they had to have greater control over their persons. This necessarily included reproduction rights—i.e., contraception and abortion—access to education, and equal opportunities in the work place. Such widespread change has occurred throughout the West. Indeed, women are widely represented in most professions and comprise more than half the student body in U.S. higher education. Western nations are richer and stronger for this evolution, which allows half the population to play a much fuller role in the economy—in contrast, for example, with some Islamic nations where women are not allowed out of the home unescorted by a male relative nor allowed to drive a car.

Gay Liberation

Gay liberation is emblematic of the empowerment of the individual because it goes to the acceptance of individual behavior at odds with the tradition of the community. Homosexuality threatened the larger society because it seemed to undermine the reproductive capacity of the societal animal, and because its occasional effeminate side seemed at odds with an essential martial vigor. Moreover, because it was generally hidden from view, the extent and the societal costs of its suppression seemed negligible. Accordingly, the fight to achieve gay liberation was—and continues to be—a telling example of the evolution of values.

While instinct, intuition, and communal values lend themselves to an aversion to homosexual behavior, it appears that a strong antipathy did not arise in the West until the late Middle Ages. In all likelihood, this was because the concept of gay "otherness" had not arisen. In early times, most men fulfilled their reproductive function; the sexual outlets and partners they selected for love were not that noteworthy.

Indeed, according to John Boswell there was no legal prohibition against same-sex physical relationships until Justinian's Codification in the 6th century A.D. Moreover, early Christians did not seem especially troubled by references in the Bible.[460]

So the modern fear of homosexuality is somewhat of a mystery. Boswell traces its roots to the late Middle Ages with an argument that is plausible, if not conclusive:

Beginning roughly in the latter half of the twelfth century, however, a more virulent hostility appeared in popular literature and eventually spread to theological and legal writings as well. The causes of this change cannot be adequately explained, but they were probably closely related to the general increase in intolerance of minority groups apparent in ecclesiastical and secular institutions throughout the thirteenth and fourteenth centuries. Crusades against non-Christians and heretics, the expulsion of the Jews from many areas of Europe, the rise of the Inquisition, efforts to stamp out sorcery and witchcraft, all testify to increasing intolerance of deviation from the standards of the majority, enforceable for the first time in the newly emerging corporate states of the High Middle Ages. This intolerance was reflected in and perpetuated by its incorporation into theological, moral, and legal compilations of the later Middle Ages, many of which continued to influence European society for centuries.[461]

These values were increasingly absorbed into societal traditions; they did not remain simply institutional pronouncements. And they were retained by Protestant communities after the Reformation, when the Western individual was increasingly empowered to think for himself in theological and economic matters. But most discussion of sex became off limits.

These repressive attitudes continued into virtually the present day. In the post-World War II era, witch hunts occurred in government to identify and eliminate gays from public employment. In the public and private sectors, jobs were lost, mental illness was exacerbated, suicides took place, and most gay activity was closeted and anonymous. The tragedy and waste of human talent was, in practical terms, pointless. These values from the Middle Ages created fears in the general population that could not—at first, anyway—be addressed rationally.

A thaw in this frozen state of affairs came about through Alfred Kinsey's revolutionary work on human sexuality. Published in 1948, *Sexual Behavior in the Human Male* presented statistics on the wide range of sexual behavior that actually existed, however out of view. Kinsey showed that as much as 37 percent of males had had at least experienced one homosexual encounter, and that perhaps 4 percent of the population was exclusively gay. Admittedly the limited sources of data available to him (e.g., many interviews occurred within prison populations) skewed the results. Nonetheless, the results shattered the prevailing mythos of what was *normal*. More importantly, debate was conducted on factual grounds rather than on irrational fears and a misreading of the Bible[462].

Two decades later, on the basis of their research, the American Psychological Association declared that homosexuality was not a mental illness—and there was no reason to believe gays experienced any more mental illness than the average person or that their states of subjective wellbeing were in any way diminished.

Gay liberation is a quintessential example of the empowerment of the individual in Western culture. It is, of course, consistent with the philosophy embodied in the phrase "pursuit of happiness." Yet the irrational but powerful fears of many were that the bedrock values of society—the cohesiveness of the family unit and morality in general—would be undermined by public sanction of a gay lifestyle. Moreover, it was not apparent that public acceptance of gays was required for society to benefit from their presence and some quarters continue to protest associated elements of institutional and legal change.

Thus this evolutionary change continues to be contentious. As Andrew Sullivan put it in the *New Republic*, the fight is more likely to be settled person by person, heart by heart. And that is how many enduring value shifts occur.

We have explored how the value system of Western civilization evolved along the trajectory from survival values to self-expression values. The starting point was our primitive, largely rural beginnings where extended family networks and clan solidarity were essential for survival. Subsequently, with greater affluence and leisure, some cultures became more introspective and aware of the powers of reason. We saw how a flowering of this stage occurred virtually simultaneously in Jewish, Greek, Hindu, and Chinese cultures about 2,500 years ago. These various cultures took different paths, with the Greek and Judaic cultures focused on rationalism and virtue, while the Hindu and Chinese cultures became largely 'other-worldly' in outlook.

At first blush, in terms of individual freedom and self-expression, there was not much to distinguish among the major cultures one millennium ago. The West was just emerging from the Dark Ages. Society was stratified in a feudal set of relationships, and a Catholic metaphysics seemed almost adequate to explain it. But it was a pinched view of sinful man as a creature preoccupied with eternal life. Still Catholic theology contained within it a neo-platonic rationalist outlook that was to prove invaluable for future evolution.

The Renaissance shifted worldviews from a preoccupation with eternal life to a focus on man in the here and now. Growing affluence, discovery of ancient Greek philosophy, and the rise of science vastly expanded man's intellectual horizons. Then the Reformation charged man with personal responsibility for discovering of truth. The ensuing splintering of sects and the bloody religious wars caused men to seek new bases for understanding men's rights and men's duties, one to another. There was a flowering of philosophic attempts, and although philosophers never succeeded in discovering an entirely coherent new metaphysics, they did illuminate the meaning of values inherent in a more mercantile, a more educated, and a more rights-oriented society. Importantly, Locke and others promulgated the view that all men were created equal and had the unalienable rights to life, liberty, and the pursuit of happiness.

After another two centuries of evolution, most Western societies agreed that these sentiments applied to women, to members of all races, and to others out of the cultural mainstream who were found not to threaten the essential well being of the societal animal. The nations holding such values have relatively increased their social capital by allowing all members of society to exercise their creativity, initiative, and productivity for the benefit of all.

Having seen how the West evolved along four paths of change, we are in a position to appreciate why value surveys detect significant differences between the affluent West and other countries. The next chapter will examine the world's principle cultural groupings to see more specifically how economic performance is tied to underlying values.

7
Cross-Cultural Performance

The central conservative truth is that it is culture, not politics, that determines the success of a society. The central liberal truth is that politics can change a culture and save it from itself. – Daniel Patrick Moynihan[463]

We have seen how the West evolved over the last thousand years or so to establish an extended economic order defined by free markets, individual freedom, and representative government, that proved to be more conducive to generating affluence for mankind than any hitherto or subsequent socio-political constructs. In that sense, this book has addressed the question of why some countries prosper. We have still to address the other side of that question—i.e., why other countries have not. Having unearthed the 'blueprint' of the extended order, and armed with the analytical tools provided by the key factors for economic growth, we are in a position to examine the track records of other countries to better understand the differing outcomes.

By contrasting the performance of other cultures, we can see more clearly the difficulties involved in other societies adopting the West's blueprint. There have been many successes. Countries, which have had a certain cultural readiness and which have emulated key aspects of the West's evolved institutions, have prospered as well. In effect, we will see that those outcomes are strongly dependent on a country's cultural readiness: cultures that evolved value systems along lines pragmatically similar to the Protestant ethic are most able to adopt the practices of the extended order. Importantly, those practices entail a large societal 'radius of trust', a drive to fulfill obligations, a sense of personal responsibility, and an ingrained work ethic. The radius of trust, while less tangible than other values, has perhaps the widest ramifications—e.g., a society's capability of developing certain key institutions such as those typical of civil society or large corporations, the willingness to abide by the results of elections, and the ability to minimize transaction costs within free markets. As we examine the world's major cultures, we shall see a wide divergence in such readiness.

Of all the societies to be examined, Japan's cultural endowment most readily provided the values essential for modernization and rapid growth. Other East Asian countries, such as the four 'dragons' (Taiwan, Hong Kong, South Korea, and Singapore), inherited a Sino Confucian culture, different in some respects from Japan, but still highly compatible with the dictates of the extended order. Other East Asian countries, with a strong Chinese presence in a largely non-Sino culture, were able to progress as well, though with differing results. Cultures lacking both the Protestant and the Confucian heritages, notably Islamic and African countries, have had the greatest difficulty in achieving economic development.

But in the construct of the laws of societal evolution, all countries to some degree will attempt to emulate the West because it will lead them to become fitter societal animals—i.e., wealthier, healthier, creative, better informed, and more powerful than before. Each country, however, follows a unique path; the Protestant/Confucian values are only part of the cultural inheritance, and economic development is only one part of national identity. While, as we saw in the West, economic development tends to drive other evolutionary trends, particularly the need for rule of law and representative government, other evolutionary trends such as the increasing empowerment of the individual may well play out differently in other cultures. In any event, emulation can be extraordinarily difficult where it is not congruent with a society's traditions and values. Success is not just a function of educating the young, investing capital, and drawing on the scientific achievements of the West. Indeed, success can be ephemeral if imposed by others before a society has achieved a necessary cultural foundation—as is illustrated by the early experience of the Britons vis-à-vis the Roman Empire.

The Difficulty of Emulating Other Cultures: The Early British Example

An example, drawn by Thomas Sowell from Britain's early existence, illuminates the difficulty of one culture emulating aspects of another more advanced culture.[1] He describes Britain's situation before, during and after the Roman conquests. Sowell writes that for about one-fifth of its recorded history, Britain was a conquered province of the Roman Empire. Britain was easily conquered by outnumbered Romans because the latter were better equipped and organized, representing a far more advanced culture than that of Britain at the time. While the British had been relatively primitive before the Roman conquest, they were by no means simple hunters and gatherers. They had agriculture, weaving, iron workers, and economic transactions utilizing coins.

At first, the Romans faced massive revolts. But the lack of unity among the Britains and Roman military superiority eventually led to the island's subjugation. Sowell writes that in the ensuing centuries, Romans conquered Britain culturally as well as militarily. Well-to-do Britains wore Roman attire, spoke Latin, and employed Roman architecture and city planning, including arcades and baths. Roads were built and commerce flourished. The Romans built a major port on the Thames, which was to become London. Nonetheless, this acculturalization did not penetrate deeply into the mass of the population.

After almost four centuries, the collapsing Empire began to withdraw its legions from Britain. By the beginning of the 6th century, British towns and roads were crumbling, the forests were reclaiming some human settlements, markets disappeared, and population declined. At the micro-economic level, examples of regression included pottery ceasing to be mass produced, and even the use of bricks disappearing for a millennium. Moreover, the population was increasingly unable to protect itself from invading barbarians from the continent – notably the Angles and the Saxons.

Sowell concludes that the general collapse occurred because the resident British culture had not sufficiently advanced to maintain the more advanced Roman culture which had been something of a veneer.

SOURCE: Thomas Sowell, *Conquests and Civilizations*, pp. 22-27

With this caution as to the difficulty of developing advanced economies, we will examine societal efforts, culture by culture, to gain an understanding of the centrality of values and worldviews to that goal. What that review will show us is that modernization is quite doable, indeed, can be achieved in the space of a generation or so, but only when there is a cultural readiness and where there is determined and inspired leadership.

Our cross-cultural examination begins with the newly advanced countries, notably Japan and other East-Asian countries; moves through Latin America, which stumbles; and on to those countries that seem to be stuck in a nondevelopmental rut: Islamic countries and sub-Saharan Africa. Finally, to reinforce the importance of values vis-à-vis growth, per se, our examination concludes with the dramatic case of Communism in the Soviet Union, a case study of how misconceived values can not only impede development but also can severely cripple the societal animal.

JAPAN

Japan is the most dramatic instance of a country successfully emulating the evolutionary changes that occurred in the West. A close look at how Japan made the transition can be particularly revealing, especially contrasted with the experience of other, less successful countries.

While Japan modernized along Western lines, it retained its distinct culture and remained a different societal animal. Its dramatic success is traceable to a unique cultural readiness to embrace the dictates of the extended order. In effect, Japan's evolution had over centuries developed values and institutions pragmatically similar to many in the West. Thus, Japan is a useful illustration of parallel societal evolution outside the West and is worthy of in-depth examination.

Japan's Threshold of Institutions and Values

At first glance, Japan in the mid-nineteenth century was a poor, isolated, backward country in the North Pacific, on the verge of suffering the same imperialist incursions that had been the fate of South Asia and China. However, Japan astonished the world by leapfrogging centuries and becoming an advanced nation within a generation. It could do so because, despite its isolation, Japan had evolved a certain 'threshold of values' that facilitated the adoption of the ways and institutions of modern society.

Japan's relevant cultural inheritance included: (a) a relatively decentralized political system inherited from its feudal past; (b) a supportive set of philosophies respecting honor and rational thinking; (c) a basic, if rudimentary, mercantile system of trade, banking, and small industry; and (d) a respect for learning—striking similarities with medieval Europe.

The Feudal Inheritance

The Japan of eleven centuries ago was in a 'Golden Age', with a government headed by an emperor, whose power was balanced by the great families of Japan. Durant writes of this age, the *Engi* period (901-922), that wealth accumulated and was centered in a fashionable life of luxury, refinement, and culture hardly equaled again until the courts of the 15th century Medici and the salons of the 18th century French enlightenment. Kyoto had by 1190 a population of half a million—more than any European city other than Constantinople and Cordova.[464]

But extravagance in the court, incompetence in the government, and corruption throughout the land lead to widespread crime, brigandage, and piracy to an extent that the emperor increasingly lost effective power: "the peasants, no longer protected from bandits by imperial armies or police, paid taxes to the shoguns, or generals, instead of to the emperor, for only the shoguns were able to protect them from robbery. The feudal system triumphed in Japan for the same reason that it had triumphed in Europe: local sources of authority grew in power as a central and distant government failed to maintain security and order."[465]

Although the institution of the emperor continued, the Emperor himself became a mere figurehead. Japan existed as a feudal state for the next several centuries, a state not dissimilar to Europe after the fall of Rome—i.e., there were multiple power centers, chaos, and intermittent civil wars.

The situation stabilized dramatically under Iyeyasu, who established the Tokugawa Shogunate in 1600. Durant writes: "The feudal order in his [Iyeyasu's] judgment was the best that could be devised for actual human beings; it provided a rational balance between central and local power, it established a natural and hereditary system of social and economic organization, and it preserved the continuity of society without subjecting it to despotic authority. It must be admitted that Iyeyasu organized the most perfect form of feudal government ever known."[466]

While the emperor resided in seclusion in Kyoto, the Shogunate, representing the provincial nobility (the Daimyo), sat in Edo (now modern Tokyo), providing the de facto governance of the nation. The peace and order provided by the Shogunate allowed the revival of trade and prosperity, analogous to the economic revival that occurred during the 12th century in Europe. Japan was here treading along a developmental path not dissimilar to Europe's in the late Middle Ages.

Philosophic Values
Japanese culture had evolved a value system, which while uniquely Eastern, embodied personal ethics that were pragmatically similar to the Protestant ethic and were to play a similar and essential role in Japan's modernization. Francis Fukuyama emphasizes the role of values in the modernization process: "If the institutions of democracy and capitalism are to work properly, they must coexist with certain premodern cultural habits that ensure their proper functioning. Law, contract, and economic rationality provide a necessary but not sufficient basis for both the stability and prosperity of postindustrial societies; they must as well be leavened with reciprocity, moral obligation, duty toward community, and trust, which are based on habit rather than rational calculation. The latter are not anachronisms in a modern society but rather the sine qua non of the latter's success."[467]

While Japan's culture was influenced by several different sets of religious teachings – notably Shintoism, Buddhism, and Confucianism, as well as the warrior code, Bushido (Way of the Knight) – Confucianism played the largest role in regard to Japan's readiness to modernize.

Confucianism
Despite Confucianism's preponderant influence in shaping the values of Japanese society, it had not been seriously considered until Tokugawa times. Its substantive incursion into Japanese value systems in the late 16th century was the result of the scion of Japan's

most famous family, Fujiwara Seigma, seeking the teachings of Confucius and gathering about him a group of young scholars. As Durant put it, they "looked upon the Chinese philosophers as the revelation of a brave new world of secular thought,"[468] rather like Western Europe's rediscovering Greek philosophy. The first Tokugawa Shoguns were also taken by these philosophies. Indeed, Durant reports that they found these teachings more persuasive than either Christianity or Buddhism. To them, Christianity appeared to be "a medley of incredible fancies," while Buddhism's otherworldly approach appeared to be "a degenerative doctrine that threatened to weaken the fibre and morale of the Japanese nation" [i.e., the Japanese societal animal].[469]

In short, Confucianism was an ethical system focused on the here and now, which required no adoption of unprovable belief in divine revelation. The Confucian ethical code, inter alia, defines duties in five relationships: father/teacher and son, ruler and subject, husband and wife, older brother and younger brother, and friend to friend—all entailing reciprocity. Its virtues were seen to have produced an evolutionary fit Chinese societal animal, which contributed to China's preeminence in East Asia for a millennium or more. Its tenets strengthened the family, enhanced a personal work ethic, and promoted general governmental stability as a result of its acceptance of authority. These values in turn led to the accumulation of wealth, and emphasized education.[470]

These features had evolved in a culturally unique way within the Chinese societal animal and possessed no intellectual link with the Protestant ethic of the West. Nonetheless, there was a pragmatic compatibility. In his anthropological studies of Japanese society, George DeVos concludes:

> The emphasis on effort and perseverance, and the manner in which this is reflected in hard work, suggest a puritan-like ethic for Niiike as a whole. As an aspect of the rapid industrialization of Japan, this Japanese ethic recalls the role of the Protestant ethic in the industrialization of Europe. In Niiike one must toil diligently, but not for God's salvation; success in hard work proves that one is dutiful toward one's parents and loves them. There is no transmutation of feelings toward one's parents into a personal relationship

with a transcendental deity, but there is instead a respectful idealization of a father image, and a loving devotion to a mother who deserves eternal gratitude.[471]

In this way, Confucianism promoted behavioral characteristics, including honoring commitments, a sense of personal responsibility, interpersonal trust, and a work ethic—all of which facilitated Japan's transition to a free market.

Beyond its influence in generating a sense of personal responsibility and a work ethic, Confucianism produced in Japan (but not in China) values consonant with a high-trust society—i.e., supporting "the expectation that arises within a community of regular, honest, and cooperative behavior, based on commonly shared norms, on the part of other members of that community."[472] In such societies, peer pressure shows little toleration for lying, for failing to meet commitments, and for making excuses that 'everyone does it'.

Fukuyama argues that the roots of Japan's high-trust culture lie in its feudal past. In contrast to China, Japanese clans did not claim ancestry from a common progenitor, and established their primary loyalty to a particular feudal lord, which produced an inclination to regimentation vis-à-vis authority that has continued to the present day. Yet at the same time, relatively weaker traditional family obligations lead the Japanese to have greater proclivity for religious, political, professional, and social organizations, as well as the possibilities for business entities.[473]

Because of this difference, Japan was able to develop practices suitable to the extended economic order. For example, in Japan, as in England, the bulk of an estate was inherited by the elder son or by an adopted heir. Younger sons were expected to leave home and establish separate households.[474] Similarly, weaker family ties resulted in Japan moving to professional management of business enterprises, even when family-owned, at an early period of modernization.[475] Altogether, Fukuyama considers Confucian values to be the basis for a wide radius of trust within Japanese society.

Confucianism also facilitated Japanese acceptance of the West's scientific tradition. Its Oyomei School, for example, emphasized teachings similar to Western thought (such as Scholasticism), and they sought to deduce right and wrong from the conscience of the

individual rather than from the traditions of society. The philosopher Nakaye propounded a philosophy in which the world was a
unity of things and reason. "God and this unity were one; the world
of things was his body, the universal law was his soul."[476]

In terms of understanding, clarity and honesty of thought and
expression were the first lessons. According to Confucius, "The
whole end of speech is to be understood ... When you know a
thing, to hold that you know it; and when you do not, to admit this
fact—this is knowledge." Durant said that obscurity of thought and
inaccuracy of speech seemed to Confucius to be national calamities.[477] While Confucianism did not lead to a deeper metaphysics
on its own, it certainly helped promote a relatively no-nonsense
approach to seeking truth. Importantly, there was no built-in bias
against science. Indeed, a belief in the unity of things embraced science once it was available.

Confucianism, however, incorporated values unconducive
to opening society to the extended order, for example, disdain of
commerce, suspicion of individual rights vis-à-vis group norms,
comfort with authoritarian government, and prizing stability over
innovation. But as happened in the West, positive experience with
modernization generated new attitudes toward commerce and entrepreneurship.

In all, the regimentation produced by feudal traditions, combined with a wide radius of trust associated with Confucianism,
contributed to Japan's ability to modernize rapidly when the time
came.

Buddhism and the Bushido Martial Code
Fukuyama also notes the importance of other religious influences in
shaping the renowned Japanese work ethic, especially Buddhism.
For example, in early Tokugawa times, Buddhist monks sanctified
mundane economic activity, which generated an ethic similar to
Puritanism. In addition, the Zen Buddhist tradition of perfection-
ism in everyday, secular activities was carried through to Japan's
industry.[478]

Another contributor to mutual trust and reciprocal obligation
in Japanese society was the Samurai tradition. Samurai warriors,
who served the nobility, accepted Bushido, a stern code of honor,

under which virtue was "deciding upon a certain course of conduct in accordance with reason, without wavering; to die when it is right to die, to strike when it is right to strike." Durant says they bore all suffering silently, and suppressed every display of emotion; their women were taught to rejoice when informed that their husbands had been killed on the battlefield. They recognized no obligation except that of loyalty to their superiors. It was common for a Samurai to disembowel himself on the death of his lord, or when disgraced for dishonor.[479] At any given time, there were a million or more Samurai, a not inconsiderable part of the population. Given the esteem with which the Samurai were held, their values of commitment, loyalty, obligation, and courage were honored in larger Japanese society as well.

This picture is borne out in the results of *The World Value Survey*. For example, all of the Confucian cultures, as all of the Protestant, have populations who trust people in general (in contrast to Islamic or historically Catholic cultures).[480] Consistent with this finding is Japan and European nations having low levels of corruption according to 'Corruption Perceptions Indices'.[481]

Trade and Industry

As we have seen, over long periods of stability in which human action is allowed free rein, wealth can increase considerably through greater productivity and economies of scale—what Deepak Lal refers to as Smithean Growth. Such growth occurred during Japan's feudal period: the population increased from 5 million in the 11th century to 18 million around 1600. During the Shogunate, between 1600 and 1850, agricultural production doubled while the population increased only 45 percent, evidence of higher productivity. Growth came about, in part, because the central government and the local *daimyo* removed internal trade barriers—abolishing tolls and breaking guild monopolies, as well as providing public goods such as flood control, fire prevention, sanitary arrangements, judicial and policing bodies.[482]

As in Medieval Europe, the growth of trade naturally led to a spontaneous growth of financial institutions. Durant wrote: "One of the most powerful of the guilds was that of the money-changers, who accepted deposits, issued vouchers and promissory notes, made loans to industry and government, and (by 1636) performed all the major functions of finance. Rich merchants and financiers rose to prominence in the cities, and began to look with jealous eye upon the exclusive political power of a feudal aristocracy that angered them by scorning the pursuit of gold. Slowly, throughout the Tokugawa era, the mercantile wealth of the nation grew..."[483]

Education and Literacy
Part of Japan's cultural readiness for modernization lay in a respect for education reflected in a core educational establishment of long tradition. This tradition extends as far back as the 8th century when emperors established the first Japanese university and the Golden Age when rich families maintained schools for their children. With time a system of provincial schools was developed, whose graduates were eligible for the university. University graduates, in turn, who passed required tests, were eligible for public office.

While much of this system broke down during centuries of civil wars, when the Tokugawa Shogunate was formed, Iyeyasu launched a number of initiatives including a training school for public administration, which later developed into the University of Tokyo. Further, students, doctors, and priests were encouraged to set up schools to provide primary education in private homes and temples, so that by 1750, 800 such schools existed, with some 40,000 students.[484] Indeed, during the Tokugawa era, Japan showed a greater interest in education than any other culture encountered by the colonialist powers.

Thus, by the end of the Shogunate in the mid-nineteenth century, Japan had many of the essential ingredients to support a modern society: cohesive cultural values, experience with decentralized power, a quasi-market economy with entrepreneurial traditions, and respect for education and literacy. But what Japan lacked was a rationalist tradition, the basis for science, representative government, and a tradition favoring individualism. Nonetheless, there was nothing inherently hostile to these factors, and, as such, they could be readily acquired by the Japanese. Indeed, at the time of the Meiji Restoration in 1868, the Japanese did not lag significantly behind the Europeans with regard to key cultural values and institutions.

The Effort to Modernize

Having the potential to modernize is one thing; making it a reality is another. From whence came the impetus and Japan's collective will to do so?

The Impetus

Japan, under the Shogunate was a homogeneous, coherent, and prosperous society with long traditions, some of which had been borrowed from Korea and China a millennium earlier. And it was not a closed society. The Japanese traded with these nations in the East Asian ambit and understood the benefits of such trade. But when Japan encountered approaches from the vastly different, and potentially more powerful, culture of the West, it made strenuous efforts to shield itself from that incursion. When those efforts crumbled, Japan reversed course in an effort to face the West on equal terms and thereby protect its sovereignty.

Initial contact with the West came via the Portuguese in 1542, but was not immediately alarming. The first meaningful incursion came with Catholic missionaries, when in 1549, St. Francis Xavier established a community of Christians that within a generation numbered 70 Jesuits and 150,000 converts. Nagasaki became a largely Christian city, its ruler actively spreading the new faith. Buddhism was suppressed in these regions, and Buddhist priests were driven away.

This assault on Japanese tradition alarmed the Shogun Hideyoshi, who issued an edict in 1587 stating: "Having learned from our faithful councilors that foreign religieux have come into our realm, where they preach a law contrary to that of Japan, and that they have even had the audacity to destroy temples dedicated to our (native gods) Kami and Hotoke; although this outrage merits the severest punishment, wishing nevertheless to show them mercy, we order them under the pain of death to quit Japan within twenty days. During that space no harm or hurt will come to them. But at the expiration of that term, we order that if any of them be found in our States, they shall be seized and punished as the greatest criminals." [485] These decrees put an end to Western religious proselytism.

Nonetheless, Iyeyasu, his successor and founder of the Tokuga-wa Shogunate, was open to expanding trade with the West when the Dutch and the English appeared early in the 17th century. But as attractive as trade opportunities might have seemed, those possibilities were overridden by the religious issues. The Japanese decided to exclude all Westerners from trade with the exception of the Dutch and even they were to be kept isolated on an artificial island built in the port of Nagasaki. Then to shield Japan further, *Seclusion Decrees* were issued over a six-year period (1633 to 1639). Under these decrees, Japanese ships were not permitted to sail overseas, and foreign captains could not employ Japanese sailors. Violators were to be put to death. Trade with the West was limited to certain goods, and all Western ships were restricted to Nagasaki.[486]

For two centuries Japan became more and more isolated. Other than limited information from castaways, crews of wrecked ships, and the occasional emissary, Japanese knowledge of the West came largely from the Dutch trading station in Nagasaki. Nonetheless, by the beginning of the 19th century, foreign intrusions became increasingly overt: Russians in the Kuril Islands in the north, British ships landing to procure provisions. Such events led to an order to expel any Westerners "without thinking twice," and any ship seen approaching the coast was to be fired upon and driven off.

But the Japanese scholar Watanabe foresaw that stubborn resistance to the outside world by the Japanese would lead to disaster. He argued that the West, with its strength in science and technology and its open class structure and effective political institutions was a more potent predator than Asia had ever known. This was not a message Japanese rulers wanted to hear. Nonetheless, his writings registered and would play a role in the national debate some years hence.[487]

Unfolding events in China—including the Opium War (1839-42, in which Britain forced China to remove trade restrictions)—reinforced Japanese fears of foreign intrusion. Growing numbers of Western ships appeared, but it was the United States that forced the issue of opening Japan to trade. In 1853, Admiral Mathew Perry arrived with four armed ships, each of which was six or more times larger than any existing Japanese vessel. Perry's mission was to gain safe treatment for shipwrecked American seamen, the right to buy coal for refueling, and to have one or more Japanese ports opened for trade with the United States. Perry did not engage in the protracted negotiations desired by the Japanese; rather he warned that failure to meet his demands would bring on a war that the Japanese would surely lose. Perry gave the Japanese a few months to consider their position before negotiations proceeded. The Japanese acquiesced, and negotiations resulted in each side achieving their minimum objectives. The Americans obtained re-supply privileges for their ships in two ports, which Perry foresaw would open the way to trade, while the Japanese managed to avoid the unequal treaty system that had been imposed on China.[488]

But as Jansen writes, further demands were not long in coming. In 1856, Townsend Harris, the new American representative, pushed for a formal agreement for the exchange of representatives and the conduct of trade. Specifically, his goals were to open four ports to trade and to secure residence rights for American representatives in each as well as in Osaka and Edo. The Japanese realized that the British, the French, and the Russians would not be far behind in wanting equivalent treatment.

Despite the skill displayed by the Japanese negotiators in playing a weak hand, Japanese ruling circles were uncertain how to respond to the American demands. Some favored accepting the demands, while others suggested prolonging the negotiations so that the Americans would give up; but most wanted to stand and fight.[489] The debate continued over a decade during which time certain ideas began to coalesce: building strength against the West, enhancing the Imperial mystique, and uniting the Shogunate and the Imperial Court.

As a program for change coalesced, the reformers looked to the Emperor's mystique for inspiring change while specifics were drawn from observations of the West. But not all the domains agreed, presumably fearing loss of power and influence. A brief Restoration War between the reformers and dissenting provinces ensued until the spring of 1869, when reforming forces were victorious. These events came to be referred to as the Meiji Restoration—i.e., restoration of the emperor as supreme authority and abolition of the Shogunate, but an emperor with sharply circumscribed powers, as will be seen.

Steps to the Modern Era

Japan's unique evolutionary track had positioned it to modernize. But it lagged behind the West in areas such as science and technology and building modern political and financial institutions. To address these gaps, Japan piggybacked on Western achievements through investigation and learning.

Learning from the West

Japan had made limited efforts to understand the West even during the period of the Seclusion Decrees. For example, each arriving captain at the Dutch trading station at Nagasaki was obliged to provide the Japanese an account of what had happened in the outside world since the previous port-of-call and they were encouraged to bring books for translation.

These efforts accelerated during the last decade of the Tokugawa Shogunate, when Japan focused on upgrading its military technology. An Institute for the Study of Barbarian Books (later to become the Institute for Western Books, and then the Institute for Development) was established based on arguments that:

> "It is urgent that we know more about the West; by studying the truly useful things like the strength and weakness, the semblance and the reality of each country, the state of its army and navy, the advantages and drawbacks of its machinery, we can adopt their strong points and avoid their shortcomings ... [We should translate] books on bombardment, on the construction of batteries, on fortifications, books on building warships and maneuvering them, books on sailing and navigation, books on training soldiers and sailors, on machinery, books that set forth the real strength and weakness, appearance and reality, of these countries."[490]

A series of missions was sent to the United States and Europe in the 1860s to examine the West's political and industrial underpinnings. The delegates, many of whom became Japan's leading managers and intellectuals in the ensuing decades, understood that industrial development was what distinguished strong from weak nations. "Paris might be more beautiful than London, but England, for all its dirt and noise and squalor of its urban poor, generated more power."[491]

One member wrote in his diary: "Nothing has more urgency for us than schools... unless we establish an unshakable national foundation we will not be able to elevate our country's prestige in a thousand years ... Our people are no different from the Americans or Europeans of today; it is all a matter of education or lack of education."[492] Members also concluded that the immediate danger to Japanese independence was less pressing than thought. Rather than undertake a crash program of militarization, they counseled 'defensive modernization' so that Japan could work its way up the ladder of development in a more coherent fashion. Equally important, they concluded that Japan had to develop representative institutions in order to build consensus for government actions. One member, having reviewed the U.S. Constitution, wrote that constitutions provided a way for the people of the whole country to express their wishes and thereby build a durable consensus.[493]

Jansen wrote: "The lessons were clear. Japan had entered a highly competitive world in which victory went to the educated and united. It should choose carefully from among the models before it: American education, British industrialization, French jurisprudence, and German representational institutions held particular promise. It would have to modernize those institutions ... thus postponing immediate gratification for the sake of long-term gain."[494] With regard to military organization and tactics, the Japanese first turned to the French and then to the Germans for land forces; for the navy, the model had always been the British.[495]

Adapting Western Models to Japan's Traditions
It was one thing for intellectuals and government officials to identify the direction of change. It was quite another to change institutions with strong vested interests. The radical changes in Japan involved: (a) dismantling the feudal structure, (b) developing a constitutional form of government, and (c) establishing representative government through elections. Japan did all this in less than a generation.

With regard to the feudal structure the question was how to disempower the daimyo (the provincial nobility) and the samurai.

One reason the Japanese reformers had more freedom of action than was often the case in the West lay in the legal status and traditional roles of the daimyo. The daimyo did not hold hereditary rights to their domains in the way that the European aristocracy did. Indeed, daimyo were often removed from their positions as events and policy dictated. In any event, daimyo were persuaded after the Restoration by financial payments to step down. In addition, the upper house of the newly created legislative body, the Diet, included many daimyo, thus allowing them their prestige and some residual power. The situation with the samurai was even easier: the samurai had lost their military role in a world with modern arms and, to ease the transition, their annual stipends were simply reconstituted as a form of pension.

The approach to establishing a constitutional order followed a track similar to the others areas of forced modernization—the best Western models were examined with an eye to integrating them with Japanese traditions. Although impressed with the American constitutional order, they focused more on the German, specifically the Prussian Constitution of 1850. The German model appeared suitable because it linked the principle of representative government with the power to tax, and it structured a government under constitutional law. Moreover, it encompassed a 'social monarchy' in which power was unified in the monarch, which coincided well with the new role envisioned for the emperor in Japan.[496] However, the emperor's new role was by no means an autocratic one. Indeed, he was to be shielded from the appearance of policy making so that he could not be faulted for bad results.

In developing Japan's constitution, the drafters showed keen insight into the difficulties of imposing a constitution on a nation without democratic traditions. Even today, we continue to overlook the importance of cultural values and traditions when we encourage democracy on merely abstract grounds. The potential problems were clearly seen at the time. Jansen writes "disparities of evolution and development combined to suggest caution. When former President Ulysses S. Grant visited Japan on his world tour in 1879, he, too, warned government figures against offering, prematurely, liberties they would not be able to take back. [Herbert] Spencer himself had warned of Japanese social fragmentation under rapid modernization ...."[497] The drafters believed that imperial sovereignty would be a rampart to prevent politics from falling into the hands of the 'uncontrollable masses'.[498] As an additional bulwark, the Japanese framers of the constitution limited the franchise to men who paid a direct national tax of 15 yen, similar to limitations employed by both the United States and Great Britain early in their evolution toward representative government.

Another feature of Japan's constitutional structure that would have major consequences in the 20th century related to the armed forces. In effect, the military was not fully subject to civilian control. Jansen noted: "ordinances stipulated that the chief of staff should be the emperor's major adviser, with direct access to him on policy and strategy. Yet, the military reported only to the emperor. The right of "direct command" might not be exercised very often by the sovereign himself, but it prevented interference in decisions affecting the military from civilian government and so gave military advisers a powerful weapon in internal political disputes."[499] The consequences of weak civilian control of the military were to become increasingly evident in the 20th century as Japan pursued its imperialist ambitions.

The new constitution was drafted largely by a small group in seclusion. Its provisions were debated in numerous meetings, many in front of the emperor, for the better part of a year. It was made official by imperial promulgation on February 11, 1889, and the new government was inaugurated the next year. First came the formation of an upper house of parliament consisting of newly appointed peers of the realm. In July 1890 the first national election of the lower chamber, the House of Representatives, was held, with more than 1,000 candidates competing for 300 seats. No such representative government existed in the world anywhere else other than in a few countries in the West.

Success

Japan's dramatic accomplishments could be seen in both the military and economic domains. The impetus for the Japanese effort to modernize had, of course, been to ensure that Japan could defend itself from Western incursions and from unequal treaties of the sort inflicted by the West on China. In short order, Japan surpassed such modest ambitions. In 1894, Japan declared war on China and won a speedy victory. A decade later in the Russo-Japanese War the Japanese defeated the Russians both on land (at Mukden) and at sea (the battle of the Straits of Tsushima), leaving Japan in the paramount position in Korea until after the Second World War, ending Russia's expansion in China, and beginning the end of Europe's rule in the East. These successes, unfortunately, were to rekindle Japanese imperialist ambitions from prior centuries and lead to the tragic consequences of the Second World War.

But it is Japan's economic achievement that is of greatest interest to this cross-cultural survey. In the space of a century, even with the devastation of World War II, Japan's economy grew to be the second largest on the planet and its people enjoyed one of the highest standards of living. This achievement was a product of (mostly) sound macroeconomic policies, the rule of law, a high savings rate, and a disciplined, hard-working population. These factors were able to come into play, because the Japanese culture, in contrast to others to be examined, was not generally antagonistic to them—i.e., to entrepreneurship, to wealth creation, to the accumulation and investment of capital, and to property rights. At the same time, the Japanese respected personal achievement and did not generally look to the state for providing for their personal needs. This is not to say that the state did not play a considerable, even dominant, role at times, but rather that it encouraged and did not stifle the workings of the market.

The two periods of Japan's most rapid economic growth were the sixty years following the Meiji Restoration and the four decades following the Second World War.[500]

The Post-Meiji Era

After the Restoration, government policy furthered the rapid industrialization of Japan in both the public and private sectors. The government built weapons factories, shipyards, post offices, railroads, and communication industries, while supporting the private sector with experts from abroad, loans, and protective tariffs.[501] Lawrence Harrison argues, however, that despite government dominance, the principal engine of growth was the extensive infrastructure of energetic, innovative, and thrifty entrepreneurs that had evolved in the later Tokugawa years. For example, the merchants and financiers from pre-restoration years founded *zaibatsu* (commercial-industrial conglomerates). Also from the military side, ex-Samurai put their management skills and payments given for relinquishing their traditional roles to work in developing new industries—e.g., ex-Samurai, Iwasaki Yataro founded Mitsubishi. The agricultural sector played an important role as well: peasants had owned their land during the Tokugawa years and had achieved sufficient affluence to diversify into commerce and industry.[502]

After a financial crisis in the late 1870s, a retrenchment program resulted in substantial privatization, with the government divesting itself of all industries except armaments, shipbuilding, communications, and public services.[503] The more traditional private sector of small enterprises continued to play a large role in meeting Japan's needs, with over one-third of workers employed in establishments numbering under ten workers. For example, in match production, teams of households were organized to work separately to split the wood, dip the heads, make matchboxes, paste labels, and pack the product.[504]

After the financial retrenchment, the economy, benefiting from sound macro-economic policies, grew rapidly. For example, the number of factories doubled from 1908 to 1918, and again from 1918 to 1924; by 1931 they had increased by another 50 percent.[505]

Japan's rapid rise to affluence and economic power was, however, catastrophically interrupted by the Second World War, during which Japan's cities were flattened, its industries ruined, and the population reduced to conditions of poverty and desperation.

Post-World War II

But Japan had a remarkable rebirth in postwar years, when Japan's political system, economy, and society were thoroughly restructured by a new constitution, imposed by the United States, which was adopted in 1947. According to Jansen: "Under its terms sovereignty was firmly invested in the people; the emperor stripped of his political prerogatives, was described as the "symbol" of the unity of the people. The capstone of demilitarization was to be found in Article 9, in which the Japanese, "aspiring sincerely to an international peace based on justice and order," "forever renounce war as a sovereign right of the nation and the threat or use of force as means of settling international disputes ... land, sea, and air forces, as well as other war potential, will never be maintained..."[506]

The new constitution also advanced the potential for greater empowerment of the individual. For example, according to Jansen, : "the entire Meiji Civil Code with its samurai-patriarchal family structure required rewriting to bring it into conformity with the constitution's assertions of equality of individuals and sexes; marriage was now to be based on mutual consent."[507]

In the economic arena, under the influence of the American occupation, the incursions of the pre-war governments into the private sector to meet military needs were undone. In addition, Americans pressed for deconcentration of conglomerate holdings and some of the giant zaibatsu were broken up. Though with time, new looser groupings called keiretsu, which were centered on large banks, arose.

Equally important, Japan's first and most influential postwar Prime Minister Shigeru Yoshida was a strong supporter of free-market policies.[508] As a result, the economy grew rapidly, benefiting from low levels of taxation, low levels of constitutionally limited defense spending, an undervalued currency that stimulated exports, and meeting the demand generated by the Korean and Viet Nam wars.

Despite the success of these policies, they faced significant political opposition at the time. Given the devastation of World War II and the resultant poverty, Japan experienced class antagonism and sharp political conflict. There was much socialist and union opposition. In addition, a new leftist intelligentsia arose for whom disapproval of Yoshida was a "badge of distinction."[509] Nonetheless, his successful policies had the support of the majority of the population, and with growing affluence class antagonism ebbed.

Some analysts credit this success less to the power of free markets than to a coordinated industrial policy led by the Ministry of International Trade and Industry (MITI). A more persuasive argument is that while MITI did a few useful things, such as provide industrial standards (notably the machine tool industry in the 1950s), its attempts to guide investment were peripheral to the larger success. The most dramatically successful business enterprises of the post-war era—Sony, Toyota, and Honda—arose from the private sector, and, if anything, were resistant to MITI pressures. For example, MITI's plan to rationalize the automobile industry by merging small producers was resisted and went nowhere.[510] Fukuyama notes that the Japanese government's role in the economy remains small. Its share of the GDP is the lowest of any member of the Organization of Economic Cooperation and Development.[511]

The above account demonstrates how Japan's unique culture, embracing most of the dictates of the extended order, powered by a high achieving population reached the pinnacle of affluence in the space of a century. This is not to argue, however, that Japan got everything right, and that there are not other elements to their culture that present problems for the future.

For example, after decades of rapid economic growth, the economic bubble burst by the 1990s, bringing a new and difficult era to Japan. In a misguided effort to stimulate growth, the government retreated from the low spending and low-taxation practices of the immediate postwar years. Economic growth stagnated, indebtedness rose, unemployment climbed.

Moreover, Japan's economic development has been narrow, compared to the United States and other countries. William Lewis' analysis of the Japanese economy notes that in industry, particularly electronics and automotive, Japan is a world leader in innovation and productivity, and these industries have helped make Japan affluent. In other sectors, however, notably farming, retailing, housing construction and banking, its productivity is substantially below that of the United States. The lagging sectors are those in which tradition, sentimentality for small operators like 'mom and pop stores', and the political clout of small farmers have led to protectionist governmental policies, leading to high prices and low productivity. Also troubling, according to Lewis, is that market distortions in these lagging sectors overpower labor and capital market factors, thus limiting the potential influence of macroeconomic policy.[512]

He speculates that Japan's failure to deal with these and other economic problems may have deeper roots in its culture and value system. Lewis states, drawing on extensive business analysis in Japan by the McKinsey Global Institute: "[Japanese colleagues], who had trained at some of the most reputable universities and business schools in the West, found it extremely difficult to dissect their own economy. The Japanese have an obsession about correctness. To dissect or analyze requires identifying causality. For less than perfect outcomes, causality implies that things could have been done better. That means there is a risk that someone has not performed as well as he should. Should that shortcoming be identified, the individual would lose face. Everyone around would be uncomfortable. The Japanese go to great lengths to avoid this discomfort. Thus they avoid causality. They avoid causality by denying the problem."[513]

Another facet, probably negative, of Japan's cultural evolution not coinciding with the West regards empowerment of the individual. Lawrence Harrison notes that Japan's strong group emphasis and suppression of individualism has reined in the type of individual creativity leading to major discoveries and inventions, resulting in many Japanese scientists leaving Japan for the United States.[514]

These shortfalls, however, do not detract from Japan's huge historic success; every country has weaknesses, and societal evolution cannot but follow a culturally unique path. The fact remains that Japan's experience has been a beacon for other developing countries—notably the seven tigers of East Asia.

SEVEN TIGERS OF ASIA

Seven East Asian countries, Hong Kong, South Korea, Taiwan, Singapore, Malaysia, Thailand, and Indonesia, often termed the seven tigers, have also achieved dramatic success in economic development in the post-World War II era. Each followed a culturally unique path, having varied colonial antecedents—British, Japanese, Dutch, or in Thailand's case, none—but as a group, they were similar, drawing to some degree on a Sino-Confucian inheritance, following a common developmental model, and establishing their vibrant new economies under the aegis of authoritarian or only quasi-free governments.

Sino-Confucian Cultural Values
Sino-Confucian culture provided the value structure—in terms of personal work ethic as well as receptivity to the macro-economic

policies and institutions of the extended order—essential to producing economic success. To be sure, only four of these countries had populations that were predominantly Chinese or Confucian in heritage: Korea, Taiwan, Hong Kong, and Singapore. But the minority Chinese populations in the other three—Malaysia (39 percent), Thailand (9 percent), and Indonesia (3 percent)—played a crucial and positively disproportionate role on the performance of these countries. Thomas Sowell writes: "The historic effect of the overseas Chinese on the region [Southeast Asia] was in some ways more profound than that of the Europeans who held imperial power in Southeast Asia."[515]

In *The Economics and Politics of Race*, Sowell presents a generic description of the Chinese immigrants wherever they migrated in Asia. Initially penniless, they would work eighteen-hour days, living austerely in overcrowded housing, to save money to begin some sort of business. Investing these savings, they began wholesale and retail distribution systems. In larger endeavors as early as the nineteenth century, they began rubber plantations and mined tin in Malaya. Eventually, according to Sowell, they came to dominate many aspects of commercial activity throughout the region.[516]

The earlier discussion of Confucianism within the context of Japan showed how its value structure contributed to this work ethic. And wherever individual Chinese escaped the otherwise rigid strictures of old Chinese societies to areas more disposed to the extended order and the exercise of their energies, they prospered.

But they had been stifled in Imperial China. Fukuyama concludes that Confucianism in China resulted in an authoritarian, bureaucratic state inimical to free markets and a rigid familism that reduced the radius of trust to the detriment of civil society and broad economic institutions—quite different from its effects in Japan. He states: "The central core of ... [Chinese Confucianism] ... was the apotheosis of the family ... as the social relationship to which all others were subordinate. Duty to the family trumped all other duties, including obligations to emperor, Heaven, or any other source of temporal or divine authority."[517] To be sure Confucianism may have played a more stifling role in the empire than elsewhere, but there is little sign that an extended order was likely to have arisen de novo in any Sino-Confucian society.

The concept of family, however, was broader than in other societies, with family lines traced back through generations of ancestors, and ties to distant, but same-named, relatives could be strong, which facilitated participation in wider commerce. Nonetheless, Sino-cultures have a narrower radius of trust than do Western cultures and Japan. These differences, in turn, caused countries having such values to industrialize differently.

For example, as argued by Fukuyama, familistic societies have greater difficulty creating large economic organizations, which in turn places constraints on the sectors of the global economy in which they are likely to compete.[518] He notes that in Taiwan, Hong Kong, and Singapore the economy is characterized by small and medium-scale companies controlled by families,[519] exhibiting a reluctance to bring in outside professional management.[520] Moreover, inhibitions on institutionalizing enterprises, combined with the Chinese custom of dividing inheritances equally among heirs, constrains the accumulation of capital[521] and generally results in the fading away of enterprises within three generations.[522] On the positive side, this pattern has made for highly flexible, fast reacting enterprises among first generation entrepreneurs.

Finally, in contrasting the evolution of Sino-cultures to the West, such familism establishes a value structure in which there is no concept of individual conscience to counter obedience to parental authority.[523] Moreover, according to Lawrence Harrison, the authoritarian family pattern applied to the whole of society, with the emperor being the father writ large. Accordingly, traditional Confucian society was authoritarian and static[524] and unlikely to evolve a vibrant extended order on its own, despite the work ethic of its people.

Thus, Confucianism appears generally to be a negative force regarding modernization. Indeed, Max Weber found the ethical system to be a principal obstacle to the development of rational enterprise capitalism.[525] But, according to Harrison: "Neutralize the forces that suppress entrepreneurship, above all bureaucratic suffocation, but also promote entrepreneurship's prestige, and you have a critical mass of achievement motivation that approximates that of Weber's Calvinists."[526]

Modernization

In the 20th century, political circumstances made it possible for each of the seven tigers to escape the economic confines of their prior societies and unleash the entrepreneurial energies of their Chinese populations: Hong Kong, Singapore, and Malaysia were freed by virtue of British colonial administration, while Taiwan and Korea began their transformation under two generations of forced exposure to Japanese organization of society and the economy as a result of Japan's colonial rule of those countries. Thailand and Indonesia's transformations were more a matter of having strong leadership that aped Japan's macro-economic policies, while they unleashed the energies of their resident Chinese populations.

Although each country differed in terms of details, and most made mistakes along the way, there is greater similarity among their paths than not. William Lewis noted with regard to successful developing countries: "They all evolve out of agriculture into manufacturing and services. Service employment always increases faster than manufacturing employment. Manufacturing employment increases for a while and then begins to decrease as a fraction of total employment."[527]

A half-century ago all these countries were poor, with agriculture providing the principal livelihood for the vast majority. The rise of manufacturing first appeared in labor-intensive industries that required relatively small amounts of capital for growth. As industrialization picked up pace, wages in industry became relatively higher than in farming, and the rural exodus to urban areas accelerated. As labor became more expensive, more capital per worker was invested by industry to utilize that labor more efficiently, leading to ever greater economic growth and income. However, only where political stability, sound currency, and property rights existed and property rights were relatively secure, did this model succeed.

While the seven tigers largely followed this path, they differed in terms of specific policies and approaches, attributable to different cultural values and traditions, resulting in some cases in relatively lower rates of economic growth.

Two important areas of difference entailed the degree to which the state intruded on the economy and the particular path taken to representative government.

State Intrusion
Virtually all the 'tigers' tended to get macro-economic policies and rule of law right, with property rights being of central importance. However, they varied in several aspects, especially with regard to the degree of state intervention in private sector decision-making— e.g., which industries to promote (if at all) and how to promote them. One impetus for government intervention is to protect infant industries from competition with world class industries in the developed world by imposing tariffs and excluding foreign competitors. The World Bank has concluded, however, that "typically the long-protected firms have not become efficient and do not in fact survive in the more competitive environment."[528]

Experience demonstrates that it is usually a mistake for developing nations to attempt to leap directly into a capital-intensive industry in which they held no comparative advantage, a decision which is most likely to occur when the government rather than private investors try to pick "winners." Hong Kong, the richest of the tigers, abstained from attempts at planning the economy, while Indonesia made numerous failed attempts. The others fall in between.

Representative Government
Earlier chapters emphasized the importance of rule of law and representative government for providing the security needed to generate and attract capital, to be responsive to the needs of the economy, and restraining the practices of the predatory state. In addition, just as the West's expansion of free markets created pressures for representative government, similar forces worked in East Asia: Japan directly aped the West; and Hong Kong and Singapore, as ex-British colonies, were essentially provided an initial democratic framework.

The other tigers developed full representative government only gradually in this initial period, being ruled by authoritarian rulers. In most of these instances, these autocratic governments provided political stability and were able to impose the macroeconomic conditions requisite for rapid economic growth. The mechanisms for representative government were later put in place, leading to free elections. Most avoided the dangers of beneficent autocracy and its tendency toward endemic corruption and cronyism. But Indonesia did not.

Hong Kong

Hong Kong is the exemplar of the seven tigers in terms of demonstrating the efficacy of the Sino-Confucian work ethic in the context of classical liberal free markets. Indeed, Hong Kong has been rated as being the most economically 'free' country in the world by both the "2001 Index of Economic Freedom" and the "Economic Freedom of the World 1997." Hong Kong's status as a British colony for about a century and a half (sovereignty was returned to China in 1997) unleashed the energies of its Chinese inhabitants from the institutional rigidities of Confucian society to become an affluent city-state. During a period of rapid growth from 1950 to 1997, it had all but closed the per capita income gap with the United States.

Not only did Hong Kong benefit from its status as a British colony, but serendipity provided a particularly apt administration—one devoted to more classically liberal economic policies than Britain's own government at home. A key role in Hong Kong's success was played by Sir John Cowperthwaite, who was Hong Kong's financial secretary from 1961 to 1971 and very much a disciple of Adam Smith.[529] Given that Hong Kong was a colony with limited representative government, the leadership had extensive scope for shaping the economy, for good or ill. Cowperthwaite balanced budgets, lowered taxes, and kept markets open. He was a dogged opponent of efforts to regulate and direct the movement of capital in Hong Kong. In his view, "in the long run, the aggregate of decisions of individual businessmen, exercising individual judgment in a free economy, even if it is mistaken, is less likely to do harm than the centralized decisions of a government, and certainly the harm is likely to be counteracted faster." He repeatedly deflected efforts to get the government to favor one line of development over another, one industry over another, and in this way, Hong Kong was notably different from some of the other tigers.

As a result, the cost of government to business and society was minimal. Milton Friedman estimated that direct government spending in 1996 constituted less than 15 percent of national income in Hong Kong, compared with 40 percent in the U.S. (and much higher in Western Europe). The costs of regulation absorb another 10 percent of national income in the U.S., while in Hong Kong, the amount is negligible.[530]

Today, with Hong Kong under the effective control of the Chinese Communist government, it is an open question if its new rulers understand the sources of Hong Kong's affluence, or whether they will gradually strangle the Golden Goose through the imposition of government control. For example, since China took over, there has been increasing political interference in the independent judiciary, restrictions on freedom of the press, and interference with academic autonomy.[531] In 2004, Human Rights Watch stated that that year "is shaping up to be the worst year for civil rights and political rights in Hong Kong since the 1997 transfer of sovereignty over the territory."[532]

Singapore

Singapore's cultural readiness for development was also derived from a Sino-British inheritance. Singapore, like Hong Kong, is a city-state populated largely by Chinese (75 percent) and developed as a British colony, incorporating features of both Western and Confucian traditions.

Singapore was a sparsely populated island when it was ceded to the British East India Company in 1819. Once it came under the complete control of the British, it grew rapidly, attracting a large Chinese population along with many Malays. By the 20th century it had become one of the world's leading ports for tin and rubber. After World War II, the city was part of a newly independent Malaysia, but became an independent republic in 1965. The separation was due largely to Malay fears that the Chinese would dominate the economy. Even after this separation, however, the remaining Chinese minority in Malaysia continues to play a predominant role there.

While Singapore ranks second, behind Hong Kong in the economic freedom rankings of the Index and the Report, it differs significantly in the degree to which the government intrudes in the economy. Government-linked corporations constitute almost 60 percent of the GDP, three-fourths of the housing units are constructed and operated by the government, and individuals are required to pay 20 percent of their earnings into a Central Provident Fund for several purposes, including retirement, education, health care, and buying a home.[533] Nevertheless, its macroeconomic policies favor growth, and in recent years, as noted by the Index, Singapore has moved to open its financial and business sectors further to wider global competition.[534]

Singapore's government resembles other tigers (at least in their earlier development) in terms of an authoritarian political environment. For example, the government freely uses libel and defamation laws against political opponents. But credit must be given to Lee Kuan Yew, the dominant figure in Singapore's essentially one-party state for 31 years (until 1990), who presided over a period of rapid growth. Thus, Singapore represents one example in which an authoritarian figure provided the political stability necessary for investment and growth without creating a corrupt, predatory state.

Taiwan

Taiwan differs from Hong Kong and Singapore by being far larger and not having had a British colonial history. Nonetheless, it shares with them an ethnic Chinese population and a Sino-Confucian culture, albeit with an overlay of Japanese tradition. The Japanese cultural overlay occurred when Taiwan was ceded by China to Japan in 1895 following the Sino-Japanese War.

Taiwan's dramatic economic development during the second half of the 20th century falls in the same league as that of Hong Kong and Singapore, and the specific path of development matches closely other successful countries such as South Korea and Spain, to be discussed later. This outcome seemed hardly likely after the Second World War, when Taiwan, freed from colonial rule, possessing no notable natural resources, densely populated, and governed by the remnants of the Chinese Nationalists who had been defeated on the mainland, had to confront the future.

Yet, critically, Taiwan had a Sino-Confucian population, whose energies were waiting to be unleashed, and it had an extensive economic infrastructure left behind by the Japanese. All that was required was stability and appropriate economic policies—i.e., in accord with the ten factors discussed in Chapter I.

To understand the result, let's begin with Taiwan's Japanese legacy. After 1895, Japan undertook a cultural transformation of the population, as well as economic development. Compulsory education in Japanese was adopted, residents were compelled to be naturalized as Japanese, and Japanese administrative mechanisms and infrastructure were put in place. This process was summarized by Lewis H. Gann:

> The Japanese ... built railways, harbors, roads, schools, agricultural research stations, clinics. Government investment played an important part in capital formation. Taiwan had traditionally formed part of China's settlement frontier; much of the island had been developed during the late seventeenth and eighteenth centuries by emigrants from the mainland who had built up a market-oriented agricultural system from the inception of Taiwan's modern economy. The Japanese found favorable conditions when they attempted to modernize traditional systems of property rights, to assist cultivators by irrigation works, and to mobilize savings to finance domestic investments. The agricultural growth rate rapidly expanded, and Taiwan became a major producer of sugar and rice. Agricultural development ... gave a boost to agricultural processing industries like sugar refining .... Private consumption rose in a striking fashion ... capital formation proceeded apace, as did the development of an indigenous bourgeoisie with a stake in both farming and industry.[535]

Thus, initially, Japan's efforts focused on agriculture and small industry, but the exigencies of preparing for and participating in the Second World War caused Japan to invest in hydroelectric power, aluminum, chemicals, and oil refining, as well.

Although Taiwan suffered considerable destruction during that war, given its cultural traditions, educational base, infrastructure, and previous economic experience, it was a good candidate to follow the Japanese model of development. Moreover, Taiwan received a boost from the United States during the Korean War and its aftermath, when the U.S. confronted a hostile Communist China, and provided Taiwan with protection, aid, and guidance.

Lawrence Harrison estimates that U.S. aid financed almost 40 percent of Taiwan's gross domestic capital formation in the 1950s. Moreover, he notes that the aid enabled thousands of Taiwanese to study in the United States, mostly at the graduate level. Those students were to take key places in Taiwan's public and private institutions (in the 1989 cabinet, 12 of the 21 ministers had studied in the United States).[536]

It was American policy guidance, however, that was instrumental in Taiwan's dramatic economic takeoff. The initial proclivity of Taiwan's authoritarian ruler, Chiang Kai-shek, was similar to many economically untutored leaders of development-aspiring countries, namely for the establishment of a regulatory, autarchic policy embracing import substitution. American advisors, however, pressed for reduced protectionism, expansion of exports, and encouragement of foreign investment. Those policies continued over the ensuing decades and are reflected by Taiwan's ratings by The Index of Economic Freedom and Economic Freedom of the World, which ranked Taiwan in 20th and 16th place, respectively, worldwide.

The new policies produced stunning economic growth: between 1951 and 1995, Taiwan experienced annual growth rates of GDP averaging 8.7 percent, the most rapid of all developing countries during that period. In the process, its industrial structure quickly left the somewhat statist inheritance from the Japanese behind. For example, in the 1950s, public-sector industries accounted for the bulk of industrial production. But by 1987, the private sector accounted for more than 85 percent of Taiwan's industrial production. As noted earlier, the vast majority of the new industry was small to medium-scale, and family owned.[537] Nonetheless, Taiwan's industry became increasingly sophisticated,[538] such that by 1995, technology-intensive products amounted to almost half of all exports.[539]

Taiwan's political transformation is also noteworthy. Most of its developmental years were under the direction of a one-party state, much like the other tigers, which produced the stability and security necessary for promoting new investments. Taiwan, however, now has made the transition to representative government. Elections for all seats in the National Assembly were held in 1991 and 1992, and in 1996, there was an election for the president. More recently, in 2000, an election of the president involved five political parties, producing a winner who was not a member of the previous ruling party.[540] A true test of a democracy is when a peaceful transfer of power to an opposition party occurs by an election. Taiwan has met that test. This transition moved the country solidly into the Western mode of economic growth and political stability.

South Korea

South Korea, while composed of a different ethnic stock than China, had a fully Sino-Confucian cultural imprint as a consequence of China's hegemony over the centuries. Indeed, Reischauer and Fairbanks concluded that "Korea ... seemed at times even more Confucian and traditionally Chinese than China itself."[541] As a result, its population had a work and savings ethic comparable to any in the Sino-cultural world. In addition, the decades of Japanese rule and the long American protectorate following the Second World War and the Korean War provided the economic infrastructure and the macro-economic policies that unleashed the energies of the Korean people to produce the dramatic growth seen in the latter half of the 20th century.

Economic development began following the Russo-Japanese War in 1905 when Korea came under Japanese control in 1910. The Japanese forced the economic development of Korea to serve the needs of the emerging Japanese Empire. Japanese industrial conglomerates, cooperating with colonial authorities, developed mines and industry, to the extent that by 1940, Korea had the best railroad system in East Asia after Japan, as well as advanced highway, electricity, and communication systems.[542] In addition, the Japanese established an education system aimed at making the Koreans more productive workers. The development, however, was highly exploitive—e.g., despite three decades of rapidly growing GDP per capita, the standard of living of most Koreans actually fell.[543] Thus, during the period of Japanese occupation, Korea may have been forced to modernize in many ways, but it had hardly established many elements of free markets.

Korea experienced widespread destruction during the Korean War of the early 1950s, leading to widespread poverty and a country divided into North and South, between a Communist dictatorship and a country allied with the democracies. In the first post-war years, South Korea's extreme poverty was somewhat alleviated by U.S. aid, but kept entrenched by the first President, Syngman Rhee, who was so focused on security that his policies erred on being statist and inward-looking. The resulting economic stagnation led Western observers to conclude wrongly that Confucianism itself was an obstacle to economic progress.[544]

That this was a misreading became evident with the government's new direction in the early 1960s. When the United States signaled an end to economic assistance, the South Korean government reversed course to impose macroeconomic policies more congruent with the extended order: in recent years, South Korea has earned economic freedom rankings of 29th and 18th among the world's countries by the Index and the Report, respectively. Given the opportunity, the population's ingrained Confucian work ethic blossomed to work, save, and invest. For example, on a per capita basis, Koreans work 40 percent more hours than do Americans and 20 percent more than the Japanese. Also, South Korea's domestic savings rate reached 15 percent in the decade following reform, and today is well above 30 percent—among the world's highest rates. (This result is in stark contrast to the early fifties when American aid was high and the Korean savings rate was only 3 percent.)[545]

Decades of dramatic economic growth followed the reforms: South Korea achieved one of the fastest growing economies in the world—averaging 9 percent GDP growth over a 30-year period—and its per capita income approached half that of the United States. This is an impressive record for a country that was impoverished and devastated only a half century ago.

The pattern of growth generally traced that of most successfully modernizing countries: a revival of agriculture, followed by light industry, heavy industry, and then service industries. Its specific path was closer to the Japanese experience than to that of the other tigers. Unlike Hong Kong, Singapore, and Taiwan, Korea's growth was not led so much by family enterprises, but rather through large conglomerate industries such as Samsung, Hyundai, and Daewoo, assisted by government intervention.

In this, the government emulated the early Japanese model rather than the post-war model. Following the Meiji Restoration, Japan had relied heavily on conglomerates called *zaibatsus*. As Lewis described this approach, the government identified strategic industries for rapid development, it nurtured large organizations in which skilled personnel and capital were concentrated, and it built favored industries such as steel and shipbuilding. Intermediary financial institutions, drawing on the high savings rate of the population, were encouraged to invest in these industries, which were shielded from foreign competition. The idea was that, through these policies, economic development would proceed faster than it would otherwise. South Korea followed the early Japanese practice of fostering conglomerates (called *chaebols* in Korea) instead of allowing the private sector and foreign investors to find areas of competitive advantage within the economy. By government direction, South Korea concentrated early on capital-intensive industries such as automobiles, semiconductors, steel, and shipbuilding.

This approach, according to William Lewis, built in future problems: government incentives lacking adequate regulation and banks providing financing without adequate risk analysis led to capacity expansion regardless of the underlying productivity and profitability. Moreover, chaebol financial reports were generally opaque, and banks were slow in discovering how poorly their loans were performing. The net result was that, while South Korea's per capita factor inputs of labor and capital were almost as high as those in the United States, the resulting productivity was only half as high as that of the U.S.[546] Indeed, in the cases of automobiles and semiconductors, the chaebols were not profitable enough to cover the costs of their bank loans. This situation could not, of course, continue indefinitely, which accounts for why South Korea was hit hard in the financial crisis of the late 1990s. In the post-crisis years, however, the South Korean government has signaled that government bailouts are not likely and has encouraged opening key sectors to outside investors.[547]

In addition to the impact of misconceived policies, an additional problem linked to culture is that values that work well for discipline, cooperation, and perseverance do not accommodate the dictates of 'creative destruction' of the modern economic world. In Korean culture, as in Japanese, failure entailed 'a loss of face', causing managers to allow failing entities to continue to operate. By contrast, in the United States, failure, in the form of bankruptcy, while perhaps devastating to the individual, can nevertheless be regarded in positive terms for society as a whole because failed business models are uncovered in a timely fashion and resources, mainly labor, can be redeployed to more productive uses.[548]

Finally, on a more positive note, South Korea followed the same path as Taiwan and the West with economic development creating pressure for representative government. The pressure emerged from ever-larger elements of society chafing at the heavy hand of the autocratic military regime. By 1985, elections for the National Assembly were held, and, in 1987, direct elections for the presidency took place. Thus had South Korea put in place a functioning democracy, which has been ratified by a number of free elections in succeeding years.[549]

Malaysia

Malaysia presents a somewhat different cultural picture: while also having been a British colony like Hong Kong and Singapore, the majority of the population consists of Muslim Malayan stock, with the Chinese constituting only a minority. As a British colony, it had gained extensive infrastructure, a professional civil service, and basic education for much of the population. Moreover, under the stability and rule of law provided by the British, Malaya's natural resource development had made it the largest dollar earner in the empire, with much of the earnings remaining in the country for re-investment. This prosperity attracted many immigrants from India and China, resulting in an ethnically diverse population.

Despite this initial leg up, Malaya had a rocky start after gaining independence from Great Britain in 1957. Guerilla warfare by the Communists and ethnic riots threatened the government. The government prevailed, but inter alia, the ethnic pressures resulted in Singapore being forced out in 1959 to leave a majority Muslim country.[550]

Malaysia was to prosper in ways similar to the other East Asian Dragons—drawing on the commercial energies of its Chinese population. The Chinese minority became richer and controlled most of the industrial and financial institutions. Sowell writes that the average Chinese earned twice the income of the average Malay in the early days of independence,[551] and by 1983, the ownership of corporations in Malaysia—including government corporations—was 27 percent Chinese and 2 percent Malay (63 percent was owned by Western investors).[552]

To address ethnic tensions, brought about in part by the disparity of economic performance, the government, representing the numerically larger Malay constituency, adopted 'affirmative action' programs. (One might wonder about the concept of affirmative action benefiting the majority of a population, rather than a minority.) For example, although the Malays were barely half the population, the Malaysian constitution reserved four-fifths of the civil service jobs for Malays, as well as three-fourths of the university scholarships. Moreover, the electoral districts were—and are—so gerrymandered that a rural Malay's vote counts twice that of an urban Chinese.[553]

Whatever the moral merits of these policies, they produced political stability under which the country grew dramatically: Malaysia's growth rate lagged only a percentage or two behind the dragons. It did so, because in still another instance the country effectively unleashed the entrepreneurial ambitions of its people within the context of macro-economic policies consistent with economic development, as observed by *The Economic Freedom of the World, 1997* report, which ranked it in 10th place, worldwide.

Since the economic crisis of the late 1990s, there appears to have been some backsliding. The *Index of Economic Freedom* recently has a less favorable view of Malaysian economic policies, rating it only in 75th place, as it was concerned by the then prime minister's prosecution of political opponents, capital controls, higher public spending, higher regulation, and higher tariffs.[554]

The recent problems notwithstanding, a lesson to be drawn from Malaysia's experience is that a country having a motivated entrepreneurial class, even if a minority, functioning within the rule of law and sound macro-economic policies can lead the entire economy into relative affluence. An observation by Fukuyama regarding the Protestant ethic appears applicable to the situations of Malaysia and other East Asian countries as well: "Weber's spirit of capitalism refers, then, not just to the work ethic narrowly defined but to other related virtues like frugality (the propensity to save), a rational approach to problem-solving, and a preoccupation with the here-and-now that inclines individuals to master their environment through innovation and labor. These are characteristics that apply primarily to entrepreneurs and owners of capital rather than to the workers they hire."[555] We shall see a similar picture in the discussions of Thailand and Indonesia.

Thailand

Thailand is a cultural case unto itself in this grouping of East Asian societies: it had never been colonized, though it was occupied by the Japanese during World War II, the population is mostly of Mongol stock, and the prevailing religion is Buddhism. But, as noted earlier, the country has a significant, more newly-arrived, Chinese minority that has disproportionately contributed to Thailand's economic growth.

Even though Thailand had not been colonized and had not enjoyed the infrastructure development and educational benefits that some colonies had gained from the British and the Japanese, the Thais were able to draw on the strengths of their unique culture to undertake many critical pre-development efforts on their own. Like the Japanese, Thailand had looked to Europe for guidance in the late 19th century: the children of its ruling class were sent to Europe to be educated, and in 1932 the country became a constitutional monarchy with representative government.

Like Malaysia, Thailand has benefited enormously from the entrepreneurial energies of its Chinese minority. Sowell highlighted the disproportionate role of the Chinese in Thailand's economic development: despite constituting only 9 percent of the population, in 1972, for example, they owned between 50 percent and 95 percent of the capital in Thailand's banking and finance industry, medicine, transportation, wholesale and retail trade, restaurants, and the import and export business.

The government, according to Sowell, "encountered the same underlying reality as other governments pursuing the same policy elsewhere in Southeast Asia—namely, that a native population from a peasant background provided relatively few people with the inclination, the money, or the experience to operate businesses, or even to perform skilled industrial labor."[556] So, it chose to reap the benefits of this commercial reality while it undertook measures that discriminated in favor of native Thais. For example, the government built and operated corporate monopolies for the sale of rice, liquor, and other commodities, excluding the Chinese from a number of occupations.

Nevertheless, despite such statist intrusions into the economy, the country generally followed a developmental model akin to the other tigers—i.g., instituting policies generally in accord with the key factors listed in the Index and the Report: Thailand is ranked 27th by the Index and 8th by the Report. Prospering in a favorable macro-economic environment, it experienced the world's highest growth rate of 9 percent annually between 1985 and 1995.

Nonetheless, Thailand is as subject to policy errors growing out of political pressures as any of the other tigers. The Index notes a general undue leniency by bankruptcy courts and a slow restructuring of the corporate sector following the East Asian financial upheaval of the late 1990s. As a result, Thailand has lagged some of the other tigers in the post-crisis years.[557]

Indonesia

Indonesia differs significantly from the other Tigers—it has no prevailing Confucian culture, has the smallest Chinese community by far, and has had two dramatically different periods of economic performance, one of abject failure and one of notable success. Its dichotomous economic performance makes Indonesia a particularly useful case study on the role of governmental policies for ill or good—as seen in the Sukarno and the Suharto presidential eras.

Sukarno

Indonesia gained its independence along with a modern institutional legacy from the Dutch following the Second World War. Theodore Friend argues that: "All the preconditions of a sophisticated capitalism, arguably, have been lurking in Southeast Asia, including Indonesia, since world market capitalism began unfolding in the region through colonial regimes in the nineteenth century. If creative arrangements between the "state" and "Chinese" could accelerate such development, capitalism should have flowered easily."[558] Here Friend seems to be referring to two ingredients that served the other developing countries well—an entrepreneurial Chinese minority and commercial traditions and institutions, left by a Western colonizer.

But problems began with Sukarno, who led the nation after independence. He was a demagogue, with no grounding in economics and no feeling for the extended order but with an affinity for elements of Marxism. As a result of the destruction of the Second World War, the Indonesian GDP was lower in 1950 than it had been before the war in 1939,[559] and Sukarno's policies worsened the situation. Friend describes some of the dysfunctional policies as too 'nationalistic' and too encumbered by "a widespread fundamental mistrust [that] tied capitalism to any kind of colonialism."[560]

An Economic Urgency Plan aimed at developing indigenous small industry, but disregarding the precepts of free markets, failed. As executed, the Plan and Sukarno's demagoguery undermined much of the country's positive Dutch legacy. In 1957 the government seized Dutch companies and expelled Dutch nationals. As one businessman put it afterwards: "It started being bad when the military took over Dutch businesses. They just ask "Where is house? Car? … But it was another "fruits of the revolution situation" … eat the fruit, plant no seed, develop no orchard."[561]

In addition, the Chinese were only 2.5 percent of the population, disliked, and not as assimilated as in other East Asian countries. In 1957 the government imposed a head tax on "aliens," which included ethnic Chinese, and banned retail trade by "aliens" outside the major cities. As a consequence, there was an exodus of over 100,000 ethnic Chinese.[562] This migration entailed, of course, a loss of capital and entrepreneurial skills. Moreover, with this track record, no foreign investors were inclined to come to Indonesia.

By the mid-1960s financial disaster loomed. Crumbling infrastructure was evident everywhere; inflation reached 640 percent in 1966 and international borrowing reached $2.1 billion by 1965, for which export earnings were inadequate to repay.[563] The per capita income fell to what it had been in 1940.[564] Life expectancy was low, and Indonesians earned less and ate less than people in the rest of Asia.[565] Despite growing poverty and a need for assistance, in a resort to the populist nationalism on which his regime was based, Sukarno rebuffed offers of assistance by the United States by saying "To hell with your aid!"[566]

Unsurprisingly in the face of this disaster, Sukarno was ousted on March 11, 1966, when the military led by General Suharto took power.

Suharto

Suharto was only one of the group of generals that seized power, but over time he became the preeminent ruler. The new leaders were confident that Western economic thinking could be applied to Indonesia. A new group of technocrats, Indonesians with degrees from the United States and known as "the Berkeley Mafia," were placed in policy positions. Friend notes that they had no nationalistic aversion to foreign aid or foreign investment. Moreover, they had no prejudice regarding the Chinese but instead saw them as critical to private-sector growth.[567]

Friend notes that the relatively small Chinese population was responsible for most of the subsequent economic takeoff. In 1997 James Castle put together a "Roadmap to Indonesian Business Groups." One hundred of the principal businesses were chiefly owned by Indonesians of Chinese ancestry.[568]

Policies undertaken incorporated many of the elements needed for sustained growth and economic stability. For example the inflation rate was brought down from the extreme levels of the Sukarno era to single digits by 1969.[569] The reforms gave more influence to domestic investors in policy setting and made exports a priority. This goal required that Indonesia attract international firms and foreign capital. In turn, Friend writes, these investors had to be assured of "low wages, a skilled workforce, efficient infrastructure, predictable taxation, acceptable terms of investment and repatriation of profits, and political stability."[570]

Despite initial low wages, the payoff to Indonesians was great: from 1970 to 1996, the per capita GDP in US dollars rose 15-fold, from $73.96 to $1,144.58.[571] This was spectacular testimony to the power of sound policies and political stability.

A Rocky Aftermath

But all did not go well—the financial problems that hit East Asia in the late 1990s did more harm to Indonesia than to the other tigers. For example, per capita GDP declined 40 percent, to US$691.68, by the year 2001.[572] While the Confucian Chinese provided the entrepreneurship required for growth, the underlying culture, the government, and most institutions were Islamic.

The predominance of an Islamic culture manifested itself in negative ways beyond the Indonesian aversion to the non-Islamic Chinese in the form of substantial levels of corruption and a predilection for cronyism. With regard to corruption, Transparency International's rankings of countries shows that Indonesia is perceived as substantially more corrupt than the other tigers. Where a high score of 10 is equivalent to 'essentially clean', Singapore had a score of 9.2; Thailand 3.2, and Indonesia 1.9.[573]

Cronyism, combined with the legacy of the later Suharto administration, was probably the most important reason for Indonesia's relative economic precariousness. Indeed, Suharto's regime could be seen as a case example of how power corrupts. He entered power as chief among equals, and as generals aged and retired and as competing politicians faded or were intimidated or bought off, Suharto quietly expanded his power and ruled virtually unchallenged for over three decades. The Cendana family, Suharto's blood relatives and cronies, came to dominate the state and the economy.[574] Friend notes: "In the 1970s his wife, Ibu Tien had earned a reputation for opening doors and being paid back in commissions. By the late 1980s and early 1990s her children went from market-nibbling to market-swallowing…"[575]In 1997, <u>Fortune</u> magazine placed Suharto's wealth at $16 billion, likely the world's sixth richest man.

Suharto also had a penchant for grandiose industrial policy, leading to substantial statist intrusion into the economy: producing planes, ships, communication equipment, and arms and subsidizing scores of uneconomic industries such as steel. But Indonesia had no comparative advantage in these areas and investments in them were ill-starred from the first.[576]

All in all, Indonesia has had dramatic economic growth, but that growth has been more precarious than that of the other tigers because of a somewhat haphazard adoption of free market policies and institutions. The dichotomous policy mix results in dramatically different rankings of economic freedom by the Index and the Report: 114th and 29th, respectively. The Index's more jaundiced view cites a lack of strong financial institutions, lagging financial reform, failure to reduce energy subsidies or open key sectors to foreign investments, as well as concerns about the judiciary vis-à-vis foreign businesses and property rights, as well as a fragility of political stability caused by sectarian violence and separatist movements.[577]

In terms of the themes of this chapter, Indonesia's post-World War II experience represents a rich contrast: the dismayingly dysfunctional approach of Sukarno followed by Suharto's adoption of some of the best practices of the seven tigers to achieve relative economic success. This dichotomy provides a framework for considering the successes and failures of other cultures and countries.

SPAIN AND LATIN AMERICA

Even though Spain has entered the ranks of the developed countries, her Latin American descendents' progress in economic development has been problematic and puzzling. To be sure, Latin America's leading countries, Argentina, Brazil, and Chile, have had periods of promising growth; yet these have, as often as not, been followed by setbacks. Consequently, whereas they once had standards of living many times that of East Asia, they now lag. Because Latin America straddles the divide of economically developed and undeveloped countries, it can provide a particular insight into the dictates of the extended order and the processes of societal evolution. The insight is grounded in cultural factors: while much of Latin America's heritage is Western and it exhibits greater readiness for modern economies than do Islamic and African cultures, it lacks the readiness for rapid development we saw in Japan and East Asia.

These problematic circumstances can be traced to deep cultural roots, viz., Hispanic/Portuguese-colonial and Catholic heritages. In particular, by virtue of having had a Catholic rather than a Protestant heritage, these countries missed out on the critical societal evolution experienced by Protestant Europe from the late 16th century onward. Lacking an inherited Protestant Ethic (or a Confucian for that matter), they have been awkwardly positioned for establishing the key elements of the extended order. Their values do not emphasize personal responsibility, exhibit limited spheres of interpersonal trust, and embody a distrust of wealth, commerce, and free markets. Moreover, even though they now mostly have constitutional representative governments, these tend to be dysfunctionally centralized in structure and lack key checks and balances for safeguards. In short, this cultural mix places most of these countries at the traditional-survival pole rather than at the secular-rational pole of the *World Values Survey*, and thus they appear, for the most part, among the partially free or mostly unfree countries ranked by the *Index of Economic Freedom*.

Furthermore, this value mix inhibits reform of their economies and political institutions. The majorities within these countries distrust free markets and globalization, and view themselves as hapless victims vis-à-vis fate or outsiders such as the United States. This mindset was highlighted by Bernard Lewis, who observed that "when people realize that things are going wrong, there are two questions they can ask. One is, 'What did we do wrong?' and the other is 'Who did this to us?' The latter leads to conspiracy theories and paranoia. The first leads to another line of thinking: 'How do we put it right?'" Landes concludes that in the latter half of the twentieth century, Latin America chose conspiracy theories and paranoia. Japan, with the Meiji Restoration, asked itself "How do we put it right?"[578]

Before examining Latin America's uneven evolutionary progress vis-à-vis the extended order, it is necessary to address the question of whether it is meaningful to treat in a unitary framework the cultural background of numerous countries which span a continent and a half. That issue was addressed in the affirmative by the anthropologist George Foster, who concluded:

> [O]verriding the Indian-based characteristics are the generic Spanish similarities, stemming from the time of the Conquest

and giving Hispanic America a cultural unity which has led anthropologists, historians, and philosophers to think in terms of a common Contemporary Hispanic American culture ...[579]

In that light, we will review the colonial and religious aspects of the Latin cultural heritage that work against the extended economic order, see how the disabling aspects of that heritage have played out in several examples, but then indicate how the disabilities can be overcome, as they largely have been in Spain and Chile.

Crippling Colonial Traditions

When Spain explored and conquered the new world, it had just come to the end of eight centuries of conflict during which it expelled the Islamic Moors from the Iberian Peninsula. In this relentless warfare, conducted by an absolute monarchy in close cooperation with the Church and the military, Spain had become in some ways a mirror image of Islam, a warrior religion predicated on converting the infidel and becoming wealthy through the acquisition of conquered territories.

This conquering mindset under a religious banner persisted during the exploration of the new world. Indeed, the stated purpose of Pope Alexander VI's Papal Bulls of 1493 was that the lands in the Indies donated to Spain by the Bull were to have their inhabitants converted to the Catholic faith.[580] In that endeavor, the monarch's power was absolute and was exercised through four viceroys. According to Jose Ignacio Garcia Hamilton, there was little opportunity in those vast territories for self-government to arise inasmuch as the crown appointed members of the town councils, and they, in turn, appointed their successors.[581]

The Spanish Crown represented the 'predatory state' writ large, not only politically, but also in the sense of literally having title to all lands: the Crown monopolized land distribution, owned all the mines (leasing their operation), and monopolized trade between Spain and the colonies. Its primary policy from the beginning was to extract wealth from the New World, notably gold and silver. Their trade and economic policies were strictly mercantilist—contrary to the extended economic order, which was arising in Protestant Europe. No colonization was allowed absent the permission of the Crown resulting in few emigrants from Spain or the rest of Europe, and the men who did go went in the role of adventurer.

The rule of law was also absent. Evasion of restrictive laws— e.g., through smuggling—was widespread. Moreover, the Crown added to the disregard of colonial law by granting the Viceroys the ability to suspend the law when its observance was dangerous, inconvenient, or troublesome.[582] Juan B. Alberdi, a critic of Spain and a drafter of a new constitution for Argentina in the 19th century wrote: "From the beginning, Spanish America was warlike; it was neither industrial, commercial nor agricultural... Its organic heritage was ignorance and disdain for work ..."[583] The net result was a stagnant, inward-looking society.

Yeatts compares the Spanish colonization with the British: "The contrast between the two processes is striking: public conquest versus private colonization; imposition of a single faith versus religious freedom; immigration of military men, noblemen, priests, and bureaucrats versus immigration of those devoted to agriculture and commerce; predominantly male immigration versus immigration of entire families; centralized administration versus autonomy of the colonies; and strong presence of the Crown in pursuit of mining rent versus low government participation."[584]

This situation was not significantly altered by the overthrow of Spanish rule early in the 19th century, because the independence movements were not the result of a shift in worldviews by the Latin American societies. Indeed, Yeatts writes that after independence, the republics were governed by authoritarian regimes typical of Iberian centralism, and the revolutionary leaders, San Martin, O'Higgins, Santa Cruz, Bolivar, and Sucre were more aligned with Spanish forms of paternalism than to Western European liberalism.[585]

Without a principled basis of government, the new entities were prone to instability and periodic violent overthrow of their governments. Among the most extreme examples, Uruguay had over forty armed struggles between 1830 and 1903, and Bolivia had no less than 178 rebellions and uprisings in the 126 years after gaining independence.[586]

During the 19ᵗʰ century, republics were formed and constitutions, partially emulating the U.S. experience, were established. But in key details, these constitutions took a different approach to governance as influenced by their colonial heritage. While the founders of the U.S. drew on British experience to develop a constitutional model that specifically circumscribed the power of central government and placed checks and balances on both the executive and the legislature, the Latin American constitutions were less federal and lacked crucial checks and balances on power.

The practical consequences led to strongmen representing oligarchic interests or to undisciplined populist governments, whose weaknesses eventually resulted in the return to power by strongmen. In the specific cases of Argentina, Chile, and Brazil, the oscillation between oligarchy and undisciplined populism continued over the course of a century or more. Most recently, between 1950 and 1990, Argentina had 19 presidents, Chile 7 (even though one, Pinochet, ruled for 17 years), and Brazil 23.

In part, this historical pattern persisted because, even when updated in recent decades, Latin American constitutions retained critical flaws. According to Mary Anastasia O'Grady: "The trouble starts with the fact that as Latin America threw off its military dictatorships and converted to democracy in the late 20ᵗʰ century, it tended to embrace a naïve form of government. Democratically elected governments were assumed to be benign and acting in the interests of the population at large and therefore were granted enormous control over economic resources. Not only are most of them now free to intervene at will but they are constitutionally assigned the obligation to act as slayer of all inequalities in life."

She particularly cites the Brazilian example. Its constitution states that Brazil's citizens have the right to "education, health, work, leisure, security, social security, protection of motherhood and childhood, and assistance to the destitute." They have a constitutional right to a "salary floor," irreducibility of wages, and a year-end salary bonus. They have the right to "overtime that must be at least 50% higher than that of normal work" and "annual vacation with remuneration at least one third higher than the normal salary." And they are guaranteed "free assistance for children and dependents from birth to six years of age, in day-care centers and pre-school facilities."[587]

This view, of course, confuses 'rights' with entitlements and goals. Human rights, as recognized in the U.S. Constitution, concern individual liberty — i.e., rights to freedom of person, freedom of speech, of religion, of assembly, all protections from potential state oppression. Logically, universal rights cannot require the rights of some (e.g., producers) to be subordinate to others (e.g., consumers). Such a view results invariably in intrusive government, and a heavily regulated economy, rife with corruption and inefficiency, and pervasive poverty — in striking contrast to the noble goals set out in the constitutions.

Indeed, despite their intentions, each of these countries has evolved economies with greater disparities of wealth than exists in any of the more developed countries. One consequence of placing specific responsibility in the central state is that economic striving shifts from individual initiative to rent-seeking through political means. Writing about Ecuador, but implying broader applicability to Latin-America, Mary Anastasia O'Grady concludes: "The country is also divided along traditional Latin American lines of haves and have-nots with domestic producers insisting on protection from imports, combative labor unions extorting high costs from society at large and much governmental profligacy. The political process is little more than an eternal battle for entitlements."[588]

And as explained by the economist Douglass North regarding all less developed countries, institutional frameworks that favor wealth distribution over wealth creation result in monopolies and restricted competition, along with transaction costs so high as to sharply curtail commerce and productive activity. [589]In effect, well intentioned regulations and high taxes ultimately result in a straight-jacket for the formal economy, forcing human ambitions and the struggle to survive into the informal one. Yeatts writes: "The absence of ... compliance with the legal norms allowed the development of an underground economy, especially in the labor market. Unionization and rigid labor laws suffocated the market, and gradually the black market became the essential component of Latin American life."[590] As a practical matter when poverty grew, despite the promises of constitutions, and as economies imploded from hyperinflation or unsustainable foreign debt, authoritarian governments tended to step in.

It is to this dynamic that one can trace Latin America's ongoing cycles between authoritarian and populist governments.

An Unhelpful Cultural Heritage

Not only did the colonial period leave a legacy of unpromising political institutions, but it left a broader cultural heritage out of step with the evolutionary changes emerging in Protestant Europe. This heritage was an amalgam of universal conservative peasant culture and the Catholic Church. Both were resistant to the dictates of the extended order regarding free markets, rule of law, and limited government.

Let's examine these two cultural strains more closely. Anthropologists have found a 'peasant society' mindset underlying Latin American culture that is common to most underdeveloped countries. As outlined in Chapter 1, the typical peasant sees little or no relationship between work and technology on one hand, and the acquisition of wealth on the other, such that the Anglo-Saxon virtues of hard work and thrift are meaningless.[591]

This pattern comports with the results of the *World Values Surveys*—i.e., less affluent countries are positioned the traditional/survival zone of values. It also evokes the spirit of medieval Europe, indeed all rural societies back to prehistoric times.

Latin America's Catholic inheritance did little to shift these views. As we saw, Catholic theology, as it evolved from medieval times to Scholasticism, found religious justification for what seemed to be universal human values. It saw human social existence as hierarchical with individuals in fixed classes, and it attempted to minimize insecurity and maximize fairness through just prices, just wages, and highly regulated terms of commerce. In so doing, it reinforced ancient views and made them resistant to change.

Yet, as we saw, Catholicism held potential for intellectual growth—indeed, one of its traditions, attempting to return to Christianity's roots, led to the Protestant Reformation. Also, earlier and more narrowly, Saint Thomas Aquinas' work opened the door for evolution of economic views, and given that opening, some societ-ies moved forward while others did not. Franciscan universities, prominent in the Netherlands, England, France, and Northern Italy, where commerce was thriving, found ways to modernize economic views (*via moderna*). Ironically, Thomistic Scholastic views, propa-gated by his fellow Dominicans, were the most static (categorized as *via antique*), and Dominican universities were found predomi-nantly in Hapsburg Europe, which languished economically.[592]

Because Spain's discovery of the New World occurred prior to the Protestant Reformation, its colonies were effectively bound by Dominican economic and social views, views of the late Middle Ages. And through the autocratic mercantilist policies discussed above, the Spanish and Portuguese colonies were untouched by the evolutionary forces at work in the rest of Western Europe.[593] The backwardness of these economic views were, however, obscured at the time because Spain commanded for a while the largest empire in the world and temporarily grew wealthy from the gold and silver found in the new colonies. But exploitation of riches in these forms engendered no impetus for new ways of understanding the world, and, more perniciously, that wealth allowed the elite to continue to denigrate entrepreneurship and general commerce. Lacking the experience of expanding commerce, Spain and its colonies failed to develop a *Protestant Ethic* (or a Catholic equivalent).

We will see more concretely how a failure to evolve such an eth-ic undermines the growth of a robust economic order. Specifically, successful economies require honoring the policies of free markets, nurturing individual initiative and the work ethic, and expanding the 'radius of trust' in society. Latin American culture has conspic-uously lagged in the development of these attributes.

Continuing Hostility to the Free Market

As discussed in Chapter III, the evolution in values supporting ex-pansion of trade and a modern economic system entailed a con-tractual rather than a personal approach to transactions, a tolerance for 'creative destruction', and devolved limited government. These values do not sit well with Latin America's Catholic heritage and, perhaps explains a certain popularity within the Latin American Church for 'liberation theology', which has a strong Marxist bent.

Carlos Alberto Montaner describes the proponents of this theology's contradictory mindset: They "are even more destructive when they attack the profit motive, competition, and consumerism. They lament the poverty of the poor, but at the same time promote the idea that owning property is sinful, as is the conduct of people who succeed in the economy by dint of hard work, saving and creativity. They preach attitudes that are contrary to the psychology of success."[594]

Such values also permeate the intellectual elite. Montaner says of these: "Most public Latin American universities and many private ones, with some exceptions, are archaic deposits of old Marxist ideas about economy and society. They continue to stress the danger of multinational investments, the damages caused by globalization, and the intrinsic wickedness of an economic model that leaves the allocation of resources to market forces."[595] The 1900 work *Ariel* by the Uruguayan Jose Enrique Rodo, which propounded the superiority of the humanist Latin culture over the pragmatic positivism of Anglo-Saxon culture and which helped support socialist, anti-"Yanqui" dependency views continues to be influential to this day.[596]

A key manifestation of these attitudes is weak property rights, ranging from a practical inability to obtain legally enforceable titles for private homes to a governmental propensity to nationalize industries and default on debt. The economist Hernando De Soto has analyzed how Latin values undermine private property rights and thereby stunt the possibilities of growth. His work found that the great majority of Peruvians—60 percent in the cities, 90 percent in rural areas—do not have secure property rights. They may have property of a sort and temporal capability to use it, but it is not legally secure. Similar to squatters, they are at risk of eviction, seizure, or inundation of new squatters.

As a practical matter, while people might have a piece of paper called a title, it can not be registered—and there is no place to go to find someone with a map willing to testify that there are not others with the similar pieces of paper giving them title to the same piece of land. As a result, few will or can make significant capital investments in such properties. Banks will not lend against that collateral, and courts cannot enforce the terms of loans. In effect, because of negative attitudes toward property rights, there is much latent capital in Latin American countries that cannot be tapped for development.[597]

In addition, De Soto's work highlights the pernicious effects of an economic regulatory system, which perversely stifles competition and enhances poverty. Inevitably, overregulation has resulted in a large informal, quasi-illegal economy. To illustrate the burdens of the regulatory state, his Institute for Liberty and Democracy set up a small garment factory to document the costs of entering the system legally. After paying essential bribes and filling out large numbers of forms, they found that one person would have to spend 289 days, working 6 hours a day, to certify a new business. In Tampa Florida, in contrast, complete legal certification of the same business took less than 4 hours.

In more sweeping terms, Yeatts writes that "the economic history of Spanish America perpetuated the centralized and bureaucratic traditions from its heritage. ... Larger operations relied on connections to local and colonial officials to facilitate virtually every aspect of business activity. Smaller ventures operated at the margins of the law; they existed only at the mercy of local powers and never with any protection from greater powers.[598]

We will see in specific examples how this mindset has resulted in protectionism, uneconomic subsidies, intrusive government regulations, uncertain property rights, and an altogether weak formal public sector of the economy.

An Unrealized Sense of Individual Responsibility

Not only has Latin America failed to adopt evolved views on economic policy, but its societies have largely missed the growing empowerment of the individual in which individuals assume greater responsibility for the conduct of their lives, are more hopeful about controlling their destinies, and demand a greater say in the conduct of political affairs. Such evolution of values was delayed for centuries in Latin America, as it was in much of Catholic Europe.

Max Weber, centuries after the Reformation, analyzing the different views held by Protestants and Catholics in Germany, found that Catholics tended to be more suspicious of wealth, less entrepreneurial, and, in education, less directed to modern education

than to classical studies. Weber concluded that the Catholic emphasis on the afterlife and a more flexible ethical system put Catholics
at a disadvantage to Protestants and Jews in modern economic systems. He stated: "The God of Calvinism demanded of his believers
not single good works, but a life of good works combined in a unified system. There was no place for the very human Catholic cycle
of sin, repentance, atonement, release, followed by renewed sin."[599]
In practice, the Protestant Ethic enhanced the virtues of truth telling, respect for the law, hard work, and living up to commitments,
thereby reducing transaction costs and increasing the economic efficiency of the societies in which it was predominant.

At the same time, Protestantism subtly decreased preoccupation with an afterlife and enhanced beliefs in the power of rationality, education, planning for the future, and saving—altogether
promoting optimism about the outcome of efforts in this life. These
attitudes were crucial for the development of social capital and the
accumulation of financial capital.[600] Lawrence Harrison argues that
in contrast to countries shaped by the Protestant Ethic, the traditional Ibero-Catholic view of work, innovation, and profit is essentially negative. Whereas the Calvinist outlook suggested that material success might be the result of God's favor, Harrison states that
Hispanic upper classes have displayed distain for physical labor,
money-making, technological skills, and non-humanistic learning.
He quotes Ortega y Gasset: "All occupations in which we engage
out of necessity are painful to us. They weigh down our life, hurt it,
tear it to pieces ... The man who works does so in the hope ... that
work will lead to liberation, that some day he will stop working
and start really living."[601] In his frustration, the Hispanic focuses on
an exaggerated sense of dignity and honor that historically has hindered cooperation within his society while it has produced a sense
of victimization vis-à-vis outsiders.

Nonetheless, these traditions have been eroding for the better.
Notably throughout Latin America in recent years, a macho male
orientation has given way to equal rights for women. For example,
the constitutions of several countries—Brazil, Cuba, Ecuador, Guatemala, Mexico, and Paraguay include gender equality as a basic
principle. Civil codes have granted women equality over the management of common property and household decision-making. In

practical terms, illiteracy among women has fallen substantially, and they make up half the students at all levels of education. In the workforce, their participation has increased from 20 percent of the labor force in 1970 to about 35 percent in 1995. Moreover, they constitute on the average 15 percent of the members of Latin American congresses.[602]

Another potentially powerful movement for change in values is the increase of the Protestant populations in Latin America during recent generations, from around 15 million in the 1960s to over 50 million in the early 1990s. They now constitute about 20 percent of the population in Brazil, Chile, and Nicaragua; and 30 percent in Guatemala. Harrison speculates that this conversion represents a desire by the lower classes for a better life by intuitively rejecting Ibero-Catholic values for the Protestant emphasis on work, education, sobriety, honesty, and community responsibility.[603]

On balance, however, Latin America continues to struggle to accept attitudes that build entrepreneurial societies within a rapidly innovating extended economic order.

Narrow Radius of Trust
Another manifestation of the Protestant (and Confucian) Ethic relates to an expansion of the 'radius of trust' operating within a society—i.e., the extent to which individuals trust other individuals and groups. The potential range of trust starts with the family, and can extend through a variety of civic and social institutions before reaching the national government. Sociologists have found that Protestant countries and Japan have large radii of trust; Hispanic countries, short ones. The *World Values Survey* reveals that Catholics in general are less trusting of their fellow men than Protestants—or Confucians for that matter.

Francis Fukuyama believes that trust arises from a set of informal values or norms—e.g., truth telling, meeting obligations, and reciprocity shared among members of a group that facilitates cooperation and makes groups function more efficiently. If members of a group come to expect that others will behave reliably and honestly, then they will come to trust one another.[604]

A short radius of trust has particular implications for how institutions beyond the family are viewed. With regard to Latin America, Mario Vargas Llosa states: "In Latin America, there is a total lack of confidence, on the part of the immense majority of the people, in institutions, and that is one of the reasons our institutions fail. Institutions cannot flourish in a country if the people don't believe in them—if, on the contrary, people have a fundamental distrust of their institutions and see in them not a guarantee of security, or of justice, but precisely the opposite."[605] One consequence is that Latin American societies have few civic organizations between the extended family and the hierarchical state.

Lower mutual trust breeds corruption. Consistent with this view, surveys by Transparency International among others, find " South America as one of the most ... corruption-plagued regions in the world."[606] Moreover, analysis shows a clear correlation between high corruption levels and low GDP growth rates.[607] One manifestation of how transaction costs are increased by corruption is the degree to which societies find it necessary to impose checking mechanisms and procedures to control dishonesty. These mechanisms, in turn, expand unproductive government, shackle private entrepreneurship, and provide new scope for corruption.[608]

The short radius of trust has broader ramifications as well. Lawrence Harrison, then a visiting scholar at MIT's Center for the International Studies wrote in 1996: "Many Latin American political, business and intellectual leaders ... increasingly acknowledge the traditional Iberian culture focuses on the individual and the family to the detriment of the broader society and does not stress such values as work, education, frugality, merit, community, and fair play. These cultural patterns are at the root of Latin America's authoritarian political traditions, its economic backwardness, the corruption of its institutions and its extreme social injustice."[609]

Given this value structure, it is understandable why it has been so difficult for Latin American societies to resist populist notions and to support necessary elements of economic and governmental reform. Yet, as we shall see, it can happen. Ample evidence exists that Catholics, when placed in countries with a predominant Protestant ethic, adopt those norms. Moreover, the examples of Spain and Chile, which conclude this section, will show how a combination of enlightened economic leadership and intrusion of the global extended order can bring reform and economic progress in its wake.

Specific Examples

A review of specific countries—Argentina, Brazil, and Chile—will show how this cultural legacy caused Latin America to languish economically. These countries contain the more advanced economies in Latin America and are especially illustrative of the frustrating pattern of growth and retrogression experienced by Latin America. The example of Spain, the cultural progenitor of most of Latin America, is added to balance the picture by showing the potential for rapid progress in Latin cultures when conditions become favorable.

Argentina

Argentina most fully illustrates the unfolding of this cultural heritage: it began its modern history as one of the poorest parts of Spain's empire, became one of the most affluent countries in the Western Hemisphere, only to sink into stagnation and relative poverty by regressing to the more dysfunctional aspects of its Hispanic/Catholic heritage.

Argentina began poor because of its lack of mineral wealth and its remoteness from the economic center of the Spanish empire. At independence in 1810, its population was smaller than its newly independent neighbors. Nonetheless, it shared the ubiquitous cultural heritage, characterized by Jose Ignacio Garcia Hamilton as including: "political absolutism, mercantilism, disregard for the law, religious uniformity, xenophobia, and social stratification."[610] Without a democratic tradition, following independence, Argentina suffered an extensive period of turmoil comparable to the other Latin American countries, culminating in a lengthy dictatorship under Juan Manuel de Rosas.

In 1853, when Rosas was ousted, Argentina was blessed by the institution of a new constitution, which while imperfect, built upon the principles of division of governmental powers, freedom of religion, support of private property and free trade, encouragement of immigration, and rule of law. As a result, Argentina was to enjoy a half century of rapid growth, known as its 'Golden Age'. With the doors open to immigration and foreign investment (heavily British), Argentina drew upon the economic advantages of its fertile pampas for producing grain and cattle, while it also developed advanced infrastructure in the form of postal service, telegraph, railways, and ports.[611]

By 1910, its GDP comprised half of that of all Hispanic America and ranked tenth among all of the world's countries. Its per capita income surpassed that of France and Italy and was many times that of Japan.[612] So it is clear that Latin America is capable of sustained growth. Unfortunately, in Argentina's case, favorable conditions were created by a landed and business elite rather than as a result of a general cultural readiness. When constitutional government was altered to reflect the whole of the population, the country regressed relative to other economically expansive countries for the remainder of the 20th century.

The details of that regression shed light on the role of culture for good or bad. The historian Carlos Rangel commented that after a populist government was elected in 1916, "Oligarchic democracy became chaotic democracy, full of inner contradictions, demagogical, ineffectual, incapable of holding in check the factions and the forces of disintegration that are characteristic of Hispanic societies."[613]

Hamilton states that the old colonial heritage re-emerged during the ensuing decades in the form of militarism, absolute political leaders, and renewed mercantilist interventions in the free market. Early examples of the growing statist intervention include rent control and marketing boards to regulate the production of meat, cereals, and other products. State intervention accelerated after Juan Peron came to power in 1946, with the nationalization of electricity, gas, and telephone utilities, as well as railroads and broadcasting. Then, in response to a flagging economy, he resorted to printing excess money, which caused inflation, followed by price controls. Rule of law suffered as well: he replaced the judges of the Supreme Court of Justice with 'friendly' judges, abolished freedom of the press, and jailed opposition leaders.[614]

A failing economy led to popular unrest and the ousting of Peron in 1955 by a military coup. Argentina was to suffer under a succession of dictatorships until 1983, when a democratic government was installed. Unfortunately, that government produced no fundamental change in economic matters.

A half-century's failures did not lead to reform, but to denial. The cause of Argentina's troubles supposedly lay not in Argentina but with others in the developed world—e.g., exploitive Yankees. Economists Raul Prebisch, Henrique Cardoso, and Enzo Faletto, for example, promoted a 'dependency theory of development', which argued that underdeveloped countries that were suppliers of raw materials to the developed world were at a strategic disadvantage that made them victims of exploitation.[615] But this theory failed to explain why Argentina had once had a standard of living higher than some of the industrialized nations, or why countries, such as Australia, which once shared economic conditions similar to Argentina's continued to prosper. The dependency theories led a number of Latin American countries in precisely the wrong economic direction—e.g., to the development of indigenous industries with government subsidies and shielded from global competition.

By the late 1980s, Argentina faced a crisis, with inflation hitting an annual rate of nearly 5,000 percent. In 1988 President Alfonsin resigned, calling the country "ungovernable." President Menem took over and implemented key reforms in macroeconomic policies. He pegged the peso to the U.S. dollar, began a major privatization program, and took other steps to open the highly protected Argentine economy.[616] He also dropped marginal tax rates: the top rate in 1984, 64 percent, was reduced to 30 percent.[617] The results were impressive. From 1991 to 1998, the Argentine GDP grew by 6 percent a year, creating optimism at home and abroad that Argentina was finally getting its economic house in order.

But this was a false dawn; the country's underlying attitudes and values had not changed. Old attitudes could be detected, for example, in the methods adopted for the privatization effort and for opening of the economy to competition from abroad. Guillermo Yeatts points out that when the government 'privatized' industries such as the utilities, railroads, broadcasting, and fuels, it simply transferred monopolies into private hands, which continued to be shielded from competitive pressures. Moreover, rather than truly opening markets to world competition, trade arrangements were made with other Latin American countries—e.g., under the Mercosur Treaty (Paraguay, Uruguay, Argentina, and Brazil), which continued barriers to the wider markets.[618]

In addition, because of tenacious resistance of special interests, the government failed to address many of Argentina's structural problems and continued Argentina's profligate policies. Brink Lindsey notes that government spending rose from 9.4 percent of the GDP in 1989 to 21 percent in 2000. In 2001, Transparency International ranked Argentina 57th out of 91 nations in terms of corruption. And featherbedding was pervasive, particularly at the state level: In the province of Tucuman "The public sector... serves primarily to enrich politicians and fund patronage jobs. Out of a formal work force of some 400,000, there are nearly 80,000 provincial and municipal government employees and another 10,000 federal government workers. Elected officials siphon off small fortunes for themselves: The annual salary for provincial legislators is roughly $300,000."

"Tucuman is by no means noteworthy for such abuses. In the impoverished province of Formosa on the country's northern border, about half of all formally employed workers are on the government payroll, and many show up only once a month—to collect their paychecks."[619]

The weight of unaddressed structural problems overwhelmed the benefits of the new reforms. The government had not dealt with a huge bureaucracy, high levels of corruption, an intrusive regulatory regime, and a system of subsidizing special interest groups. In lieu of effectively addressing the more difficult political problems, the government resorted to increasing taxes and borrowing heavily abroad. The ongoing spending was a prescription for bankruptcy, and the house of cards fell in 2002, with a run on the banks. Under a new President, Argentina devalued the peso by 75 percent, defaulted on the terms of its public debt, and essentially confiscated bank deposits (by paying them off in devalued pesos rather than according to their contractual dollar status).[620] After the economy contracted, there was a rally of sorts due to the economy being freed of debt payments. The downside would come later as foreign investors shunned the country.

The political Left would cry that Yankee market liberalization had been tried and failed. That is not true, of course. The easy political reforms were no match for the cultural heritage of intrusive central government, the power of vested interests, and hostility to free markets. Moreover, the populist rhetoric of the current President provides little hope that Argentina will attempt real reform any time soon. According to the *2009 Index*, Argentina's freedom score fell from about 70 at the year 2000 to 52.3 most recently, placing it in the mostly unfree category: in 25th place out of the 29 countries ranked in its region.[621]

A contrast with France provides a measure of Argentina's relative decline: a century ago, Argentina's per capita income exceeded that of France, but by 2001, France's was three times that of Argentina.[622] For Argentina, the 20th century was indeed a century of lost opportunity.

Brazil

Brazil, despite having a Portuguese rather than a Spanish heritage, shares similar key cultural traits—traits that have frustrated sustained economic advance. To be sure, Portugal's colonization is said to have been more tolerant than Spain's, and Brazil had a peaceful rather than revolutionary transition to independence in 1822, even retaining a royal head of state.[623] More negatively, in contrast to most of the continent, Brazil had extensive plantation slavery, which endured until 1888. Nonetheless, with regard to broad worldviews, especially political-economical, Brazil had an Ibero-Catholic anti-entrepreneurial, anti-work tradition, and had experienced Portuguese mercantilist policies, which were similar to Spain's.[624] Also, there were parallels with Argentina in terms of recurrent military authoritarianism, and periods of impressive economic growth that petered out under dysfunctional policies. Vis-à-vis the extended economic order, Brazil dramatizes the stifling effects of statist traditions, however well intentioned. Let's examine the political and the economic backgrounds to these traditions.

Because of the peaceful transition to self-government, there was little immediate shift in the cultural value system inherited from Portugal, one that endorsed slavery and concentrated land, wealth, and power in few hands. Moreover, in the ensuing century there was little movement to limited government enforced by constitutional checks and balances. While in time there was representative government—e.g., after the monarchy under Pedro II was overturned in 1889—Brazil lived for forty years under new institutions that came to be known as the "Old Republic'. And it is true that from 1930 until 1964, Brazil had a succession of elected Presidents.

Nevertheless, the military was never far removed: it ousted President Vargas in 1945 and again in 1954, as well as President Goulart in 1964, when it ruled absolutely for the next 21 years.[625] When democratic rule returned, the Constitution, as discussed earlier, established a statist order in which the central government was to be the guarantor of material well being as well as a protector of rights. Accordingly, it promoted overspending, over-taxation, over-regulation, over-protection, and fiscal precariousness.

Despite this pattern of erratic government, Brazil enjoyed some periods of sustained economic growth, notably under the administration of President Vargas and during the twenty years of military rule after 1964. Indeed, during a 68-year period, from 1920 to 1988, Brazil's GDP grew at an average of 6 percent a year, surpassed in the world only by Japan's experience. Importantly, much of the growth was industrial, in contrast to the rest of Latin America. Due to the energies of large entrepreneurial immigrant groups, notably Germans and Japanese, industrial production increased at annual rates averaging 11 percent from 1930 to 1940, and at annual rates averaging 9.9 percent from 1965 to 1980.[626] Because of these robust periods of growth, for the century as a whole, Brazil's performance has eclipsed all other Latin American countries, even oil-rich Mexico and Venezuela.[627]

Thus, as was seen in the experience of East Asia, a series of autocratic governments implementing generally sound macro-economic policies generated impressive growth. But the Brazilian pattern of robust growth was misshapen. It left much of the population outside the formal economy and, consequently, did not lead to a narrowing of income inequality, e.g., about 65 percent of the economically active population lives close to extreme poverty.[628] Moreover, as will be discussed later, the regulation and over-protectionism accompanying the growth, particularly in the hands of populist governments, contained the seeds of future problems and stagnation. Indeed, Brazil was rated among the 'least free' nations in Latin America according to "Economic Freedom of the World, 1975-1995."[629]

The resultant problems became glaring, when for twenty years, from the mid-seventies to the mid-nineties, Brazil had little economic growth. Per capita income fell an average of 0.6 percent annually throughout the eighties, even as government spending on goods and services grew steadily and inflation became endemic, hitting annual triple-digit rates.

Corrective action was essential, and it took the form of the Real Plan in 1994 under the leadership of Henrique Cardoso, Brazil's minister of finance, providing for monetary discipline and for privatizing some industry. Inflation was brought under control and growth resumed. David Landes notes the irony in this shift: Cardoso had been a leader of the 'American dependency school' that blamed others for Latin America's failure to prosper. Now he said: "Brazil has no choice. If it is not prepared to be part of the global economy, it has no way of competing ... It is not an imposition from outside. It's a necessity for us." Two years after implementing reform, he was elected president.[630] Still, that reform was only a beginning, the central state remains paramount, and a populist government under President da Silva followed Cardoso. Ominously, public debt has increased from $60 billion in 1994 to $370 billion in 2002.

Brazil's experience also illuminates the effects of an unevolved regulatory state pursuing good intentions without understanding the unintended consequences. Analysis by the McKinsey Global Institute shows how intrusive government and bad policies undermine growth and establish special interests that undermine reform. William W. Lewis notes that in terms of technology, resources, and managers Brazil has the potential to be an affluent, fully developed country. Indeed, certain sectors of the Brazilian economy—private retail banks, hyper-supermarkets, and the poultry industry—perform with a high productivity not far less than that of the United States. Brazil also maintains a substantial investment rate of 19 percent of the GDP per annum.

It is government, vested interests, and economic policies that hamstring the country. For all of the country's strengths and high levels of investment, the Brazilian GDP per capita is only 23 percent of that of the United States and half that of South Korea.

Lewis argues that, "two-thirds of the labor productivity gap not attributable to missing capital comes most importantly from inefficient organization of the activities of labor and inefficient arrangement of equipment in the production process."[631] He traces low productivity in key market sectors to poor government policies and institutional failures. Four examples are particularly telling: food retailing, automobiles, banking, and housing construction.

The food retailing sector demonstrates the negative effects of big government and high levels of taxation on the economy at the lowest level, the vast informal economy. Virtually half the Brazilian workforce works in an informal economy consisting of food stalls and small shops, which, without supporting infrastructure of computers and lacking economies of scale, is hopelessly unproductive. Their average productivity is a mere 15 percent of the average productivity of the United States and far less than the hypermarkets of Brazil.

Nonetheless, they survive principally because they pay no taxes. And they pay no taxes because they are too small, too numerous, and too dispersed for the government to monitor them effectively—even if it were politically feasible. Corporations that are part of the formal economy, on the other hand, are taxed very highly. Brazilian corporations pay 85 percent of all taxes (compared with 41 percent for US corporations). Moreover, Brazil takes a higher share of the GDP in taxes than does the United States—33 percent versus 29 percent. While Brazil's percentage take may not seem so much greater, Lewis suggests that the correct comparison is to the tax rates that held in the United States when it was at Brazil's current state of development. In 1913, for example, total tax revenues in the United States amounted to only 6 percent of the GDP.[632]

These high levels of taxation are an ineluctable result of the expansive promises of the Brazilian constitution, which requires that a certain minimum of government revenues be allocated to education; health assistance be available to all Brazilians; regional governments dedicate at least 12 percent of their revenue to health care; and basic levels of welfare and pensions be provided for everyone.[633] One consequence, for example, is that Brazil spends 11 percent of its GDP on government pensions compared with 5 percent in the United States.[634]

The automotive industry illustrates yet another example of misguided industrial policy, especially regarding attempts to shield infant industries from international competition. To be sure, the Brazilians invited large foreign automobile manufacturers to invest and set up shop in Brazil, as opposed to attempting to start the industry from scratch, as did the Koreans. But in so doing, the government for many years prohibited imports to protect the fledgling industry from global competition. The net result was an industry that fell further and further behind the world productivity norm, thus restricting output to match the relatively small Brazilian market, which in turn made operations unprofitable. Problems were compounded during inflationary periods, when Brazil adopted rigid price controls that effectively closed the door to further foreign investment. But when the government finally lifted import restrictions and price controls, the industry immediately rediscovered its competitive instincts and dramatically improved productivity. Then, as imports soared, the government reinstituted some tariffs. Where this will lead over the long-term is unclear.[635]

The banking sector is another example of the deleterious effects of government intervention. Half of all the banks in Brazil are owned by the government, and all government employee salaries and government financial assets must be deposited in these institutions. Accordingly, these financial institutions feel little competitive pressure and have made few improvements, such as computerized operations that would improve productivity, which amounts to only 40 percent of the efficiency of private retail banking in the United States. This situation is obviously not foreordained because some private banks, which are subject to competitive pressures, already approach the productivity of US banks.[636]

The housing industry is yet another example of institutional failure. Brazil lacks, as do other Latin American countries, effective institutions to secure property rights. The inability to demonstrate indisputable ownership and the failure to protect ownership rights make mortgage financing impossible. In addition, the heritage of hyperinflation has made the mortgage business impracticable for the banking industry. The inescapable result is that the building of new residential structures proceeds at the pace determined by each individual's capability to save money for the next increment. A housing industry with developers producing large numbers of houses efficiently is impractical as well.[637]

In addition to these institutional and policy failures, Brazil was affected by the widespread world economic problems in the late1990s. During this period of instability da Silva, a socialist and populist, was elected president. Given his party and his personal history, this could signal one of Latin America's frequent steps backward. On a positive note, his administration has maintained responsible financial policies, and he has risked political popularity by reforming the unsustainable pension system. There are few signs, however, that the country's spending and structural problems are being effectively addressed.

Chile
Of the Latin American countries, Chile has come closest to having overcome its cultural heritage to achieve a political-economic basis for enduring growth. To be sure it has the same Ibero-Catholic heritage, has experienced a similar succession of military and populist governments and, akin to Argentina, has had periods of sustained economic growth, only to founder under misguided policies of populist regimes. Yet, as we shall see, Chile has for the last two decades grown steadily—indeed some term it the 'poster country' of Latin America. What factors account for this apparent escape from the typical Latin pattern? Perhaps three: a culture leavened with a higher proportion of European immigrants from areas characterized by their entrepreneurial propensities, a longer tradition of constitutional government and political moderation, and a broad array of economic and institutional reforms implemented during its last period of autocratic government. We can trace the cultural attributes common to the continent that had held Chile back, while identifying the factors that have made it a leader of reform.

There are strong parallels between Chile and Argentina. Chile gained its independence in the same time period—i.e., in 1818, and was initially governed by its liberator Bernardo O'Higgins in the role of dictator. The subsequent government was ousted in 1833 by Conservatives, who promulgated a 'durable constitution' based on a strong presidency. As was the case in Argentina after it had adopted a new constitution, Chile experienced many decades of growth, based on the development and export of its copper and nitrate resources, as well as the export of agricultural products. With the emergence of a middle class, the founding of the University of Chile, and an opening of the political process to competition, many within and without the country viewed Chile as a "model republic."[638] By 1900, Chile's per capita income, while only three-quarters of Argentina's, was twice that of Brazil and greater than that of Columbia, Mexico and Peru.[639]

Chile differed somewhat from Argentina in the makeup of its immigrant stock, which may have played a role in Chile's later economic success. During the 18th century, a large proportion of the immigrant stock came from Spain's Basque country whose entrepreneurial traditions exceeded the Spanish norm. Harrison notes that the descendants of these particular immigrants have had a numerically disproportionate role in Chile's economic development. Also, he notes that later immigrants from the more entrepreneurial parts of Europe played important roles in the development of glass, ceramics, printing, chemical, paper, metallurgy, and pharmaceuticals, as well as mining and transportation.[640] In addition, Chile's cultural makeup was influenced by significant conversions from Catholicism to Protestantism during the mid-20th century. By 1990, Protestants made up 15 to 20 percent of the population.[641]

Nonetheless, from 1900 until 1987, Chile grew more slowly than all of the South American countries mentioned above, due to various combinations of uncertain politics and statist economic policies. For example, the strong presidency of the 19th century ended in 1891 with civil war and the suicide of the president. In the next century, a more parliamentary government arose, and a new constitution was ratified in 1925. These changes did not initially improve political stability: e.g., President Alessandri was ousted by the military, later restored to power, again by the military, only to be replaced by Ibanez, who ruled as a dictator from 1927 until 1931, and then, after a chaotic period during which a socialist republic was proclaimed, reelected.

But thereupon, a forty-year period of constitutional government ensued, during which governments swung between parties of the left, which included Communists and Socialists, to those of the right, notably the Christian Democrats. Unfortunately, throughout this period, policies of spending, import substitution, and state involvement in the economy led to chronic inflation and generally low growth. Chile fell well behind Brazil and the Asian Tigers.

This dysfunctional pattern did not lead to crisis until the election of Salvador Allende in 1970. Even though he was elected by a bare plurality of the vote (36.6 percent), his government embarked on a program of radical populism. This included: a redistribution of wealth, an expropriation of American copper companies, a nationalization of Chilean private companies (numbering 150 in 1971), and a vast expansion of spending for welfare, subsidized housing, health care, and education. As inevitably as night follows the day, business investment dried up, foreign exchange reserves ran out, and inflation hit a rate of 500 percent a year in 1973. Moreover, rule of law weakened, with the government looking the other way as squatters took over private property, and social unrest grew.

As happened at one time or another in virtually every other Latin American country, the military stepped in to restore stability and economic discipline; in Chile, it was under the leadership of General Pinochet. The new military regime might well have been no different than the typical Latin American—i.e., reestablishing political stability, but otherwise not significantly deviating from a statist approach to government. This transition, however, proved serendipitous in that Pinochet presided over a transformation of the economy similar to that achieved by other economically successful autocratic regimes, such as Chiang Kai-shek in Taiwan, Park Chung Hee in South Korea, and Francisco Franco in Spain. Notably to that end, he brought in experts from the "Chicago School," a leading proponent of free markets and libertarianism. Following their advice, Chile opened its markets with a policy of unilateral liberalization and reformed macroeconomic policies.

In the initial round of reforms, Chile slashed the budget deficit, instituted a restrictive monetary policy, lifted price controls, eliminated market subsidies, privatized more than 300 firms, and cut tariffs. The abrupt changes in the economy, undertaken during the economically unpropitious period of the two oil shocks of the 1970s, had high short-term social costs—e.g., domestic demand fell by 25 percent and unemployment rose to 15 percent. But then with further reforms in the early eighties, including a depreciation of the exchange rate that helped achieve a positive trade balance, the economy moved steadily ahead.[642]

A particularly notable reform involved restructuring the country's retirement pension plan from an unsustainable government defined benefit plan to one of personal retirement accounts (requiring the investment of 10 percent of salaries). One immediate result was a leap in the country's savings rate, the highest in Latin America, which greatly enhanced the availability of investment capital.

The sound macro-economic policies and structural reforms had a big payoff. According to the Index, Chile has been a model of economic performance for Latin America since the beginning of the 1980s.[643] Thereafter and until 1994, other than a recession in 1982-1983, economic growth was between 6 and 10 percent a year. Inflation was down to 8.4 percent in 1994, and the unemployment rate was brought down to less than 5 percent, one of the lowest rates among the world's less developed countries. Chile weathered the worldwide economic crisis of 1997 better than other Latin American countries and has resumed economic growth.

Just as in Taiwan, South Korea, and Spain, once the economy had been transformed and grew robust, power was returned to a constitutional government. To be sure, in 1988, Pinochet miscalculated that a plebiscite regarding his continued rule would keep him in power. The Chilean people, however, thought otherwise by electing a Christian Democrat in 1989. There have been since a number of free elections, resulting in peaceful transfers of power between parties.

Thus, Chile leads the continent in realizing free markets and effective representative government. An observation of the economist Rudiger Dornbusch is apt: "Chileans have learned how to do business and Argentines have not—Chileans are all over Argentina making deals, merging, buying, and brokering." Harrison adds: "Moreover, Protestantism is growing rapidly in Chile, bringing with it a more progressive value system that is likely to enhance the evolution of Chile's democratic political system at the same time that it promotes the work ethic and a stronger national sense of social responsibility."[644]

Spain

An examination of Spain's experience concludes this section on Hispanic/Latin American culture, because it is the most dramatic example of a country having an Ibero-Catholic heritage moving from a statist to a free market orientation. Lawrence Harrison captures Spain's dramatic transformation: "In 1950, Spain was a closed, isolated, economically backward, inequitable, rigid, and traditional authoritarian society run by the quintessential *caudillo*, Francisco Franco. In 1990 Spain was an open democracy with ample social mobility, the highest economic growth rate in the Economic Community ... How can one explain the transformation of Spain, which had until recent decades failed to create political pluralism, social equality, and economic dynamism, following essentially the same authoritarian, traditionalist path as its former colonies in the New World? A number of factors come into play, but the principal one, I believe, is Spain's decision to open itself to the mainstream ideas of the West—to permit the Enlightenment and the Industrial Revolution to come to the Pyrenees, albeit two centuries late." [645]

That transformation came from a fusion of outside pressures, positive examples from countries on Spain's doorstep, a series of enlightened decisions, as well as fortunate leadership. Harrison highlights some of the key milestones. In 1950 Spain was essentially an impoverished, underdeveloped country still recovering from the civil war of the 1930s. During the war, Spain's GDP had dropped by 25 percent and most of its gold reserves ended up in the Soviet Union. Afterwards, the country was economically isolated during the Second World War, and the United Nations voted a trade boycott of Spain in 1946 (designed to topple Franco), that deprived Spain of Marshall Plan aid. Spaniards referred to the late 1940s as the "years of hunger." [646]

Spain's isolation lessened when the United States concluded that air and naval bases in Spain would be beneficial to the West's security interests. The ensuing economic aid and the massive base construction program provided a major stimulus to the economy. Rapid, but somewhat narrow, economic growth, however, brought problems in its wake: high inflation, massive rural to urban migration along with high levels of unemployment, balance of payment difficulties, and civil unrest. Moreover, decades of protectionism had left Spain's industry uncompetitive in world markets.

At this juncture, Franco made two key appointments as Minister of Finance and Minister of Planning, and the United States put pressure on the government to make major economic policy changes. According to James Cortada, "[a]long with the

International Monetary Fund, the United States recommended that Spain dismantle state regulations that restricted trade and capital investments, devalue the peseta, curtail government spending, encourage industrial growth, and attract foreign capital. The two further urged Franco to orient Spain's economy toward greater integration with Europe's and away from its autarchic basis." [647]

The reader can see how closely these recommendations comport with the factors listed in Chapter I as essential for economic growth. As a result, from 1961 to 1973, Spain's economy grew more than 7 percent annually, the highest growth rate in Europe.[648] During this time, Spain opened its society and economy to the West. Foreign investment brought modern technology and management practices, tourism became a major industry, and one and a half million Spaniards went to work in Western Europe, where they absorbed new values and practices, which they were to bring home.

All this took place under an authoritarian government, and as happened elsewhere, the transformation of the economy brought increasing pressure for representative government with political unrest growing until Franco's death in 1975. Afterwards a modern constitution was ratified in 1978. While it was almost overturned by a military coup in 1981, the attempt was suppressed and Spain continued committed to constitutional government.[649]

Thereafter, economic growth received further impetus by Spain's entry into the European Union, which also resulted in an increasing adoption of value systems prevalent in Western Europe.

Worldviews, however, do not completely change in the space of just one generation. Harrison notes that as late as 1984, half of the respondents in a survey viewed capitalism as "illegitimate and inefficient." Such views help account for the frequent election of socialist governments. Nevertheless, under the pressure of new experience, value change does occur: Spain has grown increasingly secular[650] and increasingly commercial in its worldviews as a consequence of a half century of reform and economic prosperity.

Although Spain is an integral part of the European Union, its political and social evolution provides a positive example to all Latin America of how a beneficial movement to free markets and constitutional government is possible despite a hindering cultural heritage.

ISLAMIC STATES

Despite once having been one of the world's most advanced civilizations, and despite living alongside the evolving West, Islamic states have signally failed to develop. Their stagnant condition arises from Islamic world views that are antithetical to social evolutionary change as well as teachings that produce an environment inhospitable to the extended order.

Religious World Views

In the words of Bernard Lewis: "For a Muslim, the advent of Muhammad and the revelation of the Qur'an marks the last in a series of similar events through which God's purpose was revealed to mankind. There had been a number of prophets whom God had sent on a mission to mankind as bearers of a revealed book. Muhammad was the seal of the prophets and the Qur'an the final and perfect revelation."[651] This worldview inculcated both a sense of superiority and a mission: all mankind will accept Islam or submit to Islamic rule, and it is the religious duty of Muslims to struggle until this end is achieved. The name given by jurists to this struggle is *jihad*, An Arabic word meaning effort or striving.

The theology presents an internally consistent, logical system remarkably impervious to intellectual attack, because as the word of God, indeed God's actual spoken word, it can brook no argument. To be sure, there is some theological elaboration as contained in the reporting of Muhammad's disciples about the traditions of the prophet—i.e., in the Hadith—but there is no divergence. Their combined specificity defines a value system and specifies a code of behavior.

Since the Quran and the Hadith are the unchallengeable voice of God, they have frozen the value system and thus the cultural development of Islamic states. While some schools of Islamic theology tried to introduce greater intellectual flexibility by introducing logical devices such as analogy, subsequent tradition, or consensus of later theologians, the tether restraining change is tight. In the words of Islamicist Sayyid Qutb: "The basis for the

Islamic message is that one should accept the *shari'ah* without any question and reject all other laws, whatever their shape or form. This is Islam. There is no other meaning of Islam."[652]

In terms of the psychological hold of Islam, scholars highlight the importance of eschatology—the theology of the Last Judgment (as opposed to soteriology, the theory of salvation, in Christianity).[653] Mark Gould states: "In Islam, God's messengers, and most especially his last and final messenger, Muhammad, have told believers how they must act to be saved. God has requested nothing that believers cannot do. If they follow God's commandments (as enunciated in the Koran and the *Sunna*, the tradition), on the Day of Judgment God will judge them fairly, weighing the good against the bad."[654] In addition, if one dies as a consequence of doing God's work as in *Jihad*, one goes directly to heaven. From this perspective, the phenomenon of the suicide bomber, mystifying to other cultures, becomes explicable.

This mindset has effectively governed Islam's relations with the outside world for the last millennium or more producing a stultifying self-righteousness and insularity. We have already seen in Chapter V the closing of the Islamic mind when confronted with the forces that produced the Age of Reason in Europe. This was to have practical as well as philosophical ramifications—e.g., Muslims were discouraged from living in non-Muslim lands and there was virtually no curiosity about other cultures. Because of a sense of perfection already attained, new learning was not a priority and writings other than the Quran were deemed unimportant—e.g., a prohibition of printing existed until the 18th century,[655] and while the West produced Arabic/Western dictionaries centuries before they existed in Islamic lands, at the end of the 18th century, not a single grammar or dictionary of any Western language existed in Islamic lands either in manuscript or in print.[656] Subsequent progress has also lagged—e.g., fewer books have been translated into Arabic over the last millennium than Spain translates in an average year. Some 65 million Arabs (two of three of them women) are illiterate.[657]

Teachings Vis-à-vis the Extended Order

In terms of almost every important vector of evolutionary change experienced by the West, Islamic societies remain closer to the world of a millennium ago than the modern era. To be sure, Islam at its inception represented an evolutionary advance in strengthening Arab societal animals. For example, it enhanced the coherence of the group by reinforcing authority, minimizing dissent, and emphasizing values that permitted individuals to live peaceably together within the community. To that end, it included precepts proscribing theft, cheating, sexual license, gambling, and drinking alcohol. Such features contributed to stability in local society and to a collective sense of moral virtue that helped Islamic societies endure in a changing world. Other features, however, which effectively froze evolutionary advance, have had a major downside.

In terms of the extended order, the worldviews that are most resistant to change are those related to a free market system, democratic institutions, and empowered individuals. Regarding free markets, Islamic values remain grounded in the worldviews of earlier civilizations, in which group consensus trumps individual initiative and in which sentiment overrides the dictates of distant contractual interactions requiring honoring of agreements, and respect for the impersonal economic laws of supply and demand. For example, the extent to which the Quran values the group over the individual is evident in its stand in opposition to the "ruiner" —i.e., the selfish individualist—who jeopardizes the moral integrity of the Moslem community. "In Islam this moral distinction between socially conscious virtue and asocial individualism replicates the dichotomy between faith and unbelief that separates the social environment of Islam from that of non-Muslims."[658] Other teachings emphasize this view as well: "A faith that is not expressed in the context of structured social relationships is no faith at all."[659]

While these views have hindered entrepreneurship and the rise of modern economic institutions, they have ironically not produced societies with high mutual trust. Islamic countries uniformly are seen as having populations that suffer from a narrow radius of trust and widespread corruption.[660] In effect, Islamic societies continue to have tribal outlooks, wherein trust rarely extends beyond the extended family and clan. Their societies especially have not evolved essential elements of the Protestant and Confucian ethical systems, for example regarding truth telling and the work ethic.

Similarly, entrepreneurial ambitions are attenuated. Just as individuals are tethered by peer pressure, they are sapped of initiative and taught passivity. For example, the very meaning of the word Islam is surrender and submission to the will of God, and specific verses of the Quran undercut the concept of free will: (8:17) "when you throw (a handful of dust) it was not your act, but Allah's"; (8:10 and 3:126) "There is no triumph except that given by Allah", and (76:30) "You have no will except as Allah wills."

As a consequence, Islamic worldviews produce practical and institutional obstacles to the extended order. We have already seen Islam's hostility to charging interest on loans, a view once common to most civilizations, and clearly incompatible with the efficient deployment of capital. It is the absence of secure property rights, however, that plays a more crucial role in the languishing economic development of most Islamic countries. Deepak Lal notes: "The Islamic state, as a conquest society, had a very simple "constitutional" justification. From its inception, all land was claimed to be the property of the sovereign by right of conquest, and from the Ummayad and Abbasids down to the Ottomans in Turkey and Saffavids in Persia, state monopoly of land became a traditional legal canon of Islamic political systems.[661] He also notes: "The Sharia also lacked the Roman law concept of legal personality, which prevented the development of corporate institutions and the group loyalties they embody, and which lay at the heart of Western capitalism. It is difficult to escape the conclusion that the Islamic legal system was not conducive to development."[662]

In addition, Islamic teachings are antithetical to the democratic institutions that evolved in the West. According to Bernard Lewis, for the believing Muslim, there is no human legislative power. The divine law, the *shari'ah*, regulates all aspects of life and human powers have no right to modify it.[663] Deleterious consequences include few restraints on the predatory state, little voice for commercial interests, and frustration among the larger populous.

The net result of these values and world views is a widespread resistance to features of the extended order: *The Index of Economic*

Freedom shows that, with the exception of a few small emirates, all Islamic nations rank as "unfree" or "largely unfree." Moreover, with not one real democracy, Arab countries had the lowest UNDP "freedom score" of all of the world's regions—even lower than of sub-Saharan Africa. This resistance to the extended order, this evolutionary stagnation, has cost Islamic countries dearly in financial terms. A concrete picture of the Arab world was produced by the United Nations Development Program (UNDP) in 2002. As reported in The Wall Street Journal, the 280 million citizens of the 22-nation Arab League produced a combined GDP of $531.2 billion in 1999—less than that of Spain. The real income of the average Arab citizen was just 13.9 percent of the average citizen of the Organization for Economic Cooperation and Development countries. And if the average annual growth rate of just 0.5 percent over the past two decades continues, it will take Arabs 140 years to double their income, while other regions will achieve that in less than 10 years.

To illustrate these conclusions, let's examine the experience of Egypt, Turkey, and Saudi Arabia; but conclude with Bahrain, which provides a positive example.

Egypt

Egypt provides a graphic case of the difficulties of development in an Arab-Islamic culture, as well as the first concerted effort to so develop. Two centuries ago, the French writer Volney provided a telling insight on the cultural history underlying attempts at developing the Arab world. He was astonished by the ruined condition of Alexandria—the decayed buildings, the silted harbor. After viewing Cairo, he concluded that "the Arabs knew how to conquer, but by no means how to govern." He found that the greater part of the lands were in the hands of the beys, and the military Mamelukes. The number of proprietors was extremely small, and their property liable to a thousand impositions. There was no right of succession or for inheritance of real property.[664]

At this juncture, one individual undertook idiosyncratic first steps by an Islamic state to modernize along Western lines. This man, Muhammad Ali, overthrew the Mamelukes in the early 19th century, confiscating their lands and setting himself up as Pasha of Egypt. As an interesting historical parallel, it can be noted that Ali's efforts just predated those of Meiji Japan. But Egypt lacked the threshold of necessary values possessed by Japan. Egypt had no tradition of wider education, no Confucian or Protestant ethic, few institutions suitable for a free market system, little national unity, and little experience with dispersed centers of power. Yet, Ali had some of the necessary insights into the general direction of essential change, probably because he was an Albanian European rather than an Egyptian.

David Landes provides a cogent analysis of Ali's initiatives and their ultimate failure. Ali envisioned a comprehensive process including advances in agriculture and industry as well as innovations in schooling. Like other ambitious leaders, he included an arms program. For all these ends, he brought in expertise and machinery from Britain and France. In agriculture, he drew on work done by Jumel, a Frenchman, who had transplanted a cotton bush found originally on Reunion Island. This led to a rapid growth of mechanized cotton manufacturing—the well regarded Egyptian cotton. The earnings from this effort flowed into industry and education. By 1834, Egypt employed 400,000 machine spindles, putting it ninth in the world, and making it possible for Egypt to produce 1.2 million pieces of calico a year.

Ultimately, however, he could not jump start an ill-prepared societal animal. Landes describes the difficulties: "Native entrepreneurs were rare. Most of them were drawn from the Coptic, Jewish, and Greek minorities—outsiders who had good reason to be discreet. Local manufacturing was done in shops and cottages, by owners lacking knowledge, money, and desire to shift to machine technologies. ... Egypt had neither wood nor coal fuel, and water had to be raised before it could be used to drive wheels. So he [Ali] began with animal power—1,000 oxen to drive 250,000 cotton spindles. ... [I]t is a costly and inefficient technique, especially in hot climates. ... [C]orruption was rife. ... All this entailed the appointment of inspectors to examine accounts and niggling regulations to prevent waste and theft. ...And where would Muhammad Ali find the workers? In the best Egyptian tradition, he started by using slaves ... But, these slaves died in large numbers, which says something about working conditions. He then had recourse to forced labor torn from family and household ... Arson was an abiding threat, and maintenance was systematically neglected, the more so as bureaucratic complications within the mills (antipilferage measures) made even lubrication a monumental task. In a sandy, dusty climate, bad maintenance spelled disaster. More and more of the machines fell idle. ... Thus, output fell, as it should have."[665]

Ali's efforts left little long term imprint on Egyptian society. After the First World War, Egypt was in Britain's sphere of influence under the nominal rule of the corrupt monarchy of king Farouk. With his ouster by a military coup, Egypt gained full independence, and Abdel Nasser took power. He followed the path of the stereotypical demagogue, trying to create a pan-Arab alliance, with Egypt as its head. The focus was on past Islamic glories, Arabic honor, and demonizing Israel. Much funding went into armaments; his machinations came to a head in the 1967 war with Israel, which Israel handily won, putting an end to his larger global ambitions.

On the economic front, Egypt was greatly influenced by the socialistic thinking then current in British politics and academia. Grandiose projects such as the Aswan dam and state control of industry reflected the overall approach. Ordinary business languished because, inter alia, of a host of difficulties facing entrepreneurs as a consequence of Egypt's statist approach and cultural sensibilities. As reported by *The Washington Post*:

- Employee layoffs are banned by law
- Bureaucratic hassles, e.g. police ordered a $115 fine for "crimes against humanity"—apparently because the work force lacked the requisite number of disabled people
- Inability to match pay with performance—pay scales were based on seniority only, so that secretaries earned more than engineers
- Under the terms of purchase agreements (privatization) new owners were barred from reducing salaries or benefits, or from shrinking the work force except through attrition

- Frequent strikes with messages such as "May God punish those who exploit the workers"
- Fear of accountability—e.g., the head of one company had to sign vacation slips for his 3,200 workers because managers were too scared to do so.[666]

One can glimpse in these few examples the complete value shift that is required in the Egyptian societal animal before it can become a prosperous modern society. Under current thinking, beliefs, and approaches, modernization and Schumpeter's 'creative destruction' are virtually unattainable.

Turkey

Turkey, the principle remnant and successor to the Ottoman Empire, is the most promising case of an Islamic society modernizing, and notably its relative success stems from a concerted effort to overcome the obstacles presented by the Islamic religion. The efforts to modernize are largely attributable to one man, Mustapha Kemal, who adopted the modern name of Ataturk. He concluded that Turkey could not be both a modern and an Islamic state.

Under his leadership, in 1922 Turkey became a republic, with the office of the sultan and the caliphate abolished. He employed a full gamut of autocratic powers to give Turkey a secular government and to eliminate religious symbolism from public life. The old titles of bey, effendi, and pasha were done away with by law. Signs and symbols of old Turkey, including the harem, the veil, the fez, Moslem schools, and Moslem courts were cast away. A new system of laws, based on the European countries, was erected: they adopted the Swiss civil code, the Italian penal code, and the German commercial code. In addition, Turkey adopted the Western calendar, as well as the metric system of weights and measures.

The principles articulated by Ataturk echo strongly those of Meiji Japan: "It is an attempt to reach the level of modern civilizations, it is westernization, modernization. It requires ... experience [of] a modern social life, to establish a secular state, and to govern with a positive science mentality."[667]

Decades later, the fruit of these efforts could be seen in Turkey's relative success vis-à-vis other Islamic countries. The Index of Economic Freedom gives Turkey a ranking of 'mostly free', the highest rating of the Islamic nations and one shared with some of the emirates, Jordan, Morocco, and Tunisia. Consistent with such a ranking, Turkey has the highest GDP per capita of the Islamic states, other than the Gulf Emirates that generate substantial revenues from oil. Indeed, the country is being considered for inclusion in the European Union. The Index reports that Turkey enjoyed an economic boom in the 1980s, in part because of the economic reforms of Prime Minister Turgut Ozal. It has a rapidly growing private sector, even though the government is still heavily involved in basic industries.

The jury is still out, however, on the ultimate success of this cultural path. Islamic fundamentalism continues to rear its head in the body politic and is contained largely by the determination of the military to intervene, should it be necessary. This is hardly the basis for a fully democratic government, but it might buy the necessary time for economic development and modern culture to be solidly institutionalized.

Saudi Arabia

While Mohammed originated Islam in the Arabian Peninsula and Islam's most holy place, Mecca, is in Saudi Arabia, for centuries, the centers of the prosperous empire and the seats of learning were elsewhere—e.g., Istanbul, Baghdad, and Damascus. But following the discovery and exploitation of oil in the 20th century, Saudi Arabia gained greater prominence and influence in the Islamic world along with its new found wealth. Nonetheless, it clings to the most primitive and rigid of Islamic traditions—i.e., the Wahhabi.

The Wahhabi influence permeates society so as to preserve the ancient traditions by stymieing cultural evolution: women play almost no role in the economy, are controlled by their husbands and fathers, are kept in their homes, are not allowed to drive, and, in public, are hidden behind veils, enforced by religious police who patrol to ensure that garb and behavior is in accord with prescribed practice. Many of the schools are not centered on learning in the Western sense, but promote rote learning of the Quran. Much of the productive work in the nation is undertaken by foreign workers. The wealth is controlled by the extended Saudi royal family.

So, despite the veneer of modern society produced by oil wealth, Saudi Arabia lacks virtually all the critical elements of an evolved extended economic order. It lacks a Protestant or a Confucian work ethic, entrepreneurship, representative government, and social capital. The government relies on strict application of Islam to maintain stability and controls the allocation of wealth. Without the spontaneous order and creativity of free economies, unemployment and underemployment and nonproductive employment have continued to grow. A modern outside world continues to intrude at the same time the fundamentalist extremists try to keep it at bay.

Bahrain

Like Saudi Arabia, Bahrain gained wealth from oil, but unlike Saudi Arabia, it has embraced much of the extended order. The *Index of Economic Freedom* rates Bahrain as 'free', one of only ten countries in the world. It has strong property rights, a sound currency, modest intervention by the government in the financial sector, and low levels of taxation. This has resulted in a thriving financial sector, which now accounts for 23 percent of its GDP—a higher share than even from the oil sector.[668]

The Report is somewhat less enthusiastic because total government expenditures amount to 40 percent of the GDP, a figure similar to European welfare states, and the highest government consumption rate in the world.[669] This pattern undoubtedly is a product of an economy having unusually high revenues from petroleum.

A central question for Islamic countries, even for the whole planet, is whether Islam is capable of a reopening of its mind, a quasi-Reformation if you will. In the negative, Deepak Lal reports on reformist efforts in the 19th century to make Islamic teaching conducive to modernization. For example, Syed Ahmad Khan in India attempted to reinterpret tradition by using rationalist and historical arguments.

However, he faced the same dilemma confronted by others. Lal quotes M. Ruthven: "The gap between scientific and religious truth could only be bridged by abandoning literalistic interpretations of the divine texts, or even in the case of the Hadith, by challenging their authenticity, thus leaving much of the law open to changes which, in the circumstances, facilitated western domination and cultural penetration. This dilemma persists to this day."[670]

Moreover, a new Islamic militancy is arising as seen in the actions of al Qaeda and the Hezbollah. While these remain fringe groups, they do act in accord with a long militant tradition: according to Islamic jurists throughout centuries, the world is divided into two parts, the House of Islam and the House of War (everyone else). In this view Islamic entities reject the legitimacy of any polity outside Islam. Indeed, according to the *Sharia,* a state of war religiously and legally obligatory could end only with the conversion or subjugation of all mankind. Past military defeats, such as that of the Ottoman Empire in the First World War, and imperialist encroachment have merely led Islamic jurists to accept the possibility of truces.[671] These views are not simply a remnant of ancient theologians, but continue to be taught in mosques and madrassas throughout Islam.

As Samuel Huntington describes in *The Clash of Civilizations,* conflict presently is evident on virtually all of Islam's borders—India/Kashmir, Chechnya, Israel, Ethiopia, the Sudan, as well as in the attack on the World Trade Center.[672] There are potential problems in the heart of the West as well. In earlier eras Muslims were discouraged from living in 'The House of War', but recently they have increasingly migrated to Europe, where there are signs that they are not assimilating well. Friction and lack of assimilation could be expected in light of the teachings of the Quran, in which the doctrine of *jihad* articulates the duty of Muslims to expand the Muslim *umma,* to bring as many under its rule as possible—ultimately bringing the whole earth under the sway of Islam.[673] Muslims are motivated by a belief that they have been called by God to establish a righteous human political and social order on earth and, importantly, this order is essential to enhance each Muslim's chance at salvation.[674]

Perhaps Islam is undergoing one final convulsion in search of old glory. On the other hand, the world might well be facing an extended period of confrontation with an intransigent Islamic fanaticism.

AFRICA

In approaching Africa, a huge continent of almost 50 countries, can one meaningfully generalize about culture and value systems? Daniel Etounga-Manguelle of Cameroon[675] answered in the affirmative for sub-Saharan Africa[676], believing that none of those African nations are that far removed from a common animistic past. Just as one can generalize about Britain's value system, even though individuals may have English, Scottish, or Welsh heritages, so one can identify cross-national cultural traits in Africa. In this regard, Etounga-Manguelle believes most Africans have a relatively fatalistic view of life, accepting the uncertainty of the future rather than planning for future needs, as seen in the native African belief that only God can modify the logic of a world created for all eternity: nature is his master and sets his destiny.[677]

The absence of a future orientation combined with fewer exigent needs to plan for winter or adverse circumstance, manifests itself in traditions and traits that run counter to the Protestant and Confucian ethics. Whereas in China and Calvinist Europe, cultural values supported working, saving, and investing, African cultures placed greater emphasis on consumption geared to building and reinforcing relationships. For example, Africans have a propensity to celebrate: "birth, baptism, marriage, birthday, promotion, election, return from a short or a long trip, mourning, opening or closure of Congress, traditional and religious feasts."[678]

The animism of sub-Saharan countries goes beyond religious views to include day-to-day behaviors, forms of cooperation, and life ambitions. As discussed in the review of Latin-American cultures, 'peasant' societies, which have not much evolved from man's origins, share many traits that ill fit them for participating productively in the extended order. In particular, they characteristically have a short radius of trust, which in turn, limits the ability to cooperate beyond the extended family and the village, and nurtures a climate of corruption in artificially created larger societies that have not yet established the mores and institutions to sustain a modern economy. Where central governments are corrupt and lack historical legitimacy, political power tends to fragment, generating coups, competing armed groups, and the most extreme predatory states.

In terms of other aspects of prevailing values, Etounga-Manguelle finds African society far less individualistic and more hierarchical than Western society — in part the result of the forces of religion and tradition. He makes observations about Africans that are very close to those that describe the likely value system of early human society:

> If we had to cite a single characteristic of the African cul-ture, the subordination of the individual by the community would surely be a reference point to remember. African thought rejects any view of the individual as an autonomous and responsible being. The African is vertically rooted in his family, in the vital ancestor, if not in God; horizontally, he is linked to his group, to society, to the cosmos. The fruit of a family-individual, society-individual dynamic, all linked to the universe, the African can only develop and bloom through social and family life.[679]

Moreover, he believes that witchcraft still flourishes in the con-tinent, which Christianity with a belief in Satan, does not effectively counter. Consequently, rationalism and science play lesser roles here than in the West. He claims that sorcery becomes a mechanism for managing conflict and preserving the status quo. He reaches the harsh conclusion that the African is the intelligent being that uses his intelligence least.[680]

There are certainly virtues in such a culture. As Robert Edger-ton states: "Humans in various societies, whether urban or folk, are capable of empathy, kindness, even love, and they can some-times achieve astounding mastery of the challenges posed by their environments."[681] Indeed, these are essential characteristics of the early societal animals for surviving and flourishing in a hostile and uncertain environment. These are the values that provide for the loving care of the young, for mutual cooperation in a hunter-gatherer society, thereby increasing the efficacy of the group and the capability to fend off attacks by other groups.

However, these are values primarily for survival rather than growth. Moreover, to quote Edgerton further: "But they are also capable of maintaining beliefs, values, and social institutions that result in senseless cruelty, needless suffering, and monumental folly in their relations among themselves, as well as with other societies and the physical environment in which they live." One needs only to examine incessant warfare in modern day Africa to recognize the validity of these observations.[682]

Sadly, Africa presents the most dismal picture of the cultures surveyed in this chapter. In the fifty some nations of the continent, there are only a couple of semi-success stories. Worse still, regression seems to be the rule. In certain countries, generally those colonized by the British, colonial powers gave the indigenous peoples a leg up in terms of physical infrastructure and rudimentary educational systems. Moreover, subsequent to independence, billions of dollars of assistance have flowed from the West, seemingly to no avail. Now, with the HIV epidemic assaulting the southern half of Africa, the picture is devastating.

Before succumbing to pessimism, however, one needs to keep a long-term perspective in viewing changes required for a country to evolve to a modern society. For example, just a century and a half ago, all the peoples of sub-Saharan Africa resided in cultures akin to our most primitive forbearers. In no manner did those cultures have the threshold of values needed to advance that, for example, the Japanese had. There was incessant tribal warfare, no literacy, no philosophic base, no infrastructure, and no broad-based governments.

While it may take Africa generations longer than it did for Japan to modernize, there are reasons that it can do so, drawn from the evolutionary model discussed in this book. First, and perhaps most important, indigenous African value systems are not necessarily antithetical to those required to be build free markets and representative forms of government.

Regarding market economies, "The peoples of [pre-colonial West Africa] had economies which made agricultural produce available in amounts large enough to be sold in rural and urban markets; craft specialization often organized along the line of craft guilds, whose members manufactured goods to be sold in these markets; different kinds of currencies which were nearly always convertible one to another and, later, to European denominations of values, and elaborate trading systems, external as well as internal. Goods produced in even the smallest West African societies were circulated in local market centres, and ultimately by porters, caravans, and boats, to the large Sudanese emporiums from which they could be shipped to Mediterranean areas in exchange for foreign products."[683] Ayittey also notes that consistent with sound market economies, for centuries prices fluctuated according to supply and demand and were not fixed by any village chief or king.

Of great importance is that the means of production were owned by the natives and not by chiefs, or by tribal governments. Robert F. Gray observes of the Sonjo in Kenya: "Generally speaking, property is privately owned among the Sonjo. The only important exception is the building plots upon which the houses are built. These are owned communally. The other forms of property are owned by individuals. Thus, a piece of property such as a field, a beehive, or a goat, at any given time can be traced in ownership to an individual. According to Sonjo law, a man has ultimate ownership rights in his own property and in all property possessed by his patrilineal descendants for as long as he lives. When he dies, these rights are inherited by his heirs."[684]

With regard to government, traditional tribal cultures were not authoritarian and, indeed, tend to be highly consultative in reaching decisions. The African countries, however, have not yet institutionalized the checks and balances necessary to restrain the predatory state when it extends significantly beyond a local purview.

In many respects these values and traditions have at least a passing similarity to those of feudal Europe. Moreover, they seem in accord with Von Mises' human action and von Hayek's spontaneous order: man will work to better himself given the opportunities at hand, and will develop supporting institutions. But Africa has not on its own taken these developments to a more advanced level. In part, this has been a consequence of a cultural unreadiness common to undeveloped societies, but, in addition,

Africa suffered from deleterious political philosophies popular in the colonial powers at the time most African countries were gaining their independence.

Two of the political approaches that most hindered development included socialism and statism. Ayittey argues that post-colonial African nations fell into four groups:

- African socialism espoused by such leaders as Kwame Nkrumah of Ghana, Ahmed Sekou Toure of Guinea, Modibo Keita of Mali, Gamal Abdel Nasser of Egypt, Julius Nyerere of Tanzania, and Kenneth Kaunda of Zambia. They looked to the state to organize the economy and to supervise the societal phase of decolonization.

- Political pragmatism espoused by such leaders as Felix Houphouet-Boigny of the Ivory Coast, Abubakar Tafawa Balewa of Nigeria, Hastings Banda of Malawi, and Daniel arap Moi of Kenya. While they claimed to be non-ideological, they charged the state with the task of fostering entrepreneurship, with attracting foreign investment, and creating a climate conducive to material development. In practice, this turned out to be as statist in approach as the socialists.

- Military nationalism was pursued by leaders such as Idi Amin of Uganda, Jean-Bedel Bokassa of Central African Republic, Mobutu Sese Seko of Zaire, and Gnassingbe Eyadema of Togo. Their ideologies were bereft of intellectual content and were directed to allowing them to control the natural resources of their states. These probably accounted for the most overt forms of predation.

- Afro-Marxism was the official policy of Angola, Mozambique, Congo, and Ethiopia. It envisaged the creation of a totally new social order, in which private ownership of the means of production would be abolished and the state would become the supreme patron of economic development.[685]

All these approaches proved to be economic disasters, and the countries that employed them followed a vicious economic downward spiral. Rather than letting the private sector build on strengths, they milked the agricultural sector to build industries seen as the wave of the future, but which invariably failed. Tax rates were increased, inflation rose, price controls were imposed, bank accounts were confiscated—and in the disastrous aftermath, the private sector and 'imperialism' were blamed. When excuses failed to explain the failures, a series of coups ousted the first wave of leaders. The next wave, promising reform, were even more ignorant of the market system, and lacked the administrative experience of the original leaders. With economies deteriorating further, virtually no foreign capital was obtainable. Western institutions tried to push reforms by making them conditional for aid. Billions flowed into these countries, but there was little to show for the money because the will to reform did not come from within. Indeed, the aid relieved the local rulers of the urgency to reform.

In one of history's many unintended consequences, colonialization exacerbated the problems of evolving representative government by the imposition of large governments for which African society was unready. For example, lacking effective representation and checks and balances to control abuses by central governments, the conditions for predatory states were put in place. Consequently, thuggery and kleptocracy swept across the continent.

Out of many examples to illustrate these conclusions, this section will focus on Ghana, Nigeria, and Zimbabwe, but will conclude with Botswana, a highly promising exception.

Ghana: Promise Unfulfilled

Ghana had been a British colony, benefiting from an administrative system, transportation infrastructure, a basic educational system, and investment in agriculture. As mentioned earlier in the book, when Ghana received its independence from Britain in 1957, it enjoyed a GDP per capita on a par with South Korea. A flourishing agricultural sector featuring the production of cocoa had been created. An infrastructure of roads and railroads as well as institutions for basic schooling and health care had been established. In addition, Ghana received substantial aid from the West. In the ensuing years, Korea grew manyfold and prospered, Ghana regressed. What went wrong?

In essence, rather than allowing a free economy to grow naturally, building on strengths and competitive advantage, Ghana succumbed to the ill-considered notions of central planning and to the
predations of its elite.

Describing many African nations after independence, Ayittey
writes that the new leaders used their parliamentary majorities to
subvert their constitutions, outlaw opposition parties, and to declare their countries "one-party states". In Ghana's case, Nkrumah,
within a year of independence, introduced the Preventive Detention
Bill of July 1958 to give the government power to imprison without
trial any person suspected of activities prejudicial to the state's security. Many post-independence leaders dismissed democracy as
an alien Western concept, "a luxury Africa could not afford." But
they, Ghana included, learned all too soon that democracy was not
a luxury but a necessity.[686]

More specifically in Ghana's case, the absence of checks and balances led to a series of disastrous policy decisions. Two examples
illustrate the failure of an unchecked (other than by economic laws)
statist approach: the regulation of agriculture and the launching of
ill-conceived, grandiose industrial development projects.

Nkrumah once referred to cocoa farming as a "poor nigger's
business,"[687] a statement was made at a time when cocoa production was a significant part of the economy and a large earner of
foreign exchange. At independence, Ghana supplied two-thirds of
the world's cocoa. However, industry was thought to be the future
of the economy, and it was the job of the government to make it
happen. Cocoa farming was to be the 'milk cow' to fund that development (along with foreign aid) and to provide the governing
elites with the standard of living to which they believed they were
entitled upon independence.

Nkrumah established a Cocoa Marketing Board that bought
low from producers and sold high at the world price. In addition,
the currency was deliberately overvalued, such that at its peak, the
black market exchange rate was twenty-two times the official rate
(i.e. worth much less). Government cronies were given special li-
censes to buy at the official rate and sell at black market rates. The
net result was that whereas the cocoa producers had received 89
percent of the world market price in 1949, by 1983, they received

just 6 percent, destroying all incentive for reinvestment in this sector. Thus, while cocoa amounted to 19 percent of GDP in 1955, by 1983 it constituted only 3 percent. Easterly states: "Ghanaian cocoa is one of the classic examples of killing the goose that laid the golden egg."[688]

Other than sheer corruption, how were the agriculturally derived proceeds utilized? One major example was the Volta River Project. A large hydroelectric dam was built on the Volta River creating the world's largest man-made lake. The electricity produced was intended to supply an aluminum smelter. New bauxite mines were to be opened, along with a caustic soda plant. Railways were built and the lake was to provide a new water transportation link between north and south. Moreover, the lake was to be the basis for a new fishing industry and for large-scale irrigation. Much of this was built in the mid-1960s with the help of Western governments, the World Bank, and Kaiser Aluminum. To be sure, electricity is produced from the installation, and there has been a slow growth of aluminum production (with fluctuations). But an evaluation carried out in the 1980s noted that there were no bauxite mines, no alumina refinery, no caustic plant, no railways, the lake fishery was plagued by poor administration, the irrigation schemes never worked, the water transport system was a complete failure, and the population bordering the lake suffered from waterborne illnesses such as river blindness, hookworm, malaria, and schistosomiasis.[689]

Along with such major misallocations of capital, the socialist ideology encouraged state intervention throughout the economy with a battery of controls on prices and exchange rates. These resulted in inflation and a debased currency. From the perspective of the rulers and their politically-connected allies, however, the Byzantine maze of controls provided rich opportunities for self-aggrandizement.[690] In such a climate, foreign private investment dried up, while the country was incapable of generating fresh capital.

The obvious corruption and declining economy led to political instability. Nkrumah was ousted in a coup in 1966. Several military leaders, none of whom proved to be more clear-sighted or less corrupt, were subsequently ousted in the coming years. When Flight-Lieutenant Jerry Rawlings seized power in 1981, he imposed strict price controls and attacked private business as "dens of profiteers and capitalists." The economy sank to its nadir in 1983. The regime approached the Communist Bloc for assistance but was turned down. They then had little choice but to seek aid from Western institutions like the World Bank and the IMF, whom they had previously attacked as "imperialist institutions dedicated to the oppression and exploitation of the Third World."

While Ghana received more than 2 billion dollars from the World Bank in exchange for economic reform, all such efforts were half-hearted and incoherent given the residual socialistic philosophy. But the infusion of billions did improve the economy somewhat, and the country experienced a positive rate of growth for a decade or so. By 1997, however, the economy was once again in a shambles. Inflation was raging at 60 percent a year, unemployment had reached 30 percent, and the currency was in free-fall.[691]

So, despite a positive inheritance from colonial days in terms of infrastructure and a thriving agricultural sector, as well as substantial Western assistance, Ghana's per capita income was no greater at the end of the century than it had been four decades earlier at independence—a performance about average for sub-Saharan Africa.

Nigeria: Petroleum Wealth is not Enough

While Ghana's experience illuminated institutional and policy failures common to many African countries in the post-colonial era, Nigeria, the continent's most populous country, epitomizes how unevolved values, incompatible with those of the extended economic order, can keep a country impoverished despite extensive mineral wealth.

When Nigeria gained its independence in 1960 it had two advantages which could have been expected to speed its economic development: it had been a British colony and it possessed considerable oil reserves. As an ex- British colony, it inherited democratic institutions such as a parliament and judicial system, as well as transportation infrastructure and a system of basic education. Its oil reserves made Nigeria one of the world's largest producers of petroleum, and in the following four decades, it earned $280 billion in revenue from this source[692]—its largest source of trade revenue, by far. No other sub-Saharan country had both advantages.

Yet Nigeria experienced little net economic progress. While its per capita income grew 4.8 percent per annum between 1960 and 1980, it contracted 1.5 percent per annum between 1981 and 1998.[693] The decline of the latter years impoverished the average Nigerian— e.g., the per capita income dropped from $1,200 in 1983 to $250 in 1995.[694] An indicator of larger problems was the relative ineffectiveness of large amounts of capital investment. For example, William Easterly observes that: "Both Nigeria and Hong Kong increased their physical capital stock per worker by over 250 percent over the 1960 to 1985 time frame. The results of this massive investment were different: Nigeria's output per worker rose by 12 percent from 1960 to 1985, while Hong Kong's rose by 328 percent."[695] Effectively, the oil wealth had done little more than feed a corrupt, predatory state.

This failure can be traced to two roots—a predilection, like Ghana's, for dysfunctional policies associated with statism, and a value structure antithetical to trust and cooperation essential to the extended economic order. A relatively brief era as a British colony was insufficient to overcome value systems once common to tribal units and characterized in earlier sections as a peasant culture rife with distrust of outsiders and of individual economic success.

Moreover, the newly independent country got off on the wrong foot, having a statist bent from the start. The First Development Plan (1962-1968) stated that indigenous businessmen should control an increasing portion of the Nigerian economy, which resulted in a sharp decrease in foreign investment. The Second Development Plan (1970-1974) went further: "The interests of foreign private investors in the Nigerian economy cannot be expected to coincide at all times and in every respect with national aspirations ... It is vital therefore for Government to acquire and control on behalf of the Nigerian society the greater proportion of the productive assets of the country ..."[696]

In just a few years, the government acquired 40 percent of the largest commercial banks, 55 percent of the petroleum industry, 40 percent of the National Insurance Company of Nigeria, and 49 percent of other insurance companies.[697] Thus was a major portion of the country's economy removed from the discipline of the market and opened to the deprivations of the predatory state. In addition, Nigeria employed tactics similar to those used by Ghana regarding tariffs and import licensing for industry and price controls and marketing boards for agriculture,[698] creating in Nigeria the same potential for black markets and enrichment of special interests having ties to the government.

In terms of societal evolution, the country simply had not evolved the key features that make the modern economic extended order functional—a work ethic was lacking at the same time that the populace lacked a large radius of trust. These circumstances were compounded by the country being composed of vastly different cultural groups, who distrusted one another: Nigeria is a federation of three culturally distinct regions, having a number of different languages—Hausa, Yoruba, Edo, Ibo, Ibibido, and Ijaw (though English is the official language), and different religions—Islam is predominant in the north among the Hausa people, and Christianity and animism elsewhere. In the late 1960s, the distrust erupted in a civil war between Biafra and the dominant Hausas over control of the oil wealth, which left one million dead.[699]

Given the level of distrust within Nigerian society, it is unsurprising that the governmental institutions inherited from Britain did not produce a functioning democracy. Indeed, Nigeria has endured a series of military dictatorships (until a civilian government was elected recently in 1999). [700] And, unfortunately, the Nigerian military regimes produced no enlightened leaders, such as occasionally came to the fore in other countries, and government inevitably became the target of economic rent-seeking and personal corruption. For example, according to Easterly, "Nigerian dictator Sani Abacha allegedly accumulated billions of dollars from kickbacks on construction contracts and from diverting oil revenues to his personal account. He also diverted $2 billion from state oil refineries, leaving them unable to produce gasoline, and then, with real chutzpah, pocketed commissions on imported gasoline."[701]

Such corruption permeates government. The *2001 Index of Economic Freedom* concludes: "the government controls most large enterprises, the business environment lacks transparency, the judiciary is not independent, and corruption is rampant."[702] An intrusive government provides myriad opportunities for corruption through the regulatory process. Regarding opportunities, the Index highlights the customs clearing process and regulations governing foreign investment—e.g., "ministries charged with approving foreign investment often act arbitrarily, and there can be long delays in the project-approval process."[703]

The maze of state controls provided rich opportunities for corruption. "Because every permit has its price, Nigerian officials invent endless new rules. A guard outside a ministry demands a special permit for you to enter; a customs inspector invents an environmental regulation to let in your imports; an airline official charges passengers for their boarding cards."[704] Transparency International's Corruption Perceptions Index lists Nigeria as one of the world's most corrupt countries, viz., in 101st place out of the 102 countries ranked in 2003.[705]

Given the high transaction costs imposed by corruption, lack of mutual trust, and weak rule of law, investment—foreign or domestic—is repelled. A 1995 report of the Nigerian Institute of Social and Economic Research revealed that foreign investors were leaving the country and that there had been a total absence of new investment in 1994. Domestic investors experience the same disincentives. In 1993, the Manufacturing Association of Nigeria reported that 700 of its 1,500 members had closed their doors in the prior six years.[706] Estimates have been made that enormous sums on the order of $120 billion to $160 billion, which could potentially have been invested, have made their way into foreign bank accounts.[707]

Lack of new investment erodes the quality of Nigerian life at every level. For example, the Index states that the "infrastructure is in tatters,"[708] and Ayittey reports that the country's 38-school university system is in ruins.[709]

In such ways, value systems reflecting a lack of interpersonal trust and a lack of a Protestant or Confucian work ethic, produced a predatory state that has squandered its oil wealth, produced widespread poverty, and promises little improvement for the next generation.

Zimbabwe: Careening Toward Chaos

Whereas Ghana made many misguided decisions, and Nigeria stagnates as a consequence of corruption, Zimbabwe is virtually self-destructing, despite having the most promising post-colonial legacy of the three. Indeed, Zimbabwe's experience is reflected in the biblical adage: "Where there is no vision, the people perish." (Proverbs 29, 18)

In 1980, white minority rule in Rhodesia ended and was replaced by a black majority government under Robert Mugabe. At that time, Zimbabwe appeared to have a promising future. While the population was predominantly black, there were a significant number of British settlers, who had brought the financial and social capital to establish a modern farming sector, as well as industry and banking. The country became the 'bread basket' of Southern Africa and had extensive trade links with South Africa, the largest economy of the continent by far.

The post-independence administration of Robert Mugabe milked this endowment for a while and then finally destroyed it through demagogic policies. Mugabe overtaxed the productive sectors, engaged in military adventures in the Congo that Zimbabwe could ill-afford, debased the currency, established market-distorting price controls and regulation, and finally undermined the prosperity of the agricultural sector.

This latter effort is especially instructive of leadership that lacks a practical understanding of the values necessary for development. Having put the larger economy on a downhill course and having to confront rising unemployment and poverty, he used the white settlers and the colonial past as scapegoats for his own failures. He promised landless blacks something for nothing by confiscating the prosperous white farms.

This has proved to be a disaster of major proportions. Replacing capable, motivated, and successful owners with inexperienced and unmotivated peasants practicing traditional farming methods produced predictable results. Bank loans could no longer be repaid, black workers employed by the large farmers lost their livelihood, and the new owners with neither experience nor capital, were unable to succeed. Of course, with property rights so disregarded, there was no way to raise new capital or loans. The result was famine in a nation that had been a major food exporter.

Failure to effectively deal with the AIDS epidemic is a parallel catastrophe. Despite a forewarning of the epidemic from the early U.S. experience and knowledge that HIV had originated nearby in Africa, little was done in educational programs. Unlike Uganda, which used effective measures to forestall a major outbreak, the Mugabe government denied a problem existed and it sat on its hands. The result has been hundreds of thousands of deaths and one-quarter of the adult population infected, a dire prognosis, indeed.

At the time of this writing, Zimbabwe has the world's highest inflation rate, 80 percent unemployment, and a life expectancy that declined since 1988 from 62 to 38 years.[710] In attempts to survive, a significant fraction of the population has fled to neighboring countries. It is a case study of how a society with many developmental advantages can quickly fail under the ministrations of an unenlightened predatory state that violates virtually all the predicates of the extended order.

Botswana: A Promising Exception

Botswana, which gained independence in1966, seems to be the exception to the general evolutionary picture in Africa, and thus a sign of hope. While it seemingly had no more readiness for the extended order than the rest of Sub-Saharan Africa, it has performed well. An important contributor may be a low level of corruption, the lowest in Africa and better than some Western European countries,[711] which is evidence of a large radius of trust within its society. Equally important, in terms of governance and policy it has gotten the key things right. Indeed, if one were to revisit the world's hope for African countries as they gained their independence, it might resemble what came to be Botswana's experience. In effect, Botswana was able to draw on its British colonial institutional inheritance, without succumbing to civil wars, a thuggish predatory state, or nostrums of socialism.

As noted by the Index, for a country to prosper it must adopt most of the measures and policies associated with the extended order and economic freedom. Half-measures leave countries not much better off than the poorest, most economically repressed. The

Index's survey of Botswana's institutions and policies shows how these have contributed to its overall success—as evidenced by a market-led economy that has enjoyed one of the world's highest average growth rates during the past four decades (6.6 percent per annum over the 1990s) and a per capita GDP in 1998, which was among the highest in sub-Saharan Africa.[712]

The contributors to these track record results include rule of law, political stability, sound macro-economic policies, openness to foreign investment, and modest levels of intrusion by the state into free markets. First among these, as cited by the Index: "Botswana has Africa's oldest continuous, multi-party democratic system of government, dating back to independence in 1966. Elections are routinely free and fair.[713] This stable government in turn carried out sound policies for economic growth. These are summarized in the Index:

- A low level of protectionism in trade policy.
- A moderate fiscal burden of taxation, both personal and corporate.
- A moderate to high level of government intervention in the economy (one area of potential concern).
- Moderate levels of monetary inflation.
- Low barriers to capital flows and foreign investment.
- An advanced and competitive banking system.
- Little intervention by the government with market forces in setting prices and wages.
- A high level of protection of property rights.
- Low levels of regulations, which are transparent and evenly applied.[714]

All in all, an encouraging picture. The greatest cloud for the future lies not in its adherence to economic freedom, but its social capacity to deal with high rates of HIV infection, one of the highest on the continent, presaging a future toll on longevity and prosperity.

THE SOVIET UNION

The Soviet Union presents a special case in this survey of societal animals inasmuch as it represents not an analysis of cultural readiness and progress vis-à-vis the extended order, but rather a portrayal of a systematic attempt to overturn the extended order. Its Marxist ideological attempt to leapfrog a society to modernity misperceived the basis of economic advance in the world and misunderstood the nature of man in terms of economic motivation. The cost in lives lost and lives wasted proved to be staggering and tangentially sheds light on the general workings and pathologies of societal animals.

The Soviet system was less remarkable in its Marxist formulation than it was in the ferocity with which it was pursued. Indeed, the trappings of scientific socialism aside, Marxist ideology was just one of mankind's recurrent attempts to retreat to earlier human values of cooperative life and 'fairness'. Indeed, in Chapter III we saw how reformers in China as long as one and two millennia ago attempted to introduce quasi-socialist systems on similar grounds—and with similar results.

But seldom does one encounter in history a case where an attempt was made to supplant the value system of a culture so completely as it was by the Communists in the former Soviet Union. Aspects of Russian culture were uprooted through terror and all the tools of the modern totalitarian state, thereby destroying values, institutions, social capital, and even the élan vital that are essential for the healthy working of a societal animal, leaving behind an ailing post-communist Russia.

To achieve their ideological goals, the Communist state renounced bourgeois capitalistic values along with private property and institutions of the free market. More grievously, members of society associated with those institutions were liquidated, sent to gulags, or 'reeducated'. *The Black Book of Communism* states:

> Lenin and his comrades initially found themselves embroiled in a merciless "class war," in which political and ideological adversaries, as well as the more recalcitrant members of the general public, were branded as enemies and marked

for destruction. The Bolsheviks had decided to eliminate, by legal and physical means, any challenge or resistance, even if passive, to their absolute power. This strategy applied not only to groups with opposing political views, but also to such social groups as the nobility, the middle class, the intelligentsia, and the clergy, as well as professional groups such as the military officers and the police. Sometimes the Bolsheviks subjected these people to genocide. The policy of "de-Cossackization" begun in 1920 corresponds largely to our definition of genocide: a population group firmly established in a particular territory, the Cossacks were exterminated, the men shot, the women, children, and the elderly deported, and the villages razed or handed over to new, non-Cossack occupants. ... The "dekulakization" of 1930-1932 repeated the policy of "de-Cossackization" but on a much grander scale. Its primary objective, in accordance with the official order issued for this operation (and the regime's propaganda), was "to exterminate the kulaks as a class.[715]

Coercion was exercised on many fronts. Fear was explicitly exercised through the state security agencies—initially the NKVD and then the KGB. The pervasiveness of their influence is difficult for the Western mind to grasp. The Black Book notes that in 1939 the NKVD employed 366,000 including those personnel running the gulags. In contrast, at that time the Gestapo in Germany employed only 7,500. Moreover, party members were a ubiquitous presence and the population was given to denunciation of others as an everyday practice. Given human nature, this practice was often used for reasons of self-advancement more than ideology.[716]

The deleterious effect on mutual trust and loyalty was incalculable, and the numbers of dead are mind-boggling:

- Tens of thousands of hostages and prisoners were executed without trial, and hundreds of thousands of rebellious workers and peasants were murdered from 1918 to 1922.

- The famine of 1922 caused the deaths of 5 million people.

- The Don Cossacks were exterminated or deported in 1920.
- Tens of thousands were liquidated in concentration camps from 1918 to 1930.
- Almost 690,000 people were liquidated in the Great Purge of 1937-38.
- Two million "kulaks", i.e., relatively prosperous farmers, (and so-called kulaks) were deported in 1930-1932.
- Four million Ukrainians and two million others were starved to death by means of an artificial and systematically perpetuated famine in 1932-33.
- Thousands of Poles, Ukrainians, Balts, Moldavians, and Bessarabians were deported from 1939 to 1941, and again in 1944-45.
- The Volga Germans were deported in 1941.
- There was wholesale deportation of Crimean Tatars in 1943, and the Chechens and the Ingush in 1944....[717]

In addition to the absolute human loss, the loss of social capital was enormous. Among the groups eliminated were the business classes, which embodied free market traditions, the landed peasantry, the intelligentsia, and most of the officer corps.

But these assaults also affected the general population because of their arbitrary and random nature. Take for example the Great Terror of 1937-38. A purge calling for the arrest of all kulaks and criminals was launched on 2 July 1937. The victims of this operation were to be not only well-defined former Tsarist civil servants and White Guards, but the ambiguous categories of "socially dangerous elements" and "members of anti-Soviet parties." The Black Book states: "It appears that during 1937 and 1938, 1,575,000 people were arrested by the NKVD; of these, 1,345,000 (85.4 percent) received some sort of sentence and 681,692 (51 percent of those who were sentenced) were executed."[718]

Quotas were sent out in advance by central offices, and local NKVD often simply picked up suspects by "reactivating" old lists. If the list of names on file was insufficient, any means necessary were used to "comply with the established norms."[719] Terror is an apt term to describe this process—one that pervaded all layers of society.

Aside from the terror, the general population suffered from the bleakness created by misguided policies. Ayn Rand, who fled the Soviet Union in the 1920s, tried to capture these conditions in her book *We the Living*. Her notes for the book laid out the Soviet reality she wanted to portray: "A general misery. People driven to the point where [obtaining] the most common necessities presents a big problem. The horrible, deadening dullness of the hopeless drudgery, when all higher instincts and aspirations slowly die out, stifled by the dumb, animal struggle for a pitiful existence. And the mental atmosphere furnished by the government: a glorifying of the drudgery. A growing habit of considering all luxury—everything unnecessary and charming—to be absolutely and hopelessly out of reach. ... All the pathetic, tragic, and ridiculous efforts to make a living. Divorces to keep a job. ... The eternal fear and uncertainty."[720]

David Boaz notes how the backbone of civil society was thereby destroyed in the Soviet Union: "We can barely survive, and hardly flourish, without interacting with other people. We want to associate with others to achieve instrumental ends—producing more food, exchanging goods, developing new technology—but also because we feel a deep need for connectedness, for love and friendship and community. The associations we form with others make up what we call civil society. Those associations can take an amazing variety of forms: families, churches, schools, clubs, fraternal societies, condominium associations, neighborhood groups, and the myriad forms of commercial society, such as partnerships, corporations, labor unions, and trade associations. All of these associations serve human needs in different ways."[721]

He goes on to describe Marxism in that framework: "Ironically, Marxism promised freedom and community but delivered tyranny and atomization. The tyranny of the Marxist countries is well known, but it may not be so well understood that Marxism created a society far more atomized than anything in the capitalist world. The Marxist rulers in the Soviet empire, in the first place, believed theoretically that men under conditions of "true freedom" would have no need for organizations catering to their individual interests, and in the second place, understood practically that independent associations would threaten the power of the state. Thus, they not only eliminated private economic activity, they sought to stamp out churches, independent schools, political organizations, neighborhood associations, and everything else, down to garden clubs. ... What happened, of course, was that people deprived of any form of community and connectedness between the family and the all-powerful state became atomistic individuals with a vengeance. As the philosopher and anthropologist Ernest Gellner wrote, "The system created isolated, amoral, cynical individualists—without opportunity, skilled at double-talk and trimming." The normal ways in which people were tied to their neighbors, their fellow parishioners, the people with whom they did business were destroyed, leaving them suspicious and distrustful of one another, seeing no reason to cooperate with others or even to treat them with respect."[722]

This assault on the psychic and spiritual side of the societal animal inevitably took a physical toll. Soon the Soviet Union exhibited tangible signs of pathology—high divorce rates, high abortion rates, and a stupendous consumption of vodka. Nicholas Eberstadt reviewed statistics showing the toll on the health of individuals, especially men in recent decades. He notes that a rise in mortality combined with a drop in fertility levels has resulted in a population decline. Indeed, Russia's deaths are exceeding births by about 700,000 a year.[723] Arnold Beichman notes that only about 25 percent of Russian babies are born healthy and only 5 percent to 10 percent of Russian children are healthy. Eberstadt notes that the records of the World Health Organization do not show another instance in which the survival odds of able-bodied men are as poor as in Russia. The mortality is not a result of a leap in infectious diseases, but mostly falls in the categories of cardio-vascular disease, injuries, suicide, violence, and poisonings, the latter of which are under the control of the individual. Clearly, the picture in the immediate post-communist years is one of a disabled societal animal.[724]

Such diminished self-control can be linked to a general demoralization, which in turn can be linked to high rates of alcoholism. A national household survey showed that over 80 percent of Russian men were drinkers who consumed on the average five bottles of Vodka a week. Eberstadt notes that extraordinarily heavy drinking is implicated in Russia's explosion of deadly injuries, for many of the fatal falls, crashes, suicides, and murders. He noted further that life expectancy can be a predictor of economic growth.

Accordingly, Russian demographic prospects for the next decade or so are not promising.

So after all the Five-Year Plans, regimentation, and forced labor, Russia remains a poor country. In 2003, its per capita income was only \$2,138 as compared to over \$36,000 for the United States.[725] That is the result of an ideological and economically misguided attempt to upend the extended order.

A new chapter in Russia's history has begun, but given the country's wrenching upheaval, it is too soon to judge its likely trajectory. At the time of this writing, however, Russia has made key moves in a healthy direction: a new constitution and relatively free elections, reestablishment of private property and strengthening of the rule of law. These have had a predictable result—in terms of the expected effects of adhering to the dictates of the extended order. Given man's propensity to act economically to better to one's condition, the removal of ideological shackles of Communism and the institution of at least some key elements of free markets led to a speedy rebirth of a modest middle class.

As reported by Leon Aron, a decade after the fall of the Soviet Union, Russia had 890,000 registered businesses, mostly owned by the middle class, producing as much as 30 percent of the country's GDP. Consistent with that figure, one sees an upsurge in the use of computers and the internet, in the construction of new bedroom communities around major cities, in the purchase of new cars (a 72 percent rise from 1990 to 1998 alone), in travel abroad, and in the founding of new private schools and universities.[726]

Russia, however, is still ranked as 'mostly unfree' by the Index because of continued high levels of regulation, still weak property rights, barriers on capital flows and foreign investment, corruption, and arbitrariness of law enforcement.[727] Also, on the negative side of the ledger, President Putin made many moves to limit media freedom and to corral opposition parties. One hopes that on balance he is only following the path that other successful quasi-autocratic leaders took in modernizing their countries—i.e., stability and sound macroeconomic policies first, full democracy later.

We have seen in this cross-cultural survey how worldviews correlate with economic development. Outside the West, cultures with a strong Confucian influence present a hopeful prototype for development. Clearly, where underlying cultural value systems are congruent with those needed for modernization, societies can be transformed in a generation. Less positively, other cultures such as Latin America, generally lacking either a Protestant or a Confucian ethic, present a frustrating picture of stop-and-go economic development. The most disappointing track records are those of Islamic and African countries, in which there are few instances of significant evolution from archaic value systems to ones compatible with the extended order.

Unfortunately, in the case of lagging countries, essential values cannot be bestowed, either from the outside or internally through logic and rationality. One cannot expect to 'give' a people a democratic constitution and expect a fully functioning free society to emerge forthwith. Similarly, one cannot impose an effective system of private property without the support of the populace and the creation of an accompanying legal system to enforce associated rights. Moreover, the experience of the last five decades, in which the West undertook at great expense measures such as providing more capital or increasing educational levels, indicate extrinsic efforts are of little avail.

For a country to develop successfully, it needs a period of a generation or more experiencing sound macro-economic policies and political stability in which the populace can gain confidence in the ways of the extended order. To that end, countries that are most open to economic globalization prove to be most advantaged in making progress.

We will see in the last chapter why and how cultures resist change.

8

Innate Resistance to Change

> If we were to apply the unmodified, uncurbed, rules of the micro-cosmos (i.e. of the small band or troop, or of, say, our families) to the macro-cosmos (our wider civilization), as our instincts and sentimental yearnings often make us wish to do, *we would destroy it*. Yet if we were always to apply the rules of the extended order to our more intimate groupings, *we would crush them*. So we must learn to live in two sorts of world at once. – Friedrich von Hayek [728]

The book thus far has shown that countries that are least receptive to values of the extended order perform poorly in economic terms at the same time that other culturally-ready countries, notably Japan and those of East Asia, are markedly successful in adopting the practices necessary for economic advancement. Indeed, even when poorer countries have access to models to emulate and receive substantial financial assistance, most continue to stagnate. Clearly, there are deep-seated cultural influences at work that transcend good intentions and ambition.

Simply put, countries fail to prosper when their societies, faced with the dictates of the extended order, perceive them as threatening, in conflict with tradition, or too politically demanding. To be sure, tradition is a good thing, embodying values that equipped societal animals to survive in an often hostile and unforgiving competitive environment. Yet, if tradition is unyielding to the possibilities of the extended order, economic advancement is problematic. We need to understand better how and why tradition can be so intractable. Since billions of individuals continue to languish in poverty, despite a half-century of concerted effort by affluent countries, there is some urgency in understanding this phenomenon better.

To gain more insight, this chapter examines: (1) the persistence of atavistic value systems, (2) 20th century ideological contests between older and evolved worldviews, and (3) illustrative ongoing value contests in contemporary America.

PERSISTANCE OF ATAVISTIC VALUE SYSTEMS

Tradition, embodying the cultural strength of a society, reflects a society's survival experience, and is not easily changed. Nonetheless, the modern world has seen it as in everyone's interest that poorer countries develop economically and modify their cultures — preserving core cultural values to be sure, but adopting the ways of the extended order in wider society. To understand the nature of that challenge, we need to examine the tenacious hold of tradition when confronted with the need to evolve.

The Role of Tradition

The role of traditional values has been highlighted by anthropologists such as Ruth Benedict[729], who emphasizes that enduring cultures need to be seen as cohesive entities. Their interlocking values are coherent in a pragmatic fashion, such that it is difficult to change arbitrarily one significant value or one deep-seated practice without considering the larger context of the culture. Whatever their evolutionary path, societal animals have a system that 'works', that has enabled survival, and has undoubtedly done so through fierce competition with other groups through the ages. Traits contributing to that fitness are institutionalized through custom and religion, and are held dearly.

Societal practices and values are necessarily arranged in worldviews because that is how individuals achieve coherence to the many conclusions reached in life. The economist Thomas Sowell notes: "The ever-changing kaleidoscope of raw reality would defeat the human mind by its complexity, except for the mind's ability to abstract, to pick out parts and think of them as the whole. This is nowhere more necessary than in social visions and social theory, dealing with the complex and often subconscious interactions of millions of human beings."[730] He quotes Walter Lippman: "At the core of every moral code there is a picture of human nature, a map of the universe, and a version of history. To human nature (of the sort conceived), in a universe (of the kind imagined), after a history (so understood), the rules of the code apply."[731]

The tenacity of values in the context of tradition has great efficiency and survival value where they spur effective group action without undue delay for reflection. It is impractical and inefficient if individuals have to consider first principles in the myriad decisions, choices, and reactions demanded of them each and every day. In effect, we all act on a built-in shorthand of decision-making rules imbued by our culture, which is distinct from knowledge. Hayek notes that "Our habits and skills, our emotional attitudes, our tools, and our institutions—all are … adaptations to past experience which have grown up by selective elimination of less suitable conduct. They are as much an indispensable foundation of successful action as is our conscious knowledge."[732]

When cultural values are congruent with the range of decisions faced by society, that shorthand produces the most appropriate responses in the great preponderance of circumstances. We understand that intuitively and are reluctant to change those values on argumentation alone.

The most tenacious of values, present in every culture, are those atavistic 'survival' values, which arose from early man's successful confrontation with the very insecurity of life itself. The cohesiveness of the tribe, cooperation, sacrifice, and compassion were crucial to survival. In their way, they remain crucial—in the extended family, among friends, and among neighbors. Illness, misfortune, and bad decisions can afflict any one of us at any time. We all sense that, and there is no escaping a fundamental reliance on our fellow men.

Nonetheless, as man discovered more effective, less personal, ways of ordering his activities to generate wealth and thus, ultimately, produce an enhanced survival capability, relationships had to evolve as well. In the process, some values that were once unambiguously good—indeed essential to human survival— became only circumstantially good, and possibly circumstantially dysfunctional. Dysfunctional ones in the larger modern context—e.g., suspicion of individual initiative, of private property, and of disparate wealth—persist. They and their associated traditions yielded their hold in societies only when new approaches were demonstrably superior in producing an evolutionarily fitter society.

Even when evolved values take hold, older values and traditions persist. Indeed, as the following discussion makes clear, humans may have a 'default setting' for many older values. For example, as seen in Chapter II, our genetic makeup seems to give us an instinctual awareness of 'fairness' in interactions with one another. But what is the frame of reference for judging fairness? If a mother is dividing a pie for her children or if a tribe is dividing portions of game caught in a collective hunt, the standard is unarguably equal shares.

When early cultures established arms-length, contractual ways of cooperation to accommodate more dispersed, risk-taking, and innovative activities, however, the standard had to evolve to recognize risk-reward payoffs, even if that resulted in disparate rewards. Moreover, personal sentiment had to count for less if following abstract rules produced greater benefits for society as a whole.

Unfortunately, the dictates of the extended order can be a tough sell because they seem counterintuitive to instinctual response, absent an informed view about the workings of the market place. Employing an analogy from the physical sciences, we see uninformed individuals as having a view of economics akin to a scientific 'flat earth theory'. In physical observation, if one relies merely on one's senses and 'common sense', one concludes, as did men for millennia, that the earth is flat. But when one gains the ability to make measurements and draw inferences from those measurements, one concludes that the senses can be misleading. Such is also the case in economics and political philosophy.

Conflict of Visions

In *A Conflict of Visions*, Thomas Sowell analyzes the underlying structure of value debate in a way that provides us a means for tracking the ongoing clash between atavistic values and those of the extended order. He notes that while, in principle, there can be as many worldviews—or visions—as there are individuals, practically speaking, in debates on the contentious issues of the day, one tends to see the same faces lining up on opposite sides of the table, regardless of the issue. Thus, one can expect to find sets of values and underlying premises common to each side. Sowell's analysis divides these common groupings into *constrained* and *unconstrained* visions of life.

Sowell's constrained vision matches closely with the evolved extended order, whereas the unconstrained correspond to those forces opposing the implicit logic and the outcomes of the extended order. As discussed in prior chapters, the extended order is a product of experience, tradition, and spontaneous order, under which society functions and advances in a hazily understood, but ultimately efficient fashion. This view led, through the agency of Britain and its descendants, to a respect for common law, for constitutional traditions, for representative government, and for unfettered workings of the free market. Adam Smith, Edmund Burke, Alexander Hamilton, Friedrich von Hayek, and Milton Friedman have expounded on and defended many aspects of this worldview.

The most sophisticated unconstrained vision sprang from the *Enlightenment*, which in turn was inspired by the rise of science. Man's newfound power to understand and master his physical environment, led to the plausible belief that he could use science and logic to master his social environment as well. According to this belief, society's most intelligent and beneficent members should lead the way—notably a feature of the French Revolution.

Sowell finds an early articulation of the unconstrained view in the writings of William Godwin as expressed in "Enquiry Concerning Political Justice," published in England in 1793. Sowell writes: "Where in Adam Smith moral or socially beneficial behavior could be evoked from man only by incentives [where it did not exist unintentionally through the operation of the 'Invisible Hand'], in William Godwin man's understanding and disposition were capable of intentionally creating social benefits. Godwin regarded the *intention* to benefit others as being "of the essence of virtue," and virtue in turn as being the road to human happiness."[733] Godwin found experience to be greatly overrated. Therefore, he found the wisdom of the ages to be largely the illusions of the ignorant.[734] This view is very much an 'elitist' view. Implicit in the unconstrained view is a profound inequality between the conclusions of "persons of narrow views" and those with "cultivated" minds.[735] According to Godwin, what is needed is to infuse "just views of society" into "the liberally educated and reflecting members" of society, who in turn will be "to the people guides and instructors."[736] These views are also found in the writings of Condorcet, Rousseau, Voltaire, Robert Owen, George Bernard Shaw, Thorstein Veblen, and Ronald Dworkin.

According to Sowell these two visions are in fundamental conflict, existing at the heart of political debates of our day: on economic policy, on governmental regulation, and on judicial activism. Sowell treats the two visions evenhandedly and appears to believe that one cannot empirically choose one over the other. The entire thrust of the present book, however, is to plead the case for the constrained view.

A central difficulty with the unconstrained view is the absence of historical evidence either that an elite can provide the necessary leadership or that human nature is sufficiently malleable to be made less 'selfish' and more 'other directed'. Especially problematic is the absence of agreed-upon concrete goals for the elite to pursue; vague beneficence and a corresponding desire to redistribute wealth are insufficient. The constrained view, on the other hand, believes that, with an evolving extended order, sweeping goals are unnecessary—free markets responding to price signals produce results commensurate with the aggregate strivings of all of a society's citizens. In effect, the constrained view believes that a society's distributed intelligence harnessed in appropriate institutions is far superior to the combined intelligence of any small group of elite, however brilliant.

One does not have to dig very deep to see that the value-dynamic of the unconstrained view is little different from the tribal values of our primitive forebears or of the institutionalized religions of a millennium ago. As a practical matter, when the unevolved values of the adherents of the unconstrained cause are redeployed, people become worse off or fail to progress in economic development—*because those values have become unsuitable in an evolved, extended modern society*. They fail to achieve their own stated objectives.

Nonetheless, the arguments of the unconstrained view retain a lingering seductiveness, and so we now examine cases of clashing values in the ideological scope of the twentieth century, as well as show how the conflict of values, in the context of specific issues, plays out in modern society.

TWENTIETH CENTURY VALUE CONTESTS

Despite the towering achievement of the extended order in producing affluence and liberty for much of humankind, it has been and continues to be attacked. In part, this happens because evolution took some unfortunate turns in the early 20th century, which made progress and the benefits of the extended order seem less evident and more contentious.

At the beginning of the 20th century, the Western model of a free market economic system—democratic governance, rational thinking epitomized by the rise of science, and rights of the individual—had every sign of being the wave of the future. In pragmatic terms, income per capita increased steadily in the Western nations, classical liberalism appeared to be the most promising way for human societies to order their affairs, and scientific discovery burgeoned. Indeed, we saw how the virtues and the prospects of the Western model were so immediately apparent to Meiji Japan, that they launched an unparalleled effort to emulate the practices of the West in the economic and military spheres.

Nonetheless, the pre-World War One West was not in a 'Golden Age'. Most people were still relatively poor, the differences between rich and poor glaring, and fights between labor and management often bloody. Such circumstances spurred alternative world views such as Marxism and anarchism. While these views did not have much traction in times of growing prosperity, they were increasingly attractive following the horrors of World War I and the grinding despair of the Great Depression. Accordingly, the legitimacy of Western institutions came under wide attack, with only the United States and Great Britain (along with a few ex-colonies) remaining dedicated to democratic forms of government and free markets. Totalitarian, socialist ideologies captured much of the European continent in the forms of Fascism and Communism, while Latin American countries seemed enamored with caudillo-led, corporatist states.

So at this juncture, even after a couple of centuries of sustained advance, the extended order was in potentially desperate straits. By the early 1940s, Great Britain was under serious attack by Hitler's Germany, and the United States sat relatively unarmed in deliberate isolationism. Had Britain not had radar, had Britain not broken the German codes, had Hitler pressed the attack on Dunkirk more aggressively, and had he attacked airplane factories and bases in Britain as hard as he did London, the outcome for Western liberalism could have been dark indeed.

But the Allies prevailed, as did many of their philosophical views in the eyes of the world, Communist nations excepted. Nonetheless liberal values had been eroded during the Depression in the United States and Britain and were still being questioned in the post-war era. It took another half-century for libertarian values to regain a solid political footing, as they did with considerable success in the United States. Western Europe in some ways is more problematic.

Let's examine the partial ebb of the extended order and its resurgence in more detail to highlight ongoing tension between disparate worldviews.

The United States

The United States backtracked from its liberal heritage during the dispiriting Great Depression, which called into question the concepts and benefits of free markets. Government had neither the perspective nor the data to realize that circumstances were not the fault of the extended order, but rather resulted from calamitous errors by the federal government in the late 1920s and 1930s. The contraction of the monetary base by the Federal Reserve, the tax increases of both the Hoover and Roosevelt Administrations, and the anti-free trade stance of Congress ensured the failure of banks and the continuation of agonizing levels of unemployment.[737] In any event, as anticipatable by evolutionary theory, society scrambled to find alternative solutions to this unnerving state of affairs. In attempts to show vigor in the face of despair, the Roosevelt Administration deviated from classical liberal principles and undertook a series of actions that ran counter to the enumerated powers given to the federal government by the U.S. Constitution. These turned out to be fruitless; indeed, they probably extended the Depression, and not until the expansionary effect of World War II did unemployment significantly fall.

Even though some additional backward steps were taken under Lyndon Johnson's *Great Society* in the direction of social engineering, World War II was the low point for the democratic, free market philosophy of government. The complete victory of the Allies, followed by post-war prosperity helped Americans in particular regain confidence in their system of government. The psychological resurgence was buttressed by the philosophic work of libertarians—e.g., Friedrich von Hayek's *Road to Serfdom* published in 1944 and the creation of the Mount Pelerin Society in 1947. It took three decades for these views to slowly make their way back to the political and philosophical mainstream. But then, under the Reagan Administration's support of supply-side economic theory, a clear principled alternative to Socialism, to 'third-ways', and to intrusive large government reemerged.

Continental Western Europe

The postwar reemergence of classical liberalism was greatly reinforced by events in Europe. Special credit goes to courageous acts by the Truman Administration: President Truman recognized the aggressive actions of the Soviet Union for what they were, and worked to keep their influence out of Western Germany, halt their advance in Greece, and institute the Marshall Plan to further the growth of trade and rebuild Western Europe.

Moreover, Truman's High Commissioners in Western Germany supported the actions of Ludwig Erhard, the country's first Economics Minister and a strong libertarian. He immediately devalued the mark and created a sound currency, which was followed quickly by actions to eliminate rationing and most elements of the prior command-economy. These decisions led to two decades of

Wirtschaftswunder (Economic Miracle). Ironically, these measures were opposed by the British occupation authorities, who believed that the elimination of rationing and deregulation would lead to economic disaster. Such views were, of course, consistent with the philosophy of Britain's ruling Labor Party, and in Britain, rationing and capital controls persisted well into the 1950s—along with a stagnant economy.

In the first quarter-century after World War II, Western Europe progressed on virtually all fronts to greater prosperity, political and economic stability, and representative government. Despite France's iconoclastic foreign policy, Europe worked shoulder-to-shoulder with the United States in containing Communism, which eventually collapsed under the weight of its economic failure. With the alluring promise of Communism discredited, it seemed that serious opposition to the extended order would fade away.

So it probably will. But, as encouraging as the last half-century has been, troublesome forces continue to resist the extended order, and even undermine the cultural coherence of the West. Underlying fault lines emerged over several decades eroding libertarian principles and enhancing the power of the predatory state. Lacking an Anglo-Saxon value set of common law, individualism, and constitutional checks and balances, continental countries, including, importantly, France and West Germany, regressed in some ways along the 'survival-self expression' axis of values. The political left continually pressed for a larger role of the state in the economy, and the political right, notably in West Germany[738], often failed to offer a principled counter weight. Consequently, the share of the GDP controlled by that state increased steadily, as did inevitably, the unemployment rate. At the same time, values associated with individual responsibility diminished, with centralized planning and growing regulation producing increasingly sclerotic cultures.

Whereas in most of the post-war years Western Europe was rapidly catching up with the standard of living in the United States, now they are slowly falling behind. For example, under the initial policies of the Christian Democrats, West Germany enjoyed an 'economic miracle' with virtually no unemployment. Indeed, Germany had to import large numbers of 'guest workers' to meet the demands of an economy at full throttle. But the arrival of the Social

Democrats, under Willy Brandt, in 1969 marked a turning point. Thereafter, even under subsequent Christian Democrat administrations, government spending and unemployment rose. (Table VIII-1, which is presented later, shows the link between government spending and slower growth of GDP for the OECD nations as a whole during this period of time.) Indeed, much of Western Europe has created few net new jobs in the last three decades.

With slowing economies and continued growth of social services, most of Western Europe reduced defense spending to the point of military irrelevance. This decline of vigor and influence has gone hand in hand with stagnating population levels, a seemingly demoralized populace, diminished confidence in the roots of western culture, and a growth of moral relativism. For example, British authors John Micklethwait and Adrian Wooldridge of The Economist write: "The percentage of Americans who believe that success is determined by forces outside their control has fallen from 41 percent in 1988 to 32 percent today; by contrast, the percentage of Germans who believe it has risen from 59 percent in 1991 to 68 percent today."[739]

The loss of confidence has contributed to the Europeans' search for certainty and security at the expense of flexibility and creativity. This is evident in the path taken in the formation of the European Union, which has moved toward central planning rather than toward a devolved extended order. A piece in The Washington Times analyzed the then proposed new Constitution for the European Union to conclude that it would make the Union government more centralized, more bureaucratic, and less democratic. Rather than delineate governmental powers as does the U.S. Constitution, it is relatively silent on the enumeration of powers. Its different approach aims at a proliferation of goals and good intentions – "sustainable development," "solidarity between generations," and "the social market economy" that would inevitably produce a government with no bounds, shrinking the freedom of the individual. According to the Times: "the EU constitution is also preoccupied with the codification of welfare entitlements—i.e., redistribution claims that individuals and/or groups make against one another. For example, some of the provisions in the European Charter of Fundamental Rights, such as the right to a job, can only be guaranteed through the transfer of vast resources from some citizens to others."[740]

This does not bode well for a reinvigoration of an increasingly stagnant continental culture. Indeed, the analysis concludes that "the EU's technocratic social engineers confused their overly elaborate constitutional designs with the simple yet enlightened principles that anchor the American Constitution and underpin the very success the EU expects to emulate."

In short, recent Western European political development appears to reflect a pattern as old as history itself: attempted protection of vested interests discourages innovation and competition in the name of greater security. The agents acting for this predatory state may be different from those in ancient autocracies, but like them they do not serve the wider interests of the populace. They produce economic sclerosis and ultimately a demoralization that calls the foundations of their societies into question.

CONFLICT ARENAS

Moving our spotlight to more concrete issues, we can see how the ongoing conflict of visions is playing out in contemporary America. Some of the more illuminating of these debates involve economic policy, the judicial system, respect for truth, and assistance to developing countries.

Economic Policy

The clash of visions, or values, is probably nowhere as stark as in the arena of economic policy, which ultimately governs the production and distribution of material goods within a society as well as disparities in the distribution of wealth. The constrained view has already been broadly outlined: when creative human action is married to an efficient deployment of capital, modern science, and limited government intrusion, the most rapid growth of the economy occurs. The wealth is distributed by the workings of supply and demand for labor, and by returns to those entrepreneurs and investors who assessed circumstances most correctly. All tiers of personal income grow as productivity increases, although investors benefit relatively more. In this view, government's role is to provide security and rule of law, but disparate human talent takes it from there. Equality of opportunity is the touchstone, not equality of outcomes, and fairness attaches to equitable application of the rules established by society and not to a particular outcome of those rules.

The unconstrained view rejects a system that produces 'unfair' disparities of economic outcomes, that relies on unsentimental contractual arrangements, and that acquiesces to a Darwinian survival of the fittest among economic entities. At their core, unconstrained arguments appeal primarily to man's ancient and universal instincts of fairness and compassion, with an added assumption that government, employing modern science and management techniques, should be capable of reducing material inequality within society, minimizing economic insecurity, and sustaining the growth of the economy.

The tension between the two sets of views goes beyond competing values. Much of the emotional energy of the unconstrained views seems to be derived from an atavistic hostility to those possessing wealth, but not actually seen to be producing it, such as investors, merchants, and traders. David Brooks[741] describes the persistence of such values over the centuries, particularly as expressed by artists and intellectuals, those most disconnected from the workings of the market economy. For example in 19th century France, Stendhal said traders and merchants made him want to "weep and vomit at the same time," and Flaubert thought they were "plodding and avaricious." Hatred of the bourgeoisie, he wrote, "is the beginning of all virtue."

Such attitudes were common to all countries which were developing economically and leaving the old order behind. With regard to capitalism generally, Karl Marx claimed that commercial materialism takes all that is holy and makes it profane. This attitude is well represented among today's American intellectuals as well, even if the United States is the exemplar of a modern, creative, and affluent society. Brooks writes:

> If I pulled from my shelves all the books about the moral backwardness of the enterprising middle classes, I could stack them to the ceiling. I could start with the works of the

Transcendentalists, then move through Dreiser, Mencken, Sherwood Anderson, and Sinclair Lewis. Then we could bemoan the moral, cultural, and intellectual vapidity of suburbanites, students, middle managers, and middle Americans: Babbitt, The Man in the Gray Flannel Suit, The Souls of Black Folk, The Lonely Crowd, The Organization Man, The Catcher in the Rye, The Cultural Contradictions of Capitalism, The Affluent Society, Death of a Salesman, Soul on Ice, The Culture of Narcissism, Habits of the Heart, The Closing of the American Mind, Earth in the Balance, Slouching Towards Gomorrah, Jihad vs. McWorld, just about every word ever written by Kevin Phillips, and Michael Moore, and just about every novel of the last quarter century, from Rabbit is Rich through The Corrections. It's a Mississippi flood of pessimism.

Thus we see von Hayek's observation that evolution produces "practices, many of which men tended to dislike, whose significance they usually fail to understand, whose validity they cannot prove, and which have nonetheless fairly rapidly spread by means of an evolutionary selection."[742] Clearly, much of the artistic intelligentsia is disconnected from the underlying workings of the modern economy, and this can promote unintended, dysfunctional results. To illustrate this concern, we examine specifics of the ongoing debate in the areas of taxation, property rights, and forms of regulation such as price control, as they play out in the present day United States.

Taxation

Of the areas of contention between the constrained and unconstrained camps, tax policy is front and center, because it seems to present the greatest opportunity for those of the unconstrained views to engage in 'social engineering' that attempts to redistribute wealth and thereby achieve greater fairness of economic outcome. Those of constrained views on the other hand argue that government should be kept small so as to leave financial decisions mostly in the hands of the people, and that tax rates should be constructed to have the least deleterious effect on economic growth. In this contest, it seemed for a while that the unconstrained camp had won the argument when marginal tax rates on the wealthy in both the United States and Great Britain reached heights of 90 percent.

In time, however, economists argued with increasing persuasiveness that such rates hampered the economic growth potential of society, eventually harming all segments of society. In line with that view, a significant reduction in rates took place in 1962, when President Kennedy justified the cut on the basis that "a rising tide lifts all boats." And as predicted by supply-side theory, in response the economy began to grow smartly. Unfortunately, rates were then raised again during the Viet Nam war era, leading to the stagflation of the late-1970s. It was not until the "Supply-side Revolution" of the 1980s that tax policy was firmly linked to first economic principles compatible with rapid economic growth; principles previously formulated by the Nobel Prize-winning economist Robert Mundell. According to *The Wall Street Journal:*

> [O]ver this 25-year period [since President Reagan's policies inaugurated the supply-side policies] prosperity has been the rule, not the exception, for America—in stark contrast to the stagflationary 1970s. Perhaps the greatest tribute to Reagonomics is that, over the course of the past 276 months, the U.S. economy has been in recession for only 15. That is to say, 94 % of the time the U.S. economy has been creating jobs (43 million in all) and wealth ($30 trillion). More wealth has been created in the last quarter-century than in the previous 200 years. The policy lessons of this supply-side prosperity need to be constantly relearned, lest we return to the errors that produced the 1970s.[743]

Given the key importance of this issue, let's examine its workings at both the macro-economic and the micro-economic levels. At the macro-economic level, the issue of appropriate marginal tax rates goes to the question of how government should meet its revenue needs and provide support for the less well-off without subverting the wealth-generating capacity of the economy. While the optimum level of taxation may vary according circumstances, some economists believe that level is on the order of 20 percent of the

GDP.[744] This is to say, if rates are either higher or lower, they will produce lower amounts of revenue. When higher, tax rates slow the growth of the economy, perversely producing less revenue over the longer-term. The deleterious effect is seen in Table VIII-1, which shows how economic growth for all the OECD countries slowed dramatically over a two-decade period as average levels of taxation increased.[745]

Figure VIII-1[746] shows data over a longer 36-year period that tie national economic growth to the share of the GDP taken in taxes by the government.

Table VIII-1
Decline of OECD Economic Growth Rates: 1965-1984

Period	Government Outlays - % of GDP	GDP Annual Growth Rate
1965 - 1969	32.6	5 %
1970 - 1974	33.4	3.6 %
1975 - 1979	37.4	3.3 %
1980 -1984	41.2	1.8 %

SOURCE: Warren Brookes, "How Government Spending Affects Growth," *The Washington Times*, op-ed, June 22, 1987

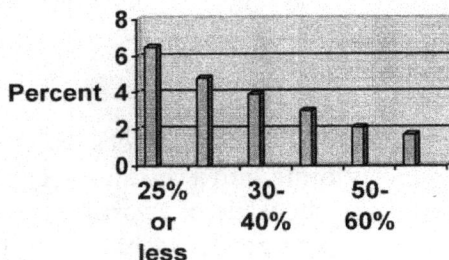

Figure VIII-1: Real GDP Growth for OECD 1960-1996

SOURCE: James Gwartney, *The Wall Street Journal*, 4/10/98

The data clearly demonstrate that high levels of taxation are a prescription for slow growth. Along with slow growth comes higher unemployment, as shown in a study performed by Bernhard Heitger, which concluded that the total tax rate was a "significant and important determinant of the total, short-term, and long-term unemployment rate."[747] So it is no surprise that, given high tax rates of Western European countries, they have experienced levels of unemployment close to twice that of the United States. They have created few net additional jobs in decades and they have large numbers on the dole.

One reason that tax rates have this impact is seen in their microeconomic effect on small businesses, which create most of the new jobs in the economy. *The Wall Street Journal* analyzed this phenomenon in the year 1988,[748] noting that there were 24 million business entities whose legal status made their profits subject to the personal income tax rate of their owners, and thus acutely sensitive to marginal tax rates.

The Journal drew on work by economists Douglas Holtz-Eakin at Syracuse University and Harvey Rosen at Princeton, who analyzed tens of thousands of income tax returns filed by sole proprietors in 1985 and 1988 to capture the effect on them of the changes of the 1986 tax laws. They specifically examined the impact of marginal tax rates on growth decisions: on whether to invest in capital assets and, if so, how much; and on whether to hire workers.

What they found was: "High marginal rates aggravated liquidity problems that entrepreneurs already had in accessing capital markets and thus dampened their capital investment, which, in turn, resulted in less output and less sales and lower payrolls. Specifically, the analysis demonstrated that the reduction in marginal tax rates had a significant impact on firm growth—the greater the percentage tax reduction, the greater the increase in business's size. Ditto for capital investment and payroll, both in the number of workers hired and salaries paid." These economists then did a back-of-the-envelope estimate of the impact of reducing the top tax bracket to 33 percent. They found that "for the 800,000 small-business people now hammered by top rates of 39.6% and 36%, the cut would increase their capital expansion by 12.5% and increase the size of their capital outlays by 11.9%. It would also give them the juice to increase their payrolls by 4%—both in the form of higher wages and more workers." Given that entrepreneurship is risky— e.g., more than one-half of all new businesses fail within 3 years, a small reduction in taxes could have a relatively large effect on the prosperity of these businesses.

With this background, some of the counterintuitive aspects of the changes in income tax revenues resulting from lower tax rates become more evident –viz., despite marginal tax rate *cuts* in the 1920s, the 1960s, and the 1980s, in every instance tax revenues *grew* briskly. Just as interesting is the fact that the top 10 percent of the population ended up paying substantially *more* both in absolute dollars and as a share of all taxes paid. If one examines IRS data for income taxes paid between 1980 and 1988, one sees that the top 10 percent of filers paid 33.7 percent more in taxes (real dollars) over that period—i.e., from $149 billion to $199.2 billion. As a consequence, their share of all income taxes paid surged from 49.3 percent to 57.2 percent.

Clearly then, high levels of taxation slow economic growth and lead to relatively high levels of unemployment. But even worse, taxation does not produce the results its advocates promise. An analysis of the share of GDP taken by the government in major western nations at three moments in time, 1870, 1960, and 1994, found that spending as a share of GDP increased an average of 19.6 percentage points between 1870 and 1960 and 19.3 percentage points from 1960 to 1994. The findings of that analysis were: "We conclude that social indicators improved the most between 1870 and 1960 when the welfare state was still in its infancy. The expansion of public expenditure and of the welfare state during the last three decades had yielded limited gains in terms of social objectives while possibly damaging the countries' economic performance. Today, countries with small governments and the newly industrialized countries show similar levels of social indicators, but these are achieved with lower expenditure, lower taxes and higher growth than countries with big government."[749]

Despite this experience, the unconstrained camp argues for higher taxes generally, and progressively higher taxes on the rich on the grounds of 'fairness', meaning to narrow the income gap between the rich and the poor. This position is incongruous, however, given that upper-income levels already pay a disproportionately high share of income taxes. For example, in the United States, the top one percent of the population pays about 36 percent of all income taxes—i.e., thirty-six times their share of the population. The bottom *one-half* pays a mere 4 percent of all income taxes.

Moreover, if the concern is the income gap, it is necessary to consider the ranks of the rich and poor over the span of lifetimes, inasmuch as the number of long-term poor in a dynamic economy is quite modest. Indeed, studies show that the ranks of the rich and the poor change continuously over time evidencing much more income mobility than is commonly perceived. One survey performed by Treasury's Office of Tax Analysis[750], for example, reviewed representative tax payers over a 10-year period (1979-1988) to track their progress through income quintiles: "In no quintile was the turnover less than 33% during the decade. In the bottom three, at least 66% of the occupants changed quintiles, generally trading up. ... What about those who started the decade in the bottom quintile? Sixty-five percent moved up at least two quintiles during the decade. Similarly, a large fraction of the most affluent in the highest quintile will move down within a comparable space in time. Thus, when we are students, or just out of school, we'll probably be in the lowest quintile. In our peak earning years, we will be in one of the two top quintiles, and in retirement, we will likely fall again.

We should also consider the accumulation of wealth in a lifetime. While retirees may have incomes that place them in lower quintiles, many of them will own their homes with all they contain and will no longer have the expenses of raising children. So, their standards of living will be higher than suggested by the income statistics. This picture suggests that the number of individuals that remain poor over a long period is a small fraction of the population. And, surely it is better to be relatively poor in an increasingly wealthy country—indeed, comparative studies show that the poor in the United States usually own their own homes and have standards of living comparable to the lower middle-class of several decades ago.

In all, experience in this particular debate shows that sentiment, uninformed by the economic laws of the extended order, is self-defeating. The impulse to tax the rich beyond a certain point hinders economic growth and produces unnecessarily high unemployment. Ironically, policies grounded in the extended order produce a robust economy and achieve a highly progressive outcome in which the most affluent pay the lion's share of the costs of central government, sparing the least affluent.

Property Rights

Unconstrained views attempt redistributing wealth by encroaching on property rights as well as through the tax system, and, in so doing, attack a central element of the extended order, namely security for the fruits of one's labor.

To provide an example of the hostility to private property by holders of the unconstrained view, Sowell cites Edward Bellamy, author of *Looking Backwards*, who argued that modern prosperity is the result of the efforts of past generations and concluded that the poor of today are or should be the co-inheritors of the prosperity of past generations—in the name of justice.[751] But this conclusion, seemingly ignorant of the workings of the market, simply draws a veil over the mechanism of past wealth generation and is cavalier about the prospects for further wealth accumulation.

To be sure, populations of affluent countries are the beneficiaries of past efforts and past capital accumulation—to the extent that current productivity is inextricably linked to availability of capital. But importantly, even if an individual owns little of that wealth, he enjoys the higher standard of living of the entire country possessing that wealth. For example, one could argue that the proposal to provide reparations to African-Americans for past slavery is misplaced because African-Americans of the current day already enjoy the higher standard of living of the United States, having incomes many times that of the descendants of those Africans who remained behind in Africa, and thus implicitly benefit from invested capital without necessarily owning it.

Nonetheless, arguments undermining property rights persist, if in somewhat more sophisticated versions. Sowell refers, for example, to John Rawls' *Theory of Justice* and the legal writings of Ronald Dworkin and Laurence Tribe. Dworkin dismisses the "silly proposition that true liberals must respect economic as well as intellectual liberty."[752] Similarly, Laurence Tribe argues that laws safeguarding property rights immunize extant distributions of wealth and economic power from a majoritarian rearrangement.[753] Indeed they do, as intended by our Founding Fathers and based on extended order tradition and experience.

Awareness of such temptations caused the British and the Americans to initially limit the voting franchise to those possessing property. They and modern day Libertarians recognize that if one tries to undo economic outcomes achieved by free markets and rule of law, virtually all economic distributions become a matter of politics. Milton Friedman stated: "A society that puts equality—in the sense of equality of outcome—ahead of freedom will end up with neither equality nor freedom. The use of force to achieve equality will destroy freedom, and the force, introduced for good purposes, will end up in the hands of people who use it to promote their own interests."[754]

The authoritarianism and failed economies of the old Soviet Union and today's Cuba are cases in point. In more of a microcosm, Tom Bethell illustrates how the initial Jamestown and Massachusetts Bay settlements almost perished when they were first established along communal lines. Not until the settlers were given their own land to cultivate did the settlements prosper. Similarly, virtually all the idealistic establishments of communes, such as by Robert Owens, failed.[755]

In the United States property rights remain secure in law and in the values of its people, although political forces continue to impinge upon them. In the most recent impingement to the time of this writing, the U. S. Supreme Court decided the *Kelo v. City of New London, Conn.* Case against property holders to the dismay of much of the country. In effect, the court agreed (only 5-4) that political entities could use the power of eminent domain to take property from owners in favor of others wanting to use it for a purpose that might generate more tax income for the government. As dissenting Justice Sandra Day O'Connor noted, under that criterion, no property is safe from the government. The American societal animal responded vigorously against this assault on private property, and at the time of this writing, many states had begun constitutional processes to prohibit such takings.

Price Control

Throughout human history, or at least since the invention of money, governments have been tempted to control prices for the seeming benefit of the largest part of the population, and the impulse for controls fits comfortably within the unconstrained worldview. Such impulses usually arise as a result of general inflation or from scarcity, such as from crop failures, which disproportionately affect the poor. The appropriate response to such circumstances, of course, is to increase production and/or curtail consumption. But this requires not controls but rather allowing free market price signals to provide necessary guidance to achieve these ends.

The economic rationale for that conclusion was articulated by David Boaz and summarized in Chapter 1 – namely: "The price system pulls together all the information available in the economy about what each person wants, how much he values it, and how it can be best produced." The rationale applies to any good desired by consumers, whether it is housing, oil, or food.[756]

Yet, in uninformed debate, arguments are made for price controls to prevent the 'hoarder' or the 'speculator' from realizing 'windfall' gain and to protect the poor. But price control and arbitrary action against commodity dealers are wrongheaded, however emotionally satisfying, because they discourage new production as well as imports, and thus end up prolonging the crisis. This is not to argue callously that in many instances, especially involving famine, public measures are not required to assist the poor. Rather measures then must not interfere with the efficient workings of the market.

While governmental regulation interfering with the forces of supply and demand in the free market is a fading impulse, it remains in the wings and is a useful example of how residual resistance to the extended order is often uninformed by economic insight. Let's examine two such residual impulses: rent control and anti-petroleum company sentiment when prices spike.

Rent Control

Political control of rents charged by the private sector is a classic case of interference with free markets by those arguing that sentiment for the less well-off trumps private property rights. Indirectly, such control represents a transfer of wealth to the tenant from the landlord, because the landlord is legally forced to receive less than the market clearing price for his property and thus a reduced rate of return on his investment. The tenant, who has made no investment and bears no risk, is the beneficiary, and the owner has fewer funds and less incentive to maintain and upgrade his property.

The impetus for rent control usually arises from a desire to protect the poor and those on fixed incomes during periods of high inflation. But rather than providing assistance to the truly needy, the political establishment imposes controls on a broad class of property because of the expedient calculation that a large group of the electorate will benefit at seemingly no cost to the taxpayer. But here again indirect costs are ignored to the detriment of larger society. Property owners let their properties run down, and they pay lower real estate taxes because their property is worth relatively less. In the worst cases, they simply abandon their properties. In any event, the "costs" are eventually shifted to the broader society: it has to in some way make up for the lost tax revenues, it has to live with a poorer housing stock; and the poor end up with fewer housing options.[757]

Not only must the larger population live with a more limited and sometimes deteriorating housing stock, but other provisions must be made for the poor. In New York, for example, that amounts to building publicly assisted units. The cost of these units, along with the loss of tax revenues from controlled units, is an ongoing drain on the fiscal health of the municipality.

Moreover, experience has shown that rent controls benefit many more tenants than are truly needy. When the communities in Massachusetts were forced to relinquish rent control by statewide legislation, there were dire predictions of "increased homelessness, rampant evictions, and mass dislocations of elderly and low income tenants." Cambridge Hospital issued a memorandum warning of massive elderly deaths as landlords raised rents and forced the elderly to move. In response, the legislature modified the decontrol legislation to provide for some assistance to low-income tenants.

Leonore Schloming, President of the Cambridge Small Property Owners Association reported the outcome[758]. Only 6 percent of the tenants qualified for protected status. Rampant evictions and mass dislocations failed to materialize. Less than one percent of the original rent-controlled households sought subsidies from city agencies. There were no reports of increase in homelessness. Not a single decontrol-related elderly death was documented. And she reports "One man, prominently featured as an elder who risked 'being thrown out on the street' without rent control, promptly went out and bought a condo after rent control's demise."

But the sun may be setting on the use of rent control. Whereas as much as 20 percent of the U.S. population was subject to rent control in the mid-1980s, a reaction set in among southern, western, and rural states. As a result, today some 30 states have laws and constitutional amendments forbidding rent control, and it is an increasingly fading phenomenon.

Petroleum
The most recent experience in the United States with wider price controls is already decades old, and not seemingly a problem. Yet impulses to control the price of energy are not that far from view.

In the early 1970s, general price controls were imposed briefly in a futile attempt to rein in inflation; futile because inflation is not a result of 'greedy producers' but is a monetary phenomenon caused by too rapid money creation by the Federal Reserve. Even though the government speedily abandoned most price controls, it continued them on petroleum for almost 10 years, resulting in distorted domestic markets, shortages, long lines at gas stations, and a falloff in new investment by petroleum companies. Once these controls were lifted, petroleum markets returned to equilibrium, shortages vanished, and prices fell.

Such lessons, however, rarely quell dysfunctional economic impulses forever. Moreover, new instances of price spikes are inevitable because petroleum is a commodity, which is subject to price swings caused by variations in supply and demand. So when oil prices spiked in 2005, because of sharply increased demand by growing economies in Asia and by supply interruptions due to hurricanes and political unrest elsewhere, some politicians forgot the earlier lessons. Despite the higher prices being a world-wide phenomenon, U.S. Senators held hearings, implying it was somehow the greed of American oil companies at fault, and suggested that imposing 'wind-fall' profit taxes was an appropriate response. Such taxes, of course, would have the same impact that they had in the 1970s—they would have reduced investment in developing new sources of energy and would have exacerbated the problem. Fortunately, this political impulse passed without any damage being done. Yet it is clear that political expediency and economic illiteracy have the potential to threaten anew.

The Courts

As we examined the evolution of the extended order, we saw how it unfolded pragmatically by an accretion of improved practices and more efficacious values, namely through tradition rather than by design. In Britain and its colonial offspring, the growing tradition was matched, step by step, with evolving common law. And, as we saw, this approach to law was in contrast to other cultures, such as on the continent of Europe, which attempted to codify law from the top down. The two approaches reflect different visions of human governance and, necessarily, different consequences: the first most compatible with classical liberal views and the other with centralized government. The tension between these judicial approaches is mirrored in the conflict between constrained and unconstrained views of the world. Let's examine conflicting philosophies of the judicial role, as well as how they play out in some illustrative contests.

Sowell finds that the constrained view is aligned with common law, which, relying on precedent, provides relatively clear requirements and enhances predictability of outcome. The unconstrained view, on the other hand, relies as well on consideration of what judges perceive as 'right', without necessarily drawing on legislative underpinning, thereby adding uncertainty and inevitable costs into the process.

Sowell cites the views of Oliver Wendell Holmes to articulate the constrained view: "The life of the law has not been logic: it has been experience. ... Many honorable and sensible judgments [express] an intuition of experience which outruns analysis and sums up many unnamed and tangled impressions; impressions which may lie beneath consciousness without losing their worth." In this view, law incorporates the experience that reflects "not only our lives but the lives of all men that have been."[759]

Then Sowell draws on Edmund Burke for an earlier expression of this view: "In a world where the individual is to be guided by the collective wisdom of his culture, in accordance with the constrained vision, culture must itself have some stability in order to serve as a guide. Without this stability, "no man could know what would be the test of honour in a nation continually varying the standard of its coin.".... To Burke, "the evils on inconstancy" were "ten thousand times worse than those of obstinacy and the blindest prejudice." In short, process costs arising from unreliable social expectations outweighed the value of incremental individual knowledge [on the part of the judge]..."[760]

Turning again to Holmes, Sowell notes that he opposed "confounding morality with law." Law existed, he said, to preserve society. Criminal justice, for example, was primarily concerned with deterring crime, not with finely adjusting punishments to the individual.[761] Sowell also cites Blackstone, the great expositor of English common law: "Blackstone's vision of man was that "his reason is corrupt, and his understanding full of ignorance and error." To Blackstone, "the frailty, the imperfection and the blindness of human reason" made it an unreliable instrument for the direct creation of law. Reason was necessary but not sufficient ... In short, like Holmes and like the constrained vision in general, Blackstone found evolved systemic rationality superior to explicitly excogitated individual rationality."[762]

The unconstrained view is philosophically different. It relies not only on tradition and precedent but also on judicial consideration of what is "right." For example, Sowell quotes Chief Justice Earl Warren's interruption of lawyers' presentation of complex legal principles to ask: "But is it right? Is it good?" He notes that, in the constrained vision, this was neither his business nor within his competence.[763] Modern writers of the unconstrained view, such as Ronald Dworkin, take this view further. Dworkin argues that courts must supply "fresh moral insight" when judging "the acts of Congress, the states, and the President."[764] Dworkin called for "a fusion of constitutional law and moral theory."[765]

The central difficulty of this view is that to the extent that it runs counter to the common law tradition it raises the question of whose morality counts. Thus, absent agreed-upon, absolute standards, applying morality in court decisions inevitably results in having political choices being made in the judicial rather than the legislative arena.

One obvious manifestation of the conflict appears in Senate hearings leading to the confirmation of federal and Supreme Court justices. In the past, the Senate often held no hearings and when they did, selection criteria focused on the nominees' competence, experience, and integrity in interpreting the law. Today, Senators apply 'litmus tests' regarding matters such as abortion, affirmative action, and views on the 'root causes of crime' in the selection of justices, reflecting the political stands of their respective parties.

Two examples serve to illuminate attempts made by the unconstrained camp to short circuit the legislative process via the judiciary to accomplish good intentions: abortion and affirmative action.

Abortion
Abortion has become the most contentious issue in the confirmation of judges to the U.S. Supreme Court, stemming, of course, from the Court's decision of some decades ago legalizing abortion, *Roe vs. Wade*. The conflict of values in the abortion debate is basic and irreconcilable. The instinct to preserve human life and particularly the life of newborns is as ancient as it is central to the value systems of virtually all societal animals. Newer competing values, associated with the empowerment of the individual, however, consider that the decision principally belongs to the mother since she bears all the material consequences, especially if it is known that the child will suffer severe mental or physical impairment.

Given the irreconcilability of these positions, society must decide which set of values trumps the other—i.e., a political decision. As society's values evolve in this matter, the legislature's reflection of those values necessarily will evolve as well. Indeed, at the time of the *Roe vs. Wade* decision, about 5 states had already made abortion legal. Nonetheless, the U.S. Supreme Court's ruling, imposing the judges' values, preempted the remaining legislatures on this issue, thereby accelerating the politization of the judicial branch of government.

Affirmative Action

The issues surrounding the concept of affirmative action have been almost equally contentious in our legal system. The constitutional position on the question of racial relations vis-à-vis the government would seem to be clear. The XIVth Amendment states: "No State shall make or enforce any law which shall abridge the privileges or immunities of citizens of the United States; ...nor deny to any person within its jurisdiction the equal protection of the laws." The XVth Amendment, with regard to voting, states that no rights may be abridged on account of race.

By the 1960s, however, impatient segments of society looked beyond the bulwarks of the Constitution to accelerate the integration of minorities into the mainstream of society, especially in the areas of education and employment. New measures, called affirmative action, provided for outreach programs in education and recruiting, and provided governmental funding to ameliorate past conditions suffered by Blacks. At first, adhering to the Constitution, such efforts specifically excluded the use of quotas or preferential treatment.

Nonetheless, special interest groups pushed for preferential treatment in a number of areas—governmental hiring, government procurement programs, private hiring decisions, and the selection of students by institutions of higher education. Inevitably, these actions resulted in displacing whites and Asians from competitive slots, and displaced groups, perceiving reverse discrimination; quickly this issue moved into the political arena and into the courts.

The disputes go to the heart of the nation's values on making judgments on the basis of merit rather than race, ethnic origin, or religion. Given the absence of a justification for preferential treatment in tradition, in common law, or in specific legislative foundation, political forces desiring preferential treatment of Blacks focused on judicial activism as the means for advancing their cause. Helping the poor and disadvantaged seemed to have priority over the values of a system built on incremental—slow but sure—rule of law. Thereby, another emotionally volatile issue added to the politization of the judiciary.

Respect for Truth

As seen in the World Values Survey, prevailing value systems of affluent countries, firmly grounded in the extended order, place importance on truth-telling and on intolerance of corruption. These values evolved because they were critical for enabling a growing circle of trust within society, which in turn facilitated the efficient functioning of an entrepreneurial and decentralized free market system. Common Law evolved in tandem by establishing strong penalties for perjury. To be sure, all societies and all segments of society have individuals that lie and defraud; it may be an unavoidable aspect of human nature. The important cultural point is how widespread negative behavior is and how well a society's mores and legal system constrain such behavior.

As self-evident as the importance of truth may now seem, it is intellectually eroded by those opposed to the outcomes of the extended order. In their eyes, the priority of achieving fairer outcomes overrides the importance for truth. So, as Sowell points out, a value contest arises wherein those of the unconstrained view hold tightly to 'sincerity', whereas those of the constrained place 'fidelity' highest on their list of virtues. For example, Sowell notes that "Godwin's whole purpose was to strengthen the individual's "sincerity, fortitude, and justice." Sincerity brings every other virtue in its train according to Godwin.[766] On the other side, those of the constrained vision rank fidelity to one's word and to one's role in life as paramount—the essence of truth and character.

Since the reality of the extended order appears at odds with their sincere good intentions, the holders of the unconstrained view end up attacking key pillars of the extended order, including truth itself. They do so not so much by denigrating the virtue of truth, but by arguing that absolute truth is not possible for the human mind to achieve, and thus arguing that other considerations should govern. For example, in philosophy the 'Deconstructionists' dispute the possibility of objective truth. We can see how these concepts have crept into popular culture. A Nobel Prize for literature was awarded to Rigoberta Menchu for her autobiographical accounts of misery in Guatemala, which turned out to consist largely of lies. But her supporters claim that the prize is deserved because "it could have been true." Similarly, the notorious CBS television report on President Bush's National Guard duty used forged documents to make its case, and when confronted on the duplicity, CBS replied that the documents were "fake but accurate."

In effect, the unconstrained camp believes that by weaning society from an undue reverence for evolving tradition, including literal interpretation of law, institutions of private property, and truth, a more just society can be created. Unfortunately, the central problem for the unconstrained view is how to establish goals to which sincerity is attached. Since absolute goals have eluded the human mind, ungrounded sincerity ends up chiefly magnifying political battles among competing rent-seeking groups.

The constrained camp expects most arguments to get settled by experiential results rather than through ideological considerations, and that approach entails a high regard for a command of facts and an analytic capability. Adherents of the unconstrained view, armed in moral certainty and unsatisfied with the outcome of the extended order, end up arguing against the importance of facts and of truth-telling.

Foreign Aid

The conflict of values plays out also in deciding how wealthy countries provide assistance to the less developed countries. The conflict does not lie in the goal of humanitarian assistance; no one quarrels with the obligation to provide help in the face of famine, disease epidemics, and natural disaster. The conflict arises in the form of the fairness issue writ large. How, it is asked, can the rich allow themselves to live comfortably when there are so many desperately poor in the world? The obvious follow-on question is usually not asked—i.e., can economic aid be given that is effective and is not merely a salve to uneasy consciences?

In any event, the affluent West has provided huge sums of assistance to poor countries, individually and through institutions, such as the World Bank, the International Monetary Fund, the United Nations, and the U.S. Agency for International Development. The economic assistance is not billed as alms, but as assistance for economic development. As a practical matter, the results have not matched the intentions.

To understand why the benevolent approach to third world development has not produced the expected results, let's review the failed attempts to develop a rationale for large-scale aid, identify problems in the concept of public aid, and examine specific instances where such aid has gone wrong.

Failed Rationales for Large-scale Aid

The hard reality is that affluence cannot be given to one country by another—it must be generated from within. For example, based on the work of the McKinsey Global Institute in many less developed countries, William W. Lewis concludes: ["Many] feel that if rich countries sent capital pouring into poor countries, the poor countries would grow richer. The solution does not start with more capital. The solution, rather, is in the country's productivity or the way it organizes and deploys both its labor and its capital. If poor countries improved productivity and balanced their budgets, they would have plenty of capital for growth from domestic savers and foreign investors..."[767]

Such a worldview, however, is not readily accepted by international assistance organizations. Given instances of grinding poverty, there is a strong urge to "do something," even if it is unclear what needs to be done. These institutions begin with a very human charitable impulse, and only then seek ways of carrying it out effectively. William Easterly describes in detail a sequence of failed rationales employed by assistance organizations.[768] The first: the concept of capital infusion.

In the post-World War II years, development experts utilized a Harrod-Domar model, which was popular because of its simplicity and because it led to the conclusion that almost any external infusion of capital would be beneficial. Basically, the model suggested that production capacity would be proportional to the stock of machinery, and to achieve a target growth rate one needed only to achieve a corresponding investment rate. Since undeveloped countries rarely seemed to be able to generate the capital for investment themselves, aid agencies were needed to fill the *financing gap*. One of many ironies in this story was that Evsey Domar admitted some years later that his work dealt with depressionary times in developed nations and thus was inapplicable to the purposes for which it had come to be used.

Part of the appeal of this model also arose from the experiences of the Great Depression and that of the Soviet Union. For example, Sir Arthur Lewis suggested that some of the unemployment of the Depression came from surplus labor, which could be 'soaked up' by building factories. Soviet economists had used similar growth-proportional-to-investment ideas. Since outsiders had at the time a positive view of the rapid industrialization of the Soviet Union, the theory seemed to have some validity.[769]

Such assistance was supposed to be temporary, with ensuing growth providing additional savings to sustain future growth. However, some prescient economists warned at the time about the burden of debt service if the capital were not wisely invested.

By the 1980s the financing gap model was clearly not working. Easterly cites the example of Guyana: total GDP in Guyana fell sharply from 1980 to 1990, as investment was increasing from 30 percent to 42 percent of GDP, and while foreign aid every year was 8 percent of GDP. Even though the model was no longer overtly cited, the underlying approach lingered. For example, a World Bank Report in 1993 argued that despite this dismal record "Guyana will continue to need substantial levels of foreign capital inflows ... to provide sufficient resources to sustain economic growth."[770]

Guyana was a spectacular failure, but what about other recipients of development aid? Easterly states that there were 88 countries that received substantial aid over a three-decade period. He noted that of these only 17 showed a positive correlation between aid and investment, and only 6 showed an increase commensurate with the amount of aid. Considering that two of the countries, Hong Kong and China, received trivial amounts, only 4 out of 88 demonstrated the investment growth predicted by the model.[771] Moreover, his analysis showed that: "The multiple factors that affect growth cause the relationship between growth and investment to be loose and unstable. Growth fluctuates around an average for each country, while investment rates drift all over the place."[772]

Easterly concludes: "Rather than worrying about how much investment is "needed" to sustain a given growth rate, we should concentrate on strengthening incentives to invest in the future and let the various forms of investment play out how they may."[773] "Moreover, giving aid on the basis of the financing gap creates perverse incentives for the recipient, as was recognized long ago. The financing gap is larger, and aid larger, [thereby lowering] ... the saving of the recipient. This creates incentives against the recipient marshaling its own resources for development."[774] This analysis highlights the inadequacy of a centralized approach, which invariably comes to rely on the use of immediately understandable, and seemingly plausible gross measures.

To be sure, most economists agree that increasing productivity requires the use of capital and technology to amplify human effort. Yet, to focus solely on the growth of capital as the central point, regardless of the incentives in the market system to deploy that capital, is asking for waste and frustration. Easterly refers to two cases. "Both Nigeria and Hong Kong increased their physical capital stock per worker by over 250 percent over the 1960 to 1985 time frame. The results of this massive investment were different: Nigeria's output per worker rose by 12 percent from 1960 to 1985, while Hong Kong's rose by 328 percent. And consider another even more capital-intensive pair: the Gambia and Japan both increased their capital stocks per worker by over 500 percent between 1960 and 1985. The result in the Gambia was that output per worker rose 2 percent from 1960 to 1985, while in Japan in rose 260 percent."[775]

Easterly further provides examples to show how investment was unproductive:

1. *Tanzania:* "The World Bank helped finance the Morogoro Shoe Factory in Tanzania in the 1970s. The shoe factory had labor, machines, and the latest in shoe-making technology. It had everything except—shoes. It never produced more than 4 percent of its installed capacity. The factory, which had planned to supply the entire Tanzanian shoe market and then export three-quarters of the planned production of 4 million shoes to Europe, never exported a single shoe. The plant was not well designed for Tanzania's climate; it had aluminum walls and no ventilation system. Production finally ceased in 1990."[776]

2. *Kenya:* The World Bank and the IMF gave Kenya 19 adjustment loans between 1979 and 1996 on the condition that they solve

the problems of poorly performing state enterprises, of which the Railways had been identified as financially troubled as early as 1972. Periodic World Bank Reports in 1983, 1989, and 1995, presumably preparatory to more lending, continued to identify the unresolved problems of the Railways. Easterly notes wryly, "At last report, at the dawn of the new millennium, Kenya Railways was still losing money and unreformed. Apparently reforming this embodiment of government patronage and inefficiency will continue to be delayed."[777] Easterly concludes: "A government that was irresponsible before the adjustment loan has unchanged incentives to be irresponsible after the adjustment loan. Only a change from a bad government to a good government will truly change policies. An unchanged irresponsible government will create the illusion of adjustment without doing the real thing. Even when donors enforce the reductions in the budget deficit, for example, the irresponsible government has every incentive to do creative fiscal accounting to avoid real adjustment."[778]

This unproductive borrowing resulted in recipients being unable to repay loans, financial crisis, and in time de facto bankruptcy. When countries as large as Mexico were unable to service their commercial loans, the extent of the debt crisis for most low income countries became starkly evident, causing the international lending agencies to scramble for a new justification for financing assistance. Easterly states: "To avert a growth collapse, we thought we had a good solution: aid and lending to developing countries conditional on their making policy reforms. Instead of aid financing investment, it was now aid financing reform."[779] So while lending previously had been conditioned on projects meeting certain rules, these adjustment loans were conditioned on the nations themselves establishing growth policies.

Easterly presents examples of the fundamental lack of seriousness by the lending agencies regarding these 'conditions'. For example, Zambia received 12 adjustment loans from the World Bank and the IMF between 1980 and 1994, such that lending and aid reached one-quarter of the Zambian GDP. One purpose of the aid was to reduce inflation. Yet Zambia had an inflation rate above 40 percent every year except two from 1985 to 1996.[780] In the 1980s the World Bank and the IMF gave an average of six adjustment loans to each country in Africa, an average of four adjustment loans to each country in Latin America, an average of four adjustment loans to each country in Asia, and an average of three adjustment loans to each country in Eastern Europe, North Africa, and the Middle East.[781]

Easterly reports that: "there was much lending, little adjustment, and little growth in the 1980s and the 1990s. A later study showed that World Bank predictions overestimated long-run growth in adjustment lending recipients by 3.5 percentage points. The per capita growth rate of the typical developing country between 1980 and 1998 was zero."[782]

Failure upon failure did not lead the World Bank and the IMF to slow lending, rather these agencies shifted to a new justification, debt relief. Poor countries now had high levels of debt and were not growing. (How could it be otherwise when loans went to corruption and patronage rather than to productive enterprise?) An array of moral leaders, from the Pope to the Dali Lama, deplored not the waste but the debt itself, and called for debt relief.

The World Bank and the IMF instituted new high profile programs along these lines, although debt relief in some form had existed for decades. The experience of those decades suggests that many countries were as highly indebted decades after relief as they were before. New borrowing simply replaced old cancelled debts. Easterly cites data showing that total debt forgiveness for 41 highly indebted poor countries from 1989 to 1997 totaled $33 billion, while their new borrowing totaled $41 billion. Notably, new borrowing was the highest in the countries that got the most debt relief. Thus, the burden of debt on the economies was in general not lessened.

The objective historical record is dismal. An immense amount of Western assistance has flowed to developing nations in the last half century: Easterly estimates that between 1950 and 1995, Western countries gave 1 trillion dollars (in 1985 dollars).[783] Tragically for their people, countries that received the most assistance in per capita terms made the least progress; indeed, in many instances, they regressed.

Lessons Learned

A number of lessons can be drawn from the experience of foreign aid. First, when an institution is distributing funds for which it is not going to be held accountable for results, it is less careful than an institution that must derive a return on investment or perish. The unfortunate reality in aid institutions is that bureaucrats are judged by the size of their budgets and the amount of assistance they provide, not on what that assistance achieves.

Secondly, international aid institutions do not seem to have a deep grasp of the sources of wealth in the advanced nations and the root causes of poverty in the less developed ones. The importance of the institutions and values that create wealth is not as ingrained in their thinking as is the charitable impulse. Moreover, they may distrust the efficacy of the free market and private corporations in addressing the size and complexity of the problems at hand, despite examples of developing countries which have demonstrated the capability to attract private investment and generate internal capital in amounts dwarfing historical flows of aid.

Thirdly, by divorcing action from results, the law of unintended consequences takes over. By providing easy money, kleptocrats are maintained in power, reform can be put off more easily, and bad investment habits are learned. Worse, when these efforts fail, the Western value system, in whose name the assistance is given, is discredited.

Given that we have highly educated, well-intentioned individuals leading the various aid agencies, what accounts for this disastrous record? Simply put, it is good intentions lacking a tether of accountability and without roots in free markets and democratic institutions. With regard to good intentions producing bad results, William W. Lewis states: "[M]ost people consider "social objectives" to be "good." Import tariffs, subsidized loans for small businesses, government disallowance of layoffs, and high minimum wage are all examples of economic policies designed to achieve social objectives. ... [But] *These measures distort markets severely and limit their productivity growth, slow overall economic growth, and cause unemployment. Rather than support these measures, it is better to level the playing field, create a bigger economic pie, and manage the distribution of that pie through the tax code for individuals.*"[784]

So this hapless track record by the affluent West in providing financial aid to poor countries underscores the theme of this chapter—i.e., good intentions, ungrounded in the rules of the extended economic order, won't achieve their intended goals and will waste much hard-earned treasure along the way. Moreover, aid-promoters undercut respect for the only system likely to let poor countries grow affluent on their own, as well as lessen the urgency for change by those countries.

The West's evolutionary advance during the last millennium moved the world in the direction of individual liberty, free markets, representative government and scientific thinking—i.e., worldviews congruent with classical Liberalism. Other countries having a cultural readiness to adopt the ways of the extended order did so with alacrity and success. Most countries, however, despite having access to the Western model, to science, and potentially to foreign investment, remain poor and seemingly stuck.

It is increasingly clear that this stagnation is rooted in a cultural unreadiness to adopt the ways of the extended order, which presents the urgent question of why cultural change is so difficult. To get at an understanding of this question, we examined the difficulty with which these values are accepted even in the affluent West itself, drawing on the ideological battles of the 20th century as well as political conflicts in contemporary America. The resistance to change was highlighted by contrasting two common sets of world views, developed by the economist Thomas Sowell: constrained world views, akin to classical liberalism, and unconstrained world views, which draw on more ancient human values together with a confidence in the efficacy of the state to ameliorate unfairness and insecurity in life.

The examination of current debate in this context shows how the unconstrained camp rejects many elements of the extended order because of a perceived unfairness in social results, particularly disparity of wealth among income classes. Yet our pragmatic review of key areas of contest—financial policy, legal philosophy, and financial aid to poor countries—showed that good intentions, disconnected from the evolved rules of the extended order simply are unable to achieve their desired ends, and, indeed, make things worse. Nonetheless, holders of the unconstrained view usually remain undissuaded, aiding weight to von Hayek's view that such intellectual disputes are not settled by reason alone. Disputes eventually get resolved through pragmatic experience—i.e., through a process of Darwinian selection of practices that work best to enhance the evolutionary fitness of our societal animal. Essentially, old soldiers simply fade into irrelevance.

So if these questions continue to be unsettled in affluent countries that have been the beneficiaries of the extended order, how much more difficult must it be for poorer countries, lacking centuries of cultural preparation, to accept the necessary values and move forward? Very difficult indeed!

With that said, poorer countries will inevitably develop economically—with an enlightened leader here, more openness to globalization there, and an incremental improvement in macro-economic policies and rule of law elsewhere. In terms of the role of affluent countries, our conclusions about the difficulties of cultural change counsel patience, caution against expensive mistakes that do more harm than good, and warn against wishful sentiment in the guise of multi-cultural equivalence.

Epilogue

This book, drawing on the concept of societal evolution, has attempted to illuminate the questions of how modern affluent societies came to be and why poorer countries continue to find prosperity and freedom so elusive. In doing so, it has distilled from the historical record the outline of an evolutionary process veiled from conventional perception – a process of considerable drama when viewed in the context of Peter Atkin's observation that humanity is in the process of evolving into a single mega-organism of potentially boundless achievement. A central role in that evolution has been that of the rise of von Hayek's economic extended order, which draws on the distributed intelligence of empowered individuals through new modes of cooperation and increasingly powerful science.

Societal evolution began to accelerate a millennium ago, when the West escaped from a cultural stasis common to the world's civilizations. The key elements of that evolutionary advance included the expansion of free markets in the face of age-old suspicion of entrepreneurs, merchants, and money-lenders; the creation of institutions to secure liberty in a world of rigid hierarchies and predatory states; the rise of science in a sea of mysticism and superstition; and the emergence of the empowered individual out of traditionally conformist societies. Taken together, these avenues of evolutionary change established the basis for humanity's towering achievements in recent centuries of escaping grinding poverty, ill health, and despotism.

We have seen how positive change occurred not because of a consensus for change, but rather because of spontaneous innovations that made societal animals evolutionarily fitter, even when running against tradition and subject to continuing dispute. Over time, these successful new practices led to societies that internalized new values and world views, which allowed them to harness the energies of their members more effectively. While this evolutionary advance initially burst forth in the Protestant West in the 17th and 18th centuries, its evident efficacy caused it to spread rapidly throughout Europe and beyond. In the 19th century, the leaders of feudal Japan coolly determined what was required to catch up with the West and launched the Meiji Restoration and other transformations of their country. In the 20th century, the Seven Tigers of East Asia adopted that model to begin their rapid ascent. Latin America, however, with the exception of Chile, lags economically and haplessly resists many dictates of free markets. Islam, after confused efforts to catch up, appears in some quarters to wish to retreat to the primitive religiosity of the 7th century, and much of Africa remains mired in a mindset resisting the predicates of the extended order. With regard to the laggards, however, there are examples in all cultures of inspired leadership that allowed modern ways to root and the foundations for economic advance to be laid. Moreover, the process of globalization brings irresistible change in its wake and can be expected to continue to do so.

But there are clouds in this generally sanguine picture. The most clearly apparent is that of fanatical Islam, which represents the antithesis of the evolved values of the extended order in governance, in individual liberty, and in institutions of free markets. Its adherents believe that the West's surpassing material strengths can be overcome through Islam's greater fervor – in service of God's command to impose Islamic religious beliefs on all humanity.

Lesser but widening threats arise from the recurrence of regressive ideologies, such as the 'Bolivarian socialism' of Venezuela's Hugo Chavez. As they undermine free institutions in their own societies, they seek to subvert their neighbors and weaken the influence of the world's democracies. Subtler still are misguided good intentions of international institutions that would drain productive wealth from the leading developed countries to aid poorer countries in ways allowing undeveloped countries to evade or postpone the hard decisions necessary for modernization. Finally, even in the heart of the extended order, each cyclical downturn of the economy invariably elicits attacks on key elements of free markets despite the powerful evidence of their achievements.

The extended order's strengths should and almost surely will prevail over time. But short term lack of resolve and confidence on the part of societies committed to free people and free markets may yet induce costly setbacks. We would do well to remember Ortega y Gassett's observation that a complacent unconcern with the defense of our evolved civilization and its freedoms can put everything that has been built up over centuries at risk.

Notes

Introduction

[1] Friedrich von Hayek, *The Fatal Conceit* (Chicago: The University of Chicago Press, 1991), 6.

[2] This statement should be tempered to reflect China and India's impressive progress in the last decade or so, such that the majority of the world's population (as opposed to number of countries) is now seeing significant growth of income.

[3] David Warsh, *Knowledge and the Wealth of Nations: A Story of Economic Discovery* (New York: W.W. Norton & Company, 2006), 380.

[4] Tom Bethell, *The Noblest Triumph: Poverty and Prosperity through the Ages* (New York: St. Martin's Press, 1998), quoting Hernando de Soto, 200.

[5] Stanley Elkins & Eric McKittrick, *The Age of Federalism: The Early American Republic, 1788-1800*. New York: Oxford University Press, 1995), quoting Walter Bagehot, 108.

[6] Lawrence E. Harrison, *Who Prospers?: How Cultural Values Shape Economic and Political Success* (New York: Basic Books, a member of the Perseus Books Group, 1992), citing George Foster, 20.

[7] Inglehart, Ronald, et al. *Human Beliefs and Values* (Ann Arbor: The University of Michigan Press, 1998), 8-10.

[8] Phillip Scribner is a retired professor of philosophy from American University, Washington, D.C., creator of the website "The Wholeness of the World" (www. twow.net), and author of *From Commonsense to Wisdom: The Path of Empirical Metaphysics* (forthcoming).

[9] Jose Ortega y Gasset (1883-1955), *The Revolt of the Masses* (New York: W.W. Norton & Company, 1932), Chapter 10.

Chapter 1

[10] Bethell, *The Noblest Triumph*, 200, quoting the economist Hernando de Soto who was lamenting slow economic development in Peru.

[11] Miles, Marc A., Holmes, Kim R., and O'Grady, Mary Anastasia. 2006 Index of Economic Freedom. Washington, DC: The Heritage Foundation and New York: The Wall Street Journal, 2006. Prepared and published annually by the Heritage Foundation and *The Wall Street Journal* since 1995.

¹² By James Gwartney and Robert Lawson. The Report parallels the Index in terms of underlying philosophy, though it employs somewhat different factors.

¹³ O'Driscoll, Gerald P. Jr., Holmes, Kim R., & Kirkpatrick, Melanie. *2001 Index of Economic Freedom.* Washington, DC: The Heritage Foundation and New York: The Wall Street Journal, 2001, 13.

¹⁴ David Warsh, *Knowledge and the Wealth of Nations*, 380, quoting the economist Elhanan Helpman, who noted that economists have been studying the wealth of nations without interruption since Adam Smith, but the subject has proved elusive and the mystery of economic growth itself has not been solved.

¹⁵ David Boaz, *Libertarianism: A Primer* (New York: The Free Press, a Division of Simon & Schuster, 1997), 83, citing the economist Ludwig von Mises.

¹⁶ Ibid., 150.

¹⁷ Ludwig von Mises, *Human Action: A Treatise on Economics* (Fourth Revised Edition, San Francisco: Fox & Wilkes, 1996),159.

¹⁸ Boaz, *Libertarianism*, 156.

¹⁹ A term coined by the economist Joseph Schumpeter describing the process whereby innovation in the market place makes economic winners of the innovators while harming some existing entities, but with net benefits for society. A common example is how the introduction of the automobile put most buggy whip manufacturers out of business.

²⁰ The World Bank, *Where is the Wealth of Nations? – Measuring Capital for the 21ˢᵗ Century* (Washington, DC: The International Bank for Reconstruction/The World Bank, 2006).

²¹ Ibid., 87.

²² Ibid., 94.

²³ Gregory Clark, *A Farewell to Alms: A Brief Economic History of the World*. Princeton and Oxford: Princeton University Press, 2007), Chapter 17.

²⁴ Harrison and Huntington, ed. *Culture Matters: How Values Shape Human Progress* (New York: Basic Books, A member of the Perseus Books Group, 2000), citing Clifford Gertz, 15.

²⁵ The results of the symposium were presented in Harrison and Huntington, *Culture Matters: How Values Shape Human Progress*.

²⁶ Ronald Inglehart is a professor of political science and program director at the Institute for Social Research at the University of Michigan. He was also chair of the steering committee of the "World Values Study."

²⁷ The material was presented in an article entitled "Culture and Democracy," which drew on data from the World Values Survey taking national-level data from 65 societies in three waves over several years. The

surveys were designed to measure values inherent in social norms to determine the nature of value differences between rich and low-income societies. His analysis drew on 22 data items used in all three waves.

[28] Francis Fukuyama is Omer L. and Nancy Hirst Professor of Public Policy at the Institute of Public Policy at George Mason University and is the author, inter alia, of *The End of History and the Last Man.*

[29] Fukuyama, "Social Capital," in *Culture Matters*, 98-99.

[30] Inglehart, in *Culture Matters*, 82-91.

[31] Lawrence E. Harrison, *Who prospers?*, 20, citing George Foster.

[32] Inglehart, *Human Values and Beliefs*, 8-10.

[33] Hayek, *The Fatal Conceit*, 18.

[34] Ibid., 12.

[35] Ibid., 13.

[36] Ibid., 19.

[37] Ibid., 6. His conception provides a richer descriptor than the more conventional term, 'capitalism', and this book will adopt the term 'extended order' as the general descriptor of modern free markets.

[38] Ibid., 14.

[39] Ibid., 9.

[40] Ibid., 103.

[41] Ibid., 15.

[42] Ibid., 127.

Chapter 2

[43] Peter Atkins, *Galileo's Finger: The Ten Great Ideas of Science*. New York: Oxford University Press, 2003), 33.

[44] Hayek, *The Fatal Conceit*, 6.

[45] Phillip Scribner, retired professor of philosophy from American University in Washington, D.C., and author of "The Wholeness of the World" (www.tWoW.net) and *From Commonsense to Wisdom: The Path of Empirical Metaphysics*, (forthcoming).

[46] Alexander Rosenberg's definition of evolution from *The Structure of Biological Science* (New York: Cambridge University Press, 1989), 167, is as follows:

1. "The number of organisms of any one type can increase in geometrical proportions. But;

2. The actual number of organisms of any one type remains close to constant over long periods.

3. No two individual members of a type of organism are identical; variation is characteristic, and some of that variation is inherited. Therefore, we may infer that:

4. Because organisms can produce more offspring than their surroundings can support, there must be a struggle among organisms to survive.

5. In this struggle, the ones whose variations best adapt them to their surroundings, the fittest, survive, whereas the less fit organisms, with less well-adapted variations, do not. And:

6. Because the variations are inheritable, there will be a change in the proportions of the variations from generation to generation: There will be evolution."

Regarding 'fitness', "each organism has a certain proportion of those properties, dispositions, and abilities, which are the causal determinants of its reproductive opportunities and thus of the number of its offspring."

[47] In the section entitled "Revolutionary evolution," in "The Wholeness of the World," Scribner outlines a framework of evolving 'part-whole complexity', wherein increasingly sophisticated 'causal connections' become more powerful in controlling salient aspects of the environment.

[48] Richard Dawkins, *The Selfish Gene* (Oxford: Oxford University Press, 1989).

[49] Ibid., 14.

[50] Ibid., 15-16.

[51] Ibid., 19.

[52] Matt Ridley, *Nature via Nurture: Genes, Experience, and What Makes Us Human* (New York: Harper Collins, 2003), 221.

[53] Scribner believes that all but a few mutations whose complexity borders on making them impossible would be tried out in a finite period of time. In effect, random variations on existing multicellular structures are continually "trying out" new powers, as if they were feeling around for new conditions that it might be useful to control. Whenever a new trait happened to control a new relevant condition (or an old condition in [a] better way), it would tend to be selected.

[54] Charles Darwin, *The Descent of Man, and Selection in Relation to Sex*, 2 Vols (London: John Murray, 1871), 166.

[55] David Sloan Wilson, *Darwin's Cathedral: Evolution, Religion, and the Nature of Society* (Chicago: University of Chicago Press, 2003).

[56] Ibid., 11.

[57] Ibid., 35.

[58] Wilson probably would be unwilling to extend this view to the level of countries and civilizations, or at least consider it too premature and hypothetical. He suggests that any rigorous analysis of the theory requires appropriate delineation of the groups in question as well as clear definition of phenotypic traits. So a rigorous expansion of the theory may ulti-

mately be undoable, given the enormous number of variables involved. Accordingly, he limits his analysis to religious groups that hold many other values and traditions in common with larger society, so that he can focus on just the differences.

[59] Richard Dawkins considers the concept of cultural evolution as well. His theory of evolution of living things accounts for the evolution of any other life in the universe, which would include societies. He states that all life evolves by the differential survival of replicating entities. In this sense culture can be seen to have replicators in the form of what he terms *memes*. He uses examples of ideas, tunes, catch-phrases, and clothes fashions. He states: "just as genes propagate themselves in the gene pool by leaping from body to body via sperms or eggs, so memes propagate themselves in the meme pool by leaping from brain to brain via a process which, in the broad sense, can be called imitation."

Darwinian selection would come from the brain's finite capacity and a person's limited time for considering ideas. In this view, ideas and values would compete to 'colonize' brain space. New memes would, like any biological replicator, have to be sufficiently enduring, fecund, and high-fidelity to survive. The individual's reason, attempting to create a coherent worldview, would weed out the failed ideas. *The Selfish Gene*, 192.

[60] Phillip Scribner, "The Wholeness of the World: Change: Epis-cause: Rational: Social Science," 5.

[61] Hayek, *The Fatal Conceit*, 25.

[62] Scribner, "The Wholeness of the World: Reflective stage, Cultural evolution, Contained Rep. Causation," 15.

[63] Such an examination is controversial in that many argue that fitness is logically indefinable, and attempts to define it in the context of evolutionary theory are tautological—i.e., what survives is fit and what allows something to survive is fitness. Nonetheless, Alexander Rosenberg argues that it is a real attribute. It cannot be more precisely defined because it is a *primitive* term, much like *force* or *magnetism*, which also can be defined only in terms of their effects. He argues that it is a *supervenient* attribute (a specialized term). This merely means that fitness relies on many more variables than one can analyze, but its effects can be imputed. For example, the relationship between Mendelian phenomena and molecular phenomena is one of supervenience. Inheritance of traits is determined by genes and Mendel identified certain principles about the inheritably of traits. Rosenberg states as an illustration: "Mendelian objects and properties supervene molecular ones: The latter fix the former ones completely, even though they cannot be connected to them in any manageable way." He states further that fitness is a relational property, reflecting the interaction of an organism and its environment. In respects it is a perfectly ordinary theoretical term, much like 'temperature', which is

determined not absolutely but by measuring changes in the properties of various substances such as the length of mercury in a tube. (*The Structure of Biological Science*, 112 and 155.) Here Rosenberg is concerned with scientific rigor. Scribner, however, notes that the process is not mysterious in that the concept of evolution unfolding in the direction of greater power to control reproductive success is intuitively straightforward.

⁶⁴ Deepak Lal, *Unintended Consequences: The Impact of Factor Endowments, Culture, and Politics on Long-Run Economic Performance* (Cambridge: The MIT Press, 1998).

⁶⁵ Book review by John J. Miller published in *The Wall Street Journal*, April 20, 2003.

⁶⁶ Richard Dawkins, in *The Selfish Gene*, characterizes the phenomenon in which genes compete to assure their survival in the next generation of their species, ranging from competition within DNA to competition between bodies containing different genes.

⁶⁷ Matt Ridley, *The Red Queen: Sex and the Evolution of Human Nature* (New York: Penguin Books, 1995),195 and 203-204.

⁶⁸ Matt Ridley, *The Origins of Virtue: Human Instincts and the Evolution of Cooperation* (New York: Penguin Books, 1998), 186-187.

⁶⁹ Jared Diamond, *The Third Chimpanzee: The Evolution and Future of the Human Animal* (New York: Harper Perennial, a division of Harper Collins, 1993), 298.

⁷⁰ Brian M. Fagan, "Lectures on Human Pre-history and the First Civilizations" offered by The Teaching Company (recorded lectures), 2003.

⁷¹ Diamond, *The Third Chimpanzee*, 285-286.

⁷² Those predecessors of ours were known as *Australopithecus africanus, Homo habilis,* and *Homo erectus.*

⁷³ *Homo erectus,* man's primitive ancestor, did kill large game by presumably driving them off cliffs or capturing them when mired in swamps. But, that is a different process in terms of the skills involved. In many ways he was still only an increasingly mobile scavenger.

⁷⁴ Diamond, *The Third Chimpanzee*, Chapter 2.

⁷⁵ Ridley, *Nature via Nurture*, 214-215.

⁷⁶ Ibid, 229.

⁷⁷ Ridley, *The Origins of Virtue*, 154-155.

⁷⁸ Ibid., 157-159.

⁷⁹ Ibid., 163.

⁸⁰ Ibid., 98.

⁸¹ Ibid., 97-98.

⁸² Wilson, *Darwin's Cathedral*, 22.

⁸³ Boyd and Richerson 1985; E.O. Wilson 1998), docility (Simon 1990), detection of cheating (Cosmides and Tooby 1992), punishment of cheating

(Boyd and Richerson 1992), symbolic thought (Deacon 1998), and explicit consensus decision-making (Boehm 1996) – Ibid., 26.

[84] Ibid., 27.

[85] Ibid., 22.

[86] Ibid., 9.

[87] Ridley, *The Origins of Virtue*, 131.

[88] Jared Diamond, *Guns, Germs and Steel: The Fates of Human Societies* (New York: W.W. Norton & Company, 1999).

[89] Ibid., 88.

[90] Diamond states: "Cereal crops have the virtues of being fast growing, high in carbohydrates, and yielding up to a ton of edible food per hectare cultivated. As a result, cereals today account for over half of all calories consumed by humans and include five of the world's leading crops (wheat, corn, rice, barley, and sorghum). Many cereal crops are low in protein, but that deficit is made up by pulses, which are often 25 percent protein (38 percent in the case of soybeans). Cereals and pulses together thus provide many ingredients of a balanced diet." Ibid., 125.

[91] Ibid., 139-140.

[92] Ibid., 136.

[93] Ibid., 125.

[94] Ibid., 159-174.

[95] Ibid., 107.

[96] Ibid., 108.

[97] Ibid., 88-91.

[98] Ibid., 154.

[99] Professor Brian M. Fagan, lectures on "Human Prehistory and the First Civilizations," Lecture 19; provided by The Teaching Company "The Great Courses."

[100] Ibid., Lecture 20.

[101] Hayek, *The Fatal Conceit*, 16.

[102] Hayek, *The Fatal Conceit*, citing Piggot's *Ancient Europe*, 40.

[103] Professor Brian M. Fagan, lectures on "Human Pre-history and the First Civilizations," Lecture 29; provided by The Teaching Company "The Great Courses."

[104] Ridley, *The Red Queen*, 188. Ridley establishes this concept with examples from gorillas and chimpanzees. The gorilla in this instance can defend an extended turf and protect several females, thereby creating a harem. The chimpanzee, however, lives in larger bands with a more dispersed food supply, and males have to share females.

[105] Ibid., 197-199.

[106] Ibid., 201. Ridley cites more of Betzig's work regarding medieval times in which she found that the countryside was heavily male-biased

because so many women were "employed" in castles. They formed a loose harem and in some instances castles contained "gynoeciums," where the harem lived in secluded luxury.

[107] By analogy, these leaps can be viewed as a form of *punctuated equilibriums* in which, because of a key mutation, rapid branching speciation occurs.

Chapter 3

[108] Hayek, *The Fatal Conceit*, 14 and 33.

[109] The economist Ludwig von Mises in his magnum opus, *Human Action: A Treatise on Economics, Fourth Revised Edition* (San Francisco: Fox & Wilkes, 1996), examined how enterprising behavior operates at the individual level. In his view, every voluntary action taken by an individual is in some measure directed to improving his condition, otherwise he would not expend the time, energy, or resources involved. Furthermore, any free act of cooperation or exchange between two individuals is seen by the parties as something that will improve the circumstances of both and, given the laws of comparative advantage, most likely will. In effect, individuals are shrewd in judging where their interests lie, which outcomes will improve those interests, and which courses of action will lead in that direction.

[110] Max Weber, *Economy and Society: An Outline of Interpretative Sociology* (Berkeley and Los Angeles: University of California Press, 1978), 630.

[111] The economist David Ricardo described the economic principle of comparative advantage as the basis for allocating effort between individuals or groups, when one is more efficient in every regard, and cooperates with another less efficient in every regard. Von Mises summarized it as follows: "The division of labor between two ... areas will ... increase the productivity of labor and is therefore advantageous to all concerned, even if the physical conditions of production for any commodity are more favorable in one of these two areas than in the other. It is advantageous for the better endowed area to concentrate its efforts upon the production of those commodities for which its superiority is greater, and to leave to the less well endowed area the production of other goods in which its superiority is less." A more concrete example is if Friday can catch twice as many fish as Crusoe but can find three times as many ripe fruits in a day, then both of them will be better off if Crusoe specializes in fishing (even though less productive) and Friday specializes in foraging. In this light, a society can lack all significant natural resources and have a relatively undereducated populace, yet be competitive in trade with others who have greater advantages. Chapter VII will provide examples of Hong Kong and

Singapore, city-states, having no natural resources, which through efforts governed by comparative advantage joined the ranks of the world's most prosperous countries.

[112] Hayek, *The Fatal Conceit*, 20.

[113] David Boaz, *The Libertarian Reader: Classic & Contemporary Writings from Lao-Tzu to Milton Friedman* (New York: The Free Press, A Division of Simon & Schuster, 1997), 422-423.

[114] Ibid.

[115] Mises, *Human Action,* 160-161.

[116] Lal, *Unintended Consequences*, 16.

[117] Lal refers to some of his earlier work in which he mathematically modeled the conditions and limitations of such rent-seeking by the state. He determined that tax rates could be so stifling as to reduce revenue from its optimum. (This could be viewed as an echo of supply-side economics.) He also indicated how the actual level of tax rates would be a function of the relative bargaining strengths of the rulers and the constituents (or prey). These strengths, in turn, are a function of entry barriers to other potential ruling powers—either from within or without.

[118] The Teaching Company, *Human Prehistory and the First Civilizations.*

[119] Russell Kirk, *The Roots of the American Order, Third Edition* (Washington, DC: Regnery Gateway, 1991).

[120] Ibid., 99.

[121] Citing M. Rostovtzeff, *The Social & Economic History of the Roman Empire*, as well as Tenney Frank, *An Economic History of Rome.*

[122] Herbert Muller, *The Uses of the Past: Profiles of Former Societies* (New York: A Mentor Book of the New American Library, 1952), 230.

[123] Will Durant, *Caesar and Christ* (New York: Simon and Schuster, 1944), 328 and 337.

[124] Bethell, *The Noblest Triumph*, 65, citing P. A. Brunt, *Italian Manpower.*

[125] Kirk, *Roots of the American Order*, 104.

[126] Ibid., 130.

[127] Ibid., 126.

[128] Lal, *Unintended Consequences*, 54, citing E. Ashtor's *A Social and Economic History of the Near East in the Middle Ages.*

[129] In its heyday, Baghdad was a city of about one million inhabitants, exceedingly large for pre-industrial times.

[130] *The Oxford History of Islam* (New York: Oxford University Press, 1999), 31-32.

[131] Ibid., 29.

[132] Ibid., 32.

[133] Weber, *Economy and Society*, 626.

[134] Lal, *Unintended Consequences*, 62.

[135] Ibid., 56.

[136] *The Oxford History of Islam*, 97.

[137] Lal, *Unintended Consequences*, 40.

[138] Ibid., 42, citing M. Elvin, *The Pattern of the Chinese Past* and *Why China Failed to Create an Endogenous Industrial Capitalism: A Critique of Max Weber's Explanation*.

[139] Ibid., Lal citing Hartwell.

[140] Ibid.

[141] Durant, *Our Oriental Heritage* (New York: Simon and Schuster, 1954), 778.

[142] Lal, *Unintended Consequences*.

[143] Ibid., 43, citing W.H. McNeill.

[144] Will Durant, *Our Oriental Heritage*, 675.

[145] Ibid., 699.

[146] Ibid., 725.

[147] Ibid., 726.

[148] Ibid., 796.

[149] Ibid., 673.

[150] Lal, *Unintended Consequences*, 47.

[151] Durant, *Our Oriental Heritage*, 673.

[152] Ibid.

[153] Ibid., 393.

[154] Ibid., 482.

[155] Ibid., 398.

[156] Ibid., 487-488.

[157] Ibid., 507.

[158] Ibid., 524-525.

[159] Lal, *Unintended Consequences*, 32, citing Y. Singh, *Modernization of Indian Tradition (1986)*.

[160] Weber, *Economy and Society*, 599.

[161] Lal, *Unintended Consequences*, 34.

[162] Weber, *Economy and Society*, 583.

[163] Ibid., 435-436.

[164] Nathan Rosenberg & L.E. Birdzell, Jr., *How the West Grew Rich: The Economic Transformation of the Industrial World* (Basic Books, a Division of Harper Collins, 1986), 39.

[165] Ibid., 43.

[166] Ibid., 51.

[167] Karl Pribram, *A History of Economic Reasoning* (Baltimore: The Johns Hopkins University Press, 1983), 6.

[168] Ibid., 12.

[169] Weber, *Economy and Society*, 584.

[170] Rosenberg and Birdzell, *How the West Grew Rich*, 52.

[171] Pribram, *A History of Economic Reasoning*, 19.

[172] Weber, *Economy and Society*, 584.

[173] Rosenberg and Birdzell, *How the West Grew Rich*, 24.

[174] Ibid.,119.

[175] Henri Pirenne, *Economic and Social History of Medieval Europe* (New York: A Harvest Book – Harcourt, Brace and Company, 1937), 40.

[176] Rosenberg and Birdzell, *How the West Grew Rich*, 60, citing British economist Sir John Hicks.

[177] Ibid., 74.

[178] Edward P. Cheyney, *The Dawn of a New Era: 1250-1453* (New York: Harper & Brothers, 1936), 64-67.

[179] Rosenberg and Birdzell, *How the West Grew Rich*, 55.

[180] Pirenne, *Economic and Social History of Medieval Europe*, 46.

[181] Cheyney, *The Dawn of a New Era*, 5-7.

[182] Pirenne, *Economic and Social History of Medieval Europe*, 10.

[183] Ibid., 33.

[184] Charles Homer Haskins, *Renaissance of the 12th Century* (Cleveland: Meridian Books, The World Publishing Company, 1955).

[185] Pirenne, *Economic and Social History of Medieval Europe*, 36.

[186] Ibid., 185.

[187] Durant, *The Age of Faith*, 728.

[188] Pirenne, *Economic and Social History of Medieval Europe*, 96-101.

[189] Cheyney, *The Dawn of a New Era*, 46.

[190] Pirenne, *Economic and Social History of Medieval Europe*, 16.

[191] Ibid., 17.

[192] Ibid., 18.

[193] Cheyney, *The Dawn of a New Era*, 11.

[194] Ibid., 14.

[195] Pirenne, *Economic and Social History of Medieval Europe*, 50.

[196] Ibid., 173-175.

[197] Ibid., 128.

[198] Durant, *The Age of Faith*, 638.

[199] Pirenne, *Economic and Social History of Medieval Europe*, 54.

[200] Ibid., 52-53.

[201] Durant, *The Age of Faith*, 640.

[202] Pirenne, *Economic and Social History of Medieval Europe*, 125.

[203] Cheyney, *The Dawn of a New Era*, 17.

[204] Pribram, *A History of Economic Reasoning*, 6.

[205] Averroes (1126-1198), a Moslem Cordoban scholar, who, inter alia, translated Aristotle's *Ethics* into Latin.

[206] Pribram, *A History of Economic Reasoning*, 5.

[207] Ibid., 6.

[208] Ibid., 8.

[209] Ibid.

[210] Ibid., 21.

[211] Ibid., 23-25.

[212] Rosenberg and Birdzell, *How the West Grew Rich*, 67.

[213] Ibid., 65-66.

[214] Ibid., 73.

[215] "In other words, measurable inputs, such as those that can be calculated in a planned economy, do not determine output. Leibenstein shows that productivity differences between workers doing the same job in a particular plant are likely to vary as much as four to one, that differences as high as 50 percent can arise between plants commanding identical equipment and the same size labor force that is paid identically. Matters of management, motivation, and spirit—and their effects on willingness to innovate and seek new knowledge—dwarf all measurable inputs in accounting for productive efficiency, both for individuals and groups, and for management and labor." – George Gilder, *Wealth and Poverty*, p. 40

[216] William W. Lewis, The Power of Productivity: Wealth, Poverty, and the Threat to Global Stability (Chicago: The University of Chicago Press, 2004), 10.

Chapter 4

[217] Martin Gilbert, *In Search of Churchill: A Historian's Journey* (New York: John Wiley & Sons, 1994),149.

[218] Similar forces leading to institutionalized forms of liberty occurred elsewhere in Europe at the time, notably the United Provinces of the Netherlands, wresting their freedom from the Hapsburg Empire, and the Helvetian Federation of the Swiss, developing forms of decentralized power combined with representative government. These countries along with Britain were, of course, all in the process of evolving a Protestant culture.

[219] The anthropologist Jane Goodall observed a range of such behaviors in bands of chimpanzees going so far as one band exterminating another, as noted by Jared Diamond, *The Third Chimpanzee*, 291.

[220] John J. Miller, *The Wall Street Journal* (April 20, 2003), reviewing *Constant Battles* by Steven LeBlanc.

[221] Diamond, *The Third Chimpanzee*, 297.

[222] Ridley, *The Origins of Virtue*, 163. Ridley states that when a group of males goes on a raid, the alpha behaves as if he must get the backing of his coalition partners before launching an attack. He cites an occasion filmed

at Gombe where the alpha, Goblin, apparently could not get the assent of some senior colleagues to pursue an action against some enemies, and the troop disengaged.

[223] Wilson, *Darwin's Cathedral*, 21.

[224] Ibid., 27.

[225] George Ayittey, *Africa in Chaos* (New York: St. Martin's Press, 1998), 87-89.

[226] Professor Brian M. Fagan's lectures on "Human Prehistory and the First Civilizations" (*The Great Courses* of the Teaching Company).

[227] Wilson, *Darwin's Cathedral*, 36.

[228] Ibid., 31.

[229] Ibid., 32.

[230] Even in the current day, totalitarian states such as Nazi Germany, the Soviet Union, and Saddam Hussein's Iraq could exert such effective control over their peoples that they had to be brought down by external pressures and force by democratic states.

[231] Durant, *Caesar and Christ*, 391.

[232] Kirk, *The Roots of American Order*, 58.

[233] Ibid., 64.

[234] Ibid., 90-91.

[235] Ibid., 91-92.

[236] Ibid.

[237] Bethell, *The Noblest Triumph*, 62-63.

[238] Kirk, *The Roots of American Order*, 98-101.

[239] A. J. Carlyle, *Political Liberty: A History of the Conception in the Middle Ages and Modern Times* (London: The Oxford University Press, 1963), 3.

[240] Ibid.

[241] Ibid.

[242] Ibid., 4-5.

[243] Ibid., 5-6.

[244] Ibid.,10-11.

[245] Ibid., 13.

[246] Ibid., 11.

[247] Kirk, *The Roots of American Order*, 108-109.

[248] Professor Daniel Robinson of Georgetown University, *The Great Ideas of Philosophy*, lectures by The Teaching Company.

[249] Kirk, *The Roots of American Order*, 108-109.

[250] Tom Bethell, *The Noblest Triumph*, 61-62.

[251] Ibid., 65.

[252] Ibid., 67-69.

[253] Durant, *Caesar and Christ*, 406.

[254] Durant, *The Age of Faith*, 36.

255 Ibid., 450.

256 Ibid., 93.

257 Ibid., 88-89.

258 Ibid., 91.

259 Ibid., 451.

260 Ibid., 453-454.

261 Ibid., 461- 472.

262 Carlyle, *Political Liberty*, 12.

263 Ibid.

264 Ibid., 14.

265 Ibid., 18-19.

266 Durant, *The Age of Faith*, 658.

267 Carlyle, *Political Liberty*, 19.

268 Ibid., 20-21.

269 H.W. Brands, *The First American: The Life and Times of Benjamin Franklin* (New York: Anchor Books, Random House, 2000), 716.

270 Kirk, *The Roots of American Order*, 180-181.

271 Ibid., 181.

272 Ibid., 193.

273 Durant, *The Age of Faith*, 674.

274 Ibid., 677.

275 Winston Churchill, *A History of the English Speaking Peoples: The Birth of Britain* (New York: Dodd, Mead & Company, 1966), 253-254.

276 Kirk, *The Roots of American Order*, 194.

277 Ibid., 195-197.

278 Churchill, *The Birth of Britain*, 308-309.

279 Kirk, *The Roots of American Order*, 198-199.

280 Winston Churchill, *A History of the English Speaking Peoples: The New World* (Princeton and Oxford: Princeton University Press, 2007), 179.

281 Will Durant, *The Age of Reason Begins* (New York: Simon and Schuster, 1961), 212.

282 Churchill, *The New World*, 275.

283 Ibid., 314.

284 Mary was married to William III of Orange, the Stadtholder (a noble, who was military leader and chief political leader of the Dutch Republic) of the United Provinces (i.e. the Netherlands).

285 John Locke, *Two Treatises of Civil Government*, as cited by Kirk, *The Roots of American Order*, 283-285.

286 Ibid.

287 It was not until a series of actions in the 19th and 20th centuries that Parliament extended the franchise to the entire adult population.

288 Kirk, *The Roots of American Order*, 298-299.

[289] Ibid., 184-187.

[290] Durant, *The Age of Reason Begins*, 54.

[291] Kirk, *The Roots of American Order*, 244-245.

[292] Ibid., 351-352.

[293] Ibid., 361.

[294] Churchill, *The Birth of Britain*, 431.

[295] Kirk, *The Roots of American Order*, 305.

[296] Ibid., 304.

[297] Ibid., 324-326.

[298] Ibid., 328.

[299] Ibid., 329.

[300] Ibid., 353.

[301] Ibid., 355-356.

[302] Ibid., 421.

[303] *The Federalist Papers*, ed. Roy P. Fairfield (New York: Anchor Books, Doubleday & Company, 1966), 160.

[304] Kirk, *The Roots of American Order*, 356.

[305] *The Federalist Papers*, 228.

[306] The number of justices was changed several times over the years, nine being the currently specified number.

[307] Samuel Eliot Morison, *The Oxford History of the American People* (New York: Oxford University Press, 1965), 363.

[308] Thomas S. Kuhn, *The Structure of Scientific Revolutions* (Chicago: The University of Chicago Press, 1970).

Chapter 5

[309] *The Columbia Encyclopedia* (Third Edition. New York: Columbia University Press, 1963), 1910.

[310] Durant, *Our Oriental Heritage*, 781-782.

[311] The term *technological* rather than *scientific* is used because the Chinese did not develop the outlook and knowledge that are prerequisites for the 'scientific method'.

[312] Lal, *Unintended Consequences*.

[313] Rosenberg & Birdzell, *How the West Grew Rich*, 87, citing Joseph Needham's, *Science and Society, East and West*.

[314] Ibid.

[315] M. Elvin, *The Pattern of the Chinese Past* (Stanford, Conn.: Stanford University Press, 1973), 233-234, as cited by Lal, *Unintended Consequences*, 43-44.

[316] *The Oxford History of Islam*, 157.

[317] Durant, *The Age of Faith*.

[318] Ibid., 240.

[319] Ibid., 257.

[320] Ibid., 249.

[321] Ibid., 241.

[322] Ibid., 242.

[323] Ibid., 244.

[324] Ibid., 244-245.

[325] Ibid., 246-249.

[326] Ibid., 243.

[327] Lal, *Unintended Consequences*, 54.

[328] Durant, *The Age of Faith*, 249.

[329] Ibid., 250.

[330] Ibid., 254.

[331] *The Oxford History of Islam*, 92.

[332] Cited by Lal, Durant, David Landes, et al.

[333] Durant, *The Age of Faith*, 332.

[334] Ibid., 251.

[335] Phillip Scribner, *Western Philosophy and the Nature of Goodness: The Search for a Wisdom Worth Loving* (draft), 18.

[336] Charles Homer Haskins, *The Renaissance of the 12th Century*, 368.

[337] Durant, *The Age of Faith*, 909.

[338] Ibid., 910-911.

[339] Ibid., 912.

[340] Ibid., 938.

[341] Ibid., 940.

[342] Ibid., 946-947.

[343] Ibid., 956.

[344] Ibid., 960-961.

[345] Ibid., 1004.

[346] Ibid., 967.

[347] Pribram, *A History of Economic Reasoning*, 5.

[348] Ibid., 6.

[349] Durant, *The Age of Faith*, 977-978.

[350] Durant, *The Age of Reason Begins*, 162.

[351] Ibid.

[352] Durant, *The Age of Faith*, 1009.

[353] Daniel Boorstin, *The Discoverers: A History of Man's Search to Know His World and Himself* (Vintage Books, a Division of Random House, 1985), 314.

[354] Ibid., 32.

[355] Ibid., 40.

[356] Ibid., 66.

357 Professor Daniel N. Robinson of Georgetown University, *The Great Courses* by The Teaching Company, Lecture Number Three, "Pythagoras and the Divinity of Numbers" presents an early classical view of reality that may have shaped the work of some early scientists.

358 Phillip Scribner, *The Wholeness of the World* (www.tWoW.net), Philosophical Stage, Function of philosophy, 14.

359 David Landes, *The Wealth and Poverty of Nations* (New York: W.W. Norton & Company, 1999), 342-344.

360 Boorstin, *The Discoverers*, 386-387.

361 Ibid., 394.

362 Private letter dated 8/13/02 from Scribner to the author.

363 Boorstin, *The Discoverers*, 294.

364 Will Durant, *The Reformation*, p. 857

365 Thomas Kuhn, *The Structure of Scientific Revolutions*, p. 69

366 Will Durant, *The Reformation* (New York: Simon and Schuster, 1957), 858.

367 Durant, *The Age of Reason Begins*, 595-597.

368 Ibid., 598.

369 Ibid., 600.

370 Ibid., 600-607.

371 As it turned out, calculus was also discovered by Leibniz in Germany about the same time, and disputes about who was first were to last many years.

372 Will Durant, *The Age of Louis XIV* (New York: Simon and Schuster, 1963), 540.

373 Ibid., 546.

374 Boorstin, *The Discoverers*, 340 and 345-347.

375 Ibid., 342.

376 Ibid., 44.

377 Ibid., 350-360.

378 Ibid., 361.

379 Ibid., 361-368.

380 Will Durant, *The Age of Voltaire* (New York: Simon and Schuster, 1965), 524.

381 Ibid., 525.

382 Kuhn, *The Structure of Scientific Revolutions*, 53-54.

383 Durant, *The Age of Voltaire*, 533-534.

384 Kuhn, *The Structure of Scientific Revolutions*, 132-134.

385 Durant, *The Age of Voltaire*, 520.

386 Kuhn, *The Structure of Scientific Revolutions*, 14.

387 Ibid., 18.

388 Durant, *The Age of Voltaire*, 522-523.

[389] Rosenberg & Birdzell, *How the West Grew Rich*, 254-255.

[390] Boaz - Article in "The Cato Policy Report" of May/June 2002 for the economic data.

Chapter 6

[391] Michael Oakeshott, *Morality and Politics in Modern Europe: The Harvard Lectures* (New Haven: Yale University Press,1993), 20-21.

[392] Wilson, *Darwin's Cathedral*, 43.

[393] Ridley, *The Origins of Virtue*, 244.

[394] Ibid., 37-38.

[395] Scribner, *The Wholeness of the World*

[396] Ibid.

[397] Herbert J. Muller, *The Uses of the Past: Profiles of Former Societies* (New York: A Mentor Book of the New American Library, 1952), 93.

[398] Ibid., 93-94.

[399] Ibid., 100.

[400] Ibid., 104-105.

[401] Ibid., 97.

[402] Scribner, *Western Philosophy and the Nature of Goodness*.

[403] Muller, *The Uses of the Past*, 154-155.

[404] Ibid., 155.

[405] Durant, *Our Oriental Heritage*, 653-654.

[406] Ibid., 656.

[407] Ibid.

[408] Ibid., 668.

[409] Ibid., 402.

[410] Ibid., 411.

[411] Ibid., 430-436.

[412] Ibid., 417.

[413] Lal, *Unintended Consequences*, citing Louis Dumont, 75.

[414] Bertrand Russell, *A History of Western Philosophy* (New York: Simon and Schuster, 1945), 598.

[415] Pribram, *A History of Economic Reasoning*, 9.

[416] Ibid., 8.

[417] Kirk, *The Roots of American Order*, 170.

[418] Scribner, *The Wholeness of the World*, Philo. Stage, Career of Epistemological philosophy, 8.

[419] Kirk, *The Roots of the American Order*, Chapter V.

[420] Lal, *Unintended Consequences*, 83, citing Jack Goody's *The Development of Family and Marriage in Europe*.

[421] Ibid., 84-89.

[422] Will Durant, *The Renaissance* (New York: Simon and Schuster, 1953), 3.
[423] Ibid., 6-9.
[424] Ibid., 77-78.
[425] Ibid., 84.
[426] Ibid., 86.
[427] Ibid., 728.
[428] Durant, *The Reformation*, 338-339.
[429] Kirk, *The Roots of the American Order*, 227-228.
[430] Ibid., 238.
[431] Durant, *The Reformation*, 340.
[432] Ibid., 345-382.
[433] Landes, *The Wealth and Poverty of Nations*, 178-180.
[434] Durant, *The Reformation*, 371-372.
[435] Kirk, *The Roots of the American Order*, 233-234.
[436] Ibid., 242.
[437] Ibid., 236.
[438] Ibid., 254-255.
[439] Landes, *The Wealth and Poverty of Nations*, 178.
[440] Kirk, *The Roots of the American Order*, 256-257.
[441] Rosenberg and Birdzell, *How the West Grew Rich*.
[442] Ibid., 123-126.
[443] Oakeshott, *Morality and Politics in Modern Europe*, 20.
[444] Will Durant, *The Life of Greece* (New York: Simon and Schuster, 1939), 646.
[445] Ibid., 652.
[446] Ibid., 654.
[447] Kirk, *The Roots of American Order*, 108.
[448] Ibid., 243-244.
[449] Oakeshott, *Morality and Politics in Modern Europe*, 63.
[450] Russell, *A History of Western Philosophy*, 605.
[451] Ibid., 610.
[452] Ibid., 615.
[453] Ibid., 632.
[454] Kirk, *The Roots of the American Order*, 288.
[455] Russell, *The History of Western Philosophy*, 597.
[456] Paul Johnson, *A History of the American People* (New York: Harper Collins, 1997), 307-310.
[457] Boaz, *The Libertarian Reader*, 78.
[458] Boaz, *The Libertarian Reader*, 63-64.
[459] Ibid., 93
[460] John Boswell, *Christianity, Social Tolerance, and Homosexuality: Gay People in Western Europe from the Beginning of the Christian Era to the Fourteenth Century* (Chicago: The University of Chicago Press, 1980).

⁴⁶¹ Ibid., 334.

⁴⁶² Boswell notes that the only place in the Old Testament that homo-sexual acts are mentioned per se is in Leviticus: "Thou shalt not lie with mankind, as with womankind: it is abomination. [18:22]" and "If a man also lie with mankind, as he lieth with a woman, both of them have com-mitted an abomination: they shall surely be put to death; their blood shall be upon them. [20:13, KJV]" (CST&H p.100) Yet, the Hebrew for abomi-nation was "Toevah" which usually represented something unclean for Jews, like eating pork or engaging in intercourse during menstruation, not something intrinsically evil like rape or theft.

Chapter 7

⁴⁶³ Harrison and Huntington, *Culture Matters*, 14.

⁴⁶⁴ Durant, *Our Oriental Heritage*, 834-835.

⁴⁶⁵ Ibid., 837.

⁴⁶⁶ Ibid., 842.

⁴⁶⁷ Fukuyama, *Trust*, 11.

⁴⁶⁸ Durant, *Our Oriental Heritage*, 866.

⁴⁶⁹ Ibid., p. 867

⁴⁷⁰ Harrison, *Who Prospers?*, 82.

⁴⁷¹ George DeVos, *Socialization for Achievement*, 67, 106, quoted in Har-rison, *Who Prospers?*, 141.

⁴⁷² Fukuyama, *Trust*, 26.

⁴⁷³ Ibid., 171-172.

⁴⁷⁴ Ibid., 174.

⁴⁷⁵ Ibid., 167.

⁴⁷⁶ Durant, *Our Oriental Heritage*, 871.

⁴⁷⁷ Ibid., 666.

⁴⁷⁸ Fukuyama, *Trust*, 183.

⁴⁷⁹ Durant, *Our Oriental Heritage*, 847.

⁴⁸⁰ Harrison and Huntington, *Culture Matters*, 90.

⁴⁸¹ Seymour Martin Lipset and Gabriel Salman Lenz, *Culture Matters*, 113, "Corruption, Culture, and Markets"

⁴⁸² Lal, *Unintended Consequences*, 142-144.

⁴⁸³ Durant, *Our Oriental Heritage*, 854.

⁴⁸⁴ Ibid., 877.

⁴⁸⁵ Ibid., 840.

⁴⁸⁶ Marius B. Jansen, *The Making of Modern Japan* (Cambridge: The Belknap Press of Harvard University Press, 2000), 78-79.

⁴⁸⁷ Ibid., 268.

⁴⁸⁸ Ibid., 278-79.

489 Ibid., 280.

490 Ibid., 318.

491 Ibid., 319.

492 Ibid., 356.

493 Ibid., 359.

494 Ibid., 360.

495 Ibid., 397.

496 Ibid., 391.

497 Ibid., 388.

498 Ibid., 394.

499 Ibid., 398.

500 During the decades leading up to the war and encompassing the war itself, the government played an increasingly central role in directing the economy to military needs, but this was not characteristic of the periods of growth.

501 Durant, *Our Oriental Heritage*, 910.

502 Harrison, *Who Prospers?*, 129.

503 Ibid.

504 Jansen, *The Making of Modern Japan*, 529.

505 Durant, *Our Oriental Heritage*, 920.

506 Jansen, *The Making of Modern Japan*, 671.

507 Ibid., 685.

508 Ibid., 691.

509 Ibid., 706.

510 Ibid., 729.

511 Fukuyama, *Trust*, 52.

512 William W. Lewis, *The Power of Productivity: Wealth, Poverty, and the Threat to Global Stability* (Chicago: The University of Chicago Press, 2004). 24.

513 Ibid., 26.

514 Harrison, *Who Prospers?*, 142.

515 Thomas Sowell, *The Economics and Politics of Race* (New York: William Morrow, 1983), 22.

516 Ibid., 24.

517 Fukuyama, *Trust*, 85.

518 Fukuyama, *Trust*, 62.

519 Ibid., 71.

520 Ibid., 74.

521 Ibid., 88.

522 Ibid., 78.

523 Ibid., 86.

524 Harrison, *Who Prospers?*, 82.

525 Ibid., 111.

[526] Ibid., 113.

[527] Lewis, *The Power of Productivity*, 159.

[528] Martin Wolf, *Why Globalization Works* (New Haven: Yale University Press, 2004), 202.

[529] Nancy DeWolf Smith, "The Wisdom that Built Hong Kong's Prosperity" *The Wall Street Journal*, July 1, 1997, A14, New York edition.

[530] David L. Littmann, *The Wall Street Journal*, op-ed, May 28, 1998, New York edition.

[531] *2001 Index of Economic Freedom*, 197.

[532] *The Wall Street Journal*, Editorial, September 4, 2004.

[533] *Economic Freedom of the World 1997*, 165.

[534] *2001 Index of Economic Freedom*, 327.

[535] Lewis H. Gann, "Western and Japanese Colonialism," *The Japanese Colonial Empire*, ed. Ramon H. Myers and Mark R. Peattie, 522-23, cited in Harrison, *Who Prospers?*, 89.

[536] Ibid., 91.

[537] Ibid., 93.

[538] Dr. Rong-I-Wu, *History of Economic Development in Taiwan, March 1997*

[539] Rong-I-Wu, *August 2003 Yearbook*, "Government Information Office," Taiwan-website.

[540] Taiwan Government Information Office.

[541] *East Asia – The Great Tradition*, p. 426, as cited by Harrison, *Who Prospers?*, 97.

[542] *Who Prospers?*, 99.

[543] Ibid., 100.

[544] Ibid., 101.

[545] Ibid., 103.

[546] Lewis, *The Power of Productivity*, 108.

[547] *2001 Index of Economic Freedom*, 231, and *Economic Freedom of the World 1997*, 171.

[548] Lewis, *The Power of Productivity*, 130.

[549] Harrison, *Who Prospers?*, 105.

[550] Charles Hirschman's review of John Drabble's *An Economic History of Malaysia, c. 1800-1990*.

[551] Sowell, *The Economics and Politics of Race*, 26.

[552] Ibid., 37.

[553] Ibid.

[554] *2001 Index of Economic Freedom*, 255 and *Economic Freedom of the World 1997*, 133.

[555] Fukuyama, *Trust*, 45.

[556] Sowell, *The Economics and Politics of Race*, 33.

[557] *2001 Index of Economic Freedom,* 357 and *Economic Freedom of the World 1997,* 187.

[558] Theodore Friend, *Indonesian Destinies* (Cambridge: The Belknap Press of Harvard University Press, 2003), 83.

[559] Ibid., 82.

[560] Ibid.

[561] Ibid., 84.

[562] Ibid., 87.

[563] Ibid.

[564] Ibid., 97.

[565] Ibid., 136.

[566] Ibid., 88.

[567] Ibid., 138.

[568] Ibid. 233.

[569] Ibid.

[570] Ibid., 241.

[571] Ibid., 510.

[572] Ibid.

[573] Ibid., 508.

[574] Ibid., 188.

[575] Ibid., 220.

[576] Ibid., 242-243.

[577] 2001 *Index,* 205; and 1997 *Report,* 117.

[578] Harrison and Huntington, *Culture Matters,* 7.

[579] George Foster, *Culture and Conquest: America's Spanish Heritage,* pp.2-3, as quoted by Lawrence Harrison in Underdevelopment is a State of Mind: The Latin American Case (Lanham: Madison Books, 2000), 145.

[580] Guillermo M. Yeatts, *The Roots of Poverty in Latin America* (Jefferson: McFarland & Company, 2005), 37.

[581] Ibid.

[582] Jose Ignacio Garcia Hamilton, "Historical Reflections on the Splendor and Decline of Argentina," *Cato Journal,* Vol. 25, No.3 (Fall 2005).

[583] Yeatts, *The Roots of Poverty in Latin America,* 36.

[584] Ibid., 48.

[585] Ibid., 52.

[586] Ibid., 53.

[587] *The Wall Street Journal,* November 16, 2001, A13.

[588] *The Wall Street Journal,* October 18, 2002, A11.

[589] Yeatts, *The Roots of Poverty in Latin America,* 88.

[590] Ibid., 76.

[591] Harrison, *Who Prospers?,* 20, citing George Foster.

[592] Pribram, *The History of Economic Reasoning,* 23.

[593] For example, contrary to the continuing Dominican view that usury was sinful, Calvin, in 1574, denied that charging interest for the use of money was inherently sinful and maintained that it could be applied to activities that produced profits. (*The Roots of Poverty in Latin America*, 32).

[594] Harrison and Huntington, *Culture Matters*, 62.

[595] Ibid., 63.

[596] Harrison, *Underdevelopment is a State of Mind*, 19.

[597] Bethell, *The Noblest Triumph*, 196-200.

[598] Yeatts, *The Roots of Poverty in Latin America*, 41.

[599] Harrison, *Who Prospers?*, 12 (quoting from *The Protestant Ethic*).

[600] Ibid., 13.

[601] Quoted from Carlos Rangel's, *The Latin Americans: Their Love-Hate Relationship with the United States*, 192, as cited by Harrison, *Who Prospers?*, 254.

[602] Mala Htun, "Culture, Institutions, and Gender Inequality in Latin America," in *Culture Matters*, 192.

[603] Lawrence E. Harrison, *The Pan-American Dream: Do Latin America's Cultural Values Discourage True Partnership with the United States and Canada?* (Boulder: Westview Press, a Division of Harper Collins, 1997), 82.

[604] Fukuyama, "Social Capital," in *Culture Matters*, 98.

[605] Ibid.

[606] Transparency International, *Global Corruption Report, 2003*, 103.

[607] Seymour Martin Lipset and Gabriel Salman Lenz, "Corruption, Culture, and Markets," in *Culture Matters*, 114.

[608] Harrison, *Who Prospers?*, 11.

[609] Harrison, "The Decline of Yanqui-bashing: To solve its problems, Latin America starts looking at itself. *The Washington Post*, C2, November, 10, 1996, C2.

[610] Hamilton, "Historical Reflections on the Splendor and Decline of Argentina."

[611] Ibid.

[612] Ibid.

[613] *The Latin Americans: Their Love-Hate Relationship with the United States*, 240-241 (Cited by Lawrence Harrison in *Underdevelopment is a State of Mind*, 108).

[614] *Cato Journal*, Volume 25, No.3.

[615] Harrison, *Underdevelopment is a State of Mind*, 113.

[616] Mary Anastasia O'Grady, "The Americas: Don't blame the free market for Agentina's woes." *The Wall Street Journal*, May 30, 1997, A19, New York edition.

[617] David R. Henderson, *The Wall Street Journal*, March 29, 1996, A11, New York edition.

[618] Yeatts, *The Roots of Poverty in Latin America,* 94 and 102.

[619] Brink Lindsey, *The Wall Street Journal,* Op-ed, January 9, 2002, New York edition.

[620] Yeatts, *The Roots of Poverty in Latin America,* 108.

[621] *2009 Index,* 75.

[622] *2001 Index of Economic Freedom*: GDP per capita: Argentina $8,475; France $27,975.

[623] Harrison, *Who Prospers?,* 31 and 36.

[624] Ibid., 30.

[625] Ibid., 30-32.

[626] Ibid., 35.

[627] Ibid., 28.

[628] Ibid., 36.

[629] David R. Henderson, *The Wall Street Journal,* March 29, 1996, A11, New York edition.

[630] David Landes in *Culture Matters,* 6.

[631] Lewis, *The Power of Productivity,* 139.

[632] Ibid., 141.

[633] Ibid., 278.

[634] Ibid., 165.

[635] Ibid., 142-143.

[636] Ibid., 147-148.

[637] Ibid., 155.

[638] Harrison, *The Pan-American Dream,* 149.

[639] Ibid., 154.

[640] Ibid., 150-152.

[641] Ibid., 153.

[642] Ibid., 161-162.

[643] *2001 Index of Economic Freedom,* 125.

[644] Harrison, *The Pan-American Dream,* 171.

[645] Harrison, *Who Prospers?,* 51-52.

[646] Ibid., 61.

[647] James W. Cortada, *Two Nations Over Time – Spain and the United States, 1776-1977,* 234, as cited by Harrison, ibid., 63.

[648] Harrison, *Who Prospers,* 63.

[649] Ibid., 74-75.

[650] Ibid., 72. Harrison cites data showing that while in 1965, over 80% of Spaniards considered themselves to be practicing Catholics, by 1983, only 31% did so. This shift is underscored by Spain's legalization of divorce in 1981 and of limited abortion in 1985.

[651] Bernard Lewis, *The Muslim Discovery of Europe* (New York: W.W. Norton & Company, 2001), 64.

[652] Sayyid Qutb, *Milestones* (American Trust Publications, 1990), as cited by Mark Gould, "Understanding Jihad", *Policy Review*, February and March, 2005.

[653] Ibid.

[654] Ibid.

[655] Boorstin, *The Discoverers*, 544.

[656] Lal, *Unintended Consequences*, 63.

[657] *The Wall Street Journal*, Editorial, July 8, 2002.

[658] *The Oxford History of Islam*, 97.

[659] Ibid., 164.

[660] See Figure II-5 for the ranking of Islamic countries vis-à-vis interpersonal trust. Also, see Transparency International's *Global Corruption Report, 2003*, 264.

[661] Lal, *Unintended Consequences*, 62.

[662] Ibid., 63.

[663] Lewis, *The Muslim Discovery of Europe*, 216.

[664] Bethell, *The Noblest Triumph*, 232.

[665] Landes, *The Wealth and Poverty of Nations*, 404-407.

[666] John Lancaster, "Decades of Doctrinaire Policies Leave Arab Economies Stalled." *The Washington Post*, August 3, 1997.

[667] Turizm.net

[668] *2001 Index of Economic Freedom*, 85.

[669] *The Economic Freedom of the World 1997*, 51.

[670] Deepak Lal, *Unintended Consequences*, 66.

[671] Lewis, *The Muslim Discovery of Europe*, 60-62.

[672] Samuel Huntington, *The Clash of Civilizations and the Remaking of the World Order* (New York: A Touchstone Book, Simon & Schuster, 1997).

[673] Gould, *Policy Review,* No. 129.

[674] Ibid.

[675] President and founder of SADEG, which is currently involved in about fifty development projects throughout Africa, and is a former member of the World Bank's Council of African Advisors.

[676] Daniel Etounga-Manguelle, in *Culture Matters*, Chapter 6.

[677] Ibid., 68-69.

[678] Ibid., 72.

[679] Ibid., 71.

[680] Ibid., 74.

[681] Harrison and Huntington, *Culture Matters*, Introduction, 25.

[682] Diamond, *The Third Chimpanzee*, 297.

[683] Elliott P. Skinner, "West African Economic Systems," as cited by Ayittey, *Africa in Chaos*.

[684] Ayittey, *Africa in Chaos*, 97.

[685] Ibid., 112-114.

[686] Ibid., 92-93.

[687] Ibid., 125.

[688] William Easterly, *The Elusive Quest for Growth* (Cambridge: The MIT Press, 2002), 256-257.

[689] Ibid., 26-27.

[690] Ayittey, *Africa in Chaos*, 176-177.

[691] Ibid., 245.

[692] Easterly, *The Elusive Quest for Growth*, 232.

[693] Ibid., 60.

[694] Ayittey, *Africa in Chaos*, 30.

[695] Easterly, *The Elusive Quest for Growth*, 67.

[696] Ayittey, *Africa in Chaos*, 162.

[697] Ibid.

[698] Ibid., 161.

[699] *The Hammond Almanac, 1982 Edition* (Maplewood: Hammond Almanac, Inc., 1982), 638.

[700] *2001 Index of Economic Freedom*, 287.

[701] Easterly, *The Elusive Quest for Growth*, 245.

[702] *2001 Index of Economic Freedom*, 287.

[703] Ibid., 287-288.

[704] *The Economist*, August 21, 1993, Survey, 5, as cited by Ayittey in *Africa in Chaos*, 177.

[705] Transparency International, *Global Corruption Report, 2003*, 265.

[706] Ayittey, *Africa in Chaos*, 213-214.

[707] Ibid., 304.

[708] *2001 Index of Economic Freedom*, 287.

[709] Ayittey, *Africa in Chaos*, 8.

[710] *Parade Magazine*, January 22, 2006, 5.

[711] Transparency International, *Global Corruption Report 2003*, 264.

[712] *2001 Index of Economic Freedom*, 103.

[713] *2006 Index of Economic Freedom*, 117.

[714] Ibid.

[715] Stephane Courtois et al., *The Black Book of Communism*, 8-9.

[716] Ibid., 16.

[717] Ibid., 9-10.

[718] Ibid., 190.

[719] Ibid., 191.

[720] Ayn Rand, *The Journals of Ayn Rand*, David Harriman, ed., 56.

[721] David Boaz, *Libertarianism: A Primer*, 127.

[722] Ibid., 129.

[723] Nicholas Eberstadt, *Policy Review*, June & July, 1999.

[724] Arnold Beichman, "Survival Odds for Russia," *Washington Times*, January 2, 2001, A14, reporting on an article by Murray Feshbach in the *Wilson Quarterly*

[725] *2006 Index of Economic Freedom*, 329.

[726] Leon Aron, *Russia's Revolution: Essays 1989-2006* (Washington, D.C.: The AEI Press, 2007), "Chapter 8: In Search of a Russian Middle Class 2000."

[727] *2009 Index*, 337.

Chapter 8

[728] Hayek, *The Fatal Conceit*, 18.

[729] Ruth Benedict, *Patterns of Culture* (Boston: Houghton Mifflin, 1959).

[730] Thomas Sowell, *A Conflict of Visions*, p. 15

[731] Walter Lippman, *Public Opinion*, p. 80

[732] Friedrich von Hayek, *The Constitution of Liberty*, p. 26

[733] Thomas Sowell, *A Conflict of Visions: Ideological Origins of Political Struggles* (New York: Quill, William Morrow, 1987), 23.

[734] Ibid., 43.

[735] Ibid., 44.

[736] Ibid., 46.

[737] Paul Craig Roberts and Lawrence M. Stratton," The Fed's Depression and the Birth of the New Deal," *Policy Review*, No. 108.

[738] The Christian Democrats' Catholic heritage often makes it as sympathetic to a paternalistic state as with free market principles

[739] George Will, *The Washington Post*, October 10, 2004.

[740] Marian Tupy and Patrick Basham, op-ed, *The Washington Times*, June 25, 2003.

[741] David Brooks, "Among the Bourgeoisophobes," *The Weekly Standard*, April 15, 2002.

[742] Hayek, *The Fatal Conceit*, 6.

[743] Editorial, *The Wall Street Journal*, January 20, 2006.

[744] Gerald Scully of The National Center for Policy Analysis estimates that the maximum growth of GNP occurs when government at all levels takes between 21.55 and 22.9% of output.

[745] This data is from a study done of seven major OECD nations by the OECD and the U. S. Chamber of Commerce examining the relationship between government spending and growth in the GDP, as cited by Warren Brookes, "How Government Spending Affects Growth," *The Washington Times*, op-ed, June 22, 1987.

[746] James Gwartney, "Less Government, More Growth", *The Wall Street Journal*, April 10, 1998.

[747] Bernhard Heitger, "The Impact of Taxation on Unemployment in OECD Countries," *The Cato Journal*, Fall 2002.

[748] "The Producers," editorial, *The Wall Street Journal*, May 15, 2001, New York edition.

[749] Bruce Bartlett, "Counterproductive Global Spending," *The Washington Times*, op-ed, September 2, 1996, A16, citing International Monetary Fund "Working Paper 95/130" by Vito Tanzi and Ludger Schuknecht.

[750] "Income Dynamics," editorial, *The Wall Street Journal*, June 16, 1991, A1, New York edition.

[751] Sowell, *A Conflict of Visions*, 192.

[752] Ibid., 188.

[753] Ibid.

[754] Ibid., 122.

[755] Bethell, *The Noblest Triumph*.

[756] Boaz, *Libertarianism*, 150-151.

[757] William Tuckery, "How Rent Control Drives Out Affordable Housing", *Policy Analysis*, Cato Institute, May 21, 1997.

[758] Lenore Schloming, "Rent-control Horrors Never Happened" *The Wall Street Journal*, July 2, 1997, A15, New York edition.

[759] Sowell, *A Conflict of Visions*, 52.

[760] Ibid., 78-79.

[761] Ibid., 176.

[762] Ibid., 178-179.

[763] Ibid., 57.

[764] Ibid., 163.

[765] Ibid., 185.

[766] Sowell, *A Conflict of Visions*, 58.

[767] Lewis, *The Power of Productivity*, 10.

[768] Easterly, *The Elusive Quest for Growth*, 35, 36.

[769] Ibid., 28-30.

[770] Ibid., 35-36.

[771] Ibid., 37-38.

[772] Ibid., 41.

[773] Ibid., 42.

[774] Ibid., 44.

[775] Ibid., 67.

[776] Ibid., 68.

[777] Ibid., 107-108.

[778] Ibid., 111.

[779] Ibid., 101.

[780] Ibid., 105.

[781] Ibid., 102.

782 Ibid.
783 Ibid., 33.
784 Lewis, *The Power of Productivity*, 10.

Works Cited

Aron, Leon. *Russia's Revolution: Essays 1989-2006*. Washington, D.C.: The AEI Press, 2007.

Atkins, Peter. *Galileo's Finger: The Ten Great Ideas of Science*. New York: Oxford University Press, 2003.

Ayittey, George B.N. *Africa in Chaos*. New York: St. Martin's Press, 1998.

Bartlett, Bruce. "Counterproductive Global Spending." *The Washington Times*, op-ed, , September 2, 1996, A16 citing International Monetary Fund "Working Paper 95/130" by Vito Tanzi and Ludger Schuknecht.

Bartley III, W.W., ed., Hayek, F.A. *The Fatal Conceit: The Errors of Socialism*. Chicago: The University of Chicago Press, 1991.

Beichman, Arnold. "Survival Odds for Russia," *Washington Times*, January 2, 2001, A14.

Benedict, Ruth. *Patterns of Culture*. Boston: Houghton Mifflin, 1959.

Bethell, Tom. *The Noblest Triumph: Poverty and Prosperity through the Ages*. New York: St. Martin's Press, 1998.

Boaz, David. *Libertarianism: A Primer*. New York: The Free Press, a Division of Simon & Schuster, 1997.

___. "The Cato Policy Report", May/June 2002.

Boaz, David, ed. *The Libertarian Reader: Classic & Contemporary Writings from Lao-Tzu to Milton Friedman*. New York: The Free Press, A Division of Simon & Schuster, 1997.

Boorstin, Daniel J. *The Discoverers: A History of Man's Search to Know His World and Himself*. New York: Vintage Books, a Division of Random House, 1985.

Boswell, John. *Christianity, Social Tolerance, and Homosexuality: Gay People in Western Europe from the Beginning of the Christian Era to the Fourteenth Century*. Chicago: The University of Chicago Press, 1980.

Brands, H.W. *The First American: The Life and Times of Benjamin Franklin*. New York: Anchor Books, Random House, 2000.

Brookes, Warren. "How Government Spending Affects Growth." *The Washington Times*. Op-ed, June 22, 1987.

Brooks, David. "Among the Bourgeoisophobes", *The Weekly Standard*, April 15, 2002.

Carlyle, A.J. *Political Liberty: A History of the Conception in the Middle Ages and Modern Times*. London: The Oxford University Press, 1963.

Cheyney, Edward P. *The Dawn of a New Era: 1250-1453*. New York: Harper & Brothers, 1936.

Churchill, Winston S. *A History of the English Speaking Peoples: The Birth of Britain*. New York: Dodd, Mead & Company, 1966.

___. *A History of the English Speaking Peoples: The New World*. New York: Dodd, Mead & Company, 1965.

Clark, Gregory. *A Farewell to Alms: A Brief Economic History of the World*. Princeton and Oxford: Princeton University Press, 2007.

The Columbia Encyclopedia. Third Edition. New York: Columbia University Press, 1963.

Courtois, Stéphane, Nicolas Werth, Jean-Louise Panné, Andrzej Paczkowski, Karel Bartosek, and Jean-Louis Margolin. *The Black Book of Communism: Crimes, Terror,*

Repression. Cambridge: Harvard University Press, 1999.

Darwin, Charles. *The Descent of Man, and Selection in Relation to Sex, 2 Vols*. London: John Murray, 1871.

Dawkins, Richard. *The Selfish Gene*. Oxford: Oxford University Press, 1989.

Diamond, Jared. *Guns, Germs, and Steel: The Fates of Human Societies*. New York: W.W. Norton & Company, 1999.

___. *The Third Chimpanzee: The Evolution and Future of the Human Animal*. New York: Harper Perennial, a division of Harper Collins, 1993.

Durant, Will. *Our Oriental Heritage*. (This and the following are parts of *The Story of Civilization*.) New York: Simon and Schuster, 1954.

___. *The Life of Greece*. New York: Simon and Schuster, 1939.

___. *Caesar and Christ*. New York: Simon and Schuster, 1944.

___. *The Age of Faith*. New York: Simon and Schuster, 1950.

___. *The Renaissance*. New York: Simon and Schuster, 1953.

___. *The Reformation*. New York: Simon and Schuster, 1957.

Durant, Will and Ariel. *The Age of Reason Begins*. New York: Simon and Schuster, 1961.

___. *The Age of Louis XIV*. New York: Simon and Schuster, 1963.

___. *The Age of Voltaire*. New York: Simon and Schuster, 1965.

Easterly, William. *The Elusive Quest for Growth*. Cambridge: The MIT Press, 2002.

Eberstadt, Nicholas. *Policy Review*, June & July, 1999.

Elkins, Stanley and McKitrick, Eric. *The Age of Federalism: The Early American Republic, 1788-1800*. New York: Oxford University Press, 1995.

Fagan, Brian M. "Human Prehistory and the First Civilizations". The Great Courses by The Teaching Company (recorded lectures), 2003.

Fairfield, Roy P., ed.,*The Federalist Papers*. New York: Anchor Books, Doubleday & Company, 1966.

Friend, Theodore. *Indonesian Destinies*. Cambridge: The Belknap Press of Harvard University Press, 2003.

Fukuyama, Francis. *Trust*. New York: Free Press Paperbacks, Simon & Schuster, 1995.

Gilbert, Martin. *In Search of Churchill: A Historian's Journey*. New York: John Wiley & Sons, 1994.

Gould, Mark. "Understanding Jihad", *Policy Review*, February and March, 2005.

Gwartney, James and Lawson, Robert. *Economic Freedom of the World*. Canada: The Frasier Institute, 1997.

Gwartney, James. "Less Government, More Growth", *The Wall Street Journal*, April, 10, 1998, p. 1, New York edition.

Hamilton, Jose Ignacio Garcia. "Historical Reflections on the Splendor and Decline of Argentina",_Cato Journal_, Vol. 25, No.3 (Fall 2005).

The Hammond Almanac, 1982 Edition. Maplewood: Hammond Almanac, Inc., 1982.

Harriman, David, ed., Rand, Ayn. *Journals of Ayn Rand*. New York: Dutton, 1997.

Harrison, Lawrence E. *Who Prospers: How Cultural Values Shape Economic and Political Success*. New York: Basic Books, a member of the Perseus Books Group, 1992.

___. *Underdevelopment is a State of Mind: The Latin American Case*. Lanham: Madison Books, 2000.

___. *The Pan-American Dream: Do Latin America's Cultural Values Discourage True Partnership with the United States and Canada?* Boulder: Westview Press, a Division of Harper Collins, 1997.

___. "The Decline of Yanqui-bashing: To solve its problems, Latin America starts looking at itself." *The Washington Post*, C2, November, 10, 1996.

Harrison, Lawrence E. and Huntington, Samuel P., ed. *Culture Matters: How Values Shape Human Progress*. New York: Basic Books, A member of the Perseus Books Group, 2000.

Haskins, Charles Homer. *The Renaissance of the 12th Century*. Cleveland: Meridian Books, The World Publishing Company, 1955.

Hayek, F.A. *The Constitution of Liberty*. Chicago: University of Chicago Press, 1960.

Heitger, Bernhard. "The Impact of Taxation on Unemployment in OECD Countries", *The Cato Journal*, Fall 2002.

Henderson, David R. *The Wall Street Journal*, March 29, 1996, A11, New York edition.

Hirschman, Charles. Review of *An Economic History of Malaysia, c. 1800-1990_by John Drabble.

Huntington, Samuel. *The Clash of Civilizations and the Remaking of the World Order.* New York: A Touchstone Book, Simon & Schuster, 1997.

Inglehart, Ronald, Basañez, Miguel, and Moreno, Alejandro. *Human Values and Beliefs: A Cross-Cultural Sourcebook.* Ann Arbor: The University of Michigan Press, 1998.

Jansen, Marius B. *The Making of Modern Japan.* Cambridge: The Belknap Press of Harvard University Press, 2000.

Johnson, Paul. *A History of the American People.* New York: Harper Collins, 1997.

Kirk, Russell. *The Roots of American Order* (Third Edition). Washington, DC: Regnery Gateway, 1991.

Kuhn, Thomas S. *The Structure of Scientific Revolutions.* Chicago: The University of Chicago Press, 1970.

Lal, Deepak. *Unintended Consequences: The Impact of Factor Endowments, Culture, and Politics on Long-Run Economic Performance.* Cambridge: The MIT Press, 1998.

Lancaster, John. "Decades of Doctrinaire Policies Leave Arab Economies Stalled." *The Washington Post*, August 3, 1997.

Landes, David S. *The Wealth and Poverty of Nations.* New York: W.W. Norton & Company, 1999.

Lewis, Bernard. *The Muslim Discovery of Europe.* New York: W.W. Norton & Company, 2001.

Lewis, William W. *The Power of Productivity: Wealth, Poverty, and the Threat to Global Stability.* Chicago: The University of Chicago Press, 2004.

Lindsey, Brink. *The Wall Street Journal*, Op-ed, January 9, 2002, New York edition.

Littmann, David L. *The Wall Street Journal*, op-ed, May 28, 1998, New York edition.

Miles, Marc A., Holmes, Kim R., and O'Grady, Mary Anastasia. *2006 Index of Economic Freedom.* Washington, DC: The Heritage Foundation and New York: The Wall Street Journal, 2006.

Miller, John J. "Review of *Constant Battles* by Steven LeBlanc," *The Wall Street Journal*, May, 20, 2003, New York edition.

Miller, Terry and Holmes, Kim R. *2009 Index of Economic Freedom.* Washington, DC: The Heritage Foundation and New York: The Wall Street Journal, 2009.

Morison, Samuel Eliot. *The Oxford History of the American People.* New York: Oxford University Press, 1965.

Muller, Herbert J. *The Uses of the Past: Profiles of Former Societies.* New York: A Mentor Book of the New American Library, 1952.

Oakeshott, Michael. *Morality and Politics in Modern Europe: The Harvard Lectures.* New Haven: Yale University Press, 1993.

O'Driscoll, Gerald P. Jr., Holmes, Kim R., & Kirkpatrick, Melanie. *2001 Index of Economic Freedom*. Washington, DC: The Heritage Foundation and New York: The Wall Street Journal, 2001.

O'Grady, Mary Anastasia. "The Americas: Don't blame the free market for Argentina's woes." *The Wall Street Journal*, May 30, 1997, A19, New York edition.

Ortega y Gasset, Jose. *The Revolt of the Masses*. New York: W.W. Norton & Company, 1932.

The Oxford History of Islam. Edited by John L. Esposito. New York: Oxford University Press, 1999.

Parade Magazine, January 22, 2006.

Pirenne, Henri. *Economic and Social History of Medieval Europe*. New York: A Harvest Book – Harcourt, Brace and Company, 1937.

Pribram, Karl. *A History of Economic Reasoning*. Baltimore: The Johns Hopkins University Press, 1983.

Ridley, Matt. *Nature Via Nurture: Genes, Experience, and What Makes Us Human*. New York: Harper Collins, 2003.

___. *The Origins of Virtue: Human Instincts and the Evolution of Cooperation*. New York: Penguin Books, 1998.

___. *The Red Queen: Sex and the Evolution of Human Nature*. New York: Penguin Books, 1995.

Roberts, Paul Craig, and Stratton, Lawrence M. "The Fed's Depression and the Birth of the New Deal" *Policy Review*, No. 108, August & September, 2001.

Robinson, Daniel N. "The Great Ideas of Philosophy". The Great Courses by the Teaching Company (recorded lectures), 1997.

Rong-I-Wu. "History of Economic Development in Taiwan". *August 2003 Yearbook, Government Information Office*, Taiwan-website.

Rosenberg, Alexander. *The Structure of Biological Science*. New York: Cambridge University Press, 1989.

Rosenberg, Nathan & Birdzell, L.E., Jr. *How the West Grew Rich: The Economic Transformation of the Industrial World*. Basic Books, a Division of Harper Collins, 1986.

Rostovtzeff, M. *The Social & Economic History of the Roman Empire*. I.S.B.N. 0-8196-2164-1

Roth, Guenther and Wittich, Claus, ed., Weber, Max. *Economy and Society: An Outline of Interpretative Sociology*. Berkeley and Los Angeles: University of California Press, 1978.

Russell, Bertrand. *A History of Western Philosophy*. New York: Simon and Schuster, 1945.

Schloming, Leonore. "Rent-control horrors never happened," *The Wall Street Journal*, July 2, 1997, A15, New York edition.

Scribner, Phillip. *Western Philosophy and the Nature of Goodness: The Search for a Wisdom Worth Loving* (forthcoming).

___. *The Wholeness of the World.* www.tWoW.net

___. Private letter to the author dated August 13, 2002.

Smith, Adam. *The Wealth of Nations, Books I-III.* London: Penguin Books, 1986.

Smith, Nancy DeWolf. "The Wisdom that Built Hong Kong's Prosperity" *The Wall Street Journal*, July 1, 1997, A14, New York edition.

Sowell, Thomas. *Conquests and Cultures: An International History.* New York: Basic Books, a Member of Perseus Books, 1998.

___. *A Conflict of Visions: Ideological Origins of Political Struggles.* New York: Quill, William Morrow, 1987.

___. *The Economics and Politics of Race.* New York: William Morrow, 1983.

Taiwan Government Information Office.

Transparency International. *Global Corruption Report 2003.* Edited by Robin Hodesa. London: Profile Books, 2003.

Tucker, William. "How Rent Control Drives Out Affordable Housing", *Policy Analysis*, Cato Institute, May 21, 1997.

Tupy, Marian, and Basham, Patrick. Op-ed article, *The Washington Times*, op-ed, June 25, 2003.

Turizm.net (Turkish Government website), regarding Ataturk's reforms.

Von Mises, Ludwig. *Human Action: A Treatise on Economics* (Fourth Revised Edition). San Francisco: Fox & Wilkes, 1996.

The Wall Street Journal, Editorial, "The Producers", May 15, 2001, New York edition.

___. Editorial, "Income Dynamics," June 16, 1991, A1, New York edition.

___. Editorial, November 16, 2001.

___. Editorial, July 8, 2002.

___. Editorial, October 18, 2002.

___. Editorial, September 4, 2004.

___. Editorial, January 20, 2006.

Warsh, David. *Knowledge and the Wealth of Nations: A Story of Economic Discovery.* New York: W.W. Norton & Company, 2006.

Will, George. *The Washington Post*, October 10, 2004.

Wilson, David Sloan. *Darwin's Cathedral: Evolution, Religion, and the Nature of Society.* Chicago: University of Chicago Press, 2003.

Wolf, Martin. *Why Globalization Works.* New Haven: Yale University Press, 2004.

The World Bank. *Where is the Wealth of Nations? – Measuring Capital for the 21st Century.* Washington, DC: The International Bank for Reconstruction/The World Bank, 2006.

Yeatts, Guillermo M. *The Roots of Poverty in Latin America.* Jefferson: McFarland & Company, 2005.

Index

Congress, U.S., 176

Constitution, U.S., features of, 174-177; Nineteenth Amendment, 270; philosophic underpinnings of, 1773-174

constitutions: Argentina's, 330; Brazilian, 321, 337; Chile's, 339; of EU countries, 389; Japan's, 291-292, 294; Roman, 142; Russia's, 376

continuity, in scientific endeavor, 209-210

cooperation, psychological testing, 63; in evolutionary process, 37

Copernicus: in development of astronomy, 215-216

corruption: Indonesia, 316; in Latin America, 329; in Nigeria, 367; and transaction costs, 329

"Corruption Perceptions Indices," 284

Cortada, James, 343

cotton manufacturing, in Egypt, 350-351

Cowperthwaite, Sir John, 302

"creative destruction," 21

Cromwell, Oliver, 163

cultural differences, between developed and underdeveloped countries, 28–33

cultural evolution, 49-51, 136

cultural map, 30 fig.

culture: definition for, 28; emulating another, 275-277; evolutionary view of, 37-38; and human capital, 28; and societal evolution, 16

D

daimyo (feudal lord), 284, 290-291

Dalton, John, 226

Dark Ages: history of, 149; pres-ervation of values through, 150-156; Roman traditions preserved in, 150-153. *See also* Medieval Europe

Darwin, Charles, 40, 46-47

data collection, in scientific development, 203, 213

da Vinci, Leonardo, 215

Dawkins, Richard, 42, 43

debt relief, foreign aid for, 413

Declaration of Independence, American, 263

dependency theories, 332

Descartes, René, 260

De Seyssel, 154

de Soto, Hernando, 2, 325-326

developed countries: and free market system, 3; and role of culture, 28–33. *see also* underdeveloped countries

developing countries: causes of poverty in, 414; per capita growth rate of, 413; successful, 300

Diamond, Jared, 54, 55, 63, 64, 65 ,66, 67, 68

Dickemann, Mildred, 72

disease, in medical understanding, 221

disparity, and social justice, 25

Domar, Evsey, 409

Dornbusch, Rudiger, 342

Dravidians, 94

Durant, Will, 82, 88, 91-95, 117, 138, 149-150, 152-153, 166, 185, 187, 189, 191, 295-198, 200-203, 217, 219, 225, 228, 240-242, 246-247, 249, 251-252, 259, 279, 281, 283, 284-285

Dutch: expelled from Indonesia, 314; trade with Japan of, 287

Dworkin, Ronald, 398, 404

www.ingramcontent.com/pod-product-compliance
Lightning Source LLC
Chambersburg PA
CBHW020330270326
41926CB00007B/116